E-COMMERCE BASICS

Technology Foundations and
E-Business Applications

E-COMMERCE BASICS

Technology Foundations and E-Business Applications

William S. Davis
Miami University, Oxford, Ohio

John Benamati
Miami University, Oxford, Ohio

Addison
Wesley

Boston San Francisco New York
London Toronto Sydney Tokyo Singapore Madrid
Mexico City Munich Paris Cape Town Hong Kong Montreal

Senior Acquisitions Editor	Maite Suarez-Rivas
Executive Editor	Susan Hartman Sullivan
Executive Marketing Manager	Michael Hirsch
Executive Development Manager	Sylvia Mallory
Development Editor	Maxine Effenson Chuck
Project Editor	Katherine Harutunian
Production Supervisor	Marilyn Lloyd
Project Manangement	Argosy Publishing
Composition and Art	Argosy Publishing
Copyeditor	Ginny Kaczmarek
Proofreader	Jeannie Smith
Design Manager	Gina Hagen Kolenda
Text Design	Susan Raymond
Cover Design	Gina Hagen Kolenda
Cover Photo	© DigitalVision
Prepress and Manufacturing	Caroline Fell

Access the latest information about Addison-Wesley titles from our World Wide Web site: http://www.aw.com/cs

Many of the designations used by manufacturers and sellers to distinguish their products are claimed as trademarks. Where those designations appear in this book, and Addison-Wesley was aware of a trademark claim, the designations have been printed in initial caps or all caps.

The programs and applications presented in this book have been included for their instructional value. They have been tested with care, but are not guaranteed for any particular purpose. The publisher does not offer any warranties or representations, nor does it accept any liabilities with respect to the programs or applications.

Library of Congress Cataloging-in-Publication Data

Davis, William S., 1943–
    E-Commerce basics: technology foundations and e-business
applications/ William S. Davis, John H. Benamati.
      p. cm.
Includes bibliographical references and index.
    ISBN 0-201-74840-1 (alk. paper)
    1. Electronic commerce. 2. Information technology. 3.
Business enterprises—Computer networks. I. Benamati, John H. II.
Title.

HF5548.32 .D376 2002
658.8'4–dc21

2002071200

ISBN 0-201-74840-1

12345678910-QWT-06050403

To my "big brother" Glenn

———————————

This book is dedicated to my loving wife, Mandy;
I could not have done this without her!

And to Bill,
for his incredible patience and mentorship during this process.

Contents

Brief Contents

Author Biographies

William S. Davis

Professor Davis wrote his first program in 1967, back in the days when the title "hacker" was considered a compliment. In 1971, he joined the faculty at Miami University in Oxford, Ohio, where he began as a teacher who writes and evolved into a writer who teaches. Addison-Wesley published his first textbook, *Operating Systems: A Systematic View* (now in its fifth edition) in 1977, and *E-Commerce Basics* is textbook number thirty-two. Today, he lives in Sarasota, Florida, writes at home, and enjoys bicycling, swimming, walking along Siesta Key Beach with his wife of thirty-six years, and regular visits from old friends and family, particularly his three terrific kids.

John "Skip" Benamati

Dr. Benamati joined IBM in 1984 as a database administrator, and left as a corporate information technology (IT) consultant in 1994 to pursue his dream of sharing his real-world experience with students at the college level. In 1997, he joined Miami University's MIS department as an assistant professor. The focus of his doctoral and ongoing research is IT change and its effects on IT management, an interest that stems from his experiences in the field. He has published articles about IT change and e-commerce in numerous journals, and he continues to provide consulting services. He was driven to write *E-Commerce Basics,* his first textbook, because of his need for an e-commerce text consistent with his conception of the course. He enjoys outdoor activities such as hunting, fishing, camping, hiking, and team sports, but his favorite activity is spending time with his wife.

Preface

The Tip of the Iceberg

It seems like only yesterday when the so-called dot-coms ruled Wall Street and e-commerce was the wave of the future. Then the bubble burst, dot-com became dot-bomb, and the latest breakthrough-technology-*du-jour* pushed e-commerce out of the limelight. For the second time in a few short years, the hype managed to get it exactly wrong.

E-commerce is much more than simply buying and selling goods and services online. The connection between a retail business and a retail customer represents the very small tip of a very large iceberg. Constructed on top of the evolving infrastructure defined by the global communication network, the Internet, and the World Wide Web, e-commerce is a new set of intra-business, business-to-business, and business-to-consumer applications that together are redefining how the business world functions.

Target Audience for This Textbook

E-Commerce Basics: Technology Foundations and E-Business Applications is written to support an introductory course in e-commerce typically offered to upper-division MIS, CIS, or information technology students, or to a broader audience as a part of the business core curriculum. This book may also be appropriate for similar courses taught by such departments and focus areas as accounting, administration, management, marketing, and production. Minimum prerequisites include an introductory course in information systems and basic computer skills.

Our Vision

E-commerce is still evolving. At first glance, it resembles a hodgepodge of tools and techniques, successes and failures, and trial-and-error initiatives, with today's breakthrough killer application rapidly becoming tomorrow's old news. Without a conceptual framework to provide a context, understanding where new ideas fit and why old ideas fail can be difficult. We believe that such a framework exists.

E-commerce is a form of business. Linking e-commerce to such basic business principles as competitive advantage, the value chain, and the supply chain gives the student a solid base for understanding why some e-commerce initiatives succeed while others fail. Within the context of that high-level structure, a layered approach allows the student to start with the underlying basics and to examine how e-commerce applications are constructed layer-by-layer, block-by-block. As a result, the student sees how the business objective, the underlying technology, and the means of achieving the business objective are related, and establishes a solid foundation for evaluating future changes in the field.

The Layered Approach

The essential purpose of layering is to utilize existing infrastructures in order to avoid re-inventing the wheel. For example, when a company builds a new headquarters, it plugs into existing power, communications, water, sewer, and transportation infrastructures rather than creating its own-in effect, the company builds on top of the existing base.

E-commerce rests on a similar infrastructure. The bottom layer is the global communication network-telephone, wireless, cable, fiber optics, and so on. The Internet is constructed on top of the communication network. The World Wide Web is an application that runs on the Internet. E-commerce business applications, in turn, plug into the World Wide Web. Understanding the underlying infrastructure makes it easier to grasp the strengths, limitations, and implications of various e-commerce solutions. We use the layered approach to provide a strong conceptual framework for the material, emphasizing how high-level business applications are built on and limited by the foundation defined by the underlying infrastructure.

Contents

The book is divided into five parts. Part 1's single chapter gives an overview of the field of e-commerce and provides a clear map for navigating the remaining chapters. Part 2 focuses on the e-commerce infrastructure, including the underlying communication network and the Internet (Chapter 2) and the World Wide Web (Chapter 3). The objective of this section is not to teach the technical details of how the evolving infrastructure works, but to provide a solid base for understanding the material that follows.

E-commerce is a layer of business applications built on top of the infrastructure described in Part 2. Because they are business applications, Part 3 opens by examining (in Chapter 4) several basic business principles that apply to any business, the impact of e-commerce on the business environment, and the business strategies that are evolving to take advantage of those changes. Next we turn to the key categories of e-commerce, including business-to-consumer (Chapter 5), intra-business (Chapter 6), and business-to-business applications (Chapter 7). After Chapter 4, the remaining Part 3 chapters can be read in any order.

E-commerce continues to experience significant growing pains, which we attempt to diagnose in Part 4. In Chapter 8, we examine cybercrime, cyberwarfare, and cyberterrorism. Chapter 9 focuses on security. Chapter 10 considers several important social and political issues, including privacy. These three chapters can be read in any order.

Part 5 consists of a single chapter that examines the future of e-commerce. It features a methodology for examining possible futures, and its intent is to spark discussion and debate. Perhaps, after reading the first 10 chapters, readers will disagree with the opinions and predictions of the authors and the experts we cite. We certainly hope so.

Chapter Features

Each chapter opens with a list of **Learning Objectives** that preview the chapter's key ideas. Each chapter ends with a **Summary**, a list of **Key Words**, a set of **Review Questions** linked to the learning objectives and designed to help the student prepare a personal summary of key topics, a set of **Exercises** suitable for class discussion or in-class assignments, and a set of **Projects** suitable for homework assignments or out-of-class research. One project category, **Building the Case**, provides continuing, hands-on activities that allow students to apply what they have learned as they progress through the course.

Spread throughout each chapter are **Feature Boxes** that explore related technologies, business issues, important numbers (such as demographic data), and clearly identified opinions that present alternative points of view.

Core-Plus-More

The e-commerce course is still evolving because e-commerce is still evolving. Often, material that seems cutting edge today is obsolete a few months later, so no matter which textbook is used, the instructor typically supplements it with outside readings, Web resources, and projects. Sometimes there seem to be as many versions of the e-commerce course as there are faculty members who teach it.

There is, however, an underlying core of material that does not change quite as rapidly. The basic architecture of the Internet and the World Wide Web are relatively stable. E-commerce applications support supply chain integration (business-to-business, or B2B), value chain integration (intra-business), and the business-to-consumer (B2C) link, all standard business ideas. Cybercrime and privacy concerns continue to plague e-commerce, and security provides perhaps the best hope of overcoming those problems. This book focuses on that underlying core and assumes that the instructor will supplement the material with current readings, references, projects, and discussions. This **Core-Plus-More** philosophy reflects our decision not to try to be everything to everyone. We believe that if we provide the basics and significant supplementary materials, the instructor can mold the course to his or her own vision.

Companion Web Site and Instructor Supplements

To help the instructor and the student build on the core, we have created a **companion Web site**. The Web site includes regularly updated suggested readings and URLs, project scenarios and pointers, the instructor supplements described below, and additional resources. Many of the supplementary materials are organized by possible course foci such as business, MIS/technology, and marketing. Appendix C in the text provides support for the hands-on task of creating a Web site. This organization effectively allows the instructor to custom-design a unique course around the core coverage provided in the textbook. In the text, end-of-chapter project suggestions grouped by course focus briefly describe the available supplementary materials and point the student to the Web site. We believe that this Core-Plus-More approach achieves a good balance between course stability and currency.

The Web site is the delivery vehicle for most of the Instructor supplements, including:

- An Instructor's Manual with lecture and discussion suggestions, solutions to the chapter review questions, comments on the end-of-chapter exercises, and projects
- Selected references and URLs
- Suggested hands-on and research projects
- Two sets of PowerPoint slides
    - A set of transparency-ready PowerPoint slides of the text's figures
    - A set of enhanced PowerPoint slides for each chapter
- A Test Bank
- A CourseCompass Web site planned for the spring 2003 semester

The Instructor Supplements are available exclusively to qualified instructors. Please contact your local sales representative or send e-mail to aw.cse@awl.com for access information.

We enjoyed writing this book, and we sincerely hope you enjoy reading it!

Acknowledgments

We would like to acknowledge our editor Maite Suarez-Rivas and our project editor Katherine Harutunian. Sylvia Mallory oversaw the manuscript development, and Maxine E. Chuck provided substantive editing. Marilyn Lloyd of Addison-Wesley helped to shepherd the manuscript through production, Ginny Kaczmarek did an excellent job of copyediting, and Karen Cheng managed the process of creating the pages. Michael Hirsch and Karen Schmitt ably handled marketing, and Jennifer Pelland was instrumental in setting up and managing the companion Web site. Our Miami University colleague Dr. T. M. Rajkumar offered much valuable feedback.

Finally, we thank the following manuscript reviewers for their constructive and timely comments

Bruce Anderson, University of North Carolina, Charlotte

Sulin Ba, Marshall School of Business, University of Southern California

Robin Burke, California State University, Fullerton

Robert Chi, California State University, Long Beach

Cyrus Daftary, Suffolk University and Northeastern University

Thomas Dillon, James Madison University

Christina Fader, University of Waterloo

Stéphane Gagnon, University of Quebec at Montreal

Hermann Gruenwald, University of Oklahoma

Kathy Harris, Northwestern Oklahoma State University

Stan Lewis, University of Southern Mississippi

Carla Meeske, University of Oregon

Makoto Nakayama, DePaul University

Irina Neuman, New Jersey Institute of Technology

William S. Davis   John "Skip" Benamati

Sarasota, FL   Oxford, OH

PART 1
Introduction

The purpose of Chapter 1 is to provide the reader with a clear map

for navigating the balance of the book.

CHAPTER 1

What Is Electronic Commerce?

When you finish reading this chapter, you should be able to:

- Distinguish between e-commerce and e-business

- Discuss how layering makes it possible to implement and maintain complex e-commerce systems

- Relate early islands of automation to organizational inefficiency

- Describe how the Internet and the World Wide Web revolutionized e-commerce

- Explain how e-commerce contributes to value chain and supply chain efficiency

- Discuss the digital nature of e-commerce

- Explain how technical innovation can be a source of competitive advantage

- Briefly describe each of the steps in the competitive advantage model and relate those steps to the stages in the technical innovation impact curve

- Distinguish the B2C, C2C, intra-business, and B2B forms of electronic commerce

The Dot-Com Debacle

In January 1999, four dot-com companies advertised on TV before, during, and immediately after Super Bowl XXXIII (Figure 1.1). A year later, that number soared by a factor of five. Perhaps you remember such classic Super Bowl XXIV spots as E*Trade's "Money out the wazoo" and Pets.com's singing sock puppet (Figure 1.2). You might even remember LifeMinders's self-proclaimed "worst commercial on the Super Bowl."

Why did all those dot-coms pay more than $2 million each for a mere thirty seconds of Super Bowl exposure? Basically, for the same reason all those automobile, beer, and soft drink companies paid more than $2 million each for their own thirty-second spots: exposure. The Super Bowl virtually guarantees a huge audience. What better way to get your name out there?

Figure 1.1 Dot-com Super Bowl advertisers.

Super Bowl XXXIII (1999)	Super Bowl XXXIV (2000)	Super Bowl XXXV (2001)
Hotbot	Agillion	E*Trade
Hotjobs	Auto Trader	Hotjobs
Monster	Britannica	Monster
Yahoo	Computer.com	
	Epidemic	
	E*Trade	
	Healtheon/WebMD	
	Hotjobs	
	Kforce	
	LifeMinders	
	MicroStrategy	
	Monster	
	Netpliance	
	OnMoney	
	OurBeginning	
	Oxygen	
	Pets.com	
	Wall Street Journal Interactive	
	WebEx	

Figure 1.2 The Pets.com sock puppet.

Photo ©1999 Nicole Nelson & J.W. Burkey.
Design: SullivanPerkins Inc.

The Myth

For those who bought into the dot-com myth, gaining national exposure seemed like a good risk. Their logic went something like this: Start with an idea for selling a product or a service over the Internet. Pitch it to a venture capitalist and collect several million dollars in seed money. Establish an online presence. (Don't worry about profits. Just "get your name out there.") Work long hours for a small salary plus stock options or equity shares. Then sell the company or issue an initial public offering (IPO), and become an instant billionaire. Jeff Bezos (Amazon.com), Steve Case (America Online), David Filo (Yahoo), and Jerry Yang (Yahoo) all made it. So can I.

Critics pointed to the historically absurd price-to-earnings (PE) ratios of the dot-com stocks and argued that even such bellwethers as Amazon.com had yet to make a profit. To a true believer, however, the critics were hopelessly mired in the past and unwilling to accept the new paradigms that drove the new economy. The old rules were obsolete. Stock prices were soaring. What more proof did they need?

The Bubble Bursts

It didn't take long for the bubble to burst. Technology stocks plummeted (Figure 1.3) and pink-slip parties replaced post-IPO celebrations. In January 2001, Super Bowl XXXV featured ads by only three dot-coms who (as the cynics gleefully pointed out) offered valuable services for the newly unemployed: job leads (Hotjobs and Monster) and a place to dump all that devalued stock (E*Trade).

What happened? Many experts blamed poor business planning on the part of the fledgling dot-coms and their venture capitalists, and the limitations imposed by a not-yet-mature technology certainly played a role. How long were customers supposed to

Figure 1.3 Technology stock prices tumbled in 2000.

Selected Year 2000 Stock Prices				
Company	**High**	**Year End**	**Loss ($)**	**Loss (%)**
Amazon	91.50	15.56	75.94	82.99
Ask Jeeves	139.75	2.44	137.31	98.25
DoubleClick	135.25	11.00	124.25	91.87
E*Trade	34.25	7.38	26.87	78.45
eBay	127.00	33.00	94.00	74.02
eToys	28.00	0.19	27.81	99.32
Hotjobs	45.50	11.44	34.06	74.86
Pets.com	14.00	0.09	13.91	99.36
Priceline	104.25	1.31	102.94	98.74
Yahoo	250.13	13.06	237.07	94.78

Source: *Sarasota Herald-Tribune*, 12/13/2000, pp. 4D-7D

wait for a not-quite-print-quality virtual product catalog to download? And was it real-istic to expect them to send their credit card numbers nonchalantly over the Web when the overhyped exploits of allegedly aggressive hackers made the term *Internet security* seem like an oxymoron? Inadequate preparation was a factor, too. Many dot-coms were started by geeks who knew technology but not business, and all too often, established businesses assigned responsibility for implementing a dot-com presence to technical novices in sales and marketing. Perhaps the originators' tunnel vision preordained the venture's eventual failure.

But greed and ignorance are powerful forces. The business world had just discovered the Internet. Entrepreneurs saw a brand-new exploding marketplace driving a new econ-omy. It looked like a sure thing. Granted, stock prices were high, but they would go even higher. Buy now, even if you know nothing about the underlying technology or the busi-ness fundamentals. Ignorance is bliss. Hop on the bandwagon before it's too late!

The result was inevitable; speculative bubbles always burst. And ignorance is *not* bliss. It's ignorance.

OPINION

What Were They Thinking?

Consider the following products and services offered by several failed dot-coms:

- AllAdvantage.com paid Web surfers 53 cents an hour to endure a barrage of advertising as they surfed the Web. Apparently, not enough advertis-ers were interested in marketing to people who were willing to work for 53 cents an hour, however.
- Arrangeonline.com, Funeral.com, Heavenly-Door.com, and Plan4ever.com marketed funeral arrange-ments and related services. Anyone for a physical/spiritual/virtual trifecta?
- BBQ.com sold barbeque products and supplies, including meat. We're not sure about propane.
- Bidforsurgery.com allowed its customers to solicit bids for certain surgical procedures.

- Furniture.com, Living.com, and UrbanDesign.com sold furniture. The virtual version of that recliner looked so comfy.
- Mylackey.com offered an online errand service. And a really neat name.
- Petstore.com offered a fish delivery service. Yes, live fish.
- Pets.com (the sock puppet people) bought Petstore.com (including the fish delivery service) for $13 million in stock. Five months later, Pets.com went out of business.

Granted, hindsight is 20/20, but what were they thinking?

Why Study E-Commerce?

In light of the recent rash of dot-com failures, why study electronic commerce? Reasonable question. Simple answer. E-commerce is much more than those dot-com failures. It is the way modern business does business. If you anticipate a business career, ignoring the basics of e-commerce makes about as much sense as ignoring the basics of accounting, finance, management, and marketing. According to Peter Drucker, "The right model for the information-based organization is… the symphony orchestra." E-commerce provides a means for blending the instruments by defining the form and structure of the next generation of information systems and enabling what Bill Gates calls a company's digital nervous system. In other words, e-commerce provides a mechanism for ensuring that the organization's various parts work together in harmony.

No matter what your major or field of emphasis, you are a future decision-maker who will help determine your employer's technical direction. Thus it is essential that you understand what modern technology can and cannot do, how your competitors are using technology, and how you can leverage technology to achieve a competitive advantage.

On a more personal level, e-commerce is changing the way we communicate, shop, invest, learn, and stay informed about the world around us. Even if you never work in a business or managerial capacity, e-commerce will affect your life. Much like the real world, cyberspace can be dangerous to the uninformed, and the more you understand, the less likely you are to fall prey to the hackers, scammers, hypesters, spoofers, and other lowlifes who populate the Internet.

If you're looking for a magic bullet that guarantees untold wealth and early retirement, a course in electronic commerce is probably not going to help you very much. If, on the other hand, you'd like some insight into how modern business does business, a solid understanding of e-commerce is a good starting point. As your career evolves, technology will change, but the underlying principles will not. Forget the dot-com hype. Electronic commerce is a source of good, old-fashioned technological innovation that improves efficiency and spawns competitive advantage. That's the reality.

The Reality of E-Commerce

E-commerce is a way of doing business. As so many dot-commers learned the hard way, a good idea, by itself, is not enough, because the underlying market parameters still matter. The ultimate objective of any business is to make a profit. Profit is revenue minus cost. Generating revenue may be glamorous, but defining e-commerce as simply buying and selling on the Internet and the World Wide Web (the traditional definition) is a form of tunnel vision akin to looking through the wrong end of a telescope. The real potential of e-commerce is improved efficiency, not revenue generation.

The definition of e-commerce is evolving to reflect this broader perspective. According to the 2001 edition of Microsoft's Encarta World English Dictionary, **e-commerce** (or **electronic commerce**) consists of "transactions conducted over the Internet, either by consumers purchasing goods and services, or directly between businesses." Webopedia (*www.webopedia.com*), an online source of technical information, defines e-commerce as "conducting business online," a definition that encompasses *any* electronic or paperless exchange of business information over *any* communication medium. Almost all business enterprises exchange goods, services, and information electronically; only a tiny fraction of these interactions directly involve retail customers, and not all of them use the Internet or the World Wide Web.

E-business (or **electronic business**) is a broader term that encompasses electronically buying, selling, servicing customers, and interacting with business partners and intermediaries over the Internet. Some experts see e-business as the objective and e-commerce as the means of achieving that objective. We will use e-commerce, the more familiar term, throughout this book, but don't lose sight of that broad, e-business perspective. Picture e-commerce as an iceberg and direct Internet-based sales to consumers as the visible tip (Figure 1.4). That is the reality of e-commerce.

Layering

The information technology and communication systems that support e-commerce are so incredibly complex that few (if any) people understand all the components in depth.

Figure 1.4 Direct business-to-customer transactions represent the visible tip of the e-commerce iceberg.

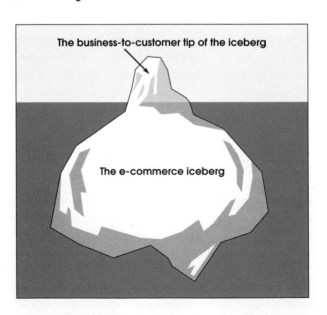

The Catalyst

If e-commerce is so good, why wasn't it common decades ago? The answer is simple: Until recently, the available technology was not up to the task. Information technology evolves quickly, however, and today's computers are sufficiently powerful and contain enough memory to support the complex software that drives e-commerce. Additionally, communication lines are now fast enough to transmit significant amounts of information between two computers in something approaching real time. Without these technological improvements, e-commerce would still be little more than an intriguing possibility.

Consequently, system developers, maintainers, and users tend to specialize. A good way to coordinate the efforts of all those specialists is to borrow an old architectural concept called **layering**, the process of adding onto or tapping into an existing infrastructure.

For example, Savannah, Georgia, is often cited as a classic example of how intelligent layering affects the way a city evolves over time. Founded in 1733 on a patch of virgin forest on the banks of the Savannah River, Savannah had no existing infrastructure to guide or constrain the city's planners. The river and the wharf were the original focal points. Running parallel to the river was a highway, an essential conduit for moving products to and from the wharf. Across the highway were several small communities, each centered on a public square. Passage through a community meant going through or around the square, but movement between communities utilized wider, less impeded thoroughfares (Figure 1.5). As Savannah grew, the underlying infrastructure imposed by the master plan acted as a spine, guiding the city's growth for the next 120 years. As new communities were added, they aligned themselves along the extended thoroughfares (allowing for rapid transit) and incorporated their own public squares (enhancing a sense of community), because doing so made sense.

Consider another example. Imagine that Wal-Mart has decided to construct a new superstore. Given a choice between locating the new store near a major interstate highway interchange or developing a more remote site, Wal-Mart is likely to choose the former, because tapping into the existing transportation infrastructure (the interstate highway system) is far less expensive than building new access roads to bring customers to an outlying site. Move on to the construction phase. Rather than creating new electric power generation, communication, water, and sewer systems, Wal-Mart will almost certainly adopt the standards documented in the local building codes and tap into the existing, standard infrastructures provided by the local electric, communication, water, and sewer utilities. (Why reinvent the wheel?) Creating a new building would be prohibitively expensive without layering.

Figure 1.5 Master plan that guided the growth of Savannah, Georgia, for 120 years.

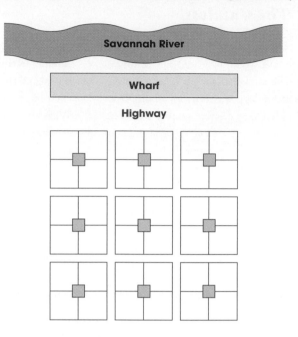

Once access to the existing infrastructures is gained, new applications can be built on top of the old layers. For example, most Wal-Mart stores have a security system that relies on both electric power and data communication. The power comes from a wall socket. Intrusions are reported via a wire plugged into a telephone jack. For all practical purposes, the services provided by the power and communication infrastructures can safely be taken for granted as they effectively fade into the background—unless, of course, they fail.

In an information system or e-commerce sense, a layer is a program or set of programs that provides services to the layer above it and uses the services provided by the layer below it. Think of each layer as a black box. To use the black box, you provide values for one or more input parameters, and it returns values for one or more output parameters. For example, if you pass a number to a square root function, the function returns the number's square root. The term *black box* implies that the contents of the box are unknown. The function (generating a square root) is known, but the user neither knows nor cares whether the function is performed by table look-up, interpolation, repetitive estimation, or an elf with a calculator. Consequently, the black box's contents can be changed without affecting the user (or any other black box) as long as the correct input parameters are supplied and the expected output parameters are produced. The result is functional independence.

Because each layer is functionally independent, stacking layers is like stacking building blocks. For example, it is possible to create a complex, integrated information system by constructing a series of applications on top of a shared information technology infrastructure (Figure 1.6). The various applications can communicate with each other through the infrastructure, and because the layers are functionally independent, each of them can be improved and upgraded without affecting the other applications or the underlying infrastructure. Also, because functions common to all the applications can be implemented in the underlying infrastructure, there is no need to repeat those functions in each program. Modern e-commerce systems would be virtually impossible to implement and maintain without layering. It is a powerful concept.

Integrating Islands of Automation

Integrated, layered information systems did not simply spring into being, of course. Instead, they evolved over time. The process started nearly half a century ago, when the earliest business computer applications focused on a single function. For example, the payroll department recognized that using computers to process and print paychecks saved money by replacing a small army of payroll clerks and typists. Other functional areas followed payroll's lead, creating applications to support accounts payable, accounts receivable, general ledger, inventory management, and similar tasks.

One legacy of this functional focus was a myriad of internal **islands of automation**, independent sets of business processes, application programs, hardware, and data that communicated with the other islands by exchanging physical (usually paper) documents. For example, imagine that sales data were input, processed, and output in printed form by the sales department on island A (Figure 1.7). Those printed reports were then delivered to islands B, C, and D, where the payroll, inventory, and accounts receivable departments respectively extracted relevant data, manually reentered that data, processed it, and produced their own printed reports. Subsequently, the accounts receivable report was delivered to island E, where the billing department extracted the data it needed to prepare bills, input and processed that data, and printed its own reports.

The problem with those islands of automation was that each one represented an internally efficient but isolated fiefdom with its own hardware, software, and data structures. For example, the sales function on island A developed computer applications to improve and integrate its sales-related processes. Meanwhile, the payroll function on island B created its own independent applications. Because each island focused on its own processes and ignored the other islands, the resulting local information systems were often incompatible, and attempts to integrate them to gain organization-wide efficiencies were thwarted by data redundancy, inconsistent data structures and data formats,

Figure 1.6 Layering.

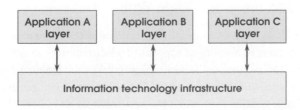

Figure 1.7 Islands of automation.

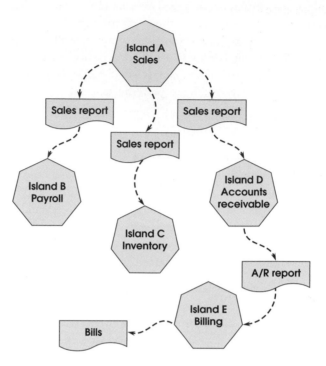

and nonstandard hardware and software. Consequently, the resulting productivity gains, though substantial, were local in scope—they stopped at the (figurative) waterline.

With apologies to English poet John Donne, no business function is an island. Sales, billing, accounts receivable, production, inventory management, order fulfillment, and other key business functions are interrelated. The key to achieving organizational (rather than local) efficiency is sharing information and using that information to coordinate those functions. In the late 1970s and early 1980s, aligning information system strategy with corporate strategy and integrating or centralizing enterprise data became the new focus, and integrating or eliminating those islands of automation by enhancing internal information sharing became an important objective. Corporate databases housed on large, centralized computers linked to the functional systems by communication lines and intermediate data conversion routines provided a means for achieving that objective (Figure 1.8). Note the layers.

The Internet and the World Wide Web

Eventually, larger firms with substantial financial resources created private proprietary communication systems to allow their suppliers and distributors to access selectively the corporate database and internal applications (Figure 1.9), thus enabling significant interorganizational efficiencies such as just-in-time (JIT) inventory management. Those proprietary communication systems were much too expensive for all but the largest companies,

Figure 1.8 Corporate databases stored on large centralized computers provided a means for integrating the islands of automation.

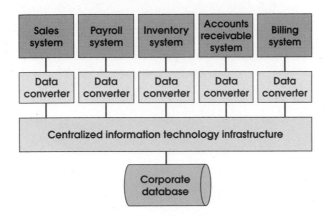

however. E-commerce did not become widely available until the Internet changed the economics of information sharing.

The **Internet** is a global network of networks defined by a set of open standards for communicating data and information between computers. It rests on top of the global data communication network (Figure 1.10). The **World Wide Web** (or just the **Web**) is a standard set of naming and linking conventions that uses the Internet to locate and transport hypertext documents and other files stored on computers located all over the world. Various Web-based application programs such as the familiar **browser**, an application program that provides a user-friendly point-and-click interface for accessing the Web, run on top of the Web. Once again, note the layers.

Figure 1.9 Private proprietary communication systems allowed suppliers and distributors to access the corporate database selectively.

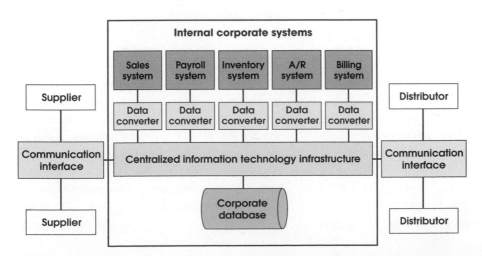

Figure 1.10 The Internet and the World Wide Web.

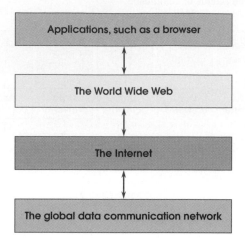

Together, the Internet and the World Wide Web created a new, inexpensive, public infrastructure that quickly replaced the private, proprietary networks used by early interorganizational applications. Big companies responded by adding economically marginal sites to their networks, thus broadening their reach. Small companies found the cost of entry to a potentially huge global marketplace no longer beyond their means. And e-commerce exploded.

Hypertext

Hypertext, the basic idea behind the World Wide Web, was proposed by Ted Nelson in the 1960s and implemented in the first Macintosh computer in 1984. Working with hypertext is like browsing an encyclopedia or a dictionary. For example, imagine you are searching for information about e-commerce and you encounter the definition *conducting business online*. Imagine further that you are not sure exactly what *online* means. Using a traditional printed encyclopedia, you might walk to the bookshelf, find the appropriate volume, open it, locate the term *online*, and read the explanation. If, however, the encyclopedia is electronic, clicking your mouse on the word

online in the e-commerce definition takes you directly to the entry for *online*.

As the term implies, hypertext was initially intended to link text entries or documents. However, the same basic idea, clicking on a logical pointer to access information, can be applied to other media as well, including graphics, sound, data, and multimedia files. On the World Wide Web, the logical pointer that connects one page to another is called a hyperlink, and clicking on a hyperlink causes a copy of the requested page to be transported across the Internet and displayed on the requestor's screen.

The Value Chain

Basketball is a team game. Consequently, a basketball team composed of five scorers and no passers is likely to lose to a balanced, well-coached team that runs precise plays. Similarly, a company that operates as a set of functionally independent islands of automation is likely to be less efficient than a competitor that effectively coordinates and balances its internal processes.

The set of integrated internal processes that combine to deliver value to customers by transforming raw materials into finished products forms a company's **value chain** (Figure 1.11). Note the arrows that link adjacent processes. Note also that all those processes are linked to the information technology infrastructure. The key to process coordination is information sharing, and the infrastructure provides a means for sharing information and for performing the necessary logic.

Incidentally, a value chain is a good example of a **model**, a simplified version of something complex used to analyze and solve problems or make predictions.[1] Models are extremely valuable because they allow us to strip away layers of detail and focus on a few essential variables. Remember, however, that a model is a simplification of reality. If the model and reality disagree, trust reality. But keep your eyes open.

Physical and Logical Data

The arrows that link adjacent value chain entities represent both product flows and data flows (Figure 1.12). Physical products such as parts, subassemblies, and finished goods are transported by truck, train, barge, airplane, forklift, assembly line, foot, or some other physical means of conveyance.[2] Physical data flows carry paper documents. In contrast, logical products and logical data flows are transferred electronically from one computer to another. A computer is a binary machine. Consequently, those logical data and product flows, whether numbers, characters, images, or sounds, exist in **digital** form as strings of binary digits, 0s and 1s. An e-commerce transaction, by definition, represents an exchange of *digital* data and information.

Figure 1.11 The value chain.

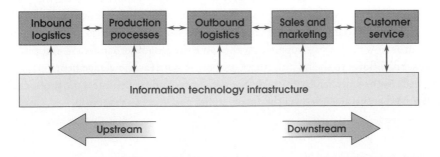

---

[1] Microsoft Encarta World English Dictionary, 2001.

[2] Except, of course, on *Star Trek*.

Figure 1.12 The arrows connecting adjacent value chain entities represent product flows and data flows.

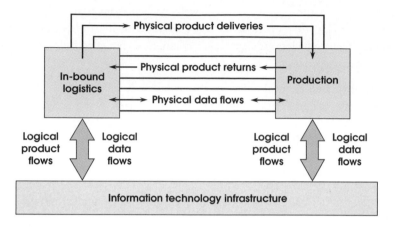

Simply replacing physical paperwork with digital data flows enhances efficiency by eliminating redundant data entry, reducing errors, minimizing paperwork clutter, and so on. More significantly, combining the digital data from related processes with other digital data such as production schedules, inventory levels, and shipping schedules makes it possible to coordinate those processes more efficiently. The result is systemwide (rather than local) efficiency.

Digital products such as software, MP3 recordings, and digital images are particularly well suited to e-commerce because, like logical data, they consist of strings of binary digits and thus can be electronically transferred between computers. Chapter 5 explores in depth the advantages associated with digital products. See Appendix A for additional information on common digital formats.

The Supply Chain

A **supply chain** is a set of business processes that allow multiple independent entities such as suppliers, manufacturers, and retailers to function as one "virtual" organization to develop and deliver products (more generally, economic value) to consumers (Figure 1.13). Like a value chain, the arrows connecting adjacent entities in the supply chain represent both product flows and data flows. Physical parts move from a supplier to the manufacturer, and returns flow back to the supplier. At the same time, data (order details, shipping documents, bills) flows to the manufacturer, and other data (acknowledgements, payments) flows back to the supplier. Increasingly, the data flows and (sometimes) the product flows are digitized and transferred via the Internet and the World Wide Web.

Bits versus Atoms

OPINION

Dell Computer has enjoyed great success marketing personal computers directly to consumers, and Amazon.com, the online bookseller, rivals Coca-Cola for brand-name recognition. Computers and bound books are physical products composed of atoms, so clearly it is possible to sell physical products online.

Remember, however, that e-commerce, the act of conducting business online, is by definition digital. Selling fifty-pound bags of dog food over the Internet makes about as much sense as selling fifty-pound bags of dog food in an airport's duty-free shop—it's the wrong marketplace. E-commerce is best for *digital* transactions, such as exchanging bits in the form of data, information, and digital products. Selling physical products online is tough unless the online experience adds enough value to the transaction to offset such negatives as shipping cost, shipping time, and the inability to physically see the product or the seller before the transaction is consummated. In other words, selling physical products online is likely to be successful only if it gives the seller a significant competitive advantage and delivers value to the customer.

Intermediaries

Note the airplane and truck icons above and below the horizontal arrows in Figure 1.13. They represent **intermediaries**, companies that assist or add value to the exchange of products and/or information. In the physical world, Wal-Mart might hire a broker to locate a supplier for some hard-to-find product, a supplier might hire a trucking firm to deliver products to Wal-Mart, and Wal-Mart might use Federal Express to send information to a supplier. With e-commerce, other intermediaries provide the hardware and software needed to store, process, and transmit information, a means for accessing the Internet and the World Wide Web, search engines, e-mail services, payment services, Web site creation and hosting services, and so on. E-commerce could not exist without the services provided by intermediaries.

Figure 1.13 The supply chain.

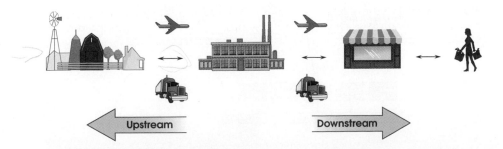

Upstream   Downstream

A Bigger Picture

Look to the right of Figure 1.13 and find the last link from the retailer to the consumer. To the uninformed, that one final link *is* e-commerce, but they are wrong. The retailer-to-consumer link (which, incidentally, accounts for the lion's share of the dot-com failures) is but one component in a much bigger system.

Each symbol on the supply chain represents a company with its own internal value chain (Figure 1.14). If the value chain links *islands* of automation, the supply chain links *continents* of automation. Additionally, the term *supply chain* (singular) is an oversimplification because it implies a single path from supplier to customer. Reality is much more complex. For example, in Figure 1.15, Wal-Mart interacts with not just one but numerous suppliers. At least some of Wal-Mart's customers buy directly from one or more of

Figure 1.14 Each symbol on the supply chain represents a company with its own value chain.

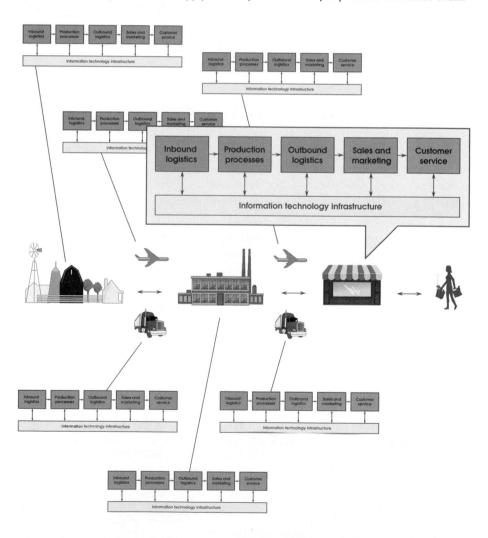

Figure 1.15 The term *supply chain* (singular) is an oversimplification.

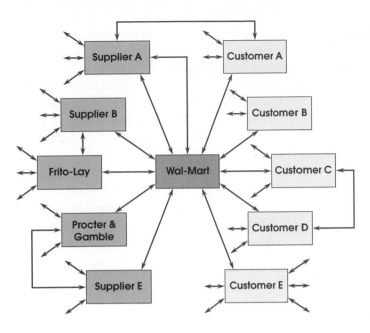

Wal-Mart's suppliers (for example, the line linking Customer A and Supplier A) and many of those suppliers interact with each other (Supplier E and Procter & Gamble). Wal-Mart, its suppliers, and its customers all utilize the services of intermediaries, and some suppliers and intermediaries are also Wal-Mart customers. Add each member organization's internal value chain, and you begin to glimpse the complexity of a real-world supply chain.

Notice how many data flows (the lines and arrows) there are in Figure 1.15. Each of those data flows represents a possible e-commerce application. Much as conducting a national census is significantly more complex than counting the number of people in a room, integrating multiple organizations is much more complex than integrating across a single company's internal value chain. E-commerce makes it *possible* to coordinate all those entities and reap the benefits resulting from improved efficiency. That is the real potential of e-commerce.

Technology as a Source of Competitive Advantage

A **competitive advantage** is a benefit derived from something a company does or has that its customers want and its competitors cannot (or choose not to) match. Your company's competitive advantage gives your customers a reason to buy from you rather than from a competitor. Consequently, companies continually seek to create and protect their own and to neutralize their competitors' competitive advantages by improving their business practices. The innovative use of information technology is a common source of such improvements. Successful e-businesses do not adopt information technology for its own sake. They do so because they see an opportunity to gain a competitive advantage.

A well-known competitive advantage model suggests a six-stage sequence for tracking the life cycle of a technical innovation (Figure 1.16).[3] During the first stage, stimulus for action, a problem or opportunity that might be addressed by an innovative application of technology is identified. Next, an organization (one of multiple competitors) makes a first major move by creating and implementing an appropriate solution, a significant investment that carries considerable risk. The third stage, customer acceptance, determines the investment's success or failure. If customers like the innovation, the first mover gains a competitive advantage and its competitors launch catch-up moves. Simultaneously, first-mover expansion moves attempt to extend or sustain the competitive advantage; think of the first mover and its competitors trading catch-up moves and expansion moves in a perpetual cycle. Eventually, given time, commoditization occurs, and the innovation becomes a normal part of doing business. At this final stage, no one enjoys a competitive advantage, but not having the innovation puts a company at a competitive disadvantage.

The adoption and impact of a technical innovation often follows a three-stage S-curve (Figure 1.17). In the initial readiness stage (Keen's stimulus for action, first major move, and customer acceptance stages), growth is slow as the technology gains acceptance and useful applications begin to evolve. Eventually, those new applications intensify acceptance of the new technology, which fuels further innovation (competitor catch-up moves

Figure 1.16 The competitive advantage model.

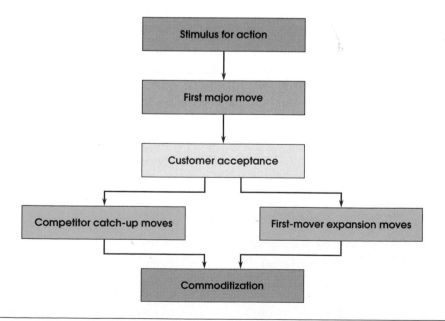

---

[3] Peter G. W. Keen, *Shaping the Future: Business Design through Information Technology* (Boston: Harvard Business School Press, 1991).

Figure 1.17 The new technology adoption curve.

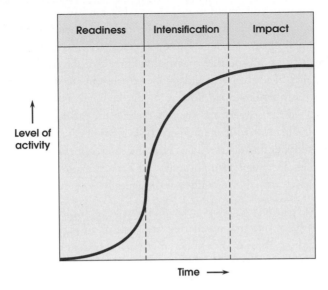

and first-mover expansion moves). During this second stage, the new technology begins to influence how companies do business. During the final impact stage, the technology becomes mainstream (commoditization).

Many experts believe that electronic commerce is just entering the intensification stage. If they are right, its full impact has yet to be determined.

BUSINESS

First Movers and First Followers

Is it best to be a first mover? Or is "wait, see, and react" a better strategy? If the innovation achieves a high level of customer acceptance, the first mover gains a competitive advantage and the competitors are reduced to playing catch-up. On the other hand, if the innovation fails, the first mover's investment is lost. Being a second mover reduces risk, but it also reduces the potential reward. It's an interesting dilemma.

Consider, for example, online retailing. The first movers included such companies as eve.com, foofoo.com, furniture.com, gazelle.com, living.com, miadora.com, Pets.com, productopia.com, and toysmart.com. A naïve belief in the magic of first mover advantage may have encouraged undue haste—get there first, then decide if it's really worth doing. But the next time you're online, don't bother trying to access those Web sites, because they no longer exist. In contrast, such "first followers" as Sears, JCPenney, Wal-Mart, and other established old-economy retailers took their time, learned from the first movers' mistakes, and leveraged their existing real-world outlets to create effective e-presences.

E-Commerce Categories

E-commerce takes many different forms (Figure 1.18), but **business-to-business** (**B2B**), the electronic exchange of information, digital products, and services between companies and across the supply chain, is by far the most significant. For example, imagine delivering parts to a manufacturer. Historically, the manufacturer sent the supplier an order (paperwork). The supplier filled the order and shipped it, accompanied by more paperwork. A bill (still more paperwork) followed, and eventually payment (even more paperwork) was made. Processing all that paperwork was expensive, error-prone, and slow. Compare the old way of doing business with the modern B2B e-commerce approach. Parts are still ordered from a supplier and delivered to a manufacturer, but the appropriate documents are exchanged digitally rather than physically. The result is lower cost, fewer errors, and faster turnaround because moving information digitally is so much more efficient.

Intra-business e-commerce, also known as **business-to-employee** (**B2E**) e-commerce, applies the same basic information-sharing principle to an organization's internal value chain, thus integrating those islands of automation you read about earlier in the chapter. Together, B2B and B2E e-commerce define the way modern business does business.

Although it represents only a small subset of e-commerce (the tip of the iceberg), **business-to-consumer** (**B2C**), the online exchange of information, goods, and services directly with the retail customer, is the best-known form. Following the dot-com shake-out, many of the weaker B2C firms are no longer in business. Natural selection suggests that the survivors are likely to be strong, however.

Recently, **consumer-to-consumer** (**C2C**) e-commerce, the direct, one-to-one exchange of electronic information between consumers, has emerged as a viable e-business model. Auction sites such as eBay, online music exchanges such as Napster and LiveWire, chat

Figure 1.18 E-commerce categories.

Category	Comments
Business-to-business (B2B)	E-commerce links between businesses. The largest and most lucrative e-commerce category. The way modern business does business.
Intra-business or business-to-employee (B2E)	Internal information sharing. B2B at the value chain level. A significant source of competitive advantage through enhanced efficiency.
Business-to-consumer (B2C)	The best known category, but a relatively small piece of the e-commerce picture. The source of the lion's share of e-commerce failures.
Consumer-to-consumer (C2C)	Direct information sharing between customers, often facilitated (but not controlled by) intermediaries. Currently a minor form of e-commerce, but with intriguing potential.

According to a summary of selected U.S. Bureau of the Census data published by *www.bizstats.com*, year 2000 retail sales in the United States totaled slightly more than $3.2 trillion. Of that total, B2C e-commerce accounted for $25.8 billion, less than 1 percent. Other e-commerce studies define retail e-commerce more broadly; for example, a September 2000 forecast by Forrester Research (published on *www.iconocast.com*) estimated year 2000 retail B2C revenues at $44.8 billion. Even if you use the higher number, B2C's slice of the pie is still only 1.4 percent, however.

Consider the results of another study published in the November 2000 issue of *Wired* (page 122). It compares the 1999 revenues generated by nineteen traditional and "new economy" business segments. Here are some selected totals:

Rank	Segment	Revenue (billions)
1	Oil	$268
2	Computers	194
3	B2B	177
14	B2C	20

The sum of B2B and B2C revenues is $197 billion. B2C's $20 billion is roughly 10 percent of that total. B2B accounts for the other 90 percent. No matter how you look at the numbers, B2B emerges as the dominant form of e-commerce.

rooms, teleconferencing, and collaborative workgroups and support groups are examples. However, although the category seems promising, there are very few pure C2C applications. For example, eBay operates an online client/server auction house that serves as a gathering point for buyers and sellers, and only the final exchange of goods and payments resembles the C2C model. Even Napster features a centralized service to match participants, and members exchange MP3 files via the Internet, a client/server network. The future of C2C e-commerce is far from clear, but its potential is intriguing.

The various e-commerce categories are discussed extensively in Chapter 5 (B2C), Chapter 6 (intra-business), and Chapter 7 (B2B).

A Plan of Attack

Together, the global communication network, the Internet, and the World Wide Web define an infrastructure for conducting e-commerce. The communication network is the foundation. The Internet defines a set of standard rules for transmitting information over the communication network. Layered on top of the Internet, the World Wide Web uses the Internet to find—and the underlying communication network to transport— hypertext documents and other files stored on computers located (literally) anywhere in the world. E-commerce is implemented by application routines that run on top of the Internet and the World Wide Web. The underlying infrastructure, e-commerce applications, and significant e-commerce growing pains are the topics of subsequent chapters.

The Infrastructure

Part 2 of this book focuses on the lowest layers, the infrastructure. Chapter 2 introduces the basics of data communication and networks, details the architecture of the Internet, and shows how the Internet is layered on top of the global data communication infrastructure. Chapter 3 addresses client server computing, the World Wide Web, and Web applications. The objective of these two chapters is not to teach you the details of the underlying technology (many schools offer independent courses on each of those topics) but to teach you enough *about* the technology so you can better appreciate the e-commerce applications that are constructed upon that base. The point is to gain a sense of what the underlying technology can and cannot reasonably be expected to do so that you can recognize good and bad e-commerce opportunities.

The Business of E-Commerce

Although some technology will be discussed, the primary focus of Part 3 is business. Just because something can be done technically does not necessarily mean that it makes business sense. From a business perspective, technology is a means to such ends as competitive advantage and (ultimately) enhanced profit. Chapter 4 reviews certain key business principles that apply to any business enterprise, be it physical or virtual, including "little" things like profit, return on investment, competitive advantage, and business planning, the underlying essentials that so many failed dot-coms either forgot, ignored, or never fully understood. Those principles establish a base for examining, from a business perspective, the various forms of e-commerce. Chapter 5 looks at the consumer-oriented B2C category, Chapter 6 focuses on intra-business e-commerce, and Chapter 7 discusses supply chain automation and B2B e-commerce. The contributions of intermediaries are highlighted throughout Part 3. Note that e-commerce applies to government and non-profit agencies, too.

Growing Pains

As you will discover, the Internet and the World Wide Web were not designed with e-commerce in mind. Instead, they were designed by academics and researchers with the highly commendable goal of furthering the exchange of ideas in a joint effort to push back the frontiers of knowledge. To the researcher, information should be freely available to all. To the entrepreneur, however, the firm's competitive advantage must be protected, and that implies secrecy. Clearly, those two worldviews are incompatible. Like a house built on sand or a square peg in a round hole, the infrastructure and the business applications layered on top of it don't always fit together perfectly.

Part 4 highlights several problems, incompatibilities, and issues that arise, at least in part, from this imperfect fit. Hacking and other forms of cybercrime, cyberterrorism, and cyberwarfare are the subjects of Chapter 8. Chapter 9 considers Internet security and examines its potential for countering the concerns raised in Chapter 9 in some detail. Chapter 10 discusses such nontechnical issues as privacy, identity theft, and online fraud that contribute to the fear, uncertainty, and doubt that shape the popular perception of cyberspace as a dangerous place .

The Future of E-Commerce

In many ways, the e-commerce infrastructure, sometimes called the information super-highway, resembles a virtual parallel to the interstate highway system that crisscrosses the United States. Conceived in the name of national defense, the interstate highway system is generally regarded a tremendous success, but consider some of its unanticipated and unintended consequences. Families left the cities and moved to the suburbs to live on what was once productive farmland. Developers responded by building new subdivisions. Beltways were constructed to ease commuting, and suburbia sprawled even more. Office parks and shopping centers sprang up, surrounded by acres of parking lots. Downtowns withered and died. And many people began to believe that we had too many automobiles, too many trucks, too many parking lots, too many urban ghettos, and too much smog.

Similarly, e-commerce will change the way we live as it changes the way we do business. Some of those changes will be good, but some won't. Understanding what e-commerce can, cannot, should, and should not do is essential if the benefits are to outweigh the costs. If you need a reason to study e-commerce, there it is.

In Part 5, Chapter 11 examines how e-commerce is likely to shape the future. It is impossible to predict the future with any precision, so this material is necessarily speculative and reflects the opinions of the authors and others. Perhaps you will disagree with some of our conclusions and speculations. Given what you have learned in Chapters 1 through 10, we sincerely hope so.

E-Commerce at Dell

BUSINESS

Dell Computer Corporation, a well-known supplier of high-quality personal and business microcomputer systems, owes much of its success to the innovative application of e-commerce principles and technology. Perhaps you have purchased a personal computer from Dell. If so, you may already be familiar with the company's highly effective B2C outlet. Internally, Dell relies on intra-business e-commerce to exchange information instantly among its value chain processes. By using the resulting current, up-to-the-minute information, Dell is able to balance and coordinate those processes to achieve impressive systemwide efficiency. Externally, Dell maintains B2B e-commerce links with the suppliers and customers that make up its supply chain, leading to additional efficiency gains. Improved efficiency implies lower costs, and those lower costs give Dell a significant, sustainable competitive advantage. Dell's e-commerce initiatives will be examined in more depth in subsequent chapters.

Summary

As a future businessperson and as a consumer, you need to understand the basics of e-commerce. E-commerce means conducting business online. E-business encompasses electronically buying, selling, servicing customers, and interacting with business partners and intermediaries over the Internet. Increasingly, e-commerce is the way business does business.

A layer is a program or set of programs that provides services to the layer above it and uses the services provided by the layer below it. Modern e-commerce systems would be virtually impossible to implement and maintain without layering.

The earliest business computer applications focused on a single function, yielding myriad internal islands of automation. The islands of automation were integrated by linking each of them to a centralized information technology infrastructure. Proprietary interorganizational systems extended access to such external entities as suppliers and distributors. Eventually, the low-cost public infrastructure enabled by layering the Internet and the World Wide Web on top of the global communication network replaced expensive proprietary systems.

A firm's value chain shows how its internal processes are linked. The arrows connecting adjacent entities represent product flows and data flows. By its very nature, e-commerce is concerned with the exchange of digital data and information. Each logical data flow represents a potential e-commerce application. Sharing information among internal processes helps to coordinate those processes, leading to productivity gains. A supply chain shows a given company's links to its suppliers and its customers. Integrating multiple organizations is much more complex than integrating a single company's internal processes, but e-commerce makes it possible to coordinate all those entities and reap the productivity gains resulting from improved efficiency. E-commerce would be impossible without the services provided by intermediaries.

Companies adopt new technology in hopes of achieving a competitive advantage; the competitive advantage model highlights the stages in the adoption process. The impact of a technical innovation often follows a three-stage S-curve as it progresses from readiness through intensification to impact.

Business-to-business (B2B) is by far the most significant form of e-commerce. Intra-business or business-to-employee (B2E) e-commerce applies B2B's information-sharing principles to an organization's internal value chain. Together, B2B and B2E e-commerce define the way modern business does business. Although it represents only a small subset of e-commerce, business-to-consumer (B2C) is the best-known form. Recently, consumer-to-consumer (C2C) e-commerce has emerged as a significant e-business model.

Key Words

browser

business-to-business (B2B) e-commerce

business-to-consumer (B2C) e-commerce

business-to-employee (B2E) e-commerce

competitive advantage

consumer-to-consumer (C2C) e-commerce

digital

e-business, or electronic business

e-commerce, or electronic commerce

intermediary

Internet

intra-business e-commerce

island of automation

layering

model

supply chain

value chain

World Wide Web

■ ■ ■
■ ■ Review Questions

You will find a set of review questions at the end of each chapter. They are designed to help you check how well you understood the chapter material. The answer to each question is in the text.

1. Briefly discuss the myth that drove so many bright people to launch a dot-com business.

2. Given the recent failures of so many dot-coms, why is it still useful to study e-commerce?

3. What is e-commerce? Distinguish between e-commerce and e-business.

4. The real potential of e-commerce lies in improved efficiency, not revenue enhancement. Do you agree or disagree? Why?

5. What is layering? Without layering, it would be next to impossible to implement and maintain a complex e-commerce system. Why?

6. What is an island of automation? Why are islands of automation inefficient from a systemwide perspective?

7. What is the Internet? What is the World Wide Web? Together, the Internet and the World Wide Web revolutionized e-commerce. How?

8. What is a value chain? How does e-commerce contribute to improving value chain efficiency?

9. Distinguish between physical and logical data. E-commerce is digital in nature. Why?

10. What is a supply chain? How does e-commerce contribute to improving supply chain efficiency?

11. What is an intermediary? Cite several examples of e-commerce intermediary services. Why are those services valuable?

12. What is a competitive advantage? Why is competitive advantage important? How does technical innovation contribute to achieving a competitive advantage?

13. Explain each of the steps in the competitive advantage model.

14. Identify and describe the stages in the technical innovation impact curve, and relate those stages to the competitive advantage model. Some experts believe that e-commerce is just entering the intensification stage. Assuming they are right, why is that significant?

15. Distinguish among the B2B, intra-business or B2E, B2C, and C2C forms of e-commerce.

■ ■ ■
■ ■ Exercises

Unlike the review questions, the answers to the exercises are not necessarily found in the text. The function of the exercises is to suggest topics for class discussion and to prompt you to think about the chapter material.

1. Why do you suppose so many dot-coms failed? What can you learn from those failures?

2. Find out which year 2000 Super Bowl XXXIV advertisers are still in business and which ones have failed. Are there any patterns that help to explain those outcomes? Can you think of other explanations to distinguish the successes from the failures?

3. Identify several examples of inappropriate e-commerce products. What makes a given product a good candidate for e-commerce success?

4. Have you ever experienced confusing instructions, lost connections, poor service, late delivery, or similar problems with a dot-com firm? How did those observations and experiences influence your personal view of e-commerce?

5. Even today, old Savannah, Georgia, remains a unique and surprisingly livable city. Visit for a few days and you quickly come to appreciate the genius of the founders' original master plan. Beyond the historic district, however, Savannah resembles most American cities. Why do you suppose that is so?

6. What is a digital product? Cite several examples. The potential for online retail sales is particularly strong for digital products. Why?

7. Is it best to be a first mover? Or is "wait, see, and react" a better strategy? What do you think?

8. Studies and demographic data consistently show that B2B is the dominant form of e-commerce. Why do you suppose that is so?

Projects

The end-of-chapter projects are divided into four groups: Broad-Based Projects, Business Projects, Information Technology Projects, and Marketing Projects. Depending on the focus of your course, your instructor might assign out-of-course work from one or more of these categories.

Some of these projects are preceded by the phrase "Building the Case," highlighted by a blue wave. These are continuing hands-on projects designed to be completed step-by-step as you master the content of each chapter. For the "Building the Case" projects, you or your instructor might choose a scenario from this textbook's companion Web site.

Broad-Based Projects

1. Ask at least ten friends and acquaintances if they use the Internet and the World Wide Web regularly, occasionally, rarely, or never, and what products (if any) they have purchased online. Then ask them how they would have answered the same questions five years ago. Write a paper to summarize your findings and explain why the responses have changed over time.

2. Ask several business professionals how e-commerce has affected their jobs or careers over the past five years. Write a paper to summarize your findings.

3. Purchase a book or a CD from Amazon.com. Visit a Barnes & Noble bookstore and the Barnes & Noble e-commerce site and purchase (physically or electronically) another book or CD. Contrast your experiences.

4. Visit a local supermarket, contact the supermarket chain's regional office, or conduct your own Internet-based research to find out how the information collected by the stores' UPC scanner checkout systems is used. Write a paper summarizing your observations and research.

5. Browse an electronic encyclopedia and compare your experience to using a traditional set of encyclopedias. Which do you prefer? Why?

6. Imagine that you are part of a consulting team competing for the opportunity to solve a potential client's e-commerce problem. Your team will be assigned a scenario describing the client's problem, organization, industry, competitive environment, existing technology infrastructure, and other information as appropriate. Your job is to prepare and present a proposal designed to convince the client that your consulting group should be selected to complete the project.

All proposals must include (as a minimum) a detailed overview of your recommended strategy and/or a preliminary version of your business plan, a prototype version of the Web site that highlights and demonstrates the most important aspects of your proposed solution, and an implementation plan. Sometime after midterm, each team will present its recommended strategy and demonstrate its prototype Web site to the class. The final step is to prepare an executive summary (no more than three pages, double spaced) of the proposed strategy and submit to your instructor the summary, a printed copy of your recommended strategy and implementation plan, a copy of your slides or other presentation materials, the URL (or a printed copy of selected pages) for your Web site, and other relevant documentation.

Start by selecting a scenario or obtaining one from your instructor. Read your scenario carefully, note any questions you might have, and find the answers to those questions. If you are part of a project team, meet with your teammates to discuss your scenario.

Business Projects

1. Review what you learned about value chains and supply chains in other business courses.

2. Over the academic term, prepare a business plan for an e-commerce firm. Start by selecting a scenario or obtaining one from your instructor. Read your scenario carefully, note any questions you might have, and find the answers to those questions. If you are part of a project team, meet with your teammates to discuss your scenario.

Information Technology Projects

1. Create a map of your school's Web site.

2. Over the academic term, create an appropriate e-commerce solution to a problem described in a scenario selected by you or obtained from your instructor. Read your scenario carefully, note any questions you might have, and find the answers to those questions. If you are part of a project team, meet with your teammates to discuss your scenario. Note that your scenario might involve B2C, intra-business, and/or B2B e-commerce.

3. Over the academic term, create a Web site for an e-commerce application. Additional details can be found in Appendix C.

Marketing Projects

1. Compile a statistical profile to describe how your classmates view the Internet. How many use it regularly, occasionally, or not at all? Why do they use the Internet? Retail purchases? Research? Entertainment? Financial transactions? Swapping MP3 files? The results might surprise you.

2. Over the academic term, design an advertising campaign for an e-commerce Web site. Start by selecting a scenario or obtaining one from your instructor. Read your scenario carefully, note any questions you might have, and find the answers to those questions. If you are part of a project team, meet with your teammates to discuss your scenario.

References

Source	URL	Comments
Addison-Wesley	*www.awl.com/ cs_supplements/davis*	Your textbook's Web site
Bizstats.com	*www.bizstats.com*	Free access to useful business statistics
Microsoft Encarta World English Dictionary	Not applicable	Microsoft's electronic dictionary
Iconocast.com	*www.iconocast.com*	Online technology/marketing magazine
Webopedia	*www.webopedia.com*	Online source of technical information

PART 2
The E-Commerce Infrastructure

E-commerce could not exist without the underlying infrastructure defined by our modern global data communication networks, the Internet (Chapter 2), and the World Wide Web (Chapter 3). The object of Part 2 is not to teach you the technical details of exactly how the evolving infrastructure works, but to provide you with a solid base for understanding the material in Parts 3, 4, and 5.

CHAPTER 2

The Infrastructure

**When you finish reading this chapter,
you should be able to:**

- List and describe the basic elements essential to data communication

- Identify several connectivity options and explain the last mile problem

- Distinguish between a LAN and a WAN

- Distinguish among token passing, collision detection, and routing

- Explain how a client/server network operates

- Explain packet switching

- Describe the services that link a user to the Internet's backbone

- List the layers in the TCP/IP model and explain what happens at each layer

- Read and understand a domain name and an IP address

- Explain how the domain name system (DNS) maps a domain name to an IP address and how the address resolution protocol (ARP) maps an IP address to a MAC (media access control) address

The Underlying Technology

This chapter introduces the underlying technology that makes e-commerce possible (Figure 2.1). Clearly, students majoring in information systems need a solid technical foundation, but what about the accounting, decision sciences, economics, finance, management, marketing, and other business students who might be taking an e-commerce course? Why should they spend time learning about data communication and Internet technology?

Consider the following scenario involving automatic teller machines (ATMs), one of the very first successful e-commerce applications. It is loosely based on a true story, although the company names have been changed. In the 1970s, the leading supplier of bank safes, safe doors, and safe deposit boxes was The Safe Company, better known as TSCo. The experts at TSCo saw the ATM as little more than a remote safe equipped with special electronics that allowed a customer to perform simple banking transactions without a teller's help. When the banks (the potential ATM purchasers) expressed concern about security, the company's sales associates had a ready answer: Nobody can break into a TSCo safe.

Based largely on its name, TSCo dominated the ATM marketplace for a time. Then an enterprising crook used a stolen card to make a cash withdrawal from one ATM, moved to a second ATM and made another withdrawal, moved to a third, and so on, netting well over $1,000. The usual limits on cash withdrawals should have restricted the crook to a few hundred dollars, but because the ATMs were independent, stand-alone devices, they knew nothing about the previous transactions. To make matters worse, the customer had already reported the stolen card, but the ATMs were not scheduled for service until later in the day, so the machines did not know the card was stolen. Word spread quickly through the criminal community, leading to a virtual epidemic of ATM attacks. As a result, TSCo's sales plummeted and the company eventually filed for bankruptcy.

Figure 2.1 This chapter introduces the underlying technology that makes e-commerce possible.

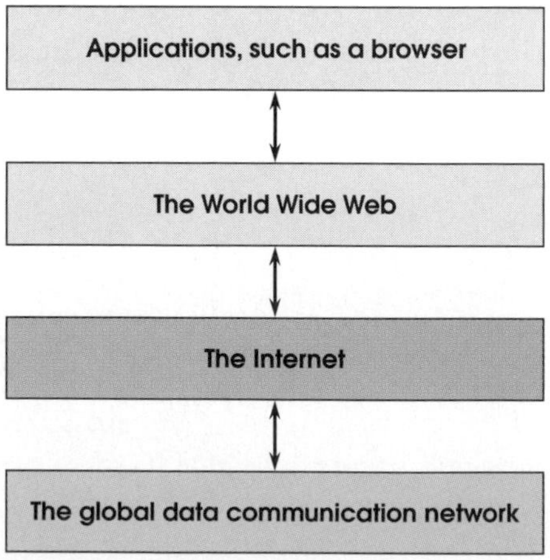

Like TSCo, Acme Safe Company, a niche player specializing in small safes, saw ATMs as a logical extension of its existing product line. Unlike TSCo, however, the company's experts listened to their potential customers and thought long and hard about the special security needs of an unattended ATM. They concluded that centralized transaction screening was an essential part of the solution. Centralized screening meant connecting remote ATMs to a central computer, which in turn meant data communication. Acme's experts knew just enough about communication technology to realize that they lacked the necessary skills, so they initiated a joint effort with the telephone company and developed a workable system of ATMs, telephone lines, and the necessary supporting software. Acme's solution sold so well that within a few years, the company was purchased by a conglomerate, making the founders instant millionaires.

To belabor a point already made in Chapter 1, ignorance is not bliss; it's ignorance. Clearly, what you don't know *can* hurt you. Neither Acme nor TSCo knew much about data communication. TSCo's people assumed (implicitly and somewhat arrogantly) that what they didn't know probably wasn't important anyway. After all, they were the experts. Acme's people, on the other hand, knew enough to realize that they needed help, and that little bit of knowledge paid dividends.

As a business student, unless your job involves designing, creating, or maintaining information systems, you probably do not need an in-depth knowledge of e-commerce technology. It is important, however, that you understand what the technology can and cannot do, when a particular technology is appropriate, and when it is not. If you recognize the potential, you can always get the necessary help. If you do not recognize the potential, however, your competitors probably will.

The objective of Chapter 2 is *not* to make you a technical expert, but to teach you enough about the underlying technology so you can understand what e-commerce can and cannot do for your company and for your career. Additionally, a basic understanding of the underlying technology will make it easier for you to grasp the e-commerce applications and issues discussed in subsequent chapters. For more technically oriented students, Appendix B offers additional depth on data communication and Internet technologies.

Data Communication

A company's value chain consists of a set of integrated processes. If the company is to succeed, those processes must be effectively balanced and coordinated; for example, if sales significantly exceed manufacturing capacity, the result can be financial disaster. A company achieves the necessary coordination by exchanging information so that each process knows the status of related processes. At one time, paper was an acceptable medium for exchanging information, but speed is essential in today's highly competitive business environment, and increasingly, electronic data communication is the accepted norm.

Data communication is the process of transferring data, information, or commands between two computers or between a computer and a terminal. Successful communication requires a message, a transmitter, a receiver, a protocol, and a medium (Figure 2.2). The **message** is the information being sent. The **transmitter** is the source of the message. The **receiver** is the destination. A **protocol** is an agreed-upon format or procedure (in effect, a set of rules) for transmitting a message over a communication medium. The **medium**, sometimes called a line, a channel, or, informally, a pipe, is the path over which the message flows in the form of a signal.

The two primary forms of data communication media are **cable** (a twisted pair of wires, a coaxial cable, a fiber optic cable, …) and **wireless** (radio, television, cell phone, microwave, satellite, infrared, …). A given cable or wireless connection transmits messages in either baseband or broadband mode. A **baseband** line carries one message at a time. **Broadband**, in contrast, divides the medium into distinct channels that act much like independent wires and transmit simultaneous messages in parallel. For example, your cable television service allows you to select from many different stations, all of which are transmitted over the same broadband cable. Some sources use the term *broadband* as a synonym for high-speed communication, perhaps because most high-speed lines are broadband.

Connectivity refers to the ability of a device or a software package to communicate with other devices or software. Physical connectivity is achieved by establishing a connection between the transmitter and the receiver over some medium. Logical connectivity is achieved by using a common set of protocols to ensure that both the transmitter and the receiver follow the same rules and speak the same language. For example, when you answer the telephone, you say "hello." You and the caller then identify yourselves, and the conversation begins. Without really thinking about it, you both use the same language, and you exchange information by taking turns. Finally, you say "goodbye" and hang up. Those informal phone etiquette rules represent a primitive communication protocol. In this example, the telephone line is the medium. Combining a medium and a protocol enables connectivity.

Plain Old Telephone Service (POTS)

Today's best-known communication option is **plain old telephone service** (**POTS**). The process of placing a call begins when the originator (a person or a computer) dials a number. The act of dialing generates a signal that travels from the originator's telephone

Figure 2.2 Communication requires a message, a transmitter, a receiver, a protocol, and a medium.

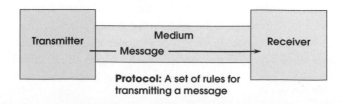

over a wire or cable to the local telephone service provider's central office (Figure 2.3). Local calls are connected directly by the local telephone service provider. Long-distance calls, however, are routed over a high-speed line to the receiving telephone's central office, which completes the call. Think of the local and long-distance segments as two independent layers. The local layer transmits the call between the sender (or the receiver) and a central office. The long-distance layer transmits the message between the two central offices.

Long-distance carriers include such companies as AT&T, MCI, Sprint, Verizon, and many others. For a given call, the local service provider and the long-distance service provider may or may not be the same company, and a long-distance connection might use almost any combination of media. To the user, however, the specific path assigned to the connection is transparent and irrelevant.

Perhaps you noticed that the long-distance layer is visualized as a cloud in Figure 2.3. The cloud image suggests that the underlying infrastructure acts like a black box, an independent layer that can be used without fully understanding what happens inside the box. For example, when you call a friend, your voices flow between the two telephones and you could care less about what happens in between; as far as you are concerned, the call disappears into a cloud and emerges at the other end. Implementing the telephone system in layers allows you to ignore the underlying technology and makes mass telephone communication possible.

Figure 2.3 Plain old telephone service (POTS).

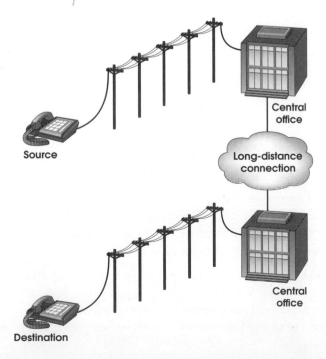

Communication Pricing

In the 1960s, the cost of a long-distance telephone call was a function of time and distance. To help control costs, many homes (and even a few businesses) kept a three-minute egg timer next to the telephone, and cross-country calls were reserved for special occasions.

Today, the major telephone service providers offer rates as low as seven cents per minute to anywhere in the United States, and in most parts of the country the local (free) calling area has expanded from a single community to a much larger region. Expect that trend to continue, with the "local" calling area expanding until, eventually, the pricing model resembles that of cable TV, with unlimited calls anywhere within the country for a fixed monthly fee, plus additional charges for extra services such as call waiting, call forwarding, voice messaging, and teleconferencing.

Why the trend toward fixed-fee pricing? Monitoring the length of individual phone calls and printing multiplepage monthly bills is expensive. Shifting to fixed-fee pricing significantly reduces administrative costs, leading to increased profits for the company and, often, lower bills for the customer—a classic win-win scenario.

Wireless Communication

In contrast to POTS, cellular telephones rely on wireless communication. When the originator dials a number on a mobile phone, an antenna picks up the signal and transmits it to a base station (Figure 2.4), which forwards the signal to a mobile switching center. If the receiving cell phone is in the same service area, the call is completed by the mobile switching center in much the same way a POTS central office completes a local call. If the call is to a wire-based telephone, it is transferred to the appropriate POTS central office, which makes the final connection. If the call is long-distance, the mobile switching center routes it to a long-distance carrier, often one of the same companies that transmit traditional wire-based telephone calls. Note that on a long-distance call, both wire-based and wireless service providers access the same long-distance infrastructure (Figure 2.5). Think of POTS and wireless services as independent layers that plug into the long-distance layer.

The Last Mile Problem

Bandwidth, a measure of the amount of data a communication medium can transmit in a given period of time, is usually expressed in bits per second (bps) or bytes per second (Bps). Each byte holds 8 bits, so 2,400 Bps is equivalent to 19,200 bps. Prefixes such as K (1,000), M (1 million), or G (1 billion) are used to indicate order of magnitude; for example, 5 Mbps means 5 *million* bits per second.

Using a modem, the current de facto standard for transmitting a message over a local telephone line is 56 Kbps. Wireless cell phones support comparable transmission rates, but quality is a problem and retransmitting errors cuts the effective speed. Once the message is transferred to a long-distance service provider, however, it is sent on its way over

Figure 2.4 Wireless communication.

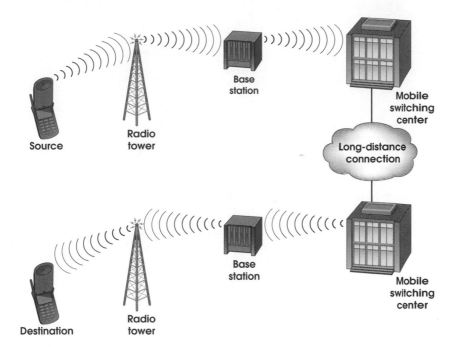

high-speed (Mbps or Gbps) lines. The enormous speed disparity between a local line and a long-distance line is called the **last mile problem**, where the "last mile" is the link between a home or office and the telephone service provider's local central office.

Promising broadband alternatives for plugging into the long-distance layer do exist (Figure 2.6). First-generation cellular phones and second-generation digital cellular services are not quite fast enough or reliable enough for serious data communication, but third-generation wireless technology should be, and new wireless options such as Bluetooth and Wi-Fi are gaining users. Another wireless option, home satellite service, is widely available today.

Figure 2.5 POTS and wireless are alternative access paths to the global data communication
infrastructure.

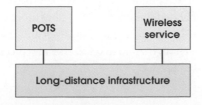

Connection Type	Bandwidth
Local telephone line	56 Kbps

Wireless
    2G digital cellullar
    2.5G digital celluar
    3G digital cellular
    Bluetooth
    Wi-Fi (802.11b)
	
	19.2 Kbps
	144 Kbps
	2 Mbps
	1 Mbps
	Up to 11 Mbps

Home satellite service	400 Kbps
DSL	1.44 Mbps
Cable service	2 to 10 Mbps
Leased line (T-1, T-3)	1.5 to 43 Mbps
Fiber optic cable	Up to 10 Gbps

A digital subscriber line (DSL) enables high-speed data communication on existing local telephone lines. Cable service bypasses the telephone company, offering connectivity from the subscriber's home or office over high-bandwidth cable. Businesses, governments, educational systems, and other large organizations sometimes bypass the last mile problem by leasing a high-speed (T-1 or T-3) line that links them directly to a central office or a long-distance carrier, and fiber optic cable looks very promising.

Unfortunately, none of these alternatives completely solves the last mile problem. Availability is a major roadblock. Not all local telephone service providers offer DSL, and even if your provider does, your home or office must lie in close proximity to a central office. Likewise, cable service is not universally available, and few homes or offices have access to fiber optic media. Third-generation wireless technology has been slow to develop. Bluetooth and Wi-Fi are short-distance technologies that operate within a limited area, such as a single building. A satellite link can be installed virtually anywhere, but setup and maintenance are difficult, a phone line is often required to upload data, and performance and reliability can be inconsistent.

Cost is another issue. Today's cable, DSL, and satellite services cost roughly the same as a telephone line plus an AOL account, but most dial-up users access the Internet over an existing already-paid-for telephone line and see the broadband options as costing twice as much. High-speed leased lines are considerably more expensive and make sense only to large organizations. Until availability improves and costs drop significantly (or high-speed services provide enough value to offset the added cost), progress toward solving the last mile problem will be slow.

The Demand for Broadband

In spite of its clear speed advantage over POTS, broadband technology's growth in market share has been disappointing. Unavailable in many parts of the United States, cable service and DSL are perceived as relatively expensive, and even the technically sophisticated regard satellite service as a last resort. Recently, the failures of cable service provider Excite@Home and DSL providers Northpoint and Flashcom have raised questions about the viability of broadband.

Today, most users seem to be content with their dial-up connections. Dial-up is adequate for e-mail and light Web browsing. Being "always on" twenty-four hours a day, another alleged broadband advantage, is not particularly persuasive, because few people actually use their computers twenty-four hours a day and leaving the system on increases its vulnerability to hackers.

The news is not entirely bad, however. According to a recent study published by *PC World*, over 70 percent of surveyed broadband customers said they were "extremely satisfied or very satisfied with their service," and a surprising number said they would never willingly go back to dial-up, which speaks well for broadband technology's staying power.[1] New alternatives are emerging, too. The carrying capacity of fiber optic cables roughly doubles every year, and sewer lines could provide inexpensive fiber pathways into homes and offices, at least in urban areas. Note that local governments, not telephone service providers, control those rights of way. Line-of-sight wireless technologies also show promise. For example, 802.11b (Wi-Fi) and 802.11a (Wi-Fi5) are open standards for short-distance wireless communication, third-generation (3G) wireless is coming, and optical laser devices might someday be used to beam a wireless broadband connection through a window.

Will broadband access ever become the connectivity norm as its proponents expect, or will it remain a niche technology? Predictions about the success or failure of a particular technology tend to be overly optimistic in the short run, but pessimistic in the long run. If the right killer application emerges, the demand for broadband service could explode, but nobody knows when (or if) that will happen.

Networks

As individuals, we tend to see communication as a two-party process involving an originator and a recipient. From an e-commerce perspective, however, a given computer or workstation must communicate with many other computers or workstations. Imagine stringing separate lines linking every computer to every other computer in the company. In addition to looking ugly and costing a fortune, the resulting spaghetti-like jumble of wires would be virtually impossible to manage and maintain.

The solution is to create a network. A **network** consists of two or more (usually more) computers or other intelligent devices linked by communication lines in a way that allows them to communicate effectively. Each device on the network is called a **node**. For a given message, one node is the transmitter and another node (or set of nodes) is the

---

[1] Brad Grimes, "Ditch Your Dial-up," *PC World* (February 2002): 68–76.

receiver. The network is the medium. The rules for sending the message from the transmitting node to the receiving node are defined in a communication protocol.

Data Communication Protocols

As stated earlier in this chapter, a data communication protocol is an agreed-upon format or procedure (a set of rules) for transmitting data between two devices. There are many different protocols, but both the transmitter and the receiver must use the same one. A protocol can be implemented in hardware, in software, or in both. Key issues include delivering messages efficiently and detecting and correcting errors.

An electronic message consists of a header, a body, and sometimes a trailer (Figure 2.7). The **header** carries information for delivering the message, such as the transmitter's address and the receiver's address. The body contains the message content; from the user's point of view, the body *is* the message. The trailer, when present, holds additional system information, such as an end-of-message marker. The precise format of the header and the trailer depends on the protocol used.

Local Area Networks (LANs)

A group of interconnected computers or workstations located in close proximity (for example, within the same building or adjacent buildings) form a **local area network**, or **LAN**. Each node has a unique address that distinguishes it from all the other nodes. The message header carries information for delivering the message, including the addresses of the source and the receiving nodes.

A LAN's topology describes its shape or form and defines its (typically baseband) connections or data paths (Figure 2.8). In a bus network, all the nodes share a common communication line, or bus. In a star network, each node is linked to a central machine; for example, a local telephone service provider operates a star network with the central office in the middle. In a ring network, the nodes form a ring, with messages moving around the ring from node to node.

Some LANs transmit messages directly from the transmitting node to the receiving node. Others broadcast messages, sending every message to every node on the network. When a message reaches a given node, the appropriate protocol checks the header, accepts or receives messages addressed to it, and ignores messages addressed to some other node.

Figure 2.7 An electronic message consists of a header, a body, and (sometimes) a trailer.

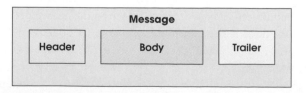

Figure 2.8 Common network topologies.

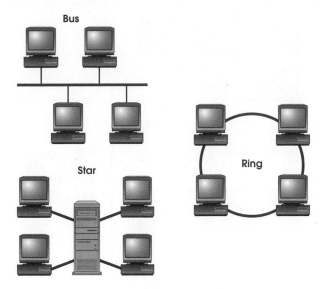

A collision occurs when two or more nodes transmit data simultaneously (or nearly simultaneously) over the same line and their messages interfere with each other, making both unreadable. One solution is collision avoidance—do not allow simultaneous transmissions. For example, on a **token passing** (or token ring) network, an electronic signal (the token) moves continuously around the network, and a node is allowed to transmit only when it holds the token. Because only one node can transmit at any given time, collisions cannot happen.

On a **collision detection** network, a given node can transmit whenever the line is clear. Because it takes time for a signal to traverse a line, however, two nodes might both sense a clear line and transmit simultaneously or nearly simultaneously, so collisions are possible. When a collision occurs, it is detected electronically and the affected messages are retransmitted.

Ethernet is a popular, inexpensive, high-speed LAN collision detection protocol designed by Xerox Corporation for a bus or star topology. An Ethernet adapter card or network interface card is installed in each network node and assigned a unique (within the LAN) address. Each station is linked to a central wiring closet. For example, Miami University's School of Business Administration network has one wiring closet per floor (Figure 2.9). The wiring closets are connected to each other and, eventually, to the network server by coaxial or fiber optic cables that stretch from floor to floor and between buildings.

Wide Area Networks (WANs)

A **wide area network**, or **WAN**, links computers or LANs that are geographically disbursed. Most WANs utilize (at least in part) high-speed, broadband public communication services such as those provided by the telephone company and other common carriers.

Figure 2.9 An Ethernet network.

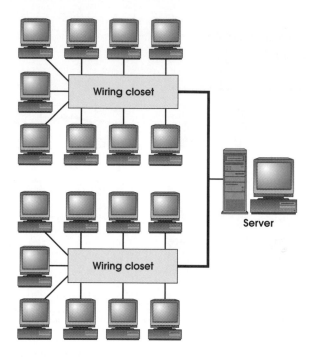

Most WANs lack an easily defined topology. For example, the Internet, a worldwide network of networks, is so vast that nobody knows exactly what it looks like. Lacking obvious connection paths, such networks (including some LANs) rely on **point-to-point transmission**, passing the message from node to node across the network in a series of hops (Figure 2.10). The process of selecting the next node or set of nodes is called **routing**.

Figure 2.10 With point-to-point transmission, the signal is routed node by node across the network.

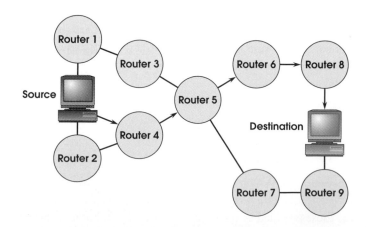

Internetworking

The process of linking two or more networks (LANs, WANs, or both) is called **internetworking**. A number of hardware devices are used to control and coordinate network-to-network communication. A bridge is a computer that links two or more similar networks (Figure 2.11). A **gateway** is a computer that links dissimilar networks; for example, a LAN might be connected to a WAN through a gateway. On the Internet (an abbreviation for *internet*working), many of the intermediate nodes are **routers**, hardware devices that accept a message, examine the header, and forward the message toward the destination node.

Client/Server Networks

In addition to their physical configuration, most networks have a logical configuration that defines the role played by each node. For example, on a **client/server network** (Figure 2.12), specialized computers called **servers** control access to all the network's shared resources and services, and the other nodes act as **clients**. When a client logs on to a network, the client node establishes a connection to a server and, subsequently, asks the server for help when it needs a shared resource. In contrast, on a peer-to-peer network, the linked computers are treated as equals and no central server provides control.

The term *server* is potentially confusing because it is commonly applied to both hardware and software; Dell sells server hardware and Microsoft sells server software. A computer designed to be a server typically has a powerful processor, considerable memory, and vast amounts of secondary storage, but it is still a computer and, given the appropriate

Figure 2.11 A bridge links similar networks. A gateway links dissimilar networks.

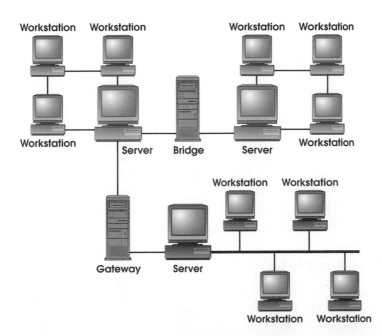

Figure 2.12 A client/server network.

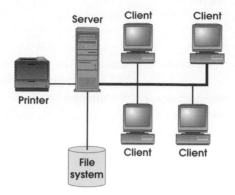

software, it could be used as a client workstation. Server software, on the other hand, is an application program that allocates shared resources and controls network communication. Server software effectively turns the computer it runs on into a server.

The Internet's Infrastructure

The Internet was initially created to solve a national defense problem. During the 1960s, at the height of the cold war, the ultimate defensive strategy was called mutually assured destruction, or MAD. Both the United States and the Soviet Union knew that if either launched a surprise nuclear attack, the other would retaliate, and *both* countries would be destroyed. There was a concern, however. If the Soviet Union were to launch a first strike against the United States, much of America's communication infrastructure would likely be destroyed, making it all but impossible to issue the commands for a counterattack. If retaliation were not certain, the MAD strategy would collapse, and the world would become an even more dangerous place.

In 1969, recognizing the need for a communication network that guaranteed message delivery even if multiple nodes were destroyed, the U.S. Department of Defense Advanced Research Projects Agency (ARPA) launched a research project called ARPANET, a network that linked four academic centers: the University of California at Los Angeles, the Stanford Research Institute, the University of California at Santa Barbara, and the University of Utah. In 1983, the project was split into a military network called MILNET and a civilian network called ARPANET, which evolved into today's Internet. This section introduces the various elements that together make up the modern Internet's physical infrastructure.

Internet Service Providers (ISPs)

The Internet is layered on top of the global data communication network described earlier in this chapter. The means used to connect to the Internet (POTS, wireless, broadband) is called the user's access network.

For residential customers and many business concerns, the access network connects to an **Internet service provider** (**ISP**) such as America Online, MSN, EarthLink, or one of thousands of others (Figure 2.13). (Like the data communication infrastructure, the Internet is sometimes visualized as a cloud.) The ISP, in turn, connects the user to the Internet, much as a POTS central office or a mobile switching center links a caller to a long-distance connection.

Most ISPs offer additional services such as e-mail, data access, training, chat rooms, and news. These services are implemented on **host** computers. A host, or end system, is a computer attached to the Internet that runs or hosts application programs such as server software. Many ISPs have separate hosts for Internet access, e-mail services, news services, and file services.

Figure 2.13 Most users access the Internet through an Internet service provider (ISP).

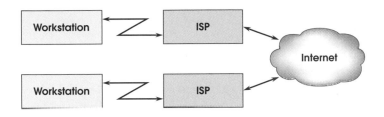

NUMBERS

The Growth of the Internet

The number of host computers directly connected to the Internet provides a good sense of the Internet's rate of growth. Consider, for example, the following data extracted from Hobbes' Internet Timeline:[2]

Year	Hosts
1969	4
1984	1,000+
1989	100,000+
1992	1,000,000+
1996	10,000,000+
2001	100,000,000+

Between 1992 and 2001, the number of hosts increased at the incredible rate of a full order of magnitude every four years. Given such a rapidly expanding pool of potential online customers, it is easy to see why so many late-1990s' entrepreneurs and venture capitalists were willing to take a risk on a dot-com.

---

[2] Robert H. Zakon, Hobbes' Internet Timeline v5.6 [cited April 9, 2002]. Available from *http://www.zakon.org/robert/internet/timeline/*.

The Backbone

The **backbone** is a network of high-speed communication lines that carries the bulk of the traffic between major segments of the Internet (Figure 2.14). In the United States, backbone service is provided by a number of commercial **network service providers** (**NSPs**). The major ISPs lease service from and access the Internet though one of the NSPs. Among the primary NSPs are such firms as AGIS, AT&T, IBM, MCI WorldCom, PSINet, SprintLink, and UUNet Technologies. Note that the list includes many long-distance telephone service providers.

Each NSP operates its own national WAN of high-speed communication lines. Because those WANs are independently owned and operated, transferring a message from one NSP to another is often necessary. The NSPs are interconnected and exchange data through **network access points** (**NAPs**). Some major ISPs and a few large organizations such as universities, research centers, and corporations connect directly to an NAP, but most go through an NSP or a regional ISP.

Regional ISPs

A **regional ISP** operates a statewide or regional backbone and typically connects to the Internet by leasing bandwidth from an NSP. Many local ISPs access the Internet through a regional ISP, and large organizations sometimes lease a direct broadband connection to a regional ISP or even an NSP. For example, at Miami University, each division (Arts and Science, Business, Education, Engineering) has its own LAN (Figure 2.15). These LANs are all linked to a university host (*muohio*) that serves as a

Figure 2.14 The backbone.

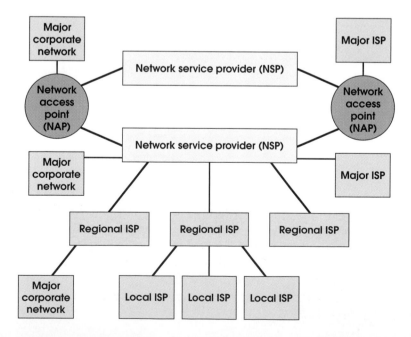

Figure 2.15 Miami University's network structure.

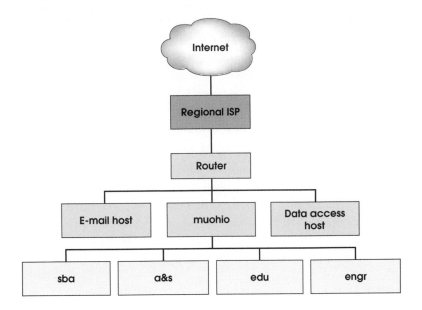

LAN-to-LAN gateway. Other university hosts support e-mail and data access. Access to the Internet (the cloud) is through a router connected to a high-speed leased line that links Miami to a regional ISP.

TCP/IP, The Internet's Protocols

As you learned earlier in this chapter, for two devices to communicate, both the transmitter and the receiver must use the same protocols. Although the Internet links millions of computers worldwide, messages still move across the Internet in a series of node-to-node hops, and the common protocol rule applies to each of those hops. The Internet simply could not exist without widely accepted protocol standards.

Packet Switching

For any given source, the typical data communication pattern consists of occasional bursts of activity separated by lengthy quiet times. The high-bandwidth lines used for long-distance communication are quite expensive, so efficiency is a priority. Local lines are relatively inexpensive, so low utilization is not a concern, but there is a risk that a single user might dominate a low-bandwidth line. **Packet switching** achieves efficient message delivery by allowing numerous messages to share the line while preventing any single user from dominating it. The Internet is a packet switching network; its protocols are designed with packet switching in mind.

On a packet switching network, a message is divided into a set of small blocks called **packets**. Picture the communication line as a continuously moving escalator-like matrix of slots, each of which can hold one packet (Figure 2.16). Some of the slots hold packets from other messages. Some are empty. The first packet from the new message is dropped into the first available slot, the second packet goes into the next available slot, and so on; note how packets from numerous messages are intermixed. At the receiving node, the packets are reassembled to form the original message. Should transmission errors occur, only lost or erroneous packets must be retransmitted, an error handling process that is much more efficient than resending the entire message.

By itself, Figure 2.16 is potentially misleading because messages rarely flow directly from the source computer to the destination computer. Instead, the packets are routed from node to node across the network (Figure 2.17). Because the packets are transmitted independently, it is possible (even likely) that the set of packets that make up a message will follow different paths from source to destination and perhaps even arrive out of order. Consequently, a packet switching protocol must be able to resequence packets by checking the sequence numbers embedded in the packet headers.

The TCP/IP or Internet Model

The **TCP/IP** (transmission control protocol/Internet protocol) or **Internet model** (Figure 2.18) specifies a set of layered packet switching protocols that define the rules for communicating over the Internet. (In fact, the Internet is sometimes defined as the set of interconnected computers that use TCP/IP.) TCP/IP resembles the International

Figure 2.16 Packet switching.

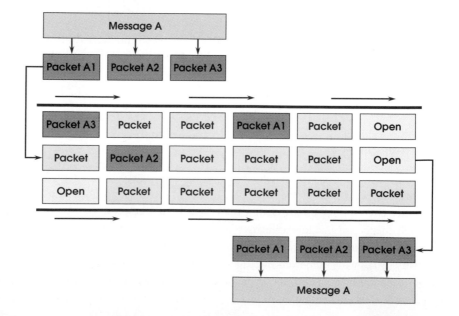

Figure 2.17 A message's packets can follow different paths through the network.

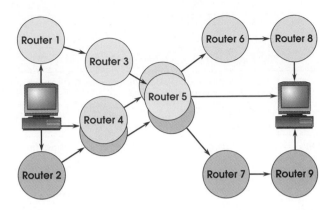

Figure 2.18 The TCP/IP model.

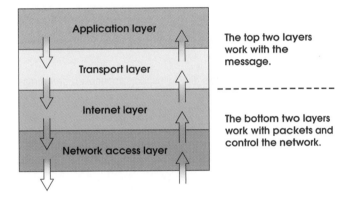

Organization for Standardization's seven-layer Open Systems Interconnect (OSI) reference model for inter-computer packet switching communication (Figure 2.19). Although rarely implemented precisely as specified, the OSI model is a useful blueprint for designing and creating networking hardware and software.

Internet access only *seems* easy; an incredible number of tasks are hidden beneath the surface. Because of TCP/IP's layered architecture, however, the underlying complexity is largely transparent, making Internet access available even to nontechnical users. As you read about the TCP/IP protocols, note how each protocol layer builds on the standards implemented in the layer below it. That is the essence of layering.

The Application Layer

The TCP/IP **application layer** holds protocols that directly support application programs (Figure 2.20). On the sending computer, an application layer protocol accepts input parameters from an application program and creates the output parameters needed

Figure 2.19 The Open Systems Interconnect (OSI) model.

OSI layer	Responsibilities
The top four layers work with the message.	
Application	Provides a logical link between an application program and the lower-level protocols.
Presentation	Performs necessary data representation and/or syntax conversions; e.g., encryption/decryption.
Session	Establishes, maintains, and terminates a connection.
Transport	Breaks the message into packets. Ensures error-free, end-to-end delivery of the complete message.
The bottom three layers work with packets and control the network.	
Network	Determines the best route for sending a packet from the source node to the destination node.
Data-link	Formats a packet for transmission to the next node.
Physical	Interfaces with the physical communication medium.

Figure 2.20 The application layer protocols directly support application programs.

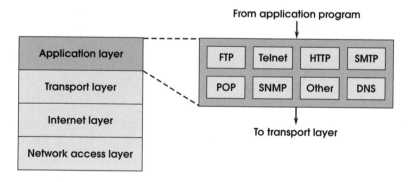

by the next layer down. At the other end of the line, the application layer protocol accepts information from the next layer down and passes it up to an equivalent application program on the receiving machine. Several well-known application layer protocols are summarized in Figure 2.21.

Understanding the difference between an application program and an application layer protocol is important. A user accesses the system by manipulating the user interface provided by an application routine such as a mailer program. An application layer protocol, subsequently, links the application program to the lower-level protocols. The user communicates directly with the application program's user interface. The application layer protocol, in contrast, is transparent to the user.

Figure 2.21 Some common application layer protocols.

Acronym	Name	Function
FTP	File transfer protocol	Download a file from or upload a file to another computer.
HTTP	Hypertext transfer protocol	Request and download a Web page. HTTP is the standard Web surfing protocol.
POP	Post office protocol	Deliver accumulated mail from a mail server to the recipient's computer.
SMTP	Simple mail transfer protocol	Send an e-mail message from the originator's computer to the recipient's mail server.
SNMP	Simple network management protocol	Monitor the activity of a network's hardware and software components.
Telnet	Terminal-emulation protocol	Log in to a remote computer. System operators use Telnet to control a server remotely.

For example, imagine using file transfer protocol (FTP) to download a set of product specifications from the corporate database to a sales associate's laptop. The sales associate (the client) starts the process by using an application routine to select the file to be downloaded. The file's path name and the addresses of the laptop and the server are passed as parameters to the application layer's FTP protocol, which adds a header containing information needed by the receiving node's FTP protocol (Figure 2.22) and passes the header and the FTP request down to the transport layer. Subsequently, the application layer FTP protocol on the receiving node (the server) strips off the header, uses the information, and passes the request up to the appropriate application program.

The Transport Layer

The next layer down, the **transport layer**, also known as the host-to-host transport layer (Figure 2.23), is responsible for ensuring successful end-to-end delivery of the complete message from an application layer protocol on the sending node to the same application layer protocol on the receiving node. For example, a message passed down to the transport layer by the application layer FTP protocol will be passed up to the receiving node's FTP protocol. Several transport layer protocols can be used, but the **transmission control protocol** (**TCP**) is by far the most common.

Figure 2.22 The application layer FTP protocol adds a header to the FTP request.

Figure 2.23 The next layer down is the transport layer.

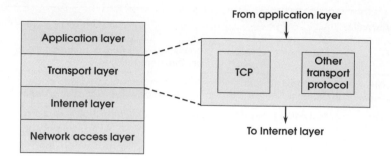

The message passed down to the transport layer consists of the application layer's header plus the content created by the user. TCP breaks the message into packets (only the first packet contains the FTP header) and adds to each one a TCP header[3] (Figure 2.24) containing information that identifies the target application layer protocol (in this case, FTP) and a sequence number. At the receiving end, the destination computer's TCP checks each packet for errors, uses the sequence numbers to reassemble the packets in the proper order, and passes the message up to the application layer protocol identified in the TCP header. On the sending side, TCP guarantees error-free message delivery by waiting to receive from the destination computer's transport layer an acknowledgement for every packet it sends. If no acknowledgement is received within a reasonable period of time, the sending computer resends the lost packets. On the receiving side, the sequence numbers in the TCP header help to ensure delivery of the *complete* message by highlighting lost packets.

Before you move on, be sure you understand that the application and transport layers deal with the entire message. When you drop below the transport layer, the Internet and network access layers, the next two topics, work with the packets created by the transport layer.

Figure 2.24 TCP adds its own header.

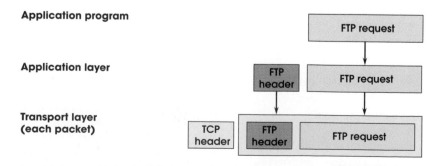

[3] See Appendix B for additional information on TCP header contents.

The Internet Layer

The **Internet layer**, or **network layer**, the second layer from the bottom (Figure 2.25), uses the **Internet protocol** (**IP**) to route packets by selecting the next node on the path that eventually leads to the receiving node. The Internet layer accepts a packet from the transport layer (the next layer up) and adds its own IP header[4] (Figure 2.26), containing the addresses of the source and destination nodes, before passing the packet down to the network access layer. At each of the intermediate nodes (and there may be many), the IP protocol selects the next node, replaces the old IP header with a new one, and passes the packet down to the network access layer. Once the packet reaches the destination node, it is passed up to the transport layer, where TCP reassembles the packets.

Note that IP routes packets, but does not deliver them. Packet delivery is the responsibility of the network access layer. Also, the source computer's IP protocol does not receive an acknowledgement from the receiving node. Guaranteeing delivery is TCP's job.

Figure 2.25 The Internet layer uses the Internet protocol (IP).

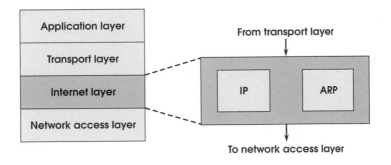

Figure 2.26 IP adds its own header.

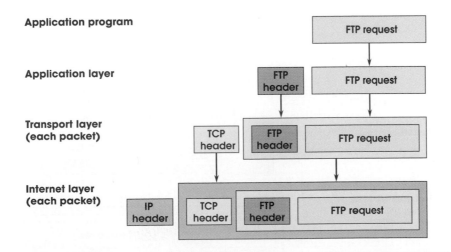

---

[4] See Appendix B for additional information on IP header contents.

The Network Access Layer

The **network access layer**, or **physical layer**, is where packets are transferred from a node to the physical communication line and sent on to the next node. Like the other layers, the network access layer accepts a message from its immediate upper layer (Internet) and adds its own header containing the address of the current node and the next node (Figure 2.27). Because the interface with the physical network is fully contained within the network access layer, the upper layers are independent of the physical network structure.

Each packet moving over a communication line to the next node has three headers, one each for the transport, Internet, and network access layers. Each header holds control information appropriate to its layer. When the message reaches the destination node, the network access layer uses the information from the network header, the Internet layer uses the information from the IP header, and so on. Once the message is reassembled at the transport layer and passed up to the application layer, the application protocol (in this case, FTP) uses the application header embedded in the message. Each layer communicates with its peer layer on the other node through the headers.

The Internet is a network of networks. Specifying a single technology that everyone must use on their LAN is impractical, so the TCP/IP model recognizes several data communication protocols that support numerous technologies (including Ethernet, collision detection, and token ring) for routing messages within a subnetwork (or subnet).

Figure 2.27 The network access layer adds yet another header.

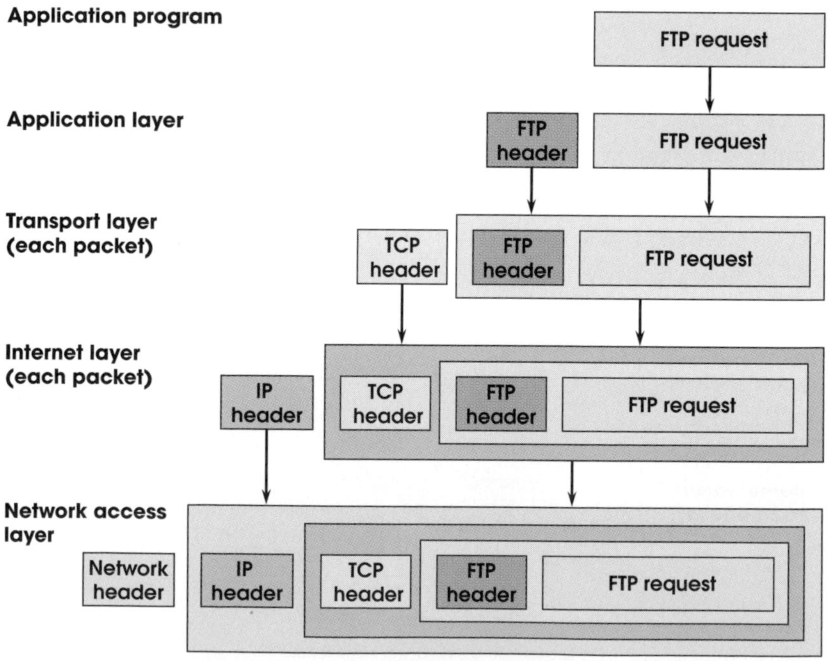

Open Standards

TCP/IP is an **open standard**; in other words, the details of the system architecture are published and freely available to everyone. Unlike proprietary standards, such as Apple's Macintosh and Microsoft's Windows, open standards promote platform independence (the ability of software to run on a variety of different computers under different operating systems) and interoperability (the ability of software to function in different environments by sharing data and resources with other software). Implementations of TCP/IP exist for virtually every computing platform in common use today.

Internet Addressing

Your school's network probably links hundreds, perhaps thousands, of computers, and a large company's network links even more. Even the biggest intracorporate network appears insignificant when compared with the Internet, however. In order to route a message across the Internet (or any network, for that matter), each connected device must have a unique address that distinguishes it from all the other nodes. An important component of the TCP/IP model is a system for assigning, maintaining, and retrieving those addresses.

Domain Names

A **domain** is a set of nodes that are administered as a unit, for example, all the networked computers belonging to Miami University or Microsoft Corporation. A **domain name** consists of two to four words separated by dots (Figure 2.28). Starting at the right is a top-level domain name such as *edu* for an educational institution, *com* for a commercial entity, *org* for a nonprofit group, and *gov* for a government service (Figure 2.29). Moving to the left are the entities within the domain. For example, in the domain name *sbaserver1.sba.muohio.edu*, *edu* is the top-level domain, *muohio* is Miami University's domain (part of the *edu* domain), *sba* is the School of Business Administration subnet (a network that forms a part of a larger network) within the *muohio* domain, and *sbaserver1* is a server within the *sba* subnet.

Figure 2.28 A domain name consists of two to four words separated by dots.

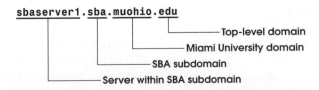

Figure 2.29 Some top-level domain names.

Domain	Signifies	Domain	Signifies
aero	Air-transport industry	au	Australia
biz	Business organization	br	Brazil
com	U.S. commercial	ca	Canada
coop	Cooperatives	cn	China
edu	U.S. educational	de	Germany
info	Unrestricted	fi	Finland
gov	U.S. government	fr	France
mil	U.S. military	gb	Great Britain
museum	Museums	in	India
name	Individuals	it	Italy
net	U.S. network	jp	Japan
org	U.S. nonprofit	ru	Russia
pro	Professionals	za	South Africa

The organization's domain name (for example, *muohio* or *aol*) is assigned to a host computer that is linked to the Internet. To the left of the domain name, the subnet and server names are assigned by the domain and, consequently, have meaning only within the domain. For example, the Internet can deliver a message to *muohio*, but it is *muohio*'s responsibility to pass the message to *sba*, and *sba*'s responsibility to pass the message to *subserver1*.

The IP Address

An **IP address** is a number that uniquely identifies a specific node. The Internet uses this number to route packets to the node. When the Internet layer's IP protocol sends a packet, it records the source and destination IP addresses in the packet's IP header using the dotted decimal format, four numbers separated by dots (Figure 2.30). For example, in the address 134.53.40.2, the first number, 134, is the top-level domain (*edu*); 53 designates Miami University's domain; 40 is the School of Business Administration subnet; and 2 is a server within this subnet.

The Domain Name System (DNS)

The actual physical transmission of messages and data requires an IP address, not a domain name. A given node's domain name and IP address convey the same information (Figure 2.31), and the **domain name system** (**DNS**) takes advantage of that relationship

Domain Name Registration

To avoid duplication, domain names are registered with a central authority and kept in a central registry. In the United States, responsibility for top-level *com*, *net*, and *org* domain name registration rests with the Department of Commerce's Internet Corporation for Assigned Names and Numbers (ICANN). Together with Network Solutions, Inc. (NSI), ICANN accredits the organizations that perform the actual registration process, usually for a fee. Other governments are responsible for allocating domain names in their own domains; for example, Japan controls the top-level domain *jp*, Germany controls *de*, and Italy controls *it*.

Because the supply of unique names is limited, an organization's domain name is a valuable piece of intellectual property that can be bought and sold,

often through a domain name brokerage. For example, Delta Airlines recently paid a great deal of money to purchase the rights to *delta.com* from the insurance company that previously (and legitimately) owned it. Less legitimate is cybersquatting, the practice of registering trademarks, company names, slogans, and celebrity names with the intent of later selling the rights. The 1999 Anti-Cybersquatting Consumer Protection Act effectively banned hoarding domain names and holding them for ransom. Additionally, recent court decisions have awarded celebrities and organizations the rights to their own name or an established trademark, and such new top-level domains as *biz*, *coop*, and *pro* should help increase the supply of appropriate domain names.

to convert domain names to IP addresses. The domain name system is implemented by a DNS protocol that resides at the TCP/IP application layer and by a hierarchy of DNS servers. The DNS servers store tables of domain-name-to-IP-address mappings that allow each layer to find the IP addresses for the next higher and next lower layers.

Figure 2.30 An IP address.

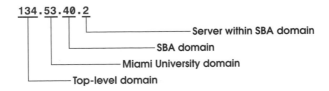

Figure 2.31 A domain name and an IP address convey the same information.

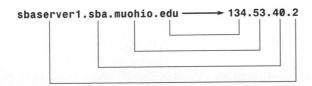

Imagine, for example, sending a message to *service.microsoft.com* from within the Miami University School of Business network (*sbaserver1.sba.muohio.edu*). The search begins with the *sba* DNS server (Figure 2.32). The *sba* DNS server knows the next higher layer's IP address, so the request is sent to *muohio*. The *muohio* DNS server knows the IP addresses of its next higher layer (the top-level domains) so it sends the request to *com* (IP address 207). The top-level DNS server knows *microsoft*'s IP address (207.46) because *microsoft* is at the next lower level, but it does not know *service* because *service* is two levels down. Thus, *com* sends Microsoft's numeric IP address (207.46) to *muohio*. Miami's DNS server then sends a request to Microsoft. *Microsoft.com* knows the IP address for *service* (one level down) and completes the address translation. The IP address (207.46.140.71) is then returned to the originating server (*sba*), which (finally) sends the message.

Following the initial address translation, the participating DNS servers **cache** or save the domain name and its matching IP address. Consequently, the next time a user in the SBA lab types *service.microsoft.com*, a cached copy is in *sba*, and the address translation is done immediately rather than being forwarded up the ladder. Similarly, if another Miami user not on the SBA subdomain requests *service.microsoft.com*, another cached copy is available on *muohio*, so the university computer's DNS server does the address translation.

Ports

As you learned earlier, the transport layer is responsible for ensuring successful end-to-end delivery of the complete message from an application layer protocol on the sending node to the same application layer protocol on the receiving node. Messages are passed to the correct application protocol by referencing a port number, the application identifier mentioned earlier. A hardware port is a physical interface or plug; for example, you probably plug your printer into a printer port. In the TCP/IP model, a **port** is also the endpoint of a *logical* connection (a program-to-program link), and all application layer protocols are associated with a logical port number (Figure 2.33). The IP address routes the message to the right node. The port number routes the message to the right application protocol on that node.

Figure 2.32 The domain name system (DNS).

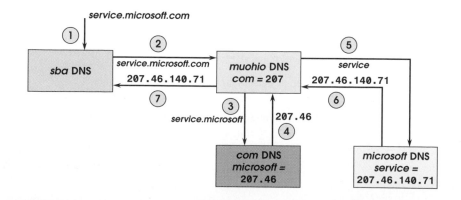

Figure 2.33 Some well-known port assignments.

Port	Used for:
5	RJE (remote job entry)
20	FTP (file transfer protocol) data
21	FTP (file transfer protocol) control
23	Telnet (terminal emulator)
25	SMTP (simple mail transfer protocol)
79	FINGER (given e-mail address, identify user)
80	HTTP (hypertext transfer protocol)
110	POP3 (post office protocol, version 3)
119	NNTP (network news transfer protocol)

The Media Access Control (MAC) Address

An IP address points to a specific computer, router, or (more generally) node. However, because the final hop is within a local domain and the IP address of the destination node (for example, a user workstation on a subnet) has meaning only within that domain, physically transmitting a message to its final destination node requires the **media access control** (**MAC**) address of that node. For example, in an Ethernet LAN, an Ethernet card is installed in each workstation, and each card has a unique MAC address that is hard-coded by the card's manufacturer. On the final hop from the destination server to the destination computer, an Internet layer TCP/IP protocol called the **address resolution protocol** (**ARP**) translates the workstation's IP address to a MAC address. The message is then routed to the destination computer.

Address Translation

Quickly review the relationship between the three types of TCP/IP addresses (Figure 2.34). The task of transmitting a message begins when a user selects the destination node's domain name. The Internet uses numeric IP addresses to route packets from node to node, so the application layer's DNS protocol converts the domain name to an IP address.

At the other end of the connection, the final hop takes the packet from a server to the destination node. Because the destination node is inside the local domain, its IP address is assigned by the domain and has meaning only within the domain. Thus the server's Internet layer ARP protocol maps the final node's IP address (which means nothing to the Internet) to a physical MAC address and passes the MAC address to the network access layer.

Figure 2.34 TCP/IP address translation.

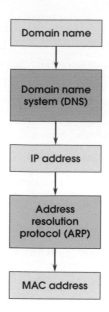

BUSINESS

Content, Connectivity, and Delivery

A successful e-commerce application requires content, connectivity, and delivery. Content is the information that supports the application. The backbone enables delivery. Connectivity links the information source and destination to the backbone.

Traditionally, content, connectivity, and delivery are viewed as independent layers created and maintained by separate businesses. A company with something to sell creates the content. Connectivity requires the specialized services of an access network provider (such as a local telephone company) and an ISP. Even more specialized are the backbone providers who operate and maintain the delivery networks.

Recently, however, a consolidation trend has emerged. Consider, for example, the series of mergers

that created AOL Time Warner. Several of the constituent companies are content providers: Turner Broadcasting and HBO are television networks, Time Inc. is a well-known publisher, Warner Music Group sells recorded music, and Warner Bros. and New Line Cinema make movies. Combining America Online, the world's biggest ISP, and Time Warner Cable, a major access network provider (Roadrunner), creates a complete connectivity solution. Consequently, AOL Time Warner controls both content and the means to deliver that content (except for the backbone) to its customers. Such mergers make good business sense. Watch for more of them, unless the courts decide that such consolidation represents an unfair restraint of trade.

The E-Commerce Infrastructure

The World Wide Web, the subject of Chapter 3, defines a set of standards for creating and accessing information over the Internet. In effect, the Web is a user interface layer constructed on top of the Internet. Evolving Web applications, another topic introduced in Chapter 3, use that Web interface to tap into the Internet and, indirectly, into the international data communication network. Together, the data communication network, the Internet, and the World Wide Web provide an infrastructure for e-commerce (Figure 2.35).

Figure 2.35 Together, the data communication network, the Internet, and the World Wide Web provide an infrastructure for e-commerce.

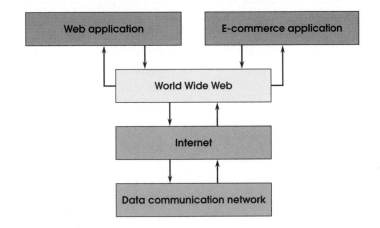

■■■ Summary

Data communication requires a message, a transmitter, a receiver, a protocol, and a medium. Today's best-known connectivity options are plain old telephone service and wireless. Broadband options such as DSL, cable service, home satellite services, and leased high-speed lines help to solve the last mile problem.

Each device on a network is called a node. A LAN's topology defines the communication links that connect its nodes. Token passing and collision detection are two options for ensuring successful message delivery on a LAN. Ethernet is a popular LAN protocol. Many WANs rely on point-to-point transmission and routing. Internetworking uses bridges, gateways, and routers to link LANs and WANs. On a client/server network, the servers control access to various services, and the clients request the services they need. On a peer-to-peer network, there is no central server.

Internet connectivity is achieved through an access network and an ISP. The Internet's backbone is maintained by a number of NSPs who lease bandwidth to regional ISPs. NSPs exchange messages at NAPs.

The TCP/IP or Internet model defines a set of standard packet switching protocols. The application layer protocols directly support application programs. The transport layer uses TCP and ensures successful end-to-end delivery of the complete message. The Internet or network layer uses IP to route packets. The network access or physical layer transfers packets to and from the physical network. Open standards promote platform independence and interoperability.

A domain is a set of nodes that are administered as a unit. Each domain is assigned a domain name. The DNS converts domain names to the numeric IP addresses used by the Internet. The ARP matches the IP address to a physical MAC address.

■■■ Key Words

address resolution protocol (ARP)
application layer
backbone
bandwidth
baseband
broadband
cable
cache
client
client/server network
collision detection
connectivity
data communication
domain
domain name
domain name system (DNS)
Ethernet
gateway
header

host
Internet layer, or network layer
Internet model
Internet protocol (IP)
Internet service provider (ISP)
internetworking
IP address
last mile problem
local area network (LAN)
media access control (MAC) address
medium
message
network
network access layer, or physical layer
network access point (NAP)
network service provider (NSP)
node
open standard
packet

packet switching
plain old telephone service (POTS)
point-to-point transmission
port (logical)
protocol
receiver
regional ISP
router
routing
server
TCP/IP, or TCP/IP model
token passing
transmission control protocol (TCP)
transmitter
transport layer
wide area network (WAN)
wireless

Review Questions

1. List and define the basic elements essential to communication.

2. List several connectivity options in bandwidth order.

3. Explain how plain old telephone service (POTS) works. Explain how wireless service works.

4. Explain the last mile problem and identify some possible solutions.

5. What is a network? Explain the difference between a LAN and a WAN.

6. Distinguish among token passing, collision detection, and routing.

7. What is a client/server network?

8. What is internetworking? Distinguish between a bridge and a gateway.

9. What functions does an Internet service provider (ISP) perform?

10. What is the Internet's backbone? Who maintains the backbone? How does a user gain access to the backbone?

11. Explain packet switching.

12. List the layers in the TCP/IP model and explain what happens at each layer.

13. What is a protocol? What functions are performed by TCP (transmission control protocol)? What functions are performed by IP (Internet protocol)?

14. Explain the process of transmitting a file from a server to a client.

15. What is an open standard? Why are open standards important?

16. What is a domain? Explain what each part of your school or organization's domain name means.

17. What is an IP address? Explain what each of the numbers in an IP address means.

18. Explain how the domain name system (DNS) maps a domain name to an IP address.

19. Explain how a logical port number establishes a link to a specific application protocol.

20. Explain how the address resolution protocol (ARP) maps an IP address to a media access control (MAC) address.

21. Identify the layers that make up the e-commerce infrastructure.

Exercises

1. A chapter sidebar suggested that communication service providers might move toward fixed-fee pricing in the near future. Do you agree or disagree? Why?

2. The federal Anti-Cybersquatting Consumer Protection Act was passed in 1999. Do you believe that such a law is necessary? Why or why not?

3. The telephone company would like to offer TV programming over its telephone lines. Meanwhile, cable TV companies are considering adding voice communication service, and wireless digital telephones already offer Internet access. How do you explain these trends?

4. One way to create a private, personal local area network (LAN) is to install a wireless communication chip in your desktop computer, your laptop, your personal digital assistant, and other personal electronic devices. Why would anyone want to do that?

5. Access the Web site *www.thelist.com* and identify several nearby Internet service providers (ISPs) and the types of services they offer.

6. Don't try to memorize all the definitions for the key terms listed at the end of this chapter. A better strategy is to visualize the terms in the context of a two-dimensional model. Start with a sketch (landscape oriented). At the upper left, label a rectangle *transmitter*. Drop down a little more than halfway and label another rectangle *ISP*. Draw a line between them. To the *ISP*'s right, near the center of the paper, add a third rectangle labeled *backbone* and draw a line connecting it to *ISP*. Add two more rectangles near the right edge. Label the top one *receiver* and the bottom one *ISP*, connect them to each other, and connect *ISP* to *backbone*.

Once you complete your sketch, go through the list of key terms and write each one where it best fits on the diagram. Skip unfamiliar terms on the first pass. Then go back for a second pass; you'll be surprised how many of the remaining terms seem to fall into place, effectively defined by related terms. If a term is still unfamiliar, reread the relevant text discussion. When you finish, your diagram will give you a context for understanding the technology.

Projects

Current references and supporting resources can be found at this textbook's companion Web site.

Broad-Based Projects

1. Describe your school's or employer's network as completely as you can. Prepare a diagram showing how the nodes are connected.

2. Check advertising and other available sources and compile a list of connectivity options for linking your computer to your school's or employer's network or to an ISP.

3. If your computer does not have Internet access, install the necessary hardware and software.

4. Write a short paper on the history of the Internet.

Building the Case:

5. Working as a team, continue with Chapter 1, Project 6. Create an initial draft of your proposed strategy by attempting to answer the following questions:
   a. What is the proposed strategy?
      (1) Where are we now?
      (2) Where do we want to be?
      (3) How can we get there?
      (4) How will we know we've arrived?
   b. What are the goals? (What are we trying to accomplish?) Remember that goals are measurable.
   c. How does the strategy add value or reduce cost?
   d. What alternatives were considered? Why was the recommended strategy chosen?
   e How will the recommended strategy help us reach the goals?
   f. What current business processes must change?

If you are unable to answer any of these questions fully, conduct the research needed to obtain the necessary information.

Business Projects

1. If DSL and/or cable service is available in your area, obtain such data as the installation cost, installation backlog (waiting time to get the service), monthly service cost, download speed, and upload speed. If multiple connectivity options are available, collect data on all of them and use the results to identify the low cost option.

Building the Case:

2. Continue with Chapter 1, Project 2 by clearly identifying your client's product or service and the potential customers for that product or service. Estimate the market size, define your client's target market share, estimate target revenue, and project the revenue stream five years into the future. Write a brief report to document your results.

Information Technology Projects

1. If you are using Windows, investigate the Internet by issuing the following commands at the MS-DOS prompt (Start/Programs/Accessories/MS-DOS Prompt). Look for Command Prompt on the Accessories menu if you are using Windows 2000 or Windows XP.
   a. Find your computer's IP address by issuing the command *ipconfig/all*. Explain what the various parts of the IP address mean.
   b. If you are using Windows 2000, issue the command *nslookup domain.top* (for example, *nslookup muohio.edu*) to find the equivalent IP address. Substitute your school's or employer's domain name.
   c. To determine whether a remote host is active, issue the command *ping domain.top* (for example, *ping muohio.edu*).
   e. Trace the path of a packet as it travels over the Internet by issuing the command *tracert www.muohio.edu*. Feel free to substitute another domain name of interest to you.

2. Investigate several wireless local area network (LAN) options such as Bluetooth, 802.11b (Wi-Fi), and 802.11a (Wi-Fi5). Write a short paper summarizing your findings.

Building the Case:

3. Continue with Chapter 1, Project 2 by outlining the primary elements of your proposed solution. Once you have a reasonable sense of your solution's components, identify your communication and connectivity options. Who are the players (customers, suppliers, employees, and so on)? What are their connectivity needs (POTS, broadband, occasional, 24/7)? Estimate the cost of providing the necessary connectivity.

Marketing Projects

1. In spite of a clear speed advantage, the market penetration of broadband continues to lag behind traditional dial-up. Do some research to determine why so many potential customers are reluctant to adopt broadband. Devise a marketing strategy to counter those issues.

Building the Case:

2. Continue with Chapter 1, Project 2 by clearly identifying your client's product or service, the potential customers for that product or service, and a preliminary set of strategies for marketing the product or service to those customers. Write a brief report to document your results.

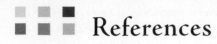 # References

Source	URL	Comments
Chicago NAP	*www.aads.net/main.html*	The Chicago NAP home page. Traffic statistics are particularly interesting.
Hobbe's Internet Timeline	*www.zakon.org/robert/ internet/timeline/*	A history of the Internet updated frequently by the author, Robert H. Zakon.
Network Engineer's Handbook	*www.wanresources.com/ tcpcell.html*	TCP/IP protocol formats, including header formats.
Thelist.com	*thelist.internet.com*	A list of worldwide ISPs grouped by country and area code.

CHAPTER 3

The World Wide Web

**When you finish reading this chapter,
you should be able to:**

- Explain how a browser and a Web server work together to transfer a Web page from a Web site to a client

- Read and understand a uniform resource locator (URL)

- Relate the process of downloading a Web page to the TCP/IP protocols introduced in Chapter 2

- Explain how Web pages are created and displayed using HTML tags and how file references and hyperlinks are inserted into a Web page

- Explain how page load time is affected by the number and size of the files referenced on the page

- Explain how applets, scripts, and plug-ins enable client-side interactivity

- Define the term Web information system and explain how middleware enables complex Web applications and the creation of dynamic Web pages

- Explain how a cookie is used to maintain state

- Identify the layers that form the e-commerce infrastructure

Business and the Internet

Until the early 1990s, the Internet was largely unknown outside government, academic, and research circles, and no commercial applications existed. In those days, data communication was relatively slow, and the dominant Internet applications (e-mail, FTP, telnet, and online bulletin boards such as Usenet) were almost exclusively text-oriented. Additionally, the user interface to the Internet, essentially a set of Unix line commands, was a bit intimidating. The potential payoff seemed not worth the effort of learning the interface, so business left the technology to the academics and the geeks.

The World Wide Web came into being in 1990. The initial response was muted until 1993, when the release of the first browser, Mosaic, changed everything. Written for the National Center for Supercomputing Applications (NCSA) by Marc Andreessen and several other University of Illinois undergraduate students, Mosaic's user-friendly point-and-click graphical user interface was a true killer application, opening Internet and Web access to virtually everyone. In short order, Andreessen started Mosaic Communications Corporation, Mosaic became Netscape, Netscape Communications Corporation went public (in 1995), Web use exploded, and business began to take notice.

Chapter 2 focused on the bottom two layers in the e-commerce infrastructure (Figure 3.1). This chapter turns to the top layers—the World Wide Web and the business applications that run on the Web.

Figure 3.1 This chapter focuses on the top layers.

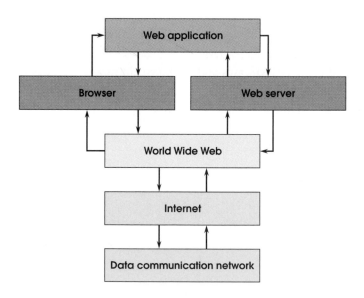

How the Web Works

The **World Wide Web** (or **Web** for short) is a client/server application layered on top of the Internet that provides simple, standardized protocols for naming, linking, and accessing virtually everything on the Internet. The basic unit of information on the Web is a **Web page**. A **Web site** is a set of closely related Web pages that are interconnected by logical pointers called **hyperlinks** (Figure 3.2). Generally, one page is designated as the Web site's **home page**, a starting point that serves as a table of contents or index for navigating the site. Most Web pages incorporate hyperlinks to pages on other Web sites, as well. The result is a vast global "web" of billions of pages.

Browsers and Web Servers

The World Wide Web supports communication between a browser and a Web server (Figure 3.3). A **browser** is an application program, such as Internet Explorer or Netscape, that runs on the client computer and requests and displays Web pages. A **Web server** is a server-side application program that runs on a host computer and manages the Web pages stored on the Web site's database.

Figure 3.2 A Web site consists of a set of related Web pages.

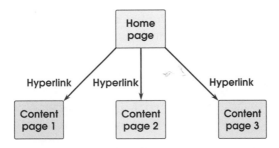

Figure 3.3 The World Wide Web supports communication between a browser and a Web server.

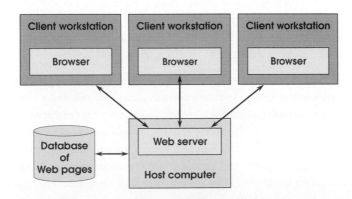

Search Engines

Given the sheer number of Web pages on the World Wide Web, finding the specific information you need is a challenge. Using a search engine can help. Some search engines, most notably Yahoo, work by maintaining a hierarchical directory that allows a user to drill down from a broad category (the United States) to specific detailed information (restaurant reviews for Sarasota, Florida). Other search engines, such as Google, accept a string of keywords as input and return a list of relevant pages; Yahoo incorporates comparable search features.

The first step in conducting a keyword search (or query) is compiling a list of relevant terms. For example, consider the following series of Google (*www.google.com*) searches for information on King Arthur and the Knights of the Round Table:

Search terms	Pages found
round table	1,980,000
"round table"	638,000
"round table" "King Arthur"	69
"round table" "King Arthur" Lancelot	25
"round table""King Arthur" Lancelot Guinevere	18

The first search returned all the indexed Web pages that contained the terms *round* and *table*. The second search treated "round table" as though it were a single word. Adding "King Arthur" eliminated furniture stores and other nonlegendary Web sites, and *Lancelot* and *Guinevere* narrowed the search even further. Checking 1,980,000 pages is impossible, but checking 18 is quite reasonable.

Typically, the browser requests and displays an initial home page, perhaps the entry page to a **portal**, a Web site that provides Internet access and offers additional services such as e-mail, a search engine, news, and local information. Once the initial home page is displayed, the user can begin surfing the Web. Hidden behind each hyperlink is the address of another Web page. Clicking on a hyperlink sends a page request from the browser (the client) to the page's Web server. The Web server responds by returning a copy of the requested page to the client's browser. The browser then displays the page.

For example, imagine requesting a Web page from Microsoft. The client workstation resides on a LAN (Figure 3.4), and a browser program is running. The user clicks on a hyperlink to Microsoft. The browser responds by generating a page request. The page request then flows from the workstation to the LAN server (hardware), crosses the Internet, and makes its way to Microsoft's host computer. On Microsoft's host (hardware), a Web server (software) retrieves the requested page from a database of Web pages and returns it over the Internet to the LAN server and on to the client workstation, where the browser displays the page.

The term *Web server* is sometimes used to refer collectively to an organization's Internet host and its hardware, software, and data components. You will find e-commerce applications much easier to understand if you clearly distinguish between server hardware and server software, however. Server hardware is designed and marketed to perform the server role in a client/server network, while server software is an application program that runs on a server or a host computer and provides the requested service. Note that without server software, server hardware is just a plain, ordinary computer. The name of a server

Figure 3.4 Downloading a Web page.

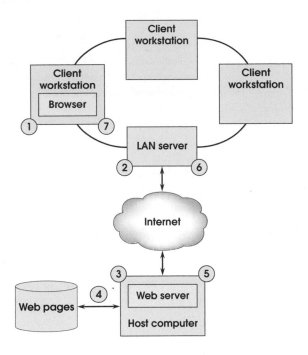

software application usually reflects its function; for example, a Web server returns Web pages, a file server retrieves files, an e-mail server manages e-mail, a database server controls access to a database, and so on. In contrast, if the reference is to server hardware, it is simply called a server.

The Uniform Resource Locator (URL)

Every page on the World Wide Web is assigned a unique address called a **uniform resource locator** (**URL**) (Figure 3.5). Starting at the left, the first parameter names the access method or protocol to be used. **Hypertext transfer protocol** (**HTTP**) is the standard TCP/IP application layer protocol for requesting and transmitting Web pages between a client browser and a Web server. The colon is a separator, and the double slash indicates that a system address (rather than a file address) follows. Next comes the host computer's domain name (Chapter 2). To the right of the domain name is the path name of the host file that holds the requested Web page. The path name is a list of subdirectories that lead to the file.

For example, in the URL *http://www.anyco.com*, *http* is the protocol, *com* is the top-level domain, *anyco* is the company or local domain, *www* (a conventional name for a public Web server) is the name of an application program that runs on the host computer holding the desired Web page, and dots or periods are used to separate the parts of the domain name. In the URL *http://employees.anyco.com/help.html*, *employees* is a different

Figure 3.5 A uniform resource locator (URL).

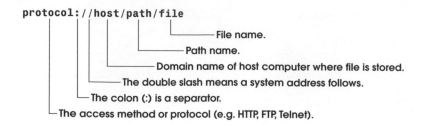

anyco Web server (perhaps a private, password-protected server for employees only) and *help.html* is the name of a Web page stored on the host. By default, if no file name is specified, the server assumes an initial page (or home page) named *index.html*, *index.htm*, *default.html*, or *default.htm*.

Although most URLs begin with HTTP, other protocols can be referenced. For example, the URL *ftp://archives.anyco.com/myfile* uses file transfer protocol (FTP) to initiate a request for a file named *myfile* from *archives*, an *anyco* file server. Once again, the leftmost parameter in a URL defines the access method or protocol that supports the transaction.

Downloading a Web Page

The task of downloading a Web page from a server to a client is accomplished by the standard protocols from the TCP/IP model introduced in Chapter 2. The process starts with the client's browser (Figure 3.6). The user identifies the desired page either by clicking on a hyperlink; by selecting a link from a bookmark or favorites file, a list of recently accessed URLs, or a history file; or by typing a URL on the address line. The request is passed to the TCP/IP application layer, where the HTTP protocol prepares a request for the selected page, calls on the domain name system (DNS) to convert the domain name specified in the URL to an equivalent IP address, adds a header, and passes the request down to the transport layer. The transport layer establishes a connection with the destination host, breaks the request into packets, and passes the first packet to the Internet layer. The Internet layer then adds its header, routes the packet to the next node, and passes the packet down to the network access layer, which adds a final header and drops the packet on the communication line.

The packet passes through numerous intermediate nodes as it moves across the Internet. Once it reaches the host, the network access layer removes it from the communication line and passes it up to the Internet layer, which checks the packet and passes it up to the transport layer. At the transport layer, the packets are collected and the message (a page request) is reassembled and passed through the application layer to the Web server, an application program. The Web server then retrieves the requested page and passes it down through the application, transport, Internet, and network access layers for transmission back to the client. When the packets that make up the requested Web page reach the client, the client's network access layer takes each packet off the line and passes

Figure 3.6 Using TCP/IP protocols to download a page.

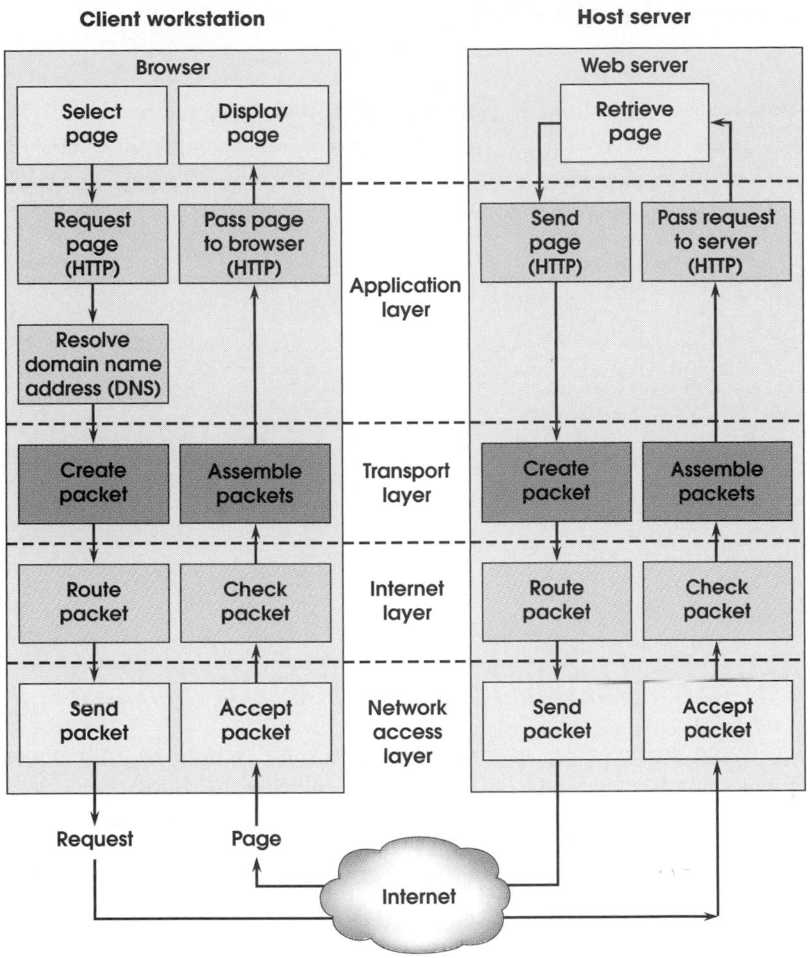

it up to the Internet layer. Subsequently, the transport layer assembles the packets and passes the message to the application layer, where HTTP passes it to the browser. Finally, the browser displays the page.

The link between the client and the server is temporary. It is established when the client sends a page request to the host server and is terminated when the requested page is returned to the client. To the user, there appears to be no difference (ignoring time delays) between loading a page from a local hard disk, from another computer on the same local area network (LAN), or from a remote host located halfway around the world, because the various lower-level protocols operate transparently and very quickly.

The number of Web servers directly connected to the Internet provides a good sense of the World Wide Web's rate of growth. Consider, for example, the following data extracted from Hobbes' Internet Timeline:[1]

Year	Web servers
1994	10,000
1995	24,000
1996	600,000
1997	1,700,000
1998	3,700,000
1999	9,500,000
2000	22,300,000

Between 1994 and 2000, the number of Web servers increased from roughly 10,000 to more than 22 million! Few technologies have ever grown that fast.

Hypertext Markup Language (HTML)

Superficially, the Web works as described in the previous section. To really understand what happens, however, you must dig a bit more deeply into the contents of a Web page. A basic Web page is a text file of **hypertext markup language** (**HTML**) tags (Figure 3.7) and embedded text that tells the client's browser how to display the page elements. HTML is a standard formatting language that all browsers understand. Consequently, any browser can display any Web page written in standard HTML.

HTML Tags

For example, consider the HTML for the intentionally oversimplified Web page pictured in Figure 3.8. The page specification begins with the opening tag *<html>*. At the bottom, the last tag, *</html>*, marks the end of the page. Everything between the opening and closing tags is part of the HTML document. The second pair of tags, *<head>* and *</head>*, encloses the page title (and usually, a great deal more); note that the title appears at the top left of the page. The *<body>* and *</body>* tags delineate the body of the page, the content to be displayed. In this example, the body consists of a few lines of text between the *<p>* and *</p>* formatting tags that denote paragraph breaks. Typically, only the first *<p>* tag is coded; the *</p>* closing tag is understood.

---

[1] Robert H. Zakon, Hobbes' Internet Timeline v5.6 [cited April 9, 2002]. Available from *http://www.zakon.org/robert/internet/timeline/*.

Figure 3.7 Web pages are created using HTML tags.

Tag	Description	Tag	Description
<APPLET>	Java applet	<HEAD>	Document header
<B>	Bold	<HTML>	HTML document
<BIG>	Big text	<I>	Italics
<BODY>	Body of document	<IMG>	Image file
 	Line break	<LINK>	Hyperlink
<CENTER>	Center element	<MENU>	Menu list
<EMBED>	Embed a plug-in	<META>	Metatag
<FIG>	Figure (gif or jpeg)	<P>	Paragraph break
<FONT>	Define type font	<SCRIPT>	Insert script
<FRAME>	Define a frame	<SMALL>	Small text
<FRAMESET>	Define a frameset	<Tab>	Insert tab
<H1>	Level 1 heading	<TABLE>	Table of data
<H2>	Level 2 heading	<TITLE>	Page title
<H3>	Level 3 heading	<U>	Underline

Source: The Willcam Group. Complete Index of HTML Tags.
http://www.willcam.com/cmat/html/crossname.html.

Figure 3.8 A simple Web page and its source HTML.

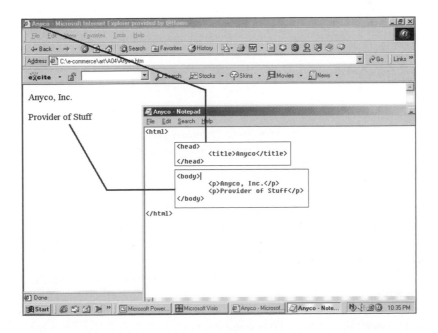

Hyperlinks

An active hyperlink that connects one Web page to another is inserted into an HTML specification between a set of anchor *<a>* tags. For example, to establish a link to Miami University's Web server, a page designer would code *<a* HREF=*"http://www.muohio.edu"*>Miami University*</a>*.

Note that the information from *HREF* to the closing quote mark is a parameter and is coded between the opening and closing angle brackets. When the page is displayed, *Miami University* will be underlined and (on most browsers) colored blue. Buried beneath that hyperlink (or "hot" link) is the parameter's value, *http://www.muohio.edu*.

Embedded Files

HTML was originally designed to support text, but plain text can be boring. To make a page more interesting (and consequently, more appealing to potential customers), the contents of image, animation, sound, and multimedia files can be added to the page by referencing the file name within the appropriate tag. For example, to insert an image file, the source file name is coded within an *<img>* (image) tag.

Imagine a real estate agency's Web site that features photographs of available properties, one per page. The HTML for each page consists of several lines of text that describe the property and an image file name embedded within an *<img>* tag (Figure 3.9). A customer selects the property to be displayed by clicking on a hyperlink. The browser responds by requesting the appropriate page, and the Web server returns an HTML file. The browser then maps the file's contents to the screen (Figure 3.10), scans the HTML for any embedded files, extracts the image file name from the *<img>* tag, and sends another request to the Web server. The Web server responds by returning the image file, and the browser displays it (Figure 3.11).

Figure 3.9 The HTML for a real estate agency page.

```
<BODY>
        <P>This charming big white house features numerous bedrooms and
        baths, a large office, and a lovely view of downtown Washington, D.C.
        <P>
        <P>Availability: Every 4 years.
        <P>
        <P>Price: If you must ask, you can't afford it.
        <P>
        <P>
        <P>
        <IMG SRC="http://www.realestate.com/properties/big-white-house.jpg">
</BODY>
```

Figure 3.10 The text is displayed first.

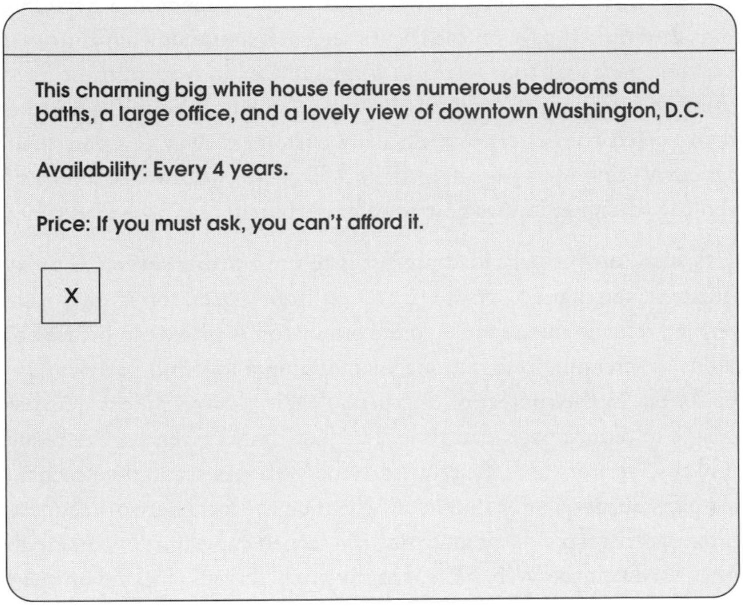

This charming big white house features numerous bedrooms and
baths, a large office, and a lovely view of downtown Washington, D.C.

Availability: Every 4 years.

Price: If you must ask, you can't afford it.

X

Figure 3.11 The browser requests the file and displays its contents.

This charming big white house features numerous bedrooms and
baths, a large office, and a lovely view of downtown Washington, D.C.

Availability: Every 4 years.

Price: If you must ask, you can't afford it.

Source: http://www.whitehouse.gov

Page Load Time

Page load time is the elapsed time between the act of clicking on a hyperlink and the appearance of the finished page on the client's screen. Because downloading each embedded file takes time, page load time increases as the number and size of those files increases. Ironically, making a page more appealing by adding graphics, sound, and other features in an effort to gain customers can actually drive customers away. If a potential customer grows impatient waiting for a page to load, he is likely to click over to another Web site. A good Web page designer knows how to balance content and page load time.

One way to speed up the page load process is to use a **proxy server**. A proxy server is an intermediate server that accepts a transaction from a user, forwards it to the appropriate server, and returns the response to the originator. A proxy can be used to perform such functions as screening transactions, maintaining a log, and performing virus and security checks, but in the context of the current topic, a proxy's most valuable function is caching pages to reduce page load time. The first time a given page is requested by a client, the proxy server forwards the request to the Web server and then caches (or saves) the returned page. Subsequently, should any client on the local network request the same page, the proxy server responds by returning the cached copy, thus bypassing the process of getting the page from the Web. Note that the proxy server is located on the client side of the connection.

TECHNOLOGY

Page Load Time and Embedded Files

Page load time is affected by the number of file references embedded in the HTML and by the size of those files, but other factors are important, too. Although thinking of each Internet and Web layer as an independent black box that performs its assigned task instantly is convenient, the reality is quite different. In Chapter 2, you learned about the numerous intermediate computers and routers that participate in transmitting packets across the Internet and the TCP/IP protocols that run on each of those machines. Keep in mind that delays are possible within any layer on any device. An unacceptably long response time might be traced to the client's browser, one or more of the client's TCP/IP layers, the client's hardware, the client's local Internet access provider, backbone congestion, an intermediate router, the server's local Internet access provider, the server's hardware, the server's TCP/IP layers, the server software, and so on.

Remember that the infrastructure is a complex, integrated system of many parts. What good is a superfast computer if excessive traffic clogs the backbone? What good is a beautifully designed, highly interactive Web page if the user's underpowered computer (or modem, or local service provider) slows the page display process to such an extent that the user abandons the download? Layering makes it possible to deal with a complex system by allowing people to focus on one layer at a time, but those layers are still interconnected, and at some point, they must function together or the system will not work well.

Client-Side Interactivity

HTML is a markup language, not a programming language. It controls the appearance of the information displayed on the client's screen, but it does not support processing or manipulating that information. Consequently, early browsers were limited to displaying **static pages** that were created in advance, stored on a Web server, and retrieved on request.

Static pages are fine for conveying information, but many business applications require interactivity; for example, to catch a potential customer's attention, an e-commerce Web page might incorporate such active elements as animation, sound, or a flashing logo. Changing an image or playing a sound implies processing, and processing implies software. The idea of having the Web server software continuously repaint the page and send each updated version to the client browser is impractical (at best). A better solution is to embed the necessary program logic in the HTML stream and let the browser execute the instructions on the client side.

In addition to adding eye-catching features, many e-commerce applications call for information to be input on the client side. For example, to purchase a product from an e-commerce company, you must enter your name, mailing address, e-mail address, credit card number, and other information on an electronic form displayed by your browser (Figure 3.12). Once again, the best solution is to embed the logic in the HTML stream and let the browser execute the supporting logic on the client side.

Figure 3.12 A data entry form.

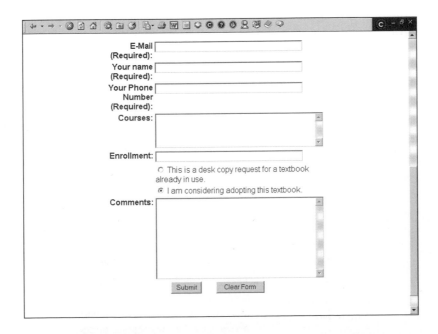

Adding Interactivity with Scripts and Applets

One way to pass logic from a Web server to a browser is to write a set of macro-like instructions called a **script** in a scripting language such as JavaScript, JScript, or VBScript. A script is normally embedded in an HTML document as a text string written between a set of <script> tags. One option is to create a script file and reference the file name between the tags. A file reference means that the client browser must request the download of the script file, however, which adds to page load time.

A script might be used to animate an image in a window, highlight an icon, or play an audio file when the mouse pointer moves over a spot on the client's screen. Scripts are also used to validate the completeness and accuracy of the data input to a browser-based form. For example, before the data is sent to the server for processing, a client-side script might check to ensure that an e-mail address field contains an "@" symbol or that a credit card field contains the correct number of digits and no nonnumeric characters. Checking the validity of the data before transmitting it to the Web server is much more efficient than retransmitting errors.

Scripting languages are not full-featured programming languages. To add more interactivity to a Web page, **applets**, small programs executed from within another program such as a browser, can be downloaded to a client. An applet can change the contents of the active Web page without requesting a complete new page: for example, periodically updating current news headlines, weather, or stock quotes in a scroll bar across the bottom of the client's screen. An applet's file name is inserted into the body of an HTML document between a set of <applet> tags. The applet itself is stored in a Web server file and downloaded to the client upon request. Most applets are written in Java, a platform-independent, object-oriented programming language developed by Sun Microsystems.

Plug-Ins

A **plug-in** is a software routine that extends the capability of a larger application. Several popular plug-ins allow a browser to process nonstandard, often proprietary animation, video, and audio files embedded in HTML documents (Figure 3.13). For example, RealAudio's RealPlayer allows a user to play streaming audio files from a distant radio station through the client computer's speakers, and Adobe's Acrobat Reader allows a user to view the contents of a Portable Document Format (PDF) file, a popular format for electronically distributing white papers and similar documents. Numerous plug-ins, many of them free, are available for downloading on the Internet.

Figure 3.13 Some popular plug-ins.

Plug-in	Supplied by	Function
Acrobat Reader	Adobe	Display PDF files
RealAudio/RealPlayer	RealAudio	Play real-time audio
Shockwave	Macromedia	Display animation
QuickTime	Apple	Animations, audio

Web Information Systems

The first Web sites were designed to convey information by exchanging simple static Web pages. Client-side scripting and applets made it possible to move beyond static Web pages and to begin to implement interactive systems. Today's state-of-the-art Web site features sophisticated, interactive, business-oriented **Web information systems** that combine client-side and server-side processing to support personalized marketing, just-in-time (JIT) inventory, JIT parts ordering, real-time intra- and inter-corporate communication, paperless transactions, and similar applications that enhance revenue and/or improve operating efficiency. This chapter considers several basic Web information system principles. Chapters 4 through 7 expand on those basics.

The Server Side

A server is an application program that runs on the server side. For example, envision several servers running on a single host computer (Figure 3.14). One Web server might manage access to the organization's public Web site. A second Web server might be available

Why the Web?

BUSINESS

Why do the Internet and the World Wide Web appeal to business? Three key reasons are low cost of entry, relatively low development and operating cost, and an accessible user interface.

Business has long known that speed counts—efficiency rises as information interchange time drops. The quickest way to exchange information is electronically, but until recently, connectivity costs were prohibitive. The Internet, a freely available open standard for accessing the underlying, public communication infrastructure, lowers the cost of entry, however, making e-commerce affordable to almost anyone.

Before the Internet became mainstream, large corporations ran their own private proprietary networks. Proprietary technology is expensive to develop and to operate, in part because people trained in a proprietary technology are (almost by definition) not widely available on the open market. Consequently, the early movers had to do their own training and pay a premium to keep their network

personnel from leaving. In contrast, the success of the Internet means that standard hardware and software are readily available at competitive prices, and people with the necessary training and skills are much more plentiful than people with proprietary skills.

In addition to the Internet's cost-reduction potential, the Web's user-friendly point-and-click interface significantly enhances the scope of a business application by increasing the number of potential users. Prior to the release of Web browsers in the early 1990s, accessing the Internet was a daunting task, but today anyone who knows the Windows or Macintosh interface can quickly learn how to surf the Web. As a result, the efficiency gains derived from quick information exchange affect more people, and a growing population of technically able customers is a possible source of significant new revenue. In other words, the Internet and the World Wide Web have the potential to enhance revenue and reduce cost. As any business major knows, profit equals revenue minus cost, and profit is the bottom line.

only to authorized customers and business partners who know the proper password, and access to a third Web server could be restricted to the organization's own employees. Add a file server to support FTP requests and an e-mail server to support e-mail delivery, and you have five server applications running on the same host. Note that running each server on a separate host (Figure 3.15) or spreading the servers over two, three, or four hosts is also possible.

Figure 3.14 Multiple servers can run on the same host.

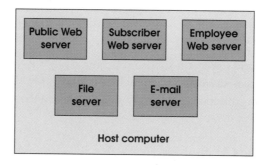

Figure 3.15 Multiple servers can run on multiple interconnected hosts.

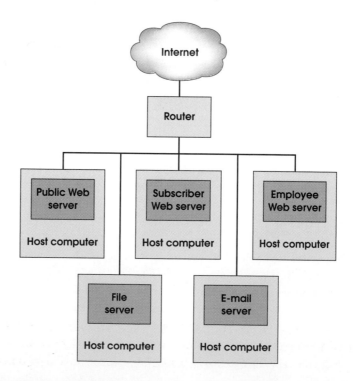

The server side also features numerous specialized hardware devices. For example, a router is often placed between the company's host or hosts and the Internet (Figure 3.15) and is assigned responsibility for exchanging packets with the outside world, passing incoming transactions to the right host or server, and sending outgoing transactions from all internal sources to the Internet. If an organization supports multiple hosts and servers, using load balancing hardware and software to distribute the processing load more evenly is another possible source of efficiency gains. Often, a Web site is mirrored or duplicated on two or more hosts to improve load balancing, particularly when page requests originate from geographically disbursed locations. Within a network, hardware devices called switches are used to move packets between the servers.

Firewalls

A **firewall** is a set of hardware and software that isolates a company's internal private network from the Internet (or any public network) by controlling external access to the organization's servers. Companies use firewalls to protect their Web information systems from hackers and other external threats. The firewall might be a separate hardware/software entity placed between the router and the Internet (Figure 3.16), or it might be implemented as software that runs on the router. Some companies follow a defend-in-depth principle, with secondary firewalls protecting each host, a third firewall layer protecting the company's internal LAN servers, and personal firewall software running on individual workstations. What slips through the top layer is likely to be stopped by a lower-level firewall.

Most firewalls work by screening packets. For example, because each packet contains a header that identifies its source and destination IP addresses, a corporate firewall might allow packets originating inside the company to flow to any server, while restricting external packets to the public Web server. Other screening criteria include protocol (accept HTTP and FTP; reject telnet), file type, message length, and so on. Some firewalls work at the application layer and filter messages based on content, rejecting pornography or MP3 files, for example.

Web Applications

Like the World Wide Web, the Web applications that support a Web information system are client/server applications. For example, consider a Web-based parts ordering system. On the client side, the manufacturer's purchasing agent (real or electronic) starts the process by launching a browser and following a hyperlink to the supplier. Subsequently, the supplier's Web server returns an order form accompanied by a supporting applet. The purchasing agent then enters the order through a browser and clicks on a Send icon. Before the order form is sent to the supplier, the applet checks to ensure that all the required information has been entered in the proper format and requests corrections if necessary.

At the supplier's end of the connection, a server-side Web application uses the information entered by the manufacturer's purchasing agent to check the available inventory, schedule a production run (if necessary), arrange for shipment, and so on. To support

Figure 3.16 A firewall protects an organization's internal network from external attack. Installing separate firewalls at each layer provides defense in depth.

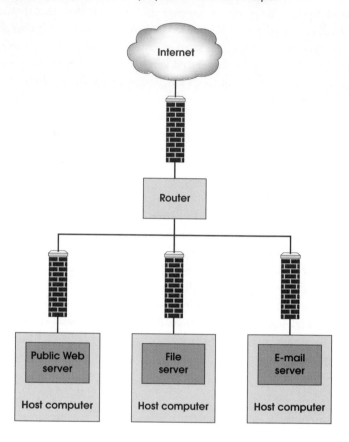

and document the transaction, the Web application generates such electronic documents as an order acknowledgement, an invoice, and a delivery schedule and returns them to the client's browser, which displays them.

Such Web applications are not quite as simple as they seem, however. The browser and the Web server work with HTML documents. HTML is a markup language, and manipulating data using a markup language is difficult. To make matters worse, database servers, not Web servers, control access to databases, and database servers cannot interpret HTML documents. In other words, translation is necessary. Thus, the order contents are converted from HTML to a format acceptable to the supplier's database server. Before it is returned to the manufacturer's browser, the information returned by the database server is converted to HTML by **middleware**, software that connects two otherwise separate applications.

For example, on the client side, order information is entered through a browser, checked by an applet (which is *not* middleware), and sent to the supplier's Web server as a set of parameters in HTTP format (Figure 3.17). The Web server passes the parameters to a middleware routine that extracts the relevant information from the parameters,

Figure 3.17 Middleware connects two otherwise separate applications.

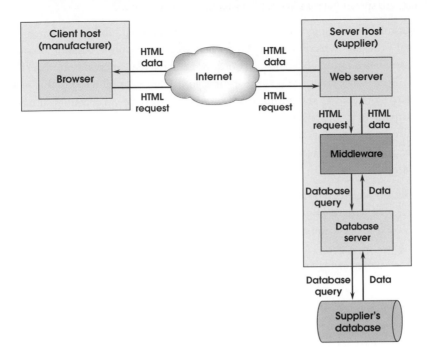

creates a database transaction, and passes the transaction to a database server. The database server, in turn, accesses the database, reads or writes the transaction data, and returns any requested data to the middleware routine. The middleware then converts the data to HTML format and returns the document to the Web server. The Web server, the middleware routine, and the database server are independent black boxes (or layers), so the Web server doesn't care whether the page comes from its own Web site database or from a middleware routine. It just accepts the page and returns it to the client's browser.

In contrast to static HTML pages, a **dynamic page** is created in real time in response to a request. The electronic documents created by the server-side middleware routine in the Web-based parts ordering system described earlier are good examples of dynamic pages; they do not exist until the client submits an order. Because the Web server has no idea whose personal data to insert until after it receives a page request from a browser, personalized Web pages that greet return customers by name are created dynamically, too.

Web applications will be covered in considerably more depth in Chapter 6.

Maintaining State

Unlike casual Web surfing, many Web applications call for performing a series of related tasks, often in a prescribed order, to achieve a specific objective, such as ordering parts, paying a bill, or maintaining a database. Some Web applications are completed during a single **session**, a relatively brief series of related transactions with a clear beginning and a clear end. Others, such as maintaining a wish list and eventually ordering from that wish list, are spread over a series of noncontiguous sessions.

Successfully performing a series of related tasks requires an ability to "remember" the results of previous steps. For example, the first step in an online banking session is to enter your identification code and password (or personal identification number) through a login screen. Once the system authenticates your identity, it allows you to check your balances, make deposits and withdrawals, transfer funds between accounts, and perform other banking functions without asking you to constantly reidentify yourself or allowing you to access anyone else's accounts. If the system is to guarantee you access to all your accounts and only your accounts, it must remember who you are as you progress from step to step.

A series of related steps are tied together by maintaining information on the application's **state** (or status). Think of the state of an executing program as a snapshot of essential operating information, such as the values of key control variables, a list of open files, a list of active print jobs, and so on. If the application is interrupted for any reason, it can be resumed by restoring those state settings.

Maintaining state is relatively simple for an application running by itself on a workstation. It is much more difficult in a client/server system, however, particularly if the server supports multiple clients. Imagine, for example, the problem faced by a popular portal such as Yahoo. At any given instant, tens (even hundreds) of thousands of visitors might be conducting a search or accessing some other service. Simultaneously maintaining the state of all those visitors is virtually impossible (and not particularly useful), so it makes little sense even to try. Instead, when the portal's Web server receives a page request, it promptly retrieves and returns the requested page and then moves on to the next transaction, essentially forgetting the transaction it just completed. Should the user subsequently click a hyperlink on the just downloaded page and generate a request for a new page, the Web server has no way of connecting the new request to the user's previous activities, even if the new page request is (from the user's perspective) part of the same session.

A system that does not monitor its state is said to be stateless. The World Wide Web is inherently stateless, which makes sense most of the time, because surfing the Web clearly does *not* require that the Web server "remember" each visitor's previous activities. Running a Web application to perform a series of related tasks in a prescribed order is a very different problem, however. Because the Web is stateless, some mechanism for maintaining state must be added to the standard protocols.

Cookies

One way to maintain state is to store a **cookie** on the client's hard disk. Created by the server, a cookie is a small text file (less than 1 KB) that holds information about the user and/or the state of the application. Subsequently, when the user's browser transmits new data or requests a new page, the cookie is returned to the server, where its contents can be used to refresh the server's memory.

Consider, for example, the familiar shopping cart metaphor used by many business-to-business (B2B) and business-to-consumer (B2C) Web sites, such as Amazon.com, to support online purchasing (Figure 3.18). As you browse through Amazon.com's Web site and identify items you wish to buy, you click on an Add to Cart button. To check on the contents of your shopping cart, you click on the View Cart icon near the top of the screen. When you finish shopping, you click on a Proceed to Checkout button to start the checkout process. Properly implemented, the shopping cart metaphor is quite effective, almost intuitive.

Let's take a closer look, however. The customer (the client) starts the shopping process by following a hyperlink to Amazon.com's Web server. Ignoring returning customers and personalized pages for the moment, the server responds by storing a set of session data (the initial contents of the currently empty shopping cart) on a database and creating a session cookie. Embedded in the cookie is the user's database access key. The session data and the cookie are then returned to the client as part of the page's HTML stream (Figure 3.19). The client's browser stores the session data and the cookie in memory and displays the Web page.

Subsequently, whenever the customer initiates an activity that changes the contents of the shopping cart (add an item, delete an item, change a quantity, and so on), the session data and the cookie are transmitted back to the server (Figure 3.20). Because the cookie holds the user's database access key, the server can read the previously stored session data, use the new session data to update the database, correct the contents of the shopping

Figure 3.18 The shopping cart metaphor.

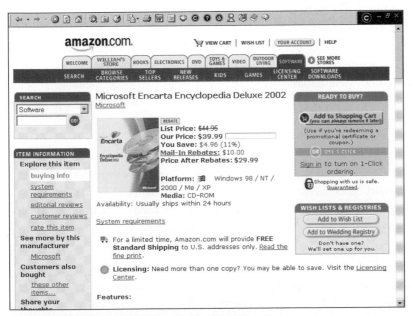

Courtesy of Amazon.com, Inc. Box shot reprinted with permission from Microsoft Corporation.

Figure 3.19 Initializing the shopping cart.

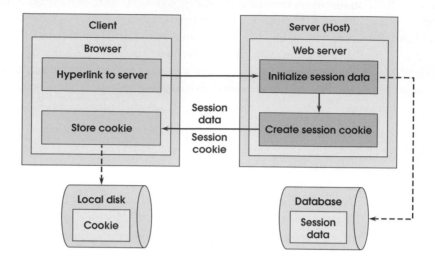

Figure 3.20 Changing the contents of the shopping cart.

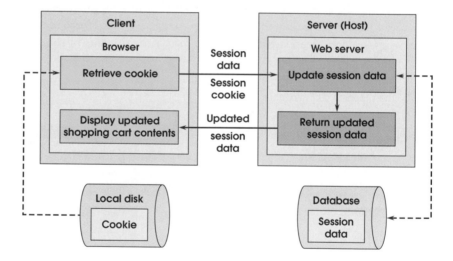

cart, and return the updated session data to the client. Eventually, the user finishes shopping and clicks on Proceed to Checkout. Once again, the cookie and the session data (the shopping cart) are sent to the server. As before, the server uses the database access key embedded in the cookie to access the session database before starting the checkout process.

Quickly review how the cookie maintains state: The server-side database holds a set of data that reflects the session contents. The cookie holds the user's database access key. Following any change to the session contents, the cookie is returned to the server, which uses the embedded access key to retrieve the session data and, effectively, reset (or remember) that particular session's state. Should the user leave the Web site or even shut down her computer, the cookie remains on the client's hard disk and the session data remains on the server's database, so the session can be resumed when the user returns.

Personalized Web Pages

Many e-commerce Web sites use cookies to identify repeat visitors. For example, when a customer purchases merchandise from Amazon.com, the Web server stores a record of the purchases on a database, creates a cookie that contains the customer's identification code, and stores the cookie on the customer's hard drive. Between visits, Amazon.com regularly analyzes (on its corporate computers) the accumulated customer data, looking for patterns that might suggest preferences.

The next time the customer accesses Amazon.com's Web site, the cookie is returned to the Web server. Because the cookie identifies a specific customer, Amazon.com's Web server can retrieve that customer's data from the database and use the data to build a dynamic page that lists books (or other products) its data analysis suggests the customer might find interesting. Note, for example, that the Web page in Figure 3.21 greets one of this textbook's authors by name, features a tab entitled William's Store, and provides hyperlinks to several book recommendations. Many Internet service providers (ISPs) offer similar features, allowing a customer to dynamically view local weather information, a list of bookmarks, starting times for the movies playing at a nearby theater, news of particular interest, and other personalized information on his initial home page. Creating a personalized Web page starts with the cookie that is uploaded to the server when the page is requested. Such personalized Web pages are a very effective marketing tool.

Figure 3.21 A personalized Web page.

Courtesy of Amazon.com, Inc.

Security

Cookies serve a useful purpose. They allow a Web application to maintain state and make personalized Web pages possible. However, because they are created by a remote server, stored on a client's hard disk, and returned to the server, cookies represent a possible invasion of privacy and enable an intrusion path that makes many users uncomfortable. One option is to set your browser to refuse all cookies, but some cookies are good. A better option is to implement reasonable security precautions.

A firewall is a good starting point. Business systems must be protected, of course, and personal firewalls are sufficiently inexpensive that they make sense even for individual users. If you use a cable or DSL connection to access the Internet, firewall protection is particularly important. Antivirus software is also essential. You simply should not surf the Internet or send and accept e-mail unless you have up-to-date antivirus software installed on your system.

Some transactions, such as the transfer of mission-critical information, trade secrets, credit card numbers, and other sensitive data, require more protection. Such data is often encrypted (converted to a secret code) before it is transmitted. Adding a digital signature verified by a digital certificate helps to ensure that the sender of a request or a response is who she claims to be. Firewalls, antivirus software, encryption, digital signatures, and digital certificates will be covered in considerably more depth in Chapter 9.

A More Complete View of the E-Commerce Infrastructure

Before you move on to Part 3, quickly review the infrastructure that supports electronic commerce (Figure 3.22). At the bottom is the data communication infrastructure. At the next level are the Internet and its many protocols. The World Wide Web forms a layer on top of the Internet and defines a platform for running a browser and a Web server. The Web, in turn, provides a base for Web applications. Such non-Web applications as e-mail and FTP communicate directly with the Internet layer without going through the World Wide Web, and a few proprietary e-commerce applications are linked directly to the data communication infrastructure. E-commerce rests on that infrastructure.

Figure 3.22 A more complete view of the e-commerce infrastructure.

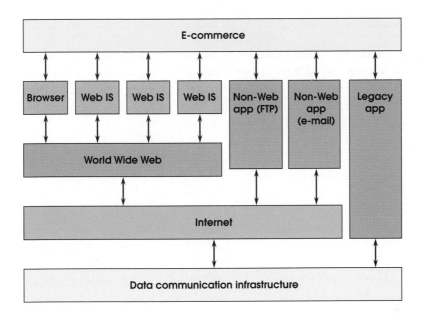

OPINION

Some Downsides

There are downsides to relying on public services and open standards such as the global data communication infrastructure, the Internet, and the World Wide Web. Much like America's interstate highway system, the e-commerce infrastructure is a commodity, available to everyone. Like a trucking company that uses the same roads, vehicles, and fuel as its competitors, leveraging technology to gain a significant, sustainable competitive advantage is difficult when everybody has equal access to the same technology.

Security is another problem. The Internet and the World Wide Web were not designed with security in mind. It is relatively easy to limit access to a private, proprietary network, but anyone with a computer, a modem, and an ISP account can access the Internet. Firewalls help to keep unauthorized hackers and other undesirables out, but the point of using the Internet and the Web is to communicate, not to block communication, and the mere act of communicating breaches the firewall. A decade ago, viruses moved from computer to computer by means of the "sneakernet," people carrying infected diskettes. Today, however, viruses are propagated much more quickly by attaching them to e-mail messages. Imagine a business concern discontinuing its e-mail service to avoid catching a virus. It's not going to happen, nor are companies going to drop FTP, telnet, or HTTP, because the benefits almost certainly outweigh the risk. Don't lose sight of the risk, though.

■ ■ ■   Summary

The basic unit of information on the World Wide Web is a Web page. A Web site consists of a set of related Web pages. Web pages and page requests are transferred between a client-side browser and a server-side Web server by following the standard TCP/IP protocols. Every page on the World Wide Web is assigned a unique address called a URL. HTTP is the standard protocol for requesting a Web page from a server. Web pages are created using HTML. File references and hyperlinks are embedded into an HTML document by coding them in the context of the appropriate tags. Page load time increases with the number and size of embedded files.

Early browsers were limited to static HTML documents. Scripts and applets enable limited client-side interactivity. A Web information system is a set of programs that runs on the platform defined by the Internet and the World Wide Web. Companies use firewalls to protect their Web information systems from hackers and other external threats. Communication between servers is performed by middleware. A dynamic page is created in response to a real-time request.

A Web application implies performing a series of related tasks, which are tied together by maintaining information on the application's state. Because the World Wide Web is inherently stateless, some Web information systems use cookies to maintain state. Personalized Web pages are an effective marketing tool. Many Web applications call for extensive security precautions.

Together, the data communication network, the Internet, the World Wide Web, and Web information systems define an infrastructure for electronic commerce.

■ ■ ■   Key Words

applet	hyperlink	static page
browser	middleware	uniform resource locator (URL)
cookie	plug-in	Web
dynamic page	portal	Web information system
firewall	proxy server	Web page
home page	script	Web server
hypertext markup language (HTML)	session	Web site
hypertext transfer protocol (HTTP)	state	World Wide Web

Review Questions

1. Distinguish among a Web page, a home page, and a Web site.

2. What is a browser? How does a browser work?

3. What is a Web server? Explain how a Web server and a browser work together to download a page from a Web site.

4. Explain each element in the URL *http://www.muohio.edu/admissions.html.*

5. Describe the process of downloading a Web page. As part of your answer, reference the TCP/IP protocols introduced in Chapter 2.

6. Explain how Web pages are created and displayed using HTML tags. Explain how file references and hyperlinks are inserted into a Web page.

7. Explain how page load time is affected by the number and size of the files referenced on a page.

8. Distinguish among an applet, a script, and a plug-in.

9. Explain how applets, scripts, and plug-ins enable client-side interactivity.

10. Distinguish between a static page and a dynamic page.

11. What is a Web information system?

12. Explain how middleware enables complex Web applications.

13. What is a firewall? Why are firewalls used?

14. The World Wide Web is inherently stateless. What does stateless mean? Why must many Web applications maintain state?

15. What is a session? Why is it sometimes necessary to maintain state throughout a session?

16. What is a cookie? Explain how a cookie is used to maintain state.

17. How do cookies make personalized Web pages possible?

18. Identify the layers that form the e-commerce infrastructure.

Exercises

1. Insert several hyperlinks into an existing or new PowerPoint presentation or word processing document. Test each hyperlink to make sure it is active.

2. Use a search engine to compile a set of at least five Web page references for a paper on the history of the Internet and the World Wide Web.

3. Use a plug-in to play music or view a video presentation over the World Wide Web.

4. E-commerce applications promise significant benefits, but not without risk. In your opinion, are the benefits worth the risk? Why or why not?

5. Display the contents of folder *c:\windows\cookies* to list the cookies stored on a Windows 9x or Windows Me computer. On a Windows 2000 computer, look for a folder named *cookies.txt*. On a Macintosh computer, look for a folder named *MagicCookie*. To see the contents of a cookie, double-click on the cookie's file name and a text editor will open. Every cookie holds the URL of the Web site that created it. The creating Web site defines the precise contents of the value field, so you may not be able to interpret all the remaining characters.

You should be able to identify the source of many of the cookies, particularly the ones placed on your system by Web sites you visit regularly. Unwanted cookies can be deleted. To delete all your cookies, open the cookies folder, select all the files (Edit/Select all or Ctrl-A), and press Delete. Some cookies are useful, so you might not want to delete them all. Instead, read through the file names, identify cookies you want to delete, and hold down the Ctrl key as you select them. When you finish, press Delete and the unwanted cookies will disappear.

■ Projects

Current references and supporting resources can be found at this textbook's companion Web site.

Broad-Based Projects

1. Write a short paper on the history of the World Wide Web.

2. Create a personal Web site consisting of at least four Web pages. The theme of your site (unless you select a different one) is you. As a minimum, your site should incorporate the following elements: text, lists or tables, columns, colors, links and navigation (internal, external), images, icons, and graphics (lines, boxes, borders). Additionally, consider including the following optional elements: interactivity using a scripting language, sound, animation, video, Java applets, frames, charts, and graphs.

3. Prepare a PowerPoint presentation on the process of downloading a Web page from a server to a client over the Internet.

Building the Case:

4. Working as a team, continue with Chapter 1, Project 6 by defining the necessary content of your prototype Web site. The prototype is a way to demonstrate the concepts underlying your proposal. Although it might be useful to show the proposed solution's overall organization and functionality, consider focusing on one area and demonstrating it in detail instead of trying to cover everything.

Business Projects

1. Three key reasons why the Internet and the World Wide Web appeal to business are low cost of entry, low development and operating cost, and an accessible user interface. Imagine that you are working for a consulting company. Do the appropriate research and write a proposal designed to convince your school's administration that registration, grade distribution, or some other administrative task should be performed online.

2. Continue with Chapter 1, Project 2 by creating a set of static Web pages (on a computer or on paper) to convey key elements of your client's product or service to the potential customers. Print copies of the Web pages.

Information Technology Projects

1. Write an applet or a script, in the language of your choice, to check the data entered client-side by a customer. The input fields are the customer's first name, last name, six-digit identification code, and e-mail address. Values must be entered in all four fields. The identification code must contain only digits. The e-mail address must contain an @ symbol.

2. Using a computer with dial-up Internet connectivity, conduct an experiment on page load time. Start by identifying ten Web sites. Type or select the URL for the first Web site, and note the time at the lower right of your screen as you press Enter or click the mouse. When the entire page is displayed, note the time again; the difference is page load time. Count the number of images, animations, sounds, and other nontext elements on the page and add the number to your data. Then repeat the process for the next Web site on your list. When you finish collecting the data for all ten Web sites, see if you can spot any patterns that you might use to predict page load time.

3. Continue with Chapter 1, Project 2 by starting a prototype of your proposed solution. For example, if your solution includes a Web site, lay out preliminary versions of key pages on paper, determine whether each page should be static, dynamic, or interactive, and explain how those choices support your strategy.

4. As a reminder, Appendix C outlines a hands-on Web site creation project.

Marketing Projects

1. Do some research and write a short paper on the tradeoff between visual impact and page load time.

2. Continue with Chapter 1, Project 2 by creating a set of static Web pages (on a computer or on paper) to convey key elements of your client's product or service. Print copies of the Web pages and study them until you are satisfied that you understand the product or service. Then review the preliminary set of marketing strategies you identified in Chapter 2 and make changes as necessary.

■ References

Web Sites

Source	URL	Comments
EarthWeb.com, Developer.com	*www.earthwebdeveloper.com*	Tools and tips for developing Web sites.
Kevin Werbach	*http://werbach.com/ barebones/barebones.txt*	The Bare Bones Guide to HTML, a good HTML reference.
The Willcam Group	*www.willcam.com/cmat/ html/crossref.html*	Willcam's Comprehensive HTML Cross Reference, a compact index of HTML tags. A complete index is available at *www.willcam.com/cmat/html/crossname.html.*
Cookie Central	*www.cookiecentral.com*	Information about cookies. Check the cookie FAQ at *www.cookiecentral.com/faq/.*

Print and White Papers

Bidigare, Sarah. 2000. "Information Architecture of the Shopping Cart," Argus Associates, Inc., *http://argus-acia.com.*

PART 3
The Business of
E-Commerce

In Part 3, the focus shifts from the underlying technology to the business applications that run on top of the e-commerce infrastructure. Because these are business applications, Chapter 4 examines selected business principles that apply to any business, describes how e-commerce changes the business environment, and considers how business strategies are evolving to take advantage of those changes. The remaining chapters in Part 3 (which can be read in any order) look more closely at the established categories of e-commerce, including business-to-consumer (Chapter 5), intra-business (Chapter 6), and business-to-business applications (Chapter 7). The contributions of intermediaries are incorporated throughout Part 3. As you read this material, try to visualize how the strengths and weaknesses of the e-commerce infrastructure shape and limit these business applications.

CHAPTER 4

The Business Environment

When you finish reading this chapter, you should be able to:

- Explain why profit is still the bottom line, even in the new economy

- Distinguish between an established company's business strategy and a startup company's business plan and explain why both are necessary

- Explain why a competitive advantage based on internal cost reduction is easier to maintain than one based on price

- Discuss how the three categories of e-commerce are really subsets of a contiguous information flow, and explain how value chain and supply chain integration help to improve efficiency

- Explain why e-commerce is essentially a digital technology

- List and describe several types of intermediary services and distinguish between disintermediation and reintermediation

- Explain how the evolving e-commerce marketplace and the accelerating pace of innovation lead to new patterns of competition

- Explain why enhancing brand-name recognition and reducing cycle time are so important to e-commerce success

- Explain why several of the qualities that make e-commerce appealing to business also represent a threat to a given firm's long-run survival

Some Underlying Business Principles

Recently, the sudden collapse of Enron, once one of the world's top companies, shocked the financial world. In spite of the human-interest stories about how Enron executives allegedly enriched themselves at the expense of their stockholders and employees, and the political stories that attempted to tie high-ranking government officials to the scandal, Enron's most lasting legacy may have been the erosion of investor confidence.

Financial markets require a steady supply of trustworthy information. Investors rely on such information to make rational decisions. They expect the companies listed on the major stock exchanges to follow certain rules in reporting their assets, liabilities, and profits. They also depend on independent auditing firms such as Arthur Andersen, Enron's auditor, to review the books and certify that a company's published reports represent a fair and accurate picture of its financial health. But Enron bent the rules, pumping assets and hiding liabilities, and Arthur Andersen either ignored certain accounting irregularities or failed to blow the whistle. Was Enron an exception, or is financial misrepresentation common? The answer to that question is crucial, because if cheating is common, investors cannot trust the available financial information, and without trustworthy information, there is little difference between investing and gambling.

What does Enron have to do with e-commerce? Plenty. Enron was more heavily involved in *trading* energy than in producing energy, dealing in futures contracts and other virtual digital commodities; in other words, Enron was largely an e-commerce company. More to the point, however, Enron's demise demonstrated in dramatic fashion what happens when a company fails to play by the rules. There were a few mini-Enrons, but most of the dot-coms you read about in Chapter 1 went out of business because they did not understand the rules (ignorance) or because they assumed that the "new" economy had changed the rules. They were wrong. E-commerce is a way of doing business, and it is subject to the rules that govern business. Technology, even innovative technology, is not enough if an e-commerce venture violates certain basic business principles. This chapter discusses some of those key principles.

The Bottom Line

"Technology changes. Economic laws do not."[1] Unprofitable businesses die because investors have better places to put their money. Investors, whether they are owners, employees, or outsiders, expect a return on their investments, and profit (revenue minus cost) is the source of that return. Thus, the ultimate objective of any business is to make a profit. Even in the so-called new economy, profit is still the bottom line.

---

[1] Carl Shapiro and Hal R. Varian. *Information Rules: A Strategic Guide to the Network Economy* (Boston: HBS Press, 1999).

Buying and selling stocks and other financial instruments based on hunches and hearsay is a bit like playing craps. Before you invest, take the time to gather enough information to really understand both the opportunity and the risk. Certain basic, standard accounting and financial practices apply to all businesses, including e-businesses. Publicly traded corporations are required to file certain documents, such as a prospectus, a quarterly report, an annual report, and information on insider trades, with the Securities and Exchange Commission (SEC). These essential documents can be found on the SEC's online Electronic Data Gathering, Analysis, and Retrieval (EDGAR) database (*www.sec.gov/edgar.shtml*) and on such sites as FreeEDGAR.com and *www.edgar-online.com*. Independent financial information is also available from such companies as Dunn & Bradstreet, Hoover's, Moody's, and Standard & Poor's.

Business Planning

Poor business planning is often cited as a primary reason for the failure of many e-commerce business ventures to make a profit. The modern e-commerce marketplace is incredibly complex, and only the efficient survive. A business enterprise achieves organizational efficiency when its functional groups work together to achieve a common set of goals. Those goals are defined during the business planning process.

Business planning is management's responsibility. At the highest level, a company's **business strategy** defines the firm's long-term vision or direction (Figure 4.1). Product, information technology, marketing, human resources, e-commerce, and other substrategies are defined within the context of the strategic plan and, thus, are consistent with that plan. At the operational level, those substrategies shape the budgets, quotas, and other specific measurable guidelines that influence day-to-day decision making. Because those guidelines are derived from the high-level business strategy, they encourage everyone to pull in the same direction.

Figure 4.1 The business planning hierarchy.

Go.com

Even successful companies are sometimes guilty of poor or inconsistent planning. For example, the Walt Disney Company paid more than $2 billion to purchase Infoseek, a World Wide Web portal. Building on that base, it launched its own portal, Go.com, in January 1999. Unfortunately, Go.com featured a distinctive traffic light logo that closely resembled the logo of another portal, GoTo.com. Faced with a legal challenge, in May 2000 Disney agreed to a $21.5 million settlement with GoTo.com, only to shut down Go.com in January 2001 and take a $790 million write-off. Two months later, however, Disney announced that Go.com would remain active (in name only) and that all search requests would be forwarded to (you guessed it) GoTo.com. It is extremely unlikely that the eventual outcome resembled the original strategic plan.

Creating a Startup Business Plan

Strategic planning provides a framework for balancing and coordinating the various parts of an existing company, but a new startup company is different. Almost by definition, a startup has no existing organization to coordinate. Instead, a primary objective of the company's founders is to convince one or more potential investors to supply the seed money needed to create the organization.

Picture yourself as an entrepreneur trying to convince a big investor to supply you with startup funding. You might have a great idea for a product or a service. You might have excellent technical and presentation skills. You might even be the first mover. But unless you can convince the potential investor that your new business is likely to become profitable, you are probably not going to get any money. What you need is a **business plan** (Figure 4.2), a document that clearly describes, at a minimum, your business, your product, your customers, your competitors (there are *always* competitors, even for a first mover), your sales and marketing plans, appropriate financial information, and the qualifications of your management team.

A business plan, sometimes called a path to profitability, is a model that defines the entrepreneur's strategy for taking the company from startup to financial success, supported by enough detail to lend credibility to that strategy. The act of creating a business plan forces the entrepreneur to consider seriously issues that might otherwise be overlooked and to think about potential problems before they become real problems. To potential investors, a well-written business plan provides information to help predict the likelihood of the venture's success or failure and enhances confidence by demonstrating the entrepreneur's grasp of essential business principles. In contrast, an entrepreneur who cannot produce a solid business plan is likely to be viewed as a novice whose lack of business acumen represents an unacceptable risk. The investor's objective is to earn a substantial return on investment, not to educate the uninformed.

Figure 4.2 The elements of a typical business plan.

Business description	Industry overview, mission statement, the company's products or services, company's position in the market, pricing strategies, competitive advantage
The product	Current status of product or service, production or service delivery process, design/development budget, labor requirements, operating expenses, capital requirements, cost of goods
The market	Target customers, market size, target market, competitors, estimated sales
Sales and marketing	Plans for identifying potential customers and converting them to actual customers, distribution channels, advertising and promotion plan
Finance	Risk assessment, cash flow, balance sheet, income statement, funding needs, return on investment, payback, net present value
Management team	Owners and controlling stockholders, management structure, board of directors, management support services

Competition

E-commerce dramatically increases competition, with companies from around the world vying for the same business. To be successful in such an environment, a company must establish and maintain a competitive advantage. As you learned in Chapter 1, a competitive advantage is a benefit derived from something a company does or has that its customers want and its competitors cannot (or choose not to) match. Businesses compete by attempting to protect and enhance their own advantages and counter those of their competitors. Success leads to profit. Failure leads to bankruptcy.

How does a company identify, protect, and enhance its own or counter a competitor's competitive advantage? Unique (the Dixie Chicks), patented (Prilosec), copyrighted (Harry Potter), or trademarked (Mickey Mouse) products or monopolistic control of a market segment help, but few companies enjoy such luxuries. Instead, they compete on price, quality, service, efficiency, product uniqueness (real or perceived), image, advertising, brand recognition, and any other attribute that gives customers a reason to select a given company's products over those of its competitors. For example, compare the price, product quality, and service provided by Wal-Mart, Sears, and Saks Fifth Avenue, and note how each of those retailers has carved out a market niche in which it enjoys a competitive advantage.

Competing on price is particularly difficult because (with very few exceptions) competitors offer identical or similar products and make their prices available for comparison. For example, if Amazon.com offers the latest Harry Potter book for 30 percent off the list price, its competitors will quickly match that offer. As a result, any competitive advantage Amazon.com might enjoy will prove short-lived.

Cost reduction is different, however. Amazon.com, Barnes & Noble, and Borders all pay about the same per copy for Harry Potter books. If, however, Amazon.com's marketing, sales, order fulfillment, and other costs are less than the competition's, then Amazon.com can sell the same product for the same price and earn a bigger profit or drop its price and go after a larger market share. A competitive advantage based on internal cost reduction is much easier to maintain than one based on price, because what happens inside the company is private and, consequently, difficult for a competitor to identify and match. In a competitive marketplace, the company that does the best job of controlling its costs is likely to be the most profitable.

Conflicting Objectives

One way to reduce cost is through process redesign. Improving an organization's processes enhances efficiency, which leads to productivity gains and lower cost, but no process stands alone. To be successful, a business concern's component parts must function together in harmony, and efficiency enhancements that cut across the value chain (Figure 4.3) and the supply chain (Figure 4.4) often yield greater productivity gains than any single process redesign.

Figure 4.3 The value chain.

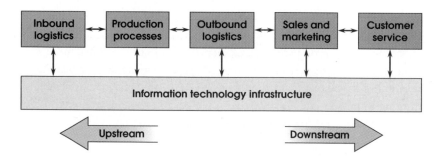

Figure 4.4 The supply chain.

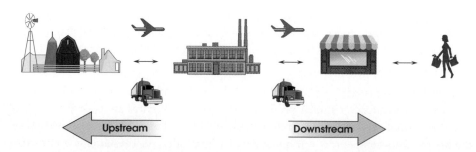

Unfortunately, the local objectives of the various value chain and supply chain components are often in conflict. For example, the sales department wants a warehouse overflowing with products so all customer orders ship immediately, but maintaining a large inventory is expensive. Consequently, companies seek to balance such **conflicting objectives** by searching for an optimal solution that maximizes total profit or minimizes total cost.

Professional systems analysts have an old saying that illuminates the conflicting objectives quandary: "You can have it fast, you can have it cheap, or you can have it right. Pick any two." If you want a quality system delivered quickly, it's going to cost you. If you want a high-quality, low-cost system, be patient because the budget won't support overtime. If you want a low-cost system delivered quickly, don't be surprised if it's full of bugs. Clearly, **trade-offs** and compromises are necessary, and those trade-offs must be based on the priorities set by management. Once again, the key is business planning.

BUSINESS

Some B2C Success Stories

The dot-com debacle marked the demise of many online retailers, but not all B2C ventures failed. Consider, for example, FTD.com. If you have ever sent flowers to someone far away, you are probably familiar with FTD, a company that manages a nationwide network of florists. Rather than targeting unsustainable growth, FTD saw the Internet as a means of leveraging its existing brand name by giving its customers online access to FTD's traditional flower delivery service. FTD knew its business, its product, its market, and its customers, and FTD's management team made sure its online venture complemented, rather than undercut, its established business.

Like FTD, E*Trade and eBay both offer a clearly defined service to clearly defined customers. E*Trade supports online stock trading, and eBay operates a virtual auction. Another key to their successes is limiting their risk. E*Trade is not responsible for its customers' financial decisions, and, although it does offer some help when things go wrong, eBay does not guarantee the items offered for bid, the delivery of those items, or the purchaser's payment. Limiting liability helps to control cost.

Self-billed as "The world's largest discount fragrance store," FragranceNet.com has thrived in spite of the failure of such competitors as BeautyJungle.com and clickmango.com. Instead of its own proprietary fragrances, FragranceNet.com decided to focus on high-markup brand names and offer them at a discount to customers already familiar with the product. Its sales and marketing plans were another reason for its success. Rather than spending a great deal of money on high-profile advertising designed to foster brand recognition, FragranceNet.com set a maximum per-customer acquisition cost and designed its advertising campaigns with that target in mind.

SmarterKids.com decided to go after a niche market: educational toys. Like FTD, the company knew its product, knew its market, and knew its customers, and it saw the Internet as a means of leveraging that knowledge. The list of failed e-commerce toy stores is legion, including such well-financed ventures as ActionAce, eToy, RedRocket, Toysmart, and ToyTime. But SmarterKids.com made it and has enjoyed slow, steady growth ever since.

What do these success stories have in common? In each case, the company understood its product, its market, and its customers and used that knowledge to set realistic, achievable goals. There is simply no substitute for solid business planning.

The E-Commerce Business Environment

Without question, e-commerce is changing the way we communicate, work, shop, invest, learn, and stay informed about the world around us. Evolving wireless communication technologies will only accelerate those trends. As the demand for online products, services, and information grows, business will find a way to meet that demand. As cost control pressures intensify, business will find a way to leverage e-commerce technology to reduce costs. In other words, e-commerce is changing the way business does business.

Given the relatively low cost of entry, virtually any business can go online. Because of the Internet's global reach, a company can reach customers and suppliers located anywhere in the world, but the competition is worldwide, too. The e-commerce business environment features both huge markets and intense competition, making a sustainable competitive advantage more important than ever.

Value Chain and Supply Chain Integration

As mentioned earlier, in a competitive marketplace, the company that does the best job of controlling its costs is likely to be the most profitable. By enabling the free flow of information, e-commerce makes it possible for a business concern to operate more efficiently by integrating its internal processes across the internal value chain. Additional efficiency gains are realized by integrating the value chains of business partners across the external, intercorporate supply chain.

Recall from Chapter 1 that there are three major categories of e-commerce: business-to-consumer (B2C), intra-business (B2E), and business-to-business (B2B). Viewing those three categories as pieces of a larger, integrated structure (Figure 4.5) may be more useful, however. B2C e-commerce, the tip of the iceberg, represents the link between a business and its customers. That link lies at the end of an internal value chain, and integration across the value chain is the essence of intra-business e-commerce. A company's

Figure 4.5 The three categories of e-commerce are pieces of a larger integrated structure.

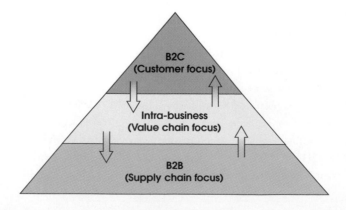

internal value chain depends upon the products and services provided by its supply chain, and the focus of B2B e-commerce is integration across the supply chain. Think of the three types of e-commerce not as independent categories, but as subsets of a single, contiguous information flow that stretches from the original raw materials to the final customer and back again, and you gain a real sense of e-commerce's potential. The various e-commerce categories are discussed extensively in Chapter 5 (B2C), Chapter 6 (intra-business), and Chapter 7 (B2B).

Be careful not to read too much into Figure 4.5. It does *not* imply that transactions flow down from the B2C layer to the intra-business layer and from there to the B2B layer. The three categories of e-commerce are interrelated, but they are all applications that occupy the same layer and communicate with each other over the lower-level infrastructure (Figure 4.6). The diagrams depicting the communication, Internet, and World Wide Web layers in Chapters 2 and 3 and the triangle shown in Figure 4.5 are models, and models simplify reality.

Consider the various categories of e-commerce from yet another perspective. Imagine that Acme's purchasing department sends an order for subassemblies to a major supplier, Soup-to-Nuts (Figure 4.7). At roughly the same time, further down the value chain, Acme's online sales department accepts an order from a retail consumer. To most observers, the transaction between Acme's purchasing department and the Soup-to-Nuts sales department is B2B e-commerce, and the customer transaction is B2C e-commerce. Essentially the same thing happens in both cases, however: one party orders products or services from a second party, and the second party fills the order. For a supplier, the sales function marks the downstream end of its value chain. For a retailer, the consumer-oriented B2C link marks the downstream end of its value chain. The manufacturer-to-supplier transaction links two value chains, so Figure 4.7 shows a portion of the supply chain. Clearly, the B2C, intra-business, and B2B e-commerce categories are far from independent.

Figure 4.6 The three e-commerce categories are applications that communicate with each other over the infrastructure.

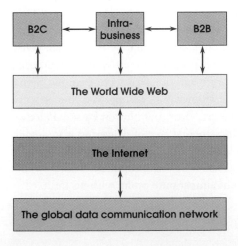

Figure 4.7 A B2C transaction and a supply chain purchasing transaction are similar.

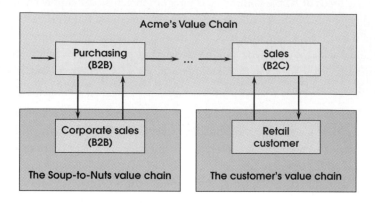

Breakthrough Products and Services

Value chain and supply chain integration promises to improve the way business does business, but breakthrough products, sometimes called **killer applications**, have the potential to totally change a market or even create a new market. For example, in the computer industry, the Apple, the Apple II, and the IBM PC established the legitimacy of personal computers and, in the process, permanently changed the industry. Similarly, the widespread acceptance of the Internet and e-mail (the Internet's first killer application) has so reduced the flow of traditional paper mail that the United States Postal Service is growing increasingly concerned about its future.

The next breakthrough product is likely to be digital. Computer software, for example, consists of strings of binary digits—0s and 1s. Do you really care if your software comes on CD-ROM or DVD? For most people, whatever medium their computer supports is fine because they want the contents, not the container. Is the container even necessary? If you have ever downloaded software over the Internet, you know the answer to that question is an emphatic no.

Digital products are particularly appealing because the law of diminishing returns does not apply to digital products, and digital assets are not consumed as they are used. Consequently, once a digital product is created, it is theoretically capable of generating infinite revenue at little or no additional cost. For example, Symantec offers a service that entitles a subscriber to electronically access upgrades to such software products as Norton System Works, Norton Anti-Virus, and Norton Personal Firewall. Once Symantec posts an update online, the incremental cost of delivering it to any given subscriber is miniscule, with no practical limit to the number of subscribers who can be served. For purely digital products such as software, once cumulative sales revenues exceed startup costs, additional sales represent almost pure profit, without limit.

Bits and Atoms

Information stored on a computer is, by definition, digital because it consists of patterns of bits. Like digital products, digital information, once created, can be distributed or exchanged almost without limit and at very little incremental cost. That is why such information-based applications as stock trading (E*Trade), auctions (eBay), dating services, and (unfortunately) pornography fit the e-commerce model so well. E-commerce is essentially a digital technology.

In contrast, physical products such as automobiles, real estate, furniture, computer components, and pet food do not fit the model. Unlike bits, atoms must be delivered physically, not electronically, and product delivery is expensive. The information (traditionally, paperwork) that describes and supports a physical transaction is easily converted to digital form, however. Electronically delivering an automobile, a building, a sofa, memory chips, or a bag of dog food may be impossible, but electronically exchanging information is certainly possible. Exchanging information may not enhance revenue, but properly applying that information can significantly reduce costs.

E-Commerce Intermediaries

E-commerce implies exchanging digital information. Intermediaries are companies that stand between the communicating parties and assist or add value to the exchange by facilitating the production, selection, delivery, or presentation of the information (Figure 4.8). Business concerns, both e-commerce and traditional, rely on intermediaries because the services they provide lie off the value chain and require expensive expertise and specialized equipment. Outsourcing such services makes good business sense.

In the e-commerce realm, connectivity and bandwidth providers (Internet service providers [ISPs], network service providers [NSPs], network access points [NAPs], and so on) provide the underlying communication infrastructure (Figure 4.9). Web site and Web information system providers facilitate the creation and organization of digital content and also develop the applications that control information exchanges. Infrastructure

Figure 4.8 E-commerce moves information between the communicating parties.

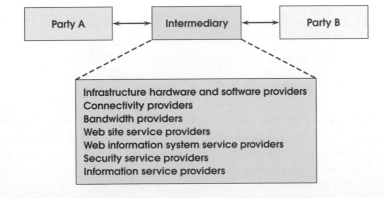

Figure 4.9 E-commerce would be all but impossible without intermediaries.

Connectivity providers	**Web information system service providers**	**Security service providers**
Telephone service providers	Application service providers	Antivirus software
Wireless service providers	System development consulting	Firewalls
Internet service providers (ISPs)	Development software	Encryption software
Cable service providers	Enterprise portal software	Identification and authentication
Common carriers	Plug-ins and gateways	Disaster recovery services
Bandwidth providers		Virtual private networks
Backbone providers	**Infrastructure hardware and software providers**	
Network service providers (NSPs)	Domain name registries	**Business service providers**
Network access points (NAPs)	Network hardware and software	Payment systems
Value-added networks	Routers and switches	Advertising services
	Load balancers	Supply chain management
Web site service providers	Client and server computers	Managed service providers
Website design and development	Peripherals	Customer relationship management
Management consulting	Operating system software	Financial software and services
Web site hosting	Communication hardware	Brokers
Content management	Communication software	Auction sites
Content distribution	Application software	
Web site usage measurement	Web browser and server software	**Information service providers**
HTML editors	Groupware	Portals, destinations, marketplaces
Storage systems		Search engines
Database software		Virtual communities
		Privacy services
		Rating services
		Shopping bots

hardware and software providers supply the hardware and software on which Web applications are constructed and through which content is delivered. Business and security service providers offer tools and services that support individual information exchanges. Information service providers help to organize, index, aggregate, and protect the content. Note that intermediaries are involved in all three categories of e-commerce.

Providing intermediary services can be lucrative. Almost by definition, however, most intermediaries lie off the value chain, and if enough customers find a less expensive or more efficient substitute for a given intermediary's services (or decide they no longer need those services), that intermediary's days are numbered. To cite a human parallel, how many blacksmiths do you know? A century ago, at least one worked in every town.

One potential benefit of many e-commerce applications is fewer intermediaries; for example, electronically downloading music eliminates the need for delivery services, warehouses, and physical retail outlets. The process of eliminating the middleman is called **disintermediation**. At first glance, the advantages seem obvious: Eliminating intermediaries saves money. E-commerce would be all but impossible without the services provided by an entirely new group of intermediaries, however. Some middlemen go only to be replaced by new middlemen, a process called **reintermediation**.

New Patterns of Competition

The e-commerce infrastructure effectively eliminates geography as a factor in many business activities. It allows a company to market worldwide, but it also exposes the company to **global competition**. Consider, for example, the process of creating a textbook, a task that has been dramatically altered over the past several years by e-commerce. To help personalize these changes, focus on the process of creating *this* textbook.

Start with the participants. The publisher, Addison-Wesley, is located in Boston. The developmental editor, copy editors, art staff, and designers were primarily Boston-area subcontractors. The reviewers were affiliated with colleges and universities throughout the United States and Canada. One coauthor worked from his office in Oxford, Ohio; the other worked from his home in Florida.

Except for a few face-to-face strategy sessions, the participants did not physically meet during the production process. Instead, the authors traded annotated Microsoft Word documents (Figure 4.10) and electronic images of the figures (Figure 4.11) as they created the manuscript. An electronic copy of the draft manuscript was sent to the publisher.

Figure 4.10 A manuscript page.

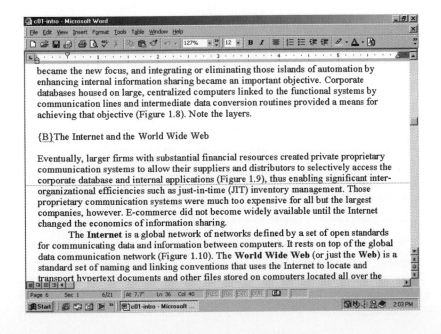

Figure 4.11 Rough art.

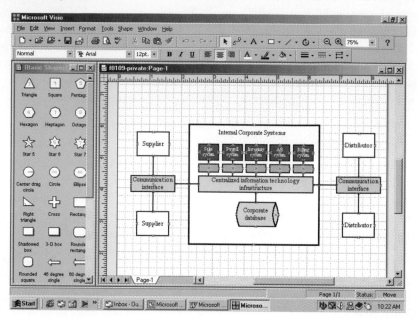

Copies were then distributed electronically to the reviewers, who returned their electronic critiques to the developmental editor. An electronic summary of the reviewers' comments helped the authors prepare a production manuscript.

A few weeks after the production manuscript was delivered, a copy editor used Word's Track Changes feature to mark suggested corrections and pose queries (Figure 4.12).

Figure 4.12 A copyedited manuscript page.

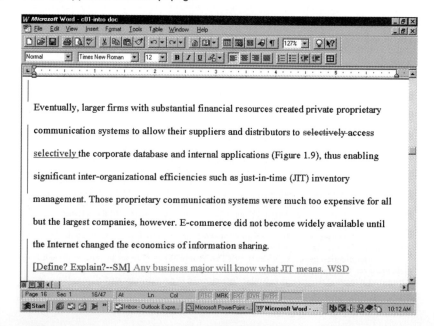

Other subcontractors converted the authors' electronic drawings, screen captures, Word tables, PowerPoint slides, and Excel spreadsheets into finished art. Near the end of the process, the page designers merged the narrative and the art to create pages in PDF format (Figure 4.13). At each stage, the authors viewed the evolving work electronically and made necessary corrections before approving the material for the next step.

Just a few years ago, the textbook production process was quite different. In those days, printed documents or diskettes were exchanged by mail, a time-consuming, expensive, and often frustrating experience. Networks existed, but they were expensive, access was limited, and the lack of established standards made exchanging documents electronically an exercise best left to specialists. The Internet (more broadly, the e-commerce infrastructure) changed the rules. Today, just about everyone involved in the textbook creation process has access to a low-cost communication network, and as long as the participants adhere (consciously or unconsciously) to the TCP/IP standard, they can, for all practical purposes, ignore the underlying complexity.

There are implications, however. For example, consider the process from a subcontractor's point of view. Historically, copy editors, artists, page designers, and other publishing service providers opened offices close to the publishers because proximity made business sense. Today, however, geography no longer matters. As you have just seen, the process of creating this textbook was performed by several specialists who rarely (if ever) met physically and who could have been working from literally anywhere in the world. Suddenly, a copy editor in Boston can accept work from a publisher in San Francisco. At the same time, a publisher in Boston can outsource work to a qualified copy editor in Atlanta, Los Angeles, or Bangalore, India. E-commerce means new opportunities, new competitors, and new risks.

Figure 4.13 A finished page.

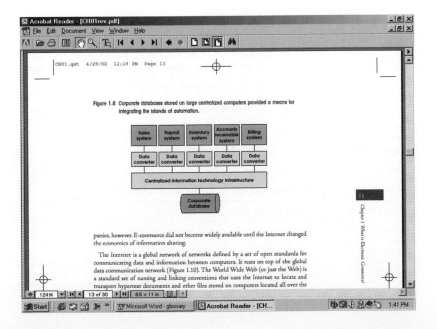

Increased Customer Power

Another implication of e-commerce is increased customer power, particularly in B2B relationships where many purchasing agents are highly techno-savvy. The e-commerce infrastructure's standard, widely available technology significantly reduces entry costs, which expands the number of competitors who can afford to play the game. Meanwhile, the Internet's worldwide scope adds global competitors to the mix and makes it possible for motivated customers to compare the offerings of all those competitors and make more informed purchasing decisions. As a result, customers have the power to demand lower prices, higher quality, and better service, all of which affect profits.

A shopping bot is an excellent example of an application that enhances customer power. A bot, a form of **intelligent agent**, is a program that uses artificial intelligence to perform a specific task, usually in the background; Figure 4.14 shows BotSpot's list of bot types. A shopping bot does comparison shopping by searching the Web and reporting back a list of sources for the desired product in reverse (lowest first) price order. The availability of such information forces a company to price its products competitively. With prices effectively fixed by the marketplace, an e-commerce firm faces considerable pressure to control its costs in order to realize a profit.

The Competitive Advantage Model

As you may recall from Chapter 1, the competitive advantage model (Figure 4.15) begins with a problem or an opportunity, the stimulus for action. If the potential reward seems worth the risk, one competitor makes a first major move. Success, as measured by

Figure 4.14 Bots.

Bot Category	Allows you to:
Chatter bots	Chat with the cyberworld
Commerce bots	Perform e-commerce activities on the Web and the Internet
Fun bots	Interact with virtual environments and virtual realities
Game bots	Monitor selected online games or act as a skilled opponent
Government bots	Find information on government Web sites
Knowledge bots	Utilize various artificial intelligence (AI) agents
News bots	Create custom newspapers or manage a clipping service
Search bots	Use an intelligent agent to search the Web
Shopping bots	Comparison shop, often by price
Software bots	Obtain software fixes, diagnose problems, and create bots
Stock bots	Monitor stock prices
Update bots	Obtain update alerts when selected Web content changes

Source: *www.botspot.com*

Figure 4.15 The competitive advantage model.

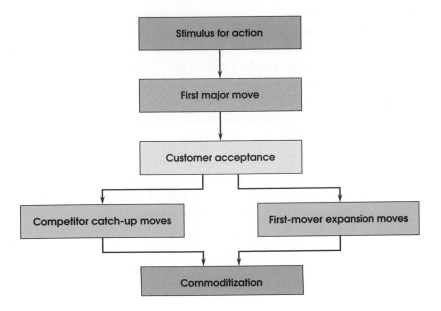

customer acceptance, creates a competitive advantage. Competitors counter by launching catch-up moves, while the first mover attempts to solidify its advantage through expansion moves. Eventually, the original innovation is adopted by all the major players and becomes a commodity, a simple cost of doing business (like an office copier) that affords no one a competitive advantage.

Look carefully at the boxes that represent competitor catch-up moves and first-mover expansion moves. They happen simultaneously, with the various competitors reacting to and building upon each other's innovations in a never-ending race for competitive advantage. Over time, as the initial innovation approaches commodity status, the relative magnitude of each new move shrinks. What were once true innovations become minor variations on a theme that affords the innovator an increasingly smaller competitive advantage, and the energy generated by the initial innovation dissipates.

E-commerce provides numerous examples of the competitive advantage model in action. Consider, for example, e-mail. Until the early 1990s, business viewed e-mail as an academic or research tool with limited practical value, until some company, influenced perhaps by a former academic (the stimulus for action), made a first major move and implemented corporatewide e-mail. The employees loved it (customer acceptance), and the improved internal communication enabled by e-mail gave the first mover a significant competitive advantage. Competitors responded by implementing their own e-mail systems (competitor catch-up moves). When commercial Internet traffic became possible, the first mover countered by expanding its e-mail system to its corporate customers (first-mover expansion moves). Additional catch-up and expansion moves followed, until eventually, an effective e-mail system became an essential cost of doing business that provided a competitive advantage to no one (commoditization).

The Accelerating Pace of Change

The competitive advantage model focuses on how competitors react to each other's catch-up and expansion moves, but it understates the effect of externally generated innovation. Long before reaching the commodity stage, many innovations are eclipsed by new ones, and the pace of such innovation is accelerating. Consider, for example, how long it took four well-known mass communication technologies to reach 50 million users (Figure 4.16). Radio needed thirty-eight years; broadcast television, thirteen years; and cable TV, ten; but the commercial Internet reached 50 million users a mere five years after its inception.

The acceleration phenomenon is not limited to major technological breakthroughs. Earlier in this chapter, you read about the process of producing a textbook. Twenty years ago, it took a full year to convert a finished manuscript into a set of pages ready for printing and binding. Ten years ago, six months was considered very fast and, if the author was willing to create camera-ready (copyedited, ready to print) master pages, three months was possible. Today, due largely to the participants' ability to exchange digital manuscripts, art, and pages electronically, three months is common, and often the finished product looks better and contains fewer typographical errors than an equivalent 1980s book.

The real point is that speed counts. In 1980, a successful, innovative textbook enjoyed a significant head start over its potential competitors. First, an editor working for a competing publisher had to find a suitable author and then negotiate a contract, a process that might take a year or more. Writing and revising the new manuscript consumed a second year, and producing it took a third. When the competitive book hit the market three years after the first book, it was likely to face a second edition of the (by now) well-known first mover's product, another classic example of the competitive advantage model in action.

Fast-forward to the present. Finding a suitable author still takes time, but the e-commerce infrastructure and e-mail can significantly accelerate the process, so nine months seems reasonable. As you read earlier in this chapter, the ability to exchange documents electronically and obtain reviewer feedback can shorten the manuscript creation process, perhaps reducing the elapsed time from a year to nine months. Add three months to convert the finished manuscript to a bound book, and the product is ready in twenty-one months, a full fifteen months faster than the old three-year standard.

Figure 4.16 Elapsed time for some well-known mass communication technologies to reach 50 million users.

Technology	First use	50M users	Elapsed years
Radio	1922	1963	38
Broadcast television	1950	1963	13
Cable TV	1976	1986	10
Commercial Internet	1994	1999	5

Based on Morgan Stanley Dean Witter. *The Global Internet Primer*. Volume I, June 2000: 12.

If you are the first mover, the **accelerating pace of innovation** made possible by e-commerce just cost you fifteen months (more than 40 percent) of your competitive advantage. How do you respond? Do you continue on track for a third-year new edition and hope that competitive products do not erode your market share too badly? Do you bring out a new edition in two years instead of three, thus sacrificing a year of potential first-edition revenue? Or do you choose to break away from the current catch-up/expansion cycle and develop an innovative, continuously updated, always current, electronically downloadable digital version of your product? If you choose the last option, are you willing to commit your company (not to mention your authors) to an expensive, risky investment that just might define a new paradigm, thus giving you (if you're lucky) a few years of market dominance? Good questions. So far, the answers are elusive.

Rapid Obsolescence

Remember the new technology adoption curve (Figure 4.17) from Chapter 1? Imagine squeezing it to compress the time scale, and you have a good visualization of the accelerating pace of innovation. The readiness stage seems to flash by. During the intensification stage, change is almost exponential, with yesterday's first major moves fueling today's catch-up/expansion cycles. By the time the original innovation's impact begins to level off, it is supplanted by a new innovation that sparks a new first major move, and the process starts all over again.

TECHNOLOGY

The Turnpike Effect

Many years ago, long before most Americans had even heard of freeways, interstate highways, and turnpikes, a team of engineers conducted a survey to determine whether people would be willing to pay a toll to drive across a city on a limited-access highway. Given the number of existing free routes, a sizable majority of those surveyed said they would not. Based on the survey, the engineers planned a long-haul road, with no increased capacity inside city limits. Then the highway opened, and people discovered firsthand the convenience of bypassing traffic lights, stop signs, and slow-moving traffic. Within months, in-city freeway traffic had exceeded the engineers' worst-case projections.

What happened to change people's minds? The preconstruction survey asked them to comment on something that did not yet exist; because drivers had never seen a limited-access highway, they had no basis for answering the question. They understood tolls, however, and they weren't about to commit their own money to some engineer's vision. Not until the road opened were they able to experience a real, concrete (no pun intended) limited-access highway and evaluate its value to them personally. For many, the highway filled a need, and they became regular users. New users bring new viewpoints, new ideas, and new innovations, and as those new innovations begin to feed on each other, demand soars, often at an accelerating rate. This phenomenon, known as the turnpike (or highway) effect, is one reason why the ultimate impact of a technical innovation, such as e-commerce, is so difficult to predict.

Figure 4.17 The accelerating pace of innovation.

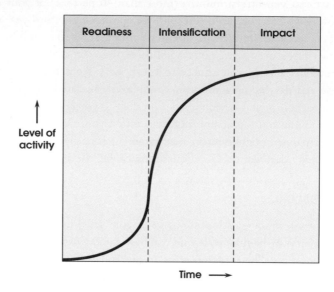

One implication of the accelerating pace of innovation is rapid obsolescence. Because technology changes so quickly, a business concern gets to enjoy the fruits of a hard-won competitive advantage for only a limited time before it is countered by a catch-up or expansion move or (even worse) made irrelevant by the emergence of a new innovation, and those catch-up moves and innovations are occurring at an accelerating rate. Consequently, **time to market** has become a key measure of e-commerce success, because delays mean opportunities permanently lost.

Evolving E-Commerce Business Strategies

Throughout this chapter, you have seen how e-commerce creates new business opportunities. Value chain and supply chain integration enable significant efficiency gains that lead to reduced costs. Electronic outlets and breakthrough digital products promise new revenue streams. The resulting lower costs and higher revenues combine to enhance the bottom line by increasing profits.

The impact of e-commerce is not entirely positive, however. Combine the competitive advantage model, the accelerating pace of change, and highly knowledgeable customers. Take the result to a logical extreme where every innovation quickly becomes a commodity and every customer has perfect information. Given such a scenario, e-commerce effectively levels the playing field, making it extremely difficult for any firm to establish and sustain a competitive advantage. Ironically, the very qualities that make e-commerce so appealing to business represent a very real threat to a particular firm's long-run survival.

Why bother? Why not just drop out of the race? Because, like such historical innovations as steam power and electricity, e-commerce has once again changed the rules of the game, and business will never be the same. Like a struggling marathon runner, a company that falls significantly behind its competitors eventually reaches the point where it can never catch up. Not only does technological innovation give the competitors a lead; it also allows the front-runners to build on that new technology and keep accelerating, widening the gap between the leaders and the also-rans. In the face of accelerating technological innovation, standing still is incredibly risky, perhaps even suicidal. E-commerce is a self-feeding phenomenon, and refusing to play the game is simply not an option. In an "innovate or die" environment, successful companies must adjust by adopting new strategies and changing the way they do business, because the alternative is failure.

Brand Recognition

With its emphasis on quick innovation, reduced cycle time, and shortened time to market, e-commerce has the seemingly inconsistent effect of enhancing the value of a well-known brand name. For example, until late 1998, the e-commerce presence of lingerie maker Victoria's Secret consisted of a simple "splash page," little more than a static, online advertisement. Then the company implemented a feature that allowed a visitor to enter her e-mail address, and within three months, Victoria's Secret had compiled a list of 80,000 potential online customers. Why did so many people willingly give their e-mail addresses to Victoria's Secret? Would they have been equally responsive if the interactive page had been on boo.com's Web site? Probably not—boo.com is not as well known and does not carry the same cachet as Victoria's Secret (which may help explain why boo.com is no longer in business). The point is that brand name matters.

What is the first name you think of when you want to buy a book online? For most people, the answer is Amazon.com. Although Amazon.com has yet to demonstrate long-term profitability, the company has successfully established a widely recognized brand name, which speaks well for its future survival. Barnes & Noble, Sears, JCPenney, Federated Department Stores, Home Depot, and several other well-known retailers have successfully established **bricks-and-clicks** Web sites that complement their physical outlets. In contrast, does anybody still recognize the names of such failed dot-coms as Eve.com, foofoo, furniture.com, gazelle.com, living.com, Miadora, Ready2Shop, RedRocket, or Toysmart?

Why is an established brand name so important to e-commerce success? Probably for the same reason brand name has always mattered—a well-known brand name reduces risk. When you walk into a McDonald's restaurant, you know exactly what you are going to get. The little diner across the road just might offer a better burger, but then again it might not, and the potential gain in value might not be enough to justify the risk. Consider a list of the twenty top technology-related brand names in the United States (Figure 4.18) and note how many you recognize. In the highly competitive business environment enabled by e-commerce, a well-known brand name matters more than ever.

Figure 4.18 The twenty top technology-related brand names in the United States.

Rank	Brand name	Rank	Brand name
1	Napster	11	Microsoft Office
2	Disney	12	Intel
3	Windows	13	WebTV
4	Microsoft	14	Sony
5	Replay TV	15	WebMD
6	TiVo	16	Yahoo
7	MP3	17	Norton
8	eBay	18	Adobe
9	Pixar	19	Palm Pilot
10	Pentium	20	Blue Mountain

Source: "Marks of Distinction, the Tech Brands That Grab Internet Users Worldwide." *Wired*, July 2001: 76.

Reducing Cycle Time

One key to surviving in today's decentralized, go-go, now-or-never, innovate-or-die business environment is reducing **cycle time**. Given the accelerating pace of change and the shrinking duration of a competitive advantage, innovations must be implemented and new products and services must be brought to market as quickly as possible. On an operational level, such B2B cross-supply-chain applications as just-in-time (JIT) manufacturing, point-of-sale ordering, and JIT inventory are manifestations of the drive to reduce cycle time. At the tactical level, decentralization has become the norm. The new economy simply will not tolerate the delays inherent in bureaucratic, centralized decision making.

Half a century ago, Thomas J. Watson, the founder of IBM Corporation, was credited, perhaps unfairly, with estimating a total world market for about five computers. He was obviously wrong, but give him (more accurately, his successor, Thomas J. Watson, Jr.) credit for keeping an open mind. If he had clung to such an erroneous view of the computer's market potential, he probably would have doomed the company, but IBM clearly survived to become a leader in information technology and e-commerce.

In Thomas Watson's days, the pace of technological innovation allowed plenty of time to recover and change directions, but e-commerce has shrunk the time horizon. In many organizations, the traditional, set in stone, three- to five-year plan has become an anachronism or has evolved into an annually updated moving target or a long-term research wish list. The future belongs to those companies that react quickly to changing markets and leverage technological innovations to take advantage of those changes.

Reacting quickly means sensing change almost as it happens. Sensing change, in turn, implies an ability to measure change. To paraphrase Bob Dylan, you may not need a weatherman to know which way the wind blows, but a good sense of direction sure helps. Sometimes, the wrong information is worse than no information at all, and in our highly competitive, adapt-or-die business environment, the old "think first, then act" adage can prove deadly. Unless, of course, you think really fast. Information technology may be a company's only hope of measuring changing business conditions and evaluating its options quickly enough to survive. A solid information technology infrastructure, coupled with effective e-commerce applications that are consistent with the firm's broader business strategies, can be leveraged to gain considerable competitive advantage.

E-Commerce at Dell

Dell started selling personal computers online in 1994, and today Internet sales account for more than 50 percent of the company's total revenues. Consumers who access Dell's state-of-the-art B2C Web site can view products, select a preconfigured system or custom design a system, order the system, and pay by credit card, all without human intervention.

The real secret to Dell's success is cost control, however. The company's ability to integrate its value chain processes is an excellent example. Orders are captured electronically (on the B2C Web site) or entered into the system by sales associates who accept telephone orders. Once an order is in the system, the associated data is used to update the production schedule almost continuously. One outcome, the result of JIT parts delivery made possible by information sharing, is a significant reduction in inventory costs.

Recently, Dell opened the OptiPlex plant, an ultra-modern manufacturing facility in Round Rock, Texas. The focus of the new plant is efficient order fulfillment. The plant's workflow is managed by a computerized control center, and many processes require little or no human intervention. The workflow controls are so efficient that only a two-hour supply of parts is needed, and finished goods inventory is essentially zero because products flow off the line and directly to the delivery trucks.

In addition to its consumer-oriented B2C and intra-business e-commerce initiatives, Dell Computer has implemented B2B applications to share information with the suppliers and business customers that make up its supply chain. For example, an e-procurement hub links customer purchasing systems to Dell's order entry system, electronically generating purchase requisitions, purchase orders, and order acknowledgements and automatically scheduling each customer's order for production. According to Dell, the new system has significantly reduced errors, which in turn reduces both Dell's and the customer's cost. Also, because of its size, Dell has enough leverage with its suppliers to require them to maintain a distribution center stocked with at least a two-week supply of parts near the Dell production facility they service. To the suppliers, Dell offers access to its internal production schedule so they can plan their own production schedules. The result is lower costs for both Dell and its suppliers.

In a highly competitive, price-sensitive marketplace, the company that does the best job of controlling its costs is likely to be the most profitable. In the personal computer marketplace, that company is Dell. At Dell, the key to cost control is integrating its B2C, intra-business, and B2C e-commerce strategies.

■■■ Summary

The objective of any business is to make a profit. Poor business planning is often cited as a primary reason for the failure of many e-commerce companies. Business planning is management's responsibility. Established companies rely on a strategic plan to coordinate their activities; startup companies need a solid business plan.

Businesses attempt to protect and enhance their own competitive advantages and counter those of their competitors. A competitive advantage based on internal cost reduction is easier to maintain than one based on price. Improving an organization's processes enhances efficiency. Improving a set of related processes to achieve systemic efficiency yields greater benefits, but requires resolving conflicting objectives.

The e-commerce infrastructure has made it possible for a business to operate more efficiently by integrating single-function islands of automation across the internal value chain, and then integrating the value chains of business partners across the external supply chain. Breakthrough products, sometimes called killer applications, have the potential to totally change a market or even create a new market. E-commerce is essentially a digital technology.

The three categories of e-commerce are really subsets of a contiguous information flow from the original raw materials to the end consumer. Intermediaries provide a variety of services at all levels of e-commerce. Disintermediation is the process of eliminating the middleman; reintermediation is the process of replacing old intermediaries with new ones.

The e-commerce infrastructure effectively eliminates geography as a factor in many business activities and enhances customer power. One implication of the accelerating pace of innovation is rapid obsolescence. Many of the qualities that make e-commerce so appealing to business represent a threat to a particular business organization's survival. E-commerce enhances the value of a well-known brand name. A solid information technology infrastructure, coupled with the right e-commerce applications that are consistent with the firm's broader business strategies, is the key to reducing cycle time and time to market.

124

■■■ Key Words

accelerating pace of innovation	cycle time	reintermediation
bricks-and-clicks	disintermediation	time to market
business plan	global competition	trade-off
business strategy	intelligent agent	
conflicting objectives	killer application	

Review Questions

1. Profit is still the bottom line, even in the new economy. Why?

2. What is the purpose of the business strategic planning process?

3. Briefly outline the primary components of a business plan. Why is it important for a startup firm to prepare a business plan?

4. A competitive advantage based on internal cost reduction is easier to maintain than one based on price. Why?

5. Explain how the three categories of e-commerce are really subsets of a contiguous information flow from the original raw materials to the final customer and back again.

6. How do value chain and supply chain integration help to improve efficiency?

7. E-commerce is a digital technology. Why? Why is the digital nature of e-commerce significant?

8. List and describe several types of e-commerce intermediaries.

9. Distinguish between disintermediation and reintermediation.

10. Explain how the evolving e-commerce marketplace leads to new patterns of competition.

11. The rate of technology-driven change is accelerating. Why?

12. Explain how the accelerating pace of innovation leads to new patterns of competition.

13. Brand-name recognition is increasingly important in e-commerce. Why?

14. Why is reducing cycle time and time to market so important to e-commerce success?

15. The very qualities that make e-commerce so appealing represent a very real threat to a given business organization's long-run survival. Do you agree or disagree? Explain why.

Exercises

1. Because business is inherently risky, business investors expect a greater return on their investments. Explain what that statement means.

2. Digital products do not experience diminishing returns and are not consumed as they are used. How do these facts help explain Microsoft's success?

3. Providing intermediary services is potentially lucrative but risky. Explain why.

4. The three categories of e-commerce are arbitrary and artificial. Do you agree? Why or why not? If the statement is true, why does this book devote a separate chapter to each category? Assuming the statement is true, what are the dangers associated with studying the three categories of e-commerce separately?

5. During World War I, horsepower was the major means of moving armaments and supplies. Two decades later, trucks and other gasoline-powered vehicles had largely supplanted the horse on the battlefield. Identify several other examples of products and industries that have been rendered obsolete by technical innovation.

6. Read through Figure 4.18, select the names of the companies that are familiar to you, and identify at least one competitive advantage enjoyed by each of those companies. The top twenty brand names were identified in a July 2001 survey. In your opinion, would the results be different if the survey was conducted today? If so, what brand names would be affected?

7. Information technology may be a company's only hope of measuring changing business conditions and evaluating its options quickly enough to survive and thrive in the new hypercompetitive e-commerce environment. Do you agree or disagree? Explain why.

▪▪▪ Projects

Current references and supporting resources can be found at this textbook's companion Web site.

Broad-Based Projects

1. You should be familiar with such basic business terms as book value, balance sheet, asset, liability, general administrative expenses, goodwill, cash flow, accounts payable, accounts receivable, and general ledger. If any of those terms seem unfamiliar, find a good introductory level business or accounting book and read the appropriate material.

2. Systems analysts have a saying that reflects the need to choose between conflicting objects: "You can have it fast, you can have it cheap, or you can have it right. Pick any two." Choose another set of conflicting objectives, such as the choice among cost, availability, and quality in health care, or the choice among fuel consumption, style, and safety in vehicle design, and write a paper on how those objectives conflict and how they can be balanced.

3. Draft a business plan for a new student co-op that plans to sell used textbooks on your campus. If you prefer, select your own product or service.

4. Imagine that your school is about to implement a broadband network that will give students living both on- and off-campus high-speed access to the university network and the Internet. Write a paper in which you consider how the turnpike effect might impact that network once it is released.

5. Use a shopping bot to obtain competitive prices for a product such as a book, a CD, a software product, or a computer.

6. Working as a team, continue with Chapter 1, Project 6 by deciding how the workload will be distributed. For example, one or two team members might assume responsibility for developing the prototype Web site, others might focus on researching the strategy and preparing the necessary written documentation, others might work on preparing and delivering the presentation, and so on. Once assignments are made, prepare a first draft of your implementation plan.

Business Projects

1. Continue with Chapter 1, Project 2 by describing your client's industry and competitors, its position in the target marketplace, and the marketplace's expected future direction (growth or contraction). Compare the results of this chapter's analysis with the revenue estimates you computed in Chapter 2 and make sure they are consistent. If necessary, modify the target revenues. Write a brief report to document your results.

Information Technology Projects

1. Continue with Chapter 1, Project 2 by rethinking your prototype to reflect the contents of Chapter 4. At this stage, your prototype exists only on paper, so changing it should be easy. After rethinking and redesigning the prototype, implement key elements of your solution. For example, if your solution includes a Web site, create preliminary static versions of key pages and identify the hyperlinks, interactive features, add-ons, and other elements your client might need to support the client's business objectives.

Marketing Projects

1. Continue with Chapter 1, Project 2 by describing your client's industry and competitors, its position in the target marketplace, and the marketplace's expected future direction (growth or contraction). Visit the competitors' Web sites, view their online ads, and study their traditional media advertisements. Reconsider your preliminary marketing strategy in the context of the competitors' existing advertising campaigns and make any necessary changes. Review the potential customers you identified in Chapter 2, make sure those customers accurately reflect the marketplace, and make sure your marketing strategy clearly distinguishes your client's product or service from the competition in a way that makes sense to the target customers. Once again, make changes as necessary. Determine reasonable targets for measuring the success or failure of the marketing campaign. Write a brief report to document your results.

References

Web Sites

Source	URL	Comments
BotSpot	*www.botspot.com*	Links to various bots, including shopping bots.
EDGAR Online	*www.edgar-online.com*	Access to the SEC's EDGAR database.
FreeEDGAR	*www.freeedgar.com*	Access to the SEC's EDGAR database.
Management Information Ltd.	*www.jks.co.uk/mi/a.htm*	A useful e-commerce glossary.
SearchEbusiness	*http://searchebusiness. techtarget.com*	Searchable database of e-business terminology.
U.S. Small Business Administration	*www.sba.gov*	Tips on creating a business plan with sample business plans.
U.S. Security and Exchange Commission	*www.sec.gov/edgar.shtml*	The SEC's EDGAR database.

Print and White Papers

Shapiro, Carl and Varian, Hal R. 1999. *Information Rules: A Strategic Guide to the Network Economy.* HBS Press: Boston.

CHAPTER 5

Consumer-Focused E-Commerce

When you finish reading this chapter, you should be able to:

- Contrast the cost of entry for a traditional bricks-and-mortar retail outlet and an e-commerce retail presence

- Describe several hooks used by consumer-focused B2C e-commerce Web sites

- Explain why reduced time to market, reduced cycle time, and first-mover status are considered important B2C e-commerce objectives

- Explain why branding is so important to e-commerce

- Describe the bricks-and-clicks strategy

- Explain how a typical B2C e-commerce firm finds potential customers and turns them into repeat customers

- Explain how a B2C e-commerce firm might achieve a sustainable competitive advantage

- Identify and describe several B2C e-commerce revenue sources

- Discuss B2C payment services and other services provided by intermediaries

The Dot-Com Revolution

In the late 1990s, extrapolations based on then-current Internet growth rates suggested that the number of Internet users would soon exceed the population of the world. Clearly, such projections were absurd and no one took them literally, but even conservative interpretations of the numbers suggested that Internet use was growing exponentially. Entrepreneurs saw those Internet users as a vast pool of potential customers in an exploding information-based global marketplace that promised to alter the very nature of modern business and make its first movers a great deal of money. After all, even a small slice is valuable if the pie is big enough, and the emerging new economy looked huge.

Other factors helped to set the stage for the dot-com revolution. In many markets, the combination of stiff competition and falling prices put a premium on cost control. One common cost-control strategy was to restrict personal contact to a company's biggest customers and to force small customers to obtain services through call centers ("operators are standing by"), interactive voice response systems ("to speak to sales, press 1"), and similar low-cost, self-serve options. Compared to such primitive (and often annoying) solutions, displaying the customer's options on a Web page seemed like a significant improvement.

There had been previous attempts to conduct business online , too. For example, in the 1980s, several online banking experiments failed miserably. Past failure normally suggests caution, but in retrospect, the 1980s user base was underprepared and insufficiently computer literate, and the technology of the time was not quite up to the task. A great deal had changed in the intervening decade, however, and Internet and Web-based e-commerce seemed different. Every Internet user was a potential customer, and every one of those potential customers owned a personal computer and a browser and knew how to use them. The time seemed right. And the revolution began.

Due in no small part to excessive hype (both on the way up and again on the way down) and a boom-to-bust stock market, the successes and failures of consumer-focused B2C e-commerce applications were very public. Subsequent stock market declines and marketplace reverses have dimmed the luster of the so-called e-commerce revolution, but the dot-coms were (and still are) a source of entrepreneurial thinking and experimentation, producing numerous innovations that carried over to other forms of e-commerce. Also, not all the dot-coms failed, and there is much to be learned from analyzing the reasons behind both the successes and the failures.

Cost of Entry

Although the "new economy" may have been overhyped, e-commerce has significantly changed at least some traditional business assumptions. For example, a physical retail outlet represents a significant startup investment. The first step in opening a new retail outlet, sometimes called a **bricks-and-mortar** presence, is to purchase or lease the necessary real estate. Location is a key to success, and obtaining space in a high-traffic location is very expensive. Once space is obtained, the merchant must purchase display tables, racks, and checkout counters; install cash registers, credit card readers, and similar payment systems; stock the shelves; and hire and train sales personnel. By the time the store opens, the merchant is deeply in debt, and recovering the startup costs through subsequent profits can take years.

Largely because of the open standard defined by the Internet and the World Wide Web, the cost of entry for an e-commerce retail presence is substantially lower. To the **e-retailer** or **e-tailer**, a company that sells retail products online, physical location does not matter, because the Internet allows any Web site to link to any other Web site, no matter where in the world those sites might be. For example, Gateway, a well-known supplier of personal computer systems, maintains a base of operations in South Dakota where real estate is relatively cheap. Because e-commerce implies a virtual "storefront," there is no need for expensive display equipment. Sophisticated payment systems and order fulfillment systems are necessary, of course, but responsibility can often be subcontracted to various intermediaries who are paid on a per transaction basis, thus reducing the need for up-front capital. Other intermediaries offer Web site hosting services, Web site design and development services, and application services.

Sources of Funding

In spite of the low-cost infrastructure, however, the entry costs for a proposed consumer-focused B2C e-commerce business venture are still substantial. Often, funding for the inevitable startup costs comes from wealthy individuals called **angels** and from **venture capitalists**, both of whom provide seed money in exchange for equity or stock options. Like the entrepreneurs, the dot-com era angels and venture capitalists were impressed by

OPINION
Wait and See

Many traditional bricks-and-mortar retailers were late entering the online marketplace, and for some, the decision to finally adopt an online presence was reluctant (at best). Were they behind the times (as customers and critics sometimes assumed) or simply biding their time? Every case is different, of course, and waiting until evolving market realities and customer expectations force a move is virtually guaranteed to yield little or no competitive advantage. But sometimes, doing it right is more important than doing it first. And sometimes not doing it at all is the best strategy.

For example, many manufacturing firms who could sell directly to consumers over the Web by using B2C e-commerce technologies have chosen not to. Few manufacturers have the logistics in place to manage individual purchases, particularly in a global marketplace, so they are dependent on physical intermediaries such as distributors. Equivalent e-commerce intermediaries do exist, but unless a significant percentage of the company's business can potentially be conducted online, the firm is understandably reluctant to jeopardize established relationships with its physical distribution channels. When it comes to e-commerce, nonparticipants are not necessarily behind the times. Sometimes they are acting in their own carefully considered best interest.

the potential of consumer-focused e-commerce and saw an opportunity to make a great deal of money. Their investments seemed like a sure thing, until the bubble burst.

The Customer's Investment

Another e-commerce advantage stems from the investment made by potential customers. Before a customer can even begin to surf the Internet, he must purchase or lease a personal computer equipped with an operating system, a browser, a modem or other connectivity hardware, and communication software (including the TCP/IP protocols). As you learned in Chapter 2, connectivity providers offer access to the communication infrastructure, an Internet service provider (ISP) serves as the user's gateway to the Internet, and both charge a monthly fee. Add those fees to the hardware and software costs, and the customer's first-year investment can easily reach $2,000 and more. Can you think of another marketplace in which the customer willingly absorbs such a major part of the cost of doing business?

Additional efficiencies are gained from the customer's willingness to do much of the initial data entry. For example, by filling out an electronic order form, the customer not only enters the data, but also assumes (implicitly or explicitly) responsibility for verifying its accuracy. To the e-retailer, the ability to capture data in electronic form at little or no cost and then reuse it in a series of sales-related processes significantly enhances the front end of the value chain.

The Hook

In the initial euphoria of an emerging marketplace, the dot-com entrepreneurs and their investors looked for a **hook**, a means of attracting potential customers. Unfortunately, many unsuccessful e-commerce ventures, particularly those launched by inexperienced business people, suffered from an excessive degree of focus on the hook. A good hook *is* important, but a hook alone is far from sufficient.

A unique product or service is a powerful hook. Truly unique products and services are rare, however, and attempting to pass off a minor improvement as a killer application or a variation on a theme as a breakthrough product simply does not work.

Another common hook is to position an e-commerce site as the price leader within a particular market niche. The risk of relying on low price as a hook is often low profit margins, however. Eventually, if price is the only variable, the product becomes a commodity, and sustaining a price-based competitive advantage in a commodity marketplace is very difficult.

Some firms assume that convenience is the answer. Once posted on the Web, a page is available twenty-four hours a day, seven days a week, 365 days a year. Given a decent selection and dependable delivery, assuming that people (like the entrepreneurs and the venture capitalists) whose everyday lives are incredibly overscheduled will be willing to pay for convenience seems reasonable. Will convenience bring in enough customers to support a viable business, however? Apparently, many dot-coms never bothered to ask that question.

Still other dot-coms rely on customer services to provide a hook. Many sites offer FAQs, help desks, online help features, account and order status tracking, targeted e-mail, and call centers to answer customer inquiries and provide information. Chat rooms and personalized Web pages are popular, too. Other Web sites offer free access to such services as e-mail, a personal appointments calendar, a personal address book, personal Web site hosting, and news delivery; note the buttons flanking the Yahoo logo in Figure 5.1. Some of these services are excellent, but quality is often an issue. Also, such services are easy to copy, and clones of popular services tend to appear quickly.

The Race to Be First

The Internet and the World Wide Web enabled an exploding global customer base, but they also brought global competition. As you learned in Chapter 4, one consequence of enhanced competition is an accelerating rate of change, leading to the rapid obsolescence of technological innovations. The time between the emergence of a competitive advantage and an effective countermove is shrinking. Consequently, time to market and reduced cycle time become key strategic objectives, because delays mean sales opportunities permanently lost.

Because of these competitive pressures, a proposed B2C venture that could legitimately claim first-mover status had relatively little trouble getting startup funding, at least until the dot-com bubble burst. "Just be first" became almost a mantra, and all too often such underlying business essentials as profit were ignored or were assumed to flow (almost as a birthright) from a first mover's competitive advantage. Perhaps more significantly, many dot-coms (and venture capitalists, for that matter) failed to ask whether the proposed product was even worth selling.

Figure 5.1 Some Web sites offer free services.

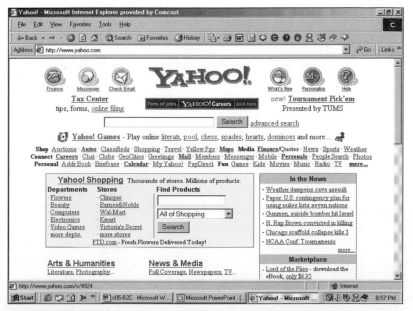

E-Shopper Demographics

A key rule of business is to know your customer. Many unsuccessful dot-coms did not know who their customers were and based key decisions (such as selecting the right hook) on demographic assumptions that turned out to be little better than guesses, stereotypes, and wishful thinking.

No one really knows the demographics of the Internet because the numbers change constantly. Initially, most Internet users were relatively young, technically sophisticated, predominantly male, relatively wealthy U.S. residents who connected through telephone lines at low transfer rates. Today, however, because of the availability of free public access, inexpensive computers, easier-to-use tools, and higher bandwidth connections, even nontechnical, lower-income people can access the Web. Recently, at least in North America, substantial numbers of senior citizens have gone online, and the number of female users now exceeds the number of male users.[1]

The U.S. dominance of the Internet is also eroding. Soon, European and Asian users will outnumber Americans.

In the long run, the distribution of potential e-commerce customers will probably evolve until it resembles the general population. Until that happens, view Internet demographic data as snapshots that are probably outdated.

U.S. Internet demographics	1999	2000	2001	2002	2003
Seniors (55+) online (millions)	12.1	16.4	19.6	24.5	27.2
Percentage e-commerce spending by seniors	21	25	28	31	32
Percentage adult male users	53.76	49.87	49.31		

Active adult users (millions)	2000	2001	2002	2003	2004
U.S.	97.7	114.4	130.8	147.7	160.6
Europe	70.1	107.8	152.7	206.5	254.9
Asia/Pacific Rim	48.7	63.8	85.4	118.8	173.0
Latin America	9.9	15.3	22.1	31.0	40.8
Africa and the Middle East	3.5	5.3	7.2	9.0	10.9

Back to Business Basics

The first-mover strategy seemed to work for a time, until the dot-com shakeout demonstrated—in the clearest possible way—the dangers associated with ignoring the underlying business basics. Unsuccessful dot-coms faded away. Successful dot-coms learned from their mistakes and the mistakes of others and changed the way they did business.

---

[1] The data in this feature was extracted from several reports published by eMarketer, Inc. (*www.eMarketer.com*, 2001). Other sources cited by eMarketer include Ovum (2000) and Jupiter Media, Metrix (2001).

Brand-Name Recognition as a Competitive Advantage

One very important lesson the successful B2C enterprises learned is that brand name matters. For example, when Amazon.com first opened for business in July 1995, it gained an immediate and significant competitive advantage over its primary competitors who lacked the ability to sell books online. Customers responded positively, and Amazon.com quickly established a recognizable brand name.

Both Barnes & Noble and Borders responded in classic catch-up fashion by begrudgingly launching their own e-commerce sites, even though they anticipated losing money. Why did they bother launching their own sites when they expected to fail? Amazon.com had redefined the marketplace, and consumers started to view booksellers who lacked an online presence as outdated and behind the times. In effect, Amazon's competitors had no choice, because failing to respond to Amazon.com's initiative threatened to undercut decades of building a recognized, respected brand name, and neither Barnes & Noble nor Borders was willing to take that risk.

As predicted, the two Web sites were not profitable. However, both Borders and Barnes & Noble combined their physical presence with their online strategies into what is now called a bricks-and-clicks strategy (Chapter 4). Ironically, Amazon.com now manages all of Borders's online sales transactions, and Borders developed a separate site, BordersStores.com, to offer customers additional services, such as access to traditional bricks-and-mortar store inventories. Barnes & Noble evolved a successful bricks-and-clicks strategy that allowed customers to research electronically and buy physically, or vice versa. As long as the revenue flows to Barnes & Noble, whether the money is filtered through the Internet or a physical checkout station doesn't really matter.

The bricks-and-clicks approach gives a tremendous competitive advantage to known brands with an established physical presence. For example, purchasing a sweater from the Sears Web site carries less risk than purchasing the equivalent sweater from some unknown e-commerce site because the Sears brand name implies stability and significantly reduces the perceived risk of fraud. Additionally, if the product ultimately proves unacceptable, the customer can always return it to a nearby shopping mall, thus minimizing the returns hassle associated with pure online shopping. The advantages are so clear that some firms have linked their online marketing, at least in part, to existing, well-known bricks-and-clicks business partners. For example, the Maytag product line is featured on the Sears Web site (Figure 5.2).

Finding Potential Customers

Figure 5.3 lists the dot-com advertisers from Super Bowl XXXIV (January 2000). Column 2 shows the products associated with each company. Although only a few years have passed since the turn of the century, how many of those companies and their products can you identify? The dot-commers advertised on the Super Bowl in hopes of quickly making an impression and becoming well known, but speed branding rarely works. How, then, can a previously unknown consumer-focused B2C e-commerce firm locate potential customers?

Figure 5.2 The Maytag product line is featured on the Sears Web site.

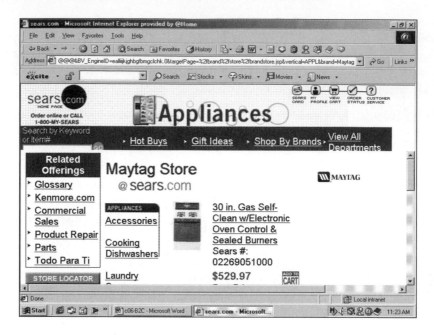

Figure 5.3 The dot-com advertisers from Super Bowl XXXIV.

Super Bowl XXXIV advertisers	Product
Agillion	Customer services
AutoTrader	Automobiles
Britannica	Encyclopedias
Computer.com	Computer information
Epidemic	Advertising services
E★Trade	Stock trading
Healtheon/WebMD	Medical information
Hotjobs	Job placement services
Kforce	Job placement services
LifeMinders	Direct marketing
MicroStrategy	Business intelligence
Monster	Job placement services
Netpliance	Internet browsing appliance
OnMoney	Personal finance
OurBeginning	Wedding invitations
Oxygen	Women's issues
Pets.com	Pet supplies
Wall Street Journal Interactive	News services
WebEx	E-meeting tools

Discount Airlines

Competing with a well-known brand is difficult, but niche marketing and cost control can contribute to a small firm's B2C e-commerce success. For example, consider discount airlines. In the 1980s, People Express established the concept, offering low-cost, no-frills flights. The company eventually went bankrupt, but today, such discounters as Southwest and JetBlue in the United States and Ryanair and easyJet in Europe are doing quite well, despite a depressed, post-9/11 air travel market.

Much of the success of these discount airlines is based on cost control. Southwest, for example, flies only one type of jet (a practice that minimizes training and maintenance costs), uses secondary airports (thus cutting landing fees), and eliminates frills like meals (thus reducing catering costs and shortening gate turnaround time). Ryanair has even dropped such services as reserved seats.

Unavailable to People Express, modern e-commerce makes additional cost cutting possible, too. For example, Ryanair has stopped dealing with travel agents (thus saving commissions) and has eliminated most of its ticket sellers. The airline has replaced those traditional booking sources with its B2C Web site, a reasonable strategy, given the target audience of young, Internet-savvy professionals. In addition to flight booking, the Web site hosts a secondary profit center by featuring special deals on hotels, rental cars, travel insurance, and similar travel-related products and services that earn Ryanair a commission. Other e-commerce applications rely on the rapid exchange of information to minimize a given plane's unproductive ground time and thus increase asset utilization. Such yield management tools are a form of intra-business e-commerce, the subject of the next chapter.

Advertising is an established tool for finding customers and building brand recognition. At the height of the dot-com boom, e-businesses advertised on other B2C Web sites, but as more and more dot-coms failed, the demand for and, hence, the revenue generated by such advertising declined. Surprisingly, given the online nature of the B2C Web sites, offline advertising on such traditional media as newspapers, magazines, television, and radio is quite common.

E-mail messages sent to both targeted and untargeted mailing lists are a relatively inexpensive alternative to traditional advertising. Unfortunately, untargeted e-mail can easily degenerate into spam, the indiscriminate mass mailing of junk e-mail to everyone on a mailing list, and the information gathering necessary to target advertisements properly has significant privacy implications. You will read more about spam and privacy in Chapter 10.

For most potential customers, the most common path to a previously unknown Web site is through a search engine. Consequently, most e-commerce companies put considerable effort into ensuring that their Web sites are listed with such well-known search engines as Google and Yahoo. A simple listing is not enough, however. The real objective is to ensure that, following a keyword search, potential customers who might actually purchase a firm's products find that firm's Web site on the list (preferably near the top) of suggested links.

One way to increase the odds that a search engine lists your Web site is to assume the potential customer's viewpoint, identify several possible key words and search criteria that a customer looking for your Web site or your product might use, arrange the search criteria in likelihood order, and then list the criteria in a set of HTML metatags. A **metatag** is a special HTML tag that allows a page designer to specify information about the Web page and, potentially, influence how the page is indexed. For example, Figure 5.4 shows a portion of the metatag entries for the Web page that describes another textbook cowritten by one of this book's authors.

Creating Repeat Customers

Potential customers are like window shoppers—they generate zero revenue until they become buyers or (even better) repeat customers. One key to converting potential customers to real customers is to create an appealing, customer-focused virtual experience that adds value from the customer's perspective.

A well-designed, well-organized, easy to navigate Web site is an essential part of that virtual experience, but a good Web site by itself is far from sufficient. Customers return to a Web site that offers real value, and simply automating the old way of doing things is not enough. Consider, for example, online catalogs. Catalog shopping and online shopping are similar. Allowing the customer to select items from a static virtual catalog, place those items in an electronic shopping cart, and then process the completed order

Figure 5.4 The metatag entries for a textbook's Web page.

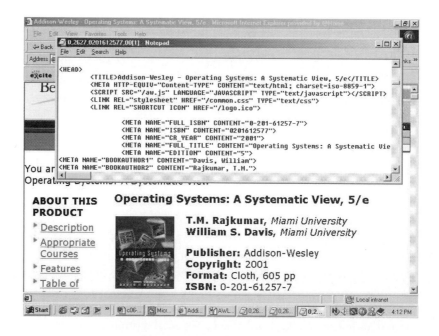

Popular Search Terms

According to Google's 2001 Year-End Zeitgeist, the twenty search terms that gained the most popularity between January 1 and December 31, 2001 are listed below.

Check Google's Web site for the current week's gaining and declining search terms. Other search engines publish similar lists, including the Lycos 50 and Yahoo's Buzz Index.

Do not be tempted to add such popular search terms to your business Web site's metatags. Doing so may produce numerous search engine hits but will almost certainly yield relatively few customers.

Think about it. If your company sells software, are your customers likely to find you by searching for anthrax, Harry Potter, Jennifer Lopez, or Nostradamus? The objective is not to generate hits, but to increase the odds that your Web site appears within the top twenty search results for a potential customer who just might be looking for something like your product. Rather than including the popular search terms, a better strategy is to exclude them and focus on search terms that uniquely identify your product.

Rank	Search term	Rank	Search term
1	Nostradamus	11	Afghanistan
2	CNN	12	Nimda [worm]
3	World Trade Center	13	American Airlines
4	Harry Potter	14	American flag
5	Anthrax	15	Aaliyah
6	Windows XP	16	FBI
7	Osama bin Laden	17	KaZaA
8	Audiogalaxy	18	Lord of the Rings
9	Taliban	19	Jennifer Lopez
10	Loft story	20	Xbox

is relatively easy. However, it is much more effective to consider the customer's previous purchasing habits and to display a personalized catalog created dynamically from up-to-the-minute information about pricing and availability and featuring products that the particular customer is likely to want. For example, Figure 5.5 shows an Amazon.com Web page customized for one of this book's authors[2]. If the assumptions about the customer's perceived needs are correct, presenting a dynamic personalized catalog saves the customer time and thus adds value. Web sites that add value tend to accumulate repeat customers.

Customer relationship management (CRM) is a powerful customer acquisition and retention tool that incorporates numerous technologies and applications to support sales and marketing. A typical CRM system captures data from all customer contact points

---

[2] No, he is not a camper, nor are any of his children. Targeted advertising does not always work well.

Figure 5.5 A personalized Web page.

Courtesy of Amazon.com, Inc.

and consolidates them in a customer database or a data warehouse. Subsequent analysis of the data allows the company to identify individual customer preferences, track demographic trends, evaluate the effectiveness of an advertising campaign, and so on. Most CRM systems also support contact management (customer name, address, telephone), sales force automation, and other tools.

Lock-In

The ultimate objective of any customer relationship effort is to add enough value to achieve **lock-in**, a state in which the customer has a vested interest to stay with a company because moving to a competitor entails significant switching costs. For example, the inconvenience associated with changing e-mail addresses (such as notifying all your contacts) tends to lock a user into her current ISP. Other examples include airline frequent flyer programs, customizable portals such as My Yahoo, and university academic programs.

Microsoft Office represents a different form of lock-in. Other office suites may be just as good (perhaps even better), but to many Office Suite users (both organizations and individuals), the cost of switching (retraining, reformatting files and documents, losing content because of incompatible data formats) is simply too high to justify. Until a product with significant measurable advantages emerges, people are reluctant to change. They are effectively locked into Microsoft.

Interconnection

Interconnection, a measure of the extent to which one company's product is linked to another company's product, is a potentially dangerous form of specialization. The classic example is the relationship between Netscape and Microsoft. As the first true point-and-click browser, Netscape almost single-handedly launched the explosion in Internet and World Wide Web use that set the stage for e-commerce. However, the most popular version of Netscape was designed to function in the context of Microsoft's Windows operating system, making Netscape vulnerable to strategic actions it did not control. Microsoft's decision to bundle Internet Explorer with Windows, in effect giving away Internet Explorer, marked the beginning of Netscape's decline. Unless pending legal action dramatically alters the browser landscape, Netscape will continue to be a minor player at best, because Internet Explorer has achieved substantial lock-in.

Is Internet Explorer better than Netscape or the other competitive browsers? Maybe, maybe not; the answer is a matter of opinion. However, there is no question that Internet Explorer is the dominant browser, and that Microsoft's ability to achieve a form of customer lock-in is a major reason for its continued success.

Achieving a Sustainable Competitive Advantage

In consumer-focused B2C e-commerce, a competitive advantage is anything that gives your customers a reason to do business with you instead of your competitors. The ideal competitive advantage is sustainable, but consumer-accessible processes are (almost by definition) publicly visible and thus relatively easy to reverse engineer or copy.

As you learned in Chapter 1, the B2C applications that drove the dot-com bubble represent the visible tip of a much larger e-commerce iceberg. A company's value chain and supply chain are largely hidden from public view, so a competitive advantage derived from improved value chain or supply chain efficiency is difficult to copy and thus relatively easy to sustain. The value chain focus of the intra-business category and the supply chain focus of the B2B e-commerce category help to explain why they have proven more successful than consumer-focused B2C applications.

Note, however, that consumer interaction, the essence of B2C e-commerce, is the front end to both the value chain (intra-business) and the supply chain (B2B); in other words, all three e-commerce categories are pieces of the same puzzle (Figure 5.6). Over the long run, the most successful e-commerce firms are likely to be the ones that successfully integrate their B2C front end with their value chain and supply chain business processes.

For example, consider Dell. At the B2C level, Dell features advanced Web applications, competitive prices, one-to-one marketing, a global reach, and effective delivery support backed by a reputation for reliability. Behind the scenes, Dell has implemented effective value chain and supply chain management tools that support the seemingly impossible—mass customization. Dell maintains little or no inventory. Instead, the company begins the process of constructing a customer's computer system when the customer places an order, relying on suppliers and business partners to deliver the right components at just

Figure 5.6 The three e-commerce categories are pieces of the same puzzle.

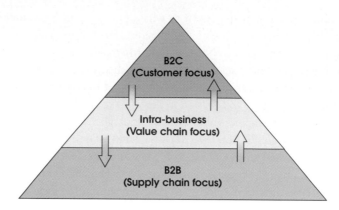

the right time. The result is a difficult-to-match combination of low cost and high quality that represents a true sustainable competitive advantage.

Customization

More generally, **customization**, the act of modifying a product or service to fit an individual customer's requirements, is a possible e-commerce source of sustainable competitive advantage. For example, to cite a familiar non-Internet example, perhaps you use a local supermarket's preferred customer card. In exchange for divulging personal information on an application form, you are given an identification card that entitles you to receive reduced prices on selected items and to participate in other incentive programs. Perhaps you are unaware that when the supermarket scans your card, it links you to your purchases and then uses that information to establish a personal shopping pattern for you. You see lower prices. The supermarket sees an opportunity to target coupons, mailers, and other forms of advertising directly to you based on your established shopping patterns, a form of one-to-one **relationship marketing**.

Similarly, Web sites use cookies and registration forms to compile personal information on their visitors and then use the information to create customer profiles. The information can be subsequently used to support targeted advertising, dynamic personalized pages, and access to special services for repeat visitors and regular customers. In other words, such relationship marketing allows a company to treat individual customers differently based on past experience, demographics, and other relevant criteria, and such customization helps to build and maintain customer loyalty. Support for relationship marketing is a component of many CRM systems.

There is a downside to customization—selling personal information. For example, targeted mailing lists and e-mail lists that categorize potential customers by their interests, income levels, shopping preferences, and similar criteria are quite valuable, and once compiled, the temptation to sell such information is difficult to resist. Even if a company's policy is not to share such information with anyone, policies can change. Recently, for example, several Web sites, including Yahoo, announced changes that give them greater freedom to share or sell personal information, and many bankrupt dot-coms discovered during the liquidation process that customer data was their most valuable asset, and destroying the data to avoid releasing it (even if the stated policy was to do exactly that) was a violation of the law. This issue will be revisited in Chapter 10.

Consumer-Focused B2C Revenue Sources

The primary objective of any business concern is to earn a profit. Consumer-focused e-commerce represents the front (downstream) end to a business organization's value and supply chains and, by definition, provides a link to the customer. Consequently, the primary focus of most B2C applications is generating revenue.

The next sections describe a variety of B2C e-commerce revenue sources. As you read, remember that few companies rely on any single revenue source. Instead, most use a hybrid approach, generating revenues in a variety of ways.

Selling Digital Products

Digital products, such as software, music, digitized images, electronic games, and (unfortunately) pornography, consist of binary digits, making them a perfect fit for consumer-focused B2C e-commerce. As you learned in Chapter 4, digital products are largely immune from diminishing returns and are not consumed as they are used. Therefore, a single copy of a digital product can potentially be distributed an infinite number of times, theoretically generating infinite revenue at little or no incremental cost.

Low distribution cost is another powerful advantage. A digital product can be transmitted over the Internet, making product distribution virtually free. Consider software, for example. Software is digital; it consists of patterns of binary digits stored on some medium. Traditionally, software is distributed on such media as diskettes, CD-ROM, and DVD. Electronically transmitting a copy directly from the supplier's file server to the customer's hard disk eliminates the need for the intermediate medium, along with such costs as creating, delivering, warehousing, handling, and returning those physical containers. Recorded music is a similar product. Most modern music is recorded digitally, copied to cassette, CD, or DVD, and distributed physically. From an efficiency standpoint, it makes much more sense to distribute music digitally by transferring a copy from the source to the customer's hard disk or onto a CD that the consumer purchased.

If the electronic distribution of digital products is so efficient, why are most digital products (books, music, movies, software, and so on) still marketed as physical media? One answer is that the Internet does not do a very good job of protecting intellectual property rights, a topic that will be discussed in depth in Chapter 11. In effect, the act of electronically storing a digital copy of a musical performance risks placing it in the public domain. Ironically, the Internet simplifies both digital distribution and digital piracy.

Until someone finds a way to preserve the creator's (and the distributor's) intellectual property rights without so inconveniencing the customer as to discourage sales, digital distribution will remain a secondary (or underground) distribution channel. Why? Think about what intellectual property means. It conveys to the product's creator an exclusive right to use, market, and distribute the product. If enough people want the product, that exclusive right is quite valuable. Just look at the revenue generated by a top musical performer, and you immediately understand why the recording industry took Napster so seriously. Simply put, without effective intellectual property protections, the risk of lost revenue due to illegal copying far outweighs any benefits gained from improved distribution efficiency.

Even excluding intellectual property rights, simply being digital is not always enough to support an effective B2C presence, however. Consider e-books, or electronic books, for example. The words and images that form the content of any book are easy to digitize. In fact, most books printed since the middle 1980s were created digitally, and a standard browser is certainly capable of displaying digitized pages. Why, then, do we continue to purchase traditional books? Have you ever read a novel on a computer screen? If not, go to *www.gutenberg.net* and download a copy of a familiar classic you once enjoyed reading. Then try reading it on the screen and compare the experience to curling up in a comfortable easy chair with a quality paperback.

In spite of the limitations of existing digital display devices, successful e-books do exist. For example, you may remember the days when a $1,000 set of encyclopedias filled a bookshelf with page after page of dead trees. Today, the equivalent of a set of encyclopedias is sold on CD-ROM for well under $100 or is even given away (for a small shipping and handling fee) as part of a credit card issuer's "customer rewards" program. The computer's ability to follow a hyperlink or to search electronically through vast amounts of digital information actually enhances the value of an online encyclopedia relative to its physical predecessors. Like encyclopedias, digital dictionaries, atlases, and similar reference books sell well. Travel books and recipe books are two other naturals—why carry dozens of physical tour books on your European vacation when a mini–CD-ROM and a compact, inexpensive reader make an equivalent body of information instantly available?

Selling Physical Products

Generating a profit by selling physical products online is more difficult, because although the customer and the e-retailer can exchange supporting information electronically, the physical product must be delivered and (occasionally) returned by means of a separate physical distribution network. In fact, some observers have suggested that such intermediaries as Federal Express, UPS, and the U.S. Postal Service are the real winners in this consumer-focused e-commerce subcategory.

Competition is intense, giving an online e-retailer very little pricing flexibility, so the key to profitability is cost control. For example, Amazon.com controls its inventory costs by stocking only a relative handful of top sellers. It relies on strategic alliances and partnerships with distributors and intermediaries to supply less-popular titles on demand from what is effectively a virtual warehouse that exists only in cyberspace (Figure 5.7). Other successful B2C e-retailers utilize business process reengineering to integrate their front (customer) and back (supplier) ends by creating efficient order fulfillment, order tracking, customer returns, and similar processes. Chapter 6 will explore business process reengineering in more detail.

Not surprisingly, the consumer-focused B2C category has accounted for a significant number of dot-com failures, and many of those failures resulted from attempting to sell an inappropriate product. For example, furniture is heavy and expensive to ship by the piece. Likewise, although fish are sometimes shipped through the mail, most live pets require costly special handling and same-day local delivery or pick-up that dissipates the Internet's global reach, and pet foods and pet supplies are conveniently available at the supermarket with no additional shipping cost. If the nature of the product gives the traditional bricks-and-mortar retail outlet a natural competitive advantage, a pure e-commerce competitor is unlikely to succeed.

Selling Services

Information-based services represent another natural source of consumer-focused e-commerce revenue because the information stored on a computer is digital. Some services, such as online stock trading (E*Trade) and electronic banking, generate revenue by charging a fixed fee for each transaction. Other B2C services, such as auction sites (eBay), travel services (Expedia, Travelocity.com), and real estate sites collect a percentage of the fee generated by each completed transaction. Job placement sites such as Hotjobs and Monster are free to the job seeker but collect a fee from the employer following a successful placement. In spite of their marginal legality and questionable morality, gambling (or gaming) sites, which often collect an admission fee in addition to the usual house advantage, have proven to be consistently profitable.

Figure 5.7 Amazon's virtual warehouse exists only in cyberspace.

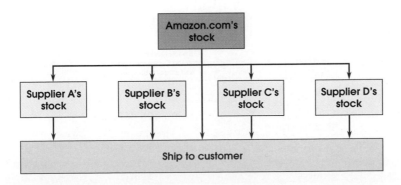

Other services are marketed over the Internet but delivered physically. For example, Peapod tried (with limited success) to establish a Web-based grocery delivery service, but flower delivery services such as FTD.com and even individual local florists (Figure 5.8) have launched highly successful online services. Additionally, many local services, such as lawn maintenance, painting, maid services, and plumbers, advertise online. Try going to *www.cityname.com*, where *cityname* is the name of your town (for example, *www.sarasota.com*) and you might be surprised at what you find. Many such Web sites resemble electronic interactive versions of the Yellow Pages.

Selling Advertising

If you have ever surfed the Web, you are familiar with **banner** ads (Figure 5.9). A relatively new technique called a surround session displays a series of related banner ads designed to build curiosity, and vertical banners, called skyscrapers, offer a change of pace. Banner ads appear in the context of a Web page. **Pop-up ads**, in contrast, are delivered in pop-up windows that can appear almost anywhere on the screen. Pop-under ads that remain hidden behind the primary window until you close your browser and pop-off ads that extend beyond the screen's right margin and force you to move them so you can see the delete button are (unfortunately) also common. Some Web sites have reciprocal agreements with other Web sites to feature each other's ads. However, most of the ads you see online are purchased.

The objective of most online ads is to entice as many potential customers as possible to the advertiser's Web site, so advertisers tend to favor high-traffic sites when placing their ads. Borrowing from the network television model, many well-known high-traffic

Figure 5.8 A local florist's Web site.

Courtesy of Twigs & Sprigs Florist, Hillsborough, NC.

Online Auctions

Online auctions take several different forms. Most people are familiar with traditional straight sale or English auctions in which the item goes to the highest bidder. Usually, the bids are open, but some auctions call for sealed bids. A Vickrey auction is similar to an English auction with one exception—the item goes to the high bidder at the *second* highest bid price. In a straight sales auction, the price is listed and the item is sold to the first qualified bidder who meets the price. In a reverse auction, the seller sets an initial price and then lowers the price until someone offers a bid. A Dutch auction is used when the seller has several identical items to sell. All the winning bidders pay the same price, the lowest successful bid amount. A variation called a Yankee auction requires each winning bidder to pay the amount he bid.

portals such as Microsoft Network, Netscape, and Yahoo offer free e-mail, online storage space, personal Web site hosting, a search engine, news, local information, and so on as a means of increasing traffic and thus boosting their advertising rates. Other Web sites offer technical (Webopedia), medical (Medscape, drkoop.com, and WebMD), financial (Hoovers Online), and other forms of information.

One problem with online advertising is a lack of widely accepted standards for measuring advertising efficiency. Figure 5.10 summarizes several widely used measures. **Hits**

Figure 5.9 A banner ad.

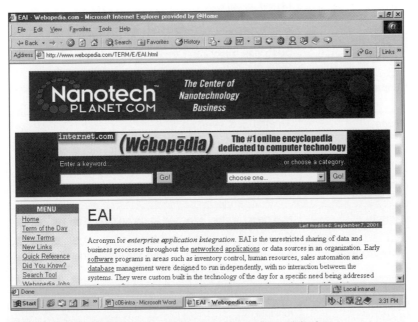

(any request for any file from a server) are easy to count, but tend to overstate the amount of traffic. An **impression**, the appearance of an advertisement on a Web page, is comparable to a print ad because, like a person flipping through the pages of a magazine, a Web surfer who views a given page is reasonably assumed to have seen any displayed ads, although many surfers set their browsers to screen out ads. The **click ratio**, the percentage of visitors to a page who click on an advertisement and go to the advertiser's Web site, is considered a better measure because those visitors clearly saw the ad and are probably interested in learning more about the product, but cases have occurred where users have been encouraged (or bribed) to click on selected ads just to boost the numbers. In fact, one reason why no single measure has emerged as a true standard is that the numbers are so easy to manipulate. At times, it seems like we measure the things we can instead of the things we should.

Figure 5.10 Several widely used measures of online advertising efficiency.

Measure	Definition
Click (or ad click)	The act of clicking on an ad.
Click ratio	Ratio of visitors to a page who click on an ad.
Click-through	The process of clicking on an ad and going to the advertiser's Web site, also known as an ad click or a request.
CPC	Cost per click.
CPM	Cost per thousand impressions.
Effective frequency	Number of times a visitor is exposed to a particular ad per unit of time.
Hit	Any request for an HTML document, such as a Web page or an embedded document. Note that a single page view might imply several hits, one for each page element.
Impression	The appearance of an ad on a Web page, also known as an ad view or a page view.
Page	An HTML document.
Page impression	An aggregate count of the number of times a Web site has been accessed or viewed by a user. Each page impression is a hit.
Page view	The act of accessing a Web page.
Reach	Number of visitors exposed to an ad over a given period of time.
Unique visitor	A person who returns to a Web site more than once during a specified period of time.
Visit	A set of requests made by one user during one continuous session. A single visit might represent multiple hits.

The lack of widely accepted standards for measuring online advertising efficiency makes it difficult to price those ads. Many pricing models have been tried, including CPM (cost per thousand impressions), click-through count, a percentage of the revenue generated as a result of a click-through, fixed monthly fees, auctions (high bidder gets the banner), and so on, but no clear standard has emerged. Perhaps a rating service comparable to ACNielson is needed.

The real potential of online advertising lies in targeting ads to very narrow market segments (market segmentation) and individuals (relationship marketing). Although some ads are displayed at random, others are selected in response to a user's actions, such as the search terms entered into a search engine, a form of customization. Relationship marketing and market segmentation take customization a step further by selecting ads based on an individual's profile or precise demographics. Unfortunately, there is a fine line between accumulating the necessary personal and demographic data and violating individual privacy. Privacy issues will be discussed in Chapter 10.

Usage Charges and Subscription Fees

Free content is a remnant of the Internet's legacy of free and open access to information. Except for limited-time promotions, free shipping is largely history, and such services as free e-mail, free online storage space, and free Web access are becoming increasingly difficult to find. The reason is simple: Advertising revenues have declined, and unless you have a reliable sponsor, giving stuff away generates more debt than profit.

Measure the Right Things

OPINION

Once upon a time, many years ago, a sawmill located somewhere in the northwest United States decided to implement an incentive pay plan in an effort to improve the productivity of its buzz saw operators. Each operator would be assigned a quota—so many board feet of lumber per day. Operators who exceeded their quotas would receive a bonus. Slackers would (eventually) receive a pink slip.

The problem was measuring the number of board feet of lumber produced by each operator. Because of physical space limitations, lumber had to be moved from the buzz saw to the lumberyard as soon as it was cut, and there was no convenient way to associate a particular piece of lumber with the buzz saw operator who cut it.

The solution: Weigh the sawdust! Every time a saw blade cut into a piece of lumber, it produced sawdust. More cuts meant both more sawdust and more board feet of lumber. So a new procedure was implemented. At regular intervals, every buzz saw operator was required to sweep up the area around his workspace and deposit the sawdust in an approved container for subsequent weighing. The result? Within two months, lumber production had declined by 10 percent, but the production of sawdust was way up.

Moral: Measure the right things, because if you measure sawdust, that's what you're going to get.

Recently, many formerly free services have begun to charge a subscription fee. For example, Major League Baseball now changes $5.95 per season for live Internet game broadcasts, and many informational sites (such as the *New York Times*) offer limited free access to selected content but charge a fee for a full range of services. Big names like Yahoo may be able to continue offering free services because they pull in enough advertising revenue, but even Yahoo is moving to subscription-based pricing on its premium services. Usage charges in the form of flat and percentage fees are also popular; for example, eBay and E*Trade charge transaction fees.

The pricing model that will eventually emerge is likely to resemble television access. Most urban residents can receive perhaps a half-dozen free, over-the-air channels. For a fee, a customer can hook into a cable TV network and access fifty or more channels, often with better reception. An additional fee entitles the viewer to one or more advertising-free premium channels such as HBO or Showtime, and at the top of the fee structure is pay-per-view programming. Don't be surprised to see comparable multitiered pricing on the Internet in the relatively near future.

Not-for-Profit Consumer Links

Consumer interaction is the essence of consumer-focused B2C e-commerce, but not-for-profit applications rely on the e-commerce infrastructure to communicate directly with consumers and clients, too. For example, although some are sponsored by commercial entities, a **virtual community** is more about social interaction and personal relationships than commercial success.

Most virtual communities focus on a single subject such as a medical condition (Alzheimer's disease, cancer, Parkinson's disease), art (the World Wide Web Artist's Consortium), ethnicity (AsianAvenue.com, BlackVoices.com), gender (iVillage.com), age groups (SeniorNet.org), intellectual discourse (The WELL), and even e-commerce research and virtual community building. Some sell advertising to cover costs; others do not allow advertising. The typical virtual community supports public, interactive communication, often in the form of a chat room with a significant number of repeat visitors. Over time, those regular visitors become community members and form lasting bonds to the virtual community and to each other.

Government-to-consumer (G2C) Web sites offer several excellent examples of nonprofit e-commerce. The official Web site of the executive branch of the United States government can be found at *www.whitehouse.gov* (Figure 5.11). Visit the Census Bureau at *www.census.gov* to access a treasure trove of demographic data. If you are thinking of starting your own business, the Small Business Administration (*www.sbaonline.sba.gov*) offers some excellent pointers. At the local level, a well-designed government Web site can

Figure 5.11 The official Web site of the executive branch of the United States government.

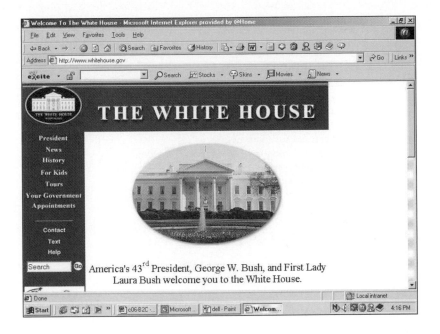

be a source of contact information, and some local government sites even allow visitors to perform such online tasks as applying for a license, registering to vote, paying taxes and utility bills, and paying a parking ticket. E-commerce allows governments to deliver their services more efficiently. In fact, you may be surprised to learn that the percentage of adult Internet users who conduct government business online exceeds the percentage of "those who performed bank transactions, paid a credit card bill, or traded stocks online."[3]

Intermediary Services

As you learned in Chapter 4, most forms of e-commerce would be impossible without the support of intermediaries, and consumer-oriented e-commerce is no exception. The first three types of intermediary services listed in Figure 5.12, infrastructure hardware and software providers, connectivity providers, and bandwidth providers, were discussed in Chapters 2 and 3, and Web information system service providers and security service providers will be covered in subsequent chapters. The three remaining types are directly relevant to B2C e-commerce and are discussed in the sections that follow.

[3] *PC World* (March 2002): 24.

Figure 5.12 Intermediary services.

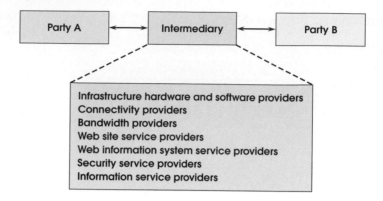

Payment Services

As the term implies, the function of a **payment service** is to collect and process customer payments. Currently, credit cards account for roughly 90 percent of total Internet payments, and Visa processes a significant percentage of those payments. Within the Visa network, issuing banks issue credit and debit cards to consumers, and acquiring banks contract with the merchants (Figure 5.13). Visa Central is a coordinating body that defines standards and a code of conduct for the issuers and acquirers. In exchange for the right to use the Visa name, those issuing and acquiring banks pay Visa Central various percentage charges, transaction fees, and service fees.

When using a credit or debit card to make an online purchase, the customer deals directly with the merchant; except for responding to a request for authorization, Visa Central is not directly involved in the process. The merchant sends completed transactions to its acquiring bank, which keeps a small percentage of the charge and transfers the remaining balance to the merchant's account. From the acquiring bank, the transaction flows to the customer's issuing bank, which accumulates purchases by customer account number, issues monthly bills, and collects customer payments.

Figure 5.13 The Visa network.

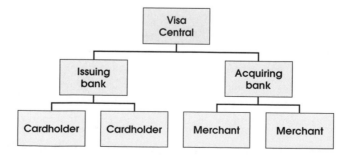

Visa was originally founded to define and administer standards, rules, and other authentication guarantees to enhance the credibility of bank credit cards. Today, as a means of overcoming consumer reluctance to send a credit card number over the Internet, Visa offers zero liability to online purchasers, and Visa Central defines minimum transaction security standards for its merchants. Often, other intermediaries provide authentication and other related security services, which will be covered in Chapter 9.

Not all online payments are made by credit card, of course. For example, online auction sales are often settled by check or money order, and unshipped merchandise, damaged merchandise, and unpaid bills are not uncommon. In exchange for a fixed transaction fee or a percentage of the payment, an **escrow service** can help reduce such risks. The escrow process begins when the buyer deposits a payment with the escrow service. The service notifies the seller that payment has been deposited, and the merchandise is shipped. The payment is released to the seller only after the buyer receives the shipment.

Internet bill presentment and payment (**IBPP**) is another option. In a direct IBPP model, the billing organization presents the bill and accepts payment on its own Web site. The service provider consolidation model adds an intermediary service that consolidates bills from various sources, presents those bills to the customer, and accepts payments. With the customer consolidation model, bills are sent directly to the customer who stores them and pays them at her convenience. Generally, payment is made by a bank-to-bank electronic funds transfer.

Because credit card payments less than $10 are not profitable, various forms of **e-cash** and **digital cash** are sometimes used to pay for microtransactions. Some services require the user to predeposit funds and then transfer individual transaction payments from the account. Others accumulate small changes and bill them or post them to a credit card at regular intervals. The common electronic purse specification (CEPS) is an open standard that has been adopted by many organizations. Other services such as Cybermoola, DoughNet, eCharge, InternetCash, PayPal, Praxicard, and RocketCash are proprietary, however, requiring all participants to install proprietary client or server software (or both). Such proprietary systems can (and do) work, but when organizations deviate from the open standards and implement proprietary solutions, they lose the advantages associated with standardization. Many potential customers are reluctant to commit to a proprietary service, particularly a payment service, because there is no guarantee that the service they choose will survive in the long run. Perhaps when a widely accepted small-transaction payment standard finally emerges, companies and customers will be more willing to participate.

Information Services

From a consumer perspective, the most heavily used intermediaries are those that help organize, find, and sift through the vast amount of information available on the Web. Many varieties of information service providers exist, but they all share a primary business objective: to attract as many visitors as possible by providing valued information services and to generate revenue through selling advertising, charging subscription fees, or selling the information collected from visitors and customers (a significant privacy concern to be explored in Chapter 10).

A **portal**—a Web site that serves as a gateway to the Internet and usually offers additional services such as e-mail, a search engine, news, and local information—is a good example of an information service provider, although some portals offer noninformation services as well. (It is not unusual for intermediary services to spill over category boundaries.) Some popular portals include America Online, Microsoft Network, Netscape, and Yahoo. Other intermediaries, such as InternetNews.com and ZDNet, organize news and other information extracted from many sources.

Shopping bots, briefly introduced in Chapter 4, are another type of information service. They are commonly used to locate the best price for a specific product, such as a Tom Clancy novel (Figure 5.14), returning a list of sources in increasing price order (Figure 5.15). Because they do such a good job of finding the best price, shopping bots tend to force prices down. Many companies view their pricing strategies as confidential, however, and resist providing information to shopping bots, thus reducing the agent's effectiveness, particularly on noncommodity products.

Figure 5.14 Typical shopping bot parameters.

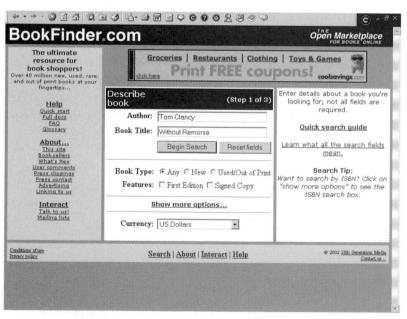

© 2002 13th Generation Media

Figure 5.15 Shopping bot results.

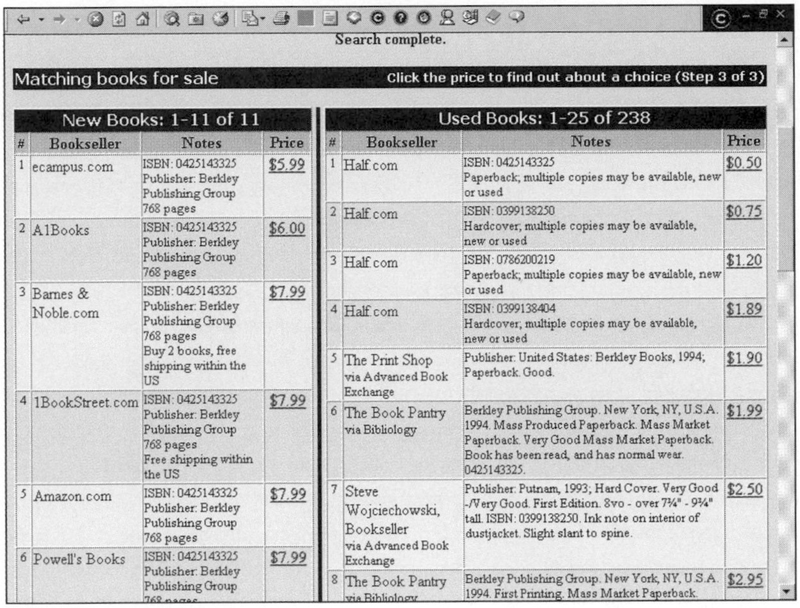

Search complete.

Matching books for sale | Click the price to find out about a choice (Step 3 of 3)

New Books: 1-11 of 11				Used Books: 1-25 of 238		
#	Bookseller	Notes	Price	#	Bookseller	Notes	Price

#	Bookseller	Notes	Price
1	ecampus.com	ISBN: 0425143325 Publisher: Berkley Publishing Group 768 pages	$5.99
2	A1Books	ISBN: 0425143325 Publisher: Berkley Publishing Group 768 pages	$6.00
3	Barnes & Noble.com	ISBN: 0425143325 Publisher: Berkley Publishing Group 768 pages Buy 2 books, free shipping within the US	$7.99
4	1BookStreet.com	ISBN: 0425143325 Publisher: Berkley Publishing Group 768 pages Free shipping within the US	$7.99
5	Amazon.com	ISBN: 0425143325 Publisher: Berkley Publishing Group 768 pages	$7.99
6	Powell's Books	ISBN: 0425143325 Publisher: Berkley Publishing Group 768 pages	$7.99

#	Bookseller	Notes	Price
1	Half.com	ISBN: 0425143325 Paperback; multiple copies may be available, new or used	$0.50
2	Half.com	ISBN: 0399138250 Hardcover; multiple copies may be available, new or used	$0.75
3	Half.com	ISBN: 0786200219 Paperback; multiple copies may be available, new or used	$1.20
4	Half.com	ISBN: 0399138404 Hardcover; multiple copies may be available, new or used	$1.89
5	The Print Shop via Advanced Book Exchange	Publisher: United States: Berkley Books, 1994; Paperback. Good.	$1.90
6	The Book Pantry via Bibliology	Berkley Publishing Group. New York, NY, U.S.A. 1994. Mass Produced Paperback. Mass Market Paperback. Very Good Mass Market Paperback. Book has been read, and has normal wear. 0425143325.	$1.99
7	Steve Wojciechowski, Bookseller via Advanced Book Exchange	Publisher: Putnam, 1993; Hard Cover. Very Good -/Very Good. First Edition. 8vo - over 7¾" - 9¾" tall. ISBN: 0399138250. Ink note on interior of dustjacket. Slight slant to spine.	$2.50
8	The Book Pantry via Bibliology	Berkley Publishing Group. New York, NY, U.S.A. 1994. First Printing. Mass Market Paperback.	$2.95

Web Site Service Providers

Many consumer-oriented B2C enterprises lack the technical expertise needed to create, manage, and maintain a Web site. Rather than investing in the necessary equipment, software, and personnel, they often turn to intermediaries to host the Web site; create, manage, and distribute the content; and provide the necessary storage systems and database software. For example, IBM's "e-business on demand" service (which supports virtually all forms of e-commerce) is advertised as "The Next Utility."

Other Forms of E-Commerce

In spite of numerous successes and an evolving sense of business reality, B2C e-commerce carries (perhaps permanently) the stigma of the dot-com era. There is no question that the dot-coms were overhyped, and that the hype fueled unrealistic expectations, leading to a speculative bubble that, in retrospect, seemed destined to burst. Remember, however, that the B2C category represents a very small part of the e-commerce picture. In contrast, the value-chain–focused intra-business and the supply-chain–focused B2B e-commerce categories (which will be covered in Chapters 6 and 7, respectively) have thrived. If B2C is the tip of the e-commerce iceberg, then intra-business and B2B e-commerce represent the primary mass hidden beneath the surface.

eBay

According to CEO Meg Whitman, eBay, the online auction site, is determined "to build the world's largest trading platform where practically anyone can trade practically anything." Already the world's largest online seller of automobiles, collectibles, computers, photographic equipment, and sporting goods, the company seems well on its way to achieving its objective. By leveraging the low communication and transaction costs made possible by the Internet, eBay was able to generate a 19 percent operating margin in 2001, and its 2005 target is 30 percent.

Cost control is one reason for eBay's success. Operating as an almost purely virtual corporation, eBay carries no inventory, owns or leases no warehouses, employs no sales personnel, and has no cost of goods sold, because its customers willingly assume responsibility for product procurement, marketing, order fulfillment, billing, and payment processing. Sources of revenue include commissions (1 to 5 percent of each transaction), listing fees, and other charges.

The incredible level of social capital (trust, goodwill, credibility) that eBay has accumulated in its few brief years of existence presages continued success. For example, the company's feedback system, which allows buyers and sellers to publicly rate each other, helps to blunt the sense—so common to online transactions—of dealing with a nameless, faceless entity somewhere in cyberspace. The network effect is another factor; more buyers attract more sellers, more sellers attract more buyers, and so on. Recently, because eBay's buyer base is sufficiently large, such giants as Dell, Disney, Home Depot, and IBM have begun selling discounted merchandise, customer returns, and overstocks through the auction site.

eBay almost perfectly illustrates the characteristics that make for a successful consumer-focused B2C e-commerce enterprise. Information, its product, is digital. Because there is no physical product, its operating expenses are low. It enjoys a recognizable brand name and a solid base of proactive, repeat customers who pay fees that generate a substantial cash flow. If you are ever asked to participate in a B2C business venture, the eBay model is an excellent place to start.

An e-retailer faces a lower cost of entry than a bricks-and-mortar retail outlet and also benefits from the investment made by potential e-commerce customers. The dot-com entrepreneurs, angels, and venture capitalists often looked for a hook as a means of attracting potential customers. Because the Web tends to shrink the time between the emergence of a competitive advantage and an effective countermove, time to market, reduced cycle time, and first-mover status became key strategic objectives.

Branding is crucial to successful consumer-focused B2C e-commerce. A bricks-and-clicks strategy gives a competitive advantage to known brands with an established physical presence. Advertising is a tool for finding customers and building brand recognition, and many potential customers are initially led to an e-retailer's Web site by the results of a key word search. A metatag is a special HTML tag that allows a page designer to specify information about a Web page and, potentially, influence how the page is indexed by the popular search engines.

One key to converting potential customers to real customers is to create an appealing, customer-focused virtual experience that adds value for the customer. CRM is a powerful customer acquisition and retention tool that can help an e-retailer achieve lock-in by enhancing customer value. Over the long run, the most successful e-commerce firms are likely to be the ones that successfully integrate their consumer-focused B2C front end with their value chain (intra-business) and supply chain (B2B) business processes. Customization and one-to-one relationship marketing are possible sources of sustainable competitive advantage.

The primary objective of most B2C applications is generating revenue. Digital products are a good fit for e-commerce. When selling physical products online, the key to profitability is cost control. Because information is digital, information-based services represent a natural source of consumer-focused e-commerce revenue. Many Web sites feature free services supported by advertising. Recently, however, many formerly free services have begun to charge a subscription fee. Although their objectives are different, virtual communities, government sites, and other not-for-profit Web sites resemble B2C Web sites.

Payment services, an example of intermediary business services, are crucial to B2C e-commerce. Most online payments are made by credit card, but online auction sales are typically settled person to person by check, and various forms of e-cash and digital cash are used to pay for smaller transactions. From a consumer perspective, the most heavily used intermediaries are those that help organize, find, and sift through the vast amount of information available on the Web. Portals and shopping bots are other popular information services.

▪ ▪ ▪ Key Words

angel	e-retailer or e-tailer	metatag
banner	escrow service	payment service
bricks-and-mortar	hit	pop-up ad
click ratio	hook	portal
customer relationship management (CRM)	impression	relationship marketing
customization	interconnection	venture capitalist
digital cash	internet bill presentment and payment (IBPP)	virtual community
e-cash	lock-in	

1. Given the failure of so many dot-coms, why is it still useful to study consumer-focused B2C e-commerce?

2. Contrast the cost of entry for a traditional bricks-and-mortar retail outlet with that of an e-commerce retail outlet.

3. Before participating in an e-commerce transaction, a potential customer must make a substantial up-front investment. Describe this investment and explain its significance.

4. What is a hook? Describe several hooks used by consumer-focused B2C e-commerce Web sites.

5. Why are reduced time to market, reduced cycle time, and first-mover status considered important B2C e-commerce objectives?

6. Why is branding so important to B2C e-commerce?

7. Describe the bricks-and-clicks strategy.

8. Identify several strategies that a consumer-focused B2C e-commerce firm might use to find potential customers.

9. What is the purpose of an HTML metatag?

10. Identify several strategies that a B2C e-commerce firm might use to turn potential customers into repeat customers.

11. Explain how a B2C e-commerce enterprise might achieve a sustainable competitive advantage.

12. What are customization and relationship marketing?

13. Identify and describe several B2C e-commerce revenue sources.

14. Explain how the effectiveness of online advertising is measured.

15. Cite several examples of B2C-like not-for-profit Web sites. What is a virtual community?

16. Identify several online payment options.

17. What is the business objective of an information provider? Identify at least two examples of information provider services.

Exercises

1. Identify the regular e-shoppers in your class and develop a demographic profile based on the characteristics of those individuals. Include age, gender, previous computer experience, and any other characteristics the class might consider significant.

2. Recently, the number of adult female Internet users exceeded the number of adult male Internet users in the United States. Does that surprise you? Why or why not? How might the surge in adult female users affect Internet demographics and target markets?

3. Some Internet users run software that blocks banner and pop-up ads when a Web page is displayed. Perhaps you are familiar with television technologies such as TiVo that allow a viewer to record many hours of programming, replay the programs at the viewer's convenience, and skip over the ads. What are the implications of such technologies for the future of advertising?

4. Using the widely accepted TCP/IP standard is much less expensive than relying on a proprietary network, but some companies continue to use their proprietary systems. Why?

Projects

Current references and supporting resources can be found at this textbook's companion Web site.

Broad-Based Projects

1. Stop by your favorite video rental outlet and check out a documentary film called Startup.com. After viewing it, write a review.

2. Visit www.gutenberg.net, locate a classic novel you once enjoyed reading, and download a copy to your hard disk. Then try reading the first chapter onscreen. When you finish, write a paper comparing your online experience to reading a traditional bound version of the same novel.

3. Conduct some research into the current state-of-the-art digital text readers and write a paper summarizing your findings.

4. The existing network of gas stations effectively locks us into gasoline-powered vehicles. Identify several other aspects of your everyday life that exhibit lock-in. Is lock-in good or bad?

5. Would you be willing to sign up for an IBPP or digital cash service? Why or why not?

6. In your opinion, what does the use of auctions to set advertising rates say about the viability of online advertising as a revenue source?

7. Select a favorite e-commerce Web site, identify at least three competitive sites, and conduct a comparative analysis of the sites. For example, compare unique features, common features, visual interest, ease of use, selection, security features, page loading speed, price, and so on. Write a paper summarizing your findings. Add to your paper your assessment of each Web site's competitive advantage or advantages.

Building the Case:

8. Working as a team, continue with Chapter 1, Project 6 by carefully reviewing your Web site's customer interface to make sure it supports your strategy. Change your strategy, your implementation plan, and your Web site as necessary.

Business Projects

1. Conduct some research into the various forms of online payment services and determine how each form charges for its service. Write a paper or prepare a PowerPoint presentation summarizing your findings.

2. Continue with Chapter 1, Project 2 by explaining how your client will find potential customers and convert them to repeat customers, outlining an appropriate advertising campaign, and identifying your client's distribution channels. Estimate the cost of designing and developing (or purchasing) a customer relationship solution and the continuing costs of operating and maintaining that solution. Write a brief report to document your results.

Information Technology Projects

1. Determine how data is collected on hits and other measures of advertising effectiveness. Download from the Web an applet that counts hits and insert it into a Web page.

2. Continue with Chapter 1, Project 2 by rethinking your prototype to reflect the contents of Chapter 5. For example, make sure you have considered such factors as the nature of your customer interface, revenue sources, and functions that might be outsourced to an intermediary. Depending on your background, available time, and your instructor's preference, if your solution includes a Web site, you might create or modify the appropriate static pages or incorporate Java, JavaScript, or VBScript code to support true interactivity.

Marketing Projects

1. Conduct some research into the various forms of online advertising. Determine how the effectiveness of online advertising is measured, how online advertisements are created, and how host sites charge for online advertising. Write a paper or prepare a PowerPoint presentation summarizing your findings.

2. Imagine that you have been charged with marketing the course you are currently taking. Working with your class or a subgroup of your classmates, develop a list of search terms that might be included in the course Web site's metatag.

3. Continue with Chapter 1, Project 2 by preparing a storyboard outlining the proposed advertising campaign, including preliminary versions of Web pages, online advertisements, and traditional media ads. Estimate a budget for the advertising campaign.

References

Web Sites

Source	URL	Comments
eMarketer, Inc.	*www.emarketer.com*	A good source of demographic and other marketing information.
Google	*www.google.com/ press/zeitgeist2001.html*	Google's Year-End Zeitgeist for 2001. For the most current version, delete the year 2001 in the URL.
Project Gutenberg	*www.gutenberg.net*	A digital library of classic books.
U.S. Census Bureau	*www.census.gov*	A treasure trove of demographic data.
U.S. Small Business Administration	*www.sbaonline.sba.gov*	An excellent source of small business startup information and advice.

Print and White Papers

Schonfeld, Erick. March 2002. "eBay's Secret Ingredient." *Business 2.0*: 52–58.

CHAPTER 6

Intra-Business
E-Commerce

**When you finish reading this chapter,
you should be able to:**

- Explain how intra-business e-commerce can enhance an organization's efficiency and effectiveness

- Explain how integrating the value chain helps to solve the islands of automation problem and leads to new approaches to information system development

- Explain how such server-side tools as common gateway interface (CGI) and Active Server Pages (ASP) contribute to client/server application development

- Explain how a client/server application's presentation, business, and information/data logic can be partitioned to distribute the workload

- Distinguish between a thin client and a fat client

- Distinguish among two-tier, three-tier, and n-tier applications

- Explain enterprise application integration (EAI)

- Distinguish between a first-generation intranet and a second-generation intranet

- Identify several problems associated with intranet content management

- Describe the functions performed by an enterprise portal

Internal Communication

Not too many years ago, most internal business communication was paper-based. Paper worked well for letters, memos, and similar one-time transactions, but because no printed document can possibly reflect changes that occur after its publication date, paper is not an effective medium for longer lasting information.

For example, until recently, when a new employee first arrived on Miami University's campus, he was issued a binder containing an up-to-date loose-leaf copy of the university procedures manual. Several times a year, printed copies of changed pages were mailed to each faculty member, along with instructions for updating the manual. Surprisingly, a few people actually kept their personal copy up-to-date, but most found other things to do with their time. Consequently, when questions about personnel policies, promotion, tenure, research support, and other career-affecting issues arose, finding an up-to-date manual was difficult. All too often, decisions were based on outdated information, leading to misunderstandings, incorrect personnel and funding decisions, and even the occasional threat of legal action.

Today, such documents as the procedures manual, the campus telephone book, the undergraduate and graduate bulletins, various reports and fact sheets, and the student handbook are available online on Miami University's Web site (Figure 6.1). The contents are maintained centrally and continuously, so new employees and students are quickly listed in the electronic telephone directory, name and address changes are posted as soon as they are reported, and the electronic copy of the procedures manual is always current.

Figure 6.1 Miami University's online publications and policies.

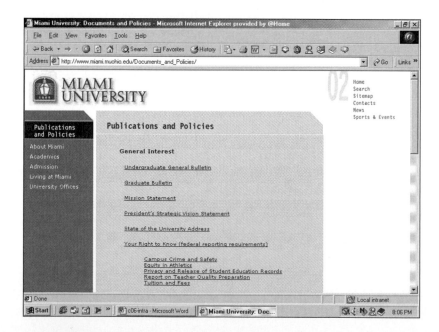

At first glance, posting key documents online seems almost trivial, and from the viewpoint of a single individual, perhaps it is. The issue, however, is volume: Repeat any activity enough times and it becomes significant. For example, counting the number of people in a room is easy, but (as we learn every ten years) conducting a national census is not. When you consider the cost of printing and distributing thousands of copies of a procedures manual and its subsequent changes, the time spent by employees updating the manual, and the mistakes resulting from the (understandable) failure to keep the manual current, the economic benefits derived from online access to key publications and procedures are substantial.

Providing employee information online was an early **intra-business e-commerce** application. Subsequently, such human resource applications as internal job postings, benefit selection, and expense account management and such productivity tools as e-mail, electronic calendars, contact management, and so on were added to what are sometimes called **business-to-employee (B2E) e-commerce** systems.

Today, intra-business e-commerce is increasingly used to integrate processes across the value chain, enabling just-in-time (JIT) inventory management, real-time order tracking, improved production scheduling, and similar applications, many of which involve little or no human intervention. Given those automated applications, a B2E focus seems a bit incomplete, so the term *intra-business e-commerce* will be used throughout this book. Note, however, that neither intra-business nor B2E are as widely accepted as B2B and B2C.

The Evolutionary Nature of Intra-Business E-Commerce

In contrast to the entrepreneurial, revolutionary, public, and sometimes chaotic development of consumer-oriented B2C e-commerce (covered in Chapter 5), both intra-business e-commerce and business-to-business (B2B) e-commerce (discussed in Chapter 7) enjoyed the luxury of evolving in private, in the context of traditional business planning with appropriate attention paid to such good old-fashioned business principles as profit and return on investment. Together, intra-business and B2B e-commerce represent natural steps in the continuing evolution of information technology as a strategic resource. Intra-business e-commerce (Figure 6.2), the subject of this chapter, is conducted within a business organization and numbers communicating with employees and improving the efficiency of the internal value chain among its primary objectives.

The Value Chain

An organization's value chain (Figure 6.3) is the set of integrated internal processes that combine to transform raw materials into finished products or services. Together, those processes define how the organization operates internally. Consider, for example, the

Figure 6.2 This chapter discusses intra-business e-commerce.

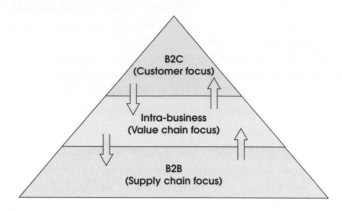

Figure 6.3 The value chain.

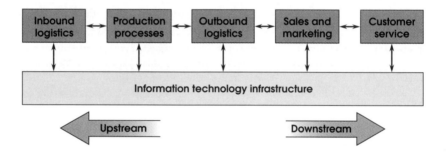

value chain for a personal computer manufacturer (Figure 6.4). The high-level processes form a logical chain from purchasing components and raw materials through production, marketing, order entry, order fulfillment, and ongoing customer service. Each of those processes consists of numerous subprocesses (Figure 6.5), many of which can be broken down into still smaller subprocesses and so on, yielding thousands of discrete business processes within a single organization's value chain.

Efficiency and Effectiveness

The objective of many intra-business e-commerce applications is to reduce internal operating costs through efficiency gains both within the individual processes and across the value chain. A competitive advantage derived from improved efficiency is relatively easy to sustain because a company exerts primary control over its own internal processes and what happens within the organization is largely hidden from public view. In contrast, consumer-focused B2C applications must communicate with the external public marketplace, so (as you learned in Chapter 5) a competitive advantage, even one based on a true innovation, is difficult to sustain, because successful innovations are quickly cloned or reverse-engineered by competitors.

Figure 6.4 The value chain for a personal computer manufacturer.

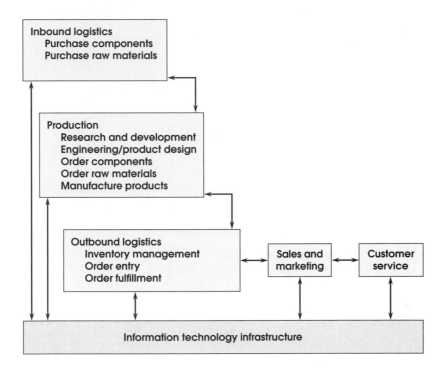

This chapter spotlights trends in the innovative use of information technology to improve efficiency and effectiveness within and across the value chain. Over time, the focus of these improvements has evolved from the individual processes to interprocess integration through the electronic (or paperless) exchange of business information. Perhaps the best way to grasp the significance of these changes is to follow the evolution of intra-business e-commerce.

The Beginnings

Long before computers were invented, large business concerns dealt with the complexity of commercial activity by organizing along functional lines (sales, manufacturing, purchasing, inventory, accounting, and so on), defining the work to be done as a series of related single-function processes and assigning each of those sets of processes to the appropriate functional group or department (Figure 6.6). The functional groups communicated with each other by exchanging paperwork. For example, in a typical manufacturing company, a salesperson hand-wrote a customer order on a paper form and turned in accumulated orders to the sales office secretary at the end of the day or the week. The secretary, in turn, delivered the order forms (by courier or mail) to the manufacturing

Figure 6.5 Each value chain process consists of numerous subprocesses.

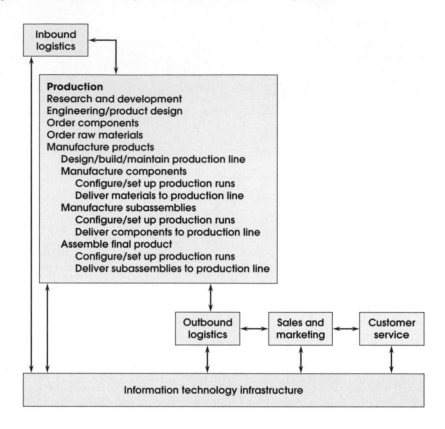

plant, where people in other departments performed such processes as order entry, scheduling, procuring raw materials, manufacturing, and managing inventory, until the finished product was delivered to the customer.

Single-Function Applications

Half a century ago, when modern computers first arrived on the scene, early business applications reflected that functional orientation by focusing on individual processes and automating selected manual tasks. For example, imagine a precomputer, manual payroll system that consisted of five discrete processes (Figure 6.7). Payroll clerks collected employee time sheets on Friday morning. In a second process, the clerks copied the labor data from the individual time sheets to spreadsheet-like paper forms on Friday afternoon. Starting on Monday morning, the payroll clerks used paper, pencil, desktop calculators, and paper forms to compute and record the previous week's payroll, finishing their work by quitting time on Thursday. On Friday, while the payroll clerks started on the *next* week's payroll, a group of secretaries typed or handwrote the current paychecks. Finally, the checks were distributed to the employees.

Figure 6.6 The organizational pyramid.

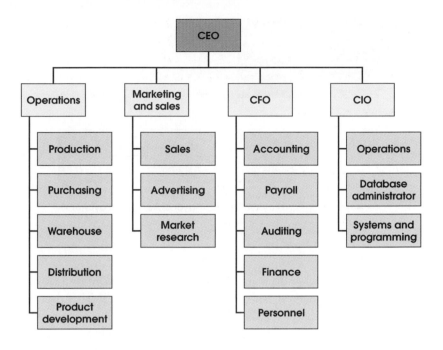

Figure 6.7 A manual payroll system.

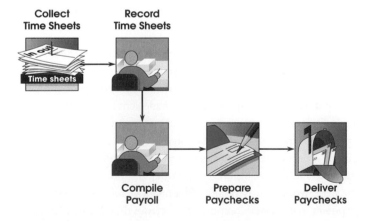

Because it was clearly the payroll department's most expensive process, the first payroll application program (Figure 6.8) automated the Compile Payroll process and the ability to print paychecks on a high-speed printer automated the Print Paychecks (formerly Prepare Paychecks) process. The Record Time Sheets process shifted from paper and pencil to keyboarding, but it remained essentially manual. Although some payroll clerks and secretaries lost their jobs, the new system was clearly more efficient than the old one, delivering improved service at a lower cost.

Figure 6.8 Automating selected processes made the payroll system more efficient.

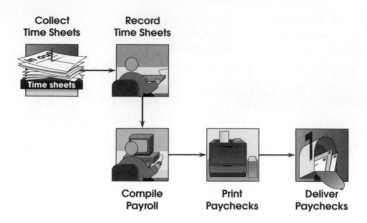

Study the payroll system flow diagram (Figure 6.8) and try to imagine ways to automate the remaining manual procedures. For example, if some or all of the labor data were collected electronically through a terminal of some type, the Collect Time Sheets and Record Time Sheets processes could be further streamlined or perhaps fully automated, and if a significant number of employees were persuaded to allow the company to directly deposit their paychecks in a bank, fewer checks would remain to be distributed manually. Such a process-by-process approach is how the early system developers attacked the problem of improving efficiency within a functionally related group of processes. Their objective was to **optimize** the operation of their function by performing their assigned tasks in the most cost-efficient way possible.

Similar efficiency gains were realized by automating such business functions as order entry, accounts receivable, accounts payable, purchasing, inventory control, and general ledger. Given the existing functionally oriented business environment, automating (and optimizing) each functional group's processes made sense. Each department or function was, in effect, an independent black box that communicated with other departments by exchanging paperwork (a primitive form of layering), and as long as the paperwork flows were maintained, a department's processes could be modified without affecting the rest of the organization. In fact, computerizing individual processes tended to improve the quality of the paperwork because many documents were printed rather than handwritten, and computers made fewer computational errors than human clerks.

The functional focus worked well in its day. An accounting program running on a computer can resolve accounting entries and generate financial reports more quickly and more accurately than a human clerk. The same was true for time recording, generating paychecks, monitoring inventory levels, and so on. Each efficiency gain represented a potential competitive advantage. The race to automate business processes was on.

Islands of Automation

As you learned in Chapter 1, one legacy of this functional focus was a myriad of internal islands of automation (Figure 6.9): isolated sets of business processes, each with its own unique application programs, hardware, and data that communicated with the other islands by exchanging paper documents. For example, every process pictured in Figure 6.8 was the responsibility of payroll, and nonpayroll processes were of no interest to the payroll department. A payroll process might import data (for example, printed sales reports yielded the data needed to compute sales commissions) and export printed documents such as paychecks and accounting reports. But how sales compiled those input documents, and what the accounting department did with the output reports was not payroll's concern. And what happened on the payroll island was payroll's business and no one else's.

Other functional groups, such as sales, inventory control, accounts receivable, and billing, took exactly the same proprietary view of their own processes and data, and with good reason. For example, to prevent employee fraud, standard operating procedures typically prohibit the same person from issuing a bill and collecting the payment. What better way to uphold the principle of functional segregation than to place responsibility for issuing bills and collecting payments in separate departments?

Figure 6.9 Islands of automation.

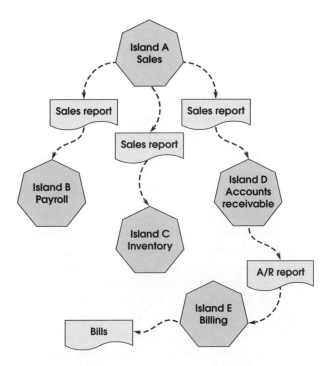

A 1970s-era computer had significantly less computing power than a modern entry-level PC. In those days, memory cost about "a buck a byte," a machine with 512 KB (about $500,000 worth) of memory was state-of-the-art, and most computers had significantly less. For example, in 1975, one of this book's authors wrote an inventory analysis application on an IBM System 3 with 16 KB (yes, *kilobytes!*) of memory. With such limited memory, the machine could execute only one application program at a time in batch mode, so there was no way to integrate the results generated by the inventory analysis program with related applications in anything remotely approaching real time. Back in the 1970s, independent single-function applications were about the best we could do.

Those independent single-function applications were consistent with the prevailing business climate,

however. In the 1970s, most companies were organized functionally, a management structure that implicitly encouraged the development of isolated islands of automation. Given all those single-function fiefdoms, today's highly integrated systems probably would have enjoyed limited support at best. In other words, the technology fit the times, and there was little pressure for immediate technological improvement.

Did technology force business to change over the past three decades? Or did the evolving business need force technology to change? The answer to both questions is probably yes. Technological innovation suggests new applications, and new applications suggest new innovations. The result is a powerful positive feedback loop that drives an accelerating rate of change.

Suboptimization

Viewing a system (such as an organization) as a set of independent departments inevitably leads to **suboptimization**, the optimization of a single component, often at the expense of systemwide efficiency. Each island represented an internally efficient but isolated domain with its own policies, operating procedures, reward structures, hardware, software, and data structures. The sales function on island A might develop computer applications to improve and integrate its sales-related processes, but the resulting productivity gains were local in scope—they stopped (figuratively) at the waterline.

Sales, billing, accounts receivable, production, inventory management, order fulfillment, payroll, and other key business functions are not truly independent, however; they are highly interrelated. Coordinating those functions is the key to overcoming local suboptimization and achieving organizational efficiency, and sharing information is the key to coordination. Unfortunately, attempts to integrate the various islands' systems and gain organization-wide efficiencies were thwarted by data redundancy, inconsistent data structures and data formats, incompatible hardware and software, and office politics. The severity of the suboptimization problem varied widely. The more disparate an island, the more difficult and expensive it was to integrate its functions into the organization. To complicate matters, office political considerations often proved more difficult to overcome than incompatible technology, because each functional area tended to be comfortable within its own fiefdom and (understandably) reluctant to sacrifice its established power base for the good of the organization. The reward structure also worked against functional integration by defining success relative to how well a department performed its assigned task. For example, a warehouse manager whose salary and promotion opportunities depend on how well he controls inventory costs is unlikely to support a proposal to increase inventory levels for the benefit of production or sales, even if doing so enhances corporatewide profits.

Integrating the Value Chain

As hardware and software continued to improve, management slowly began to realize the strategic value of information technology and the potential for leveraging technological innovation to achieve a competitive advantage. One of those innovative ideas was to add value by increasing the electronic sharing of information among the various value chain processes. For example, information sharing between the order entry and inventory management processes enables an order taker to inform a customer immediately if a product is in stock, and information sharing between order entry and customer service allows a service representative to access a customer's previous purchases or check on the status of a current order in real time. Such innovations create a competitive advantage by increasing customer satisfaction. As you learned in Chapter 1, once a first mover implements a technical innovation and, as a result, gains a competitive advantage, competitors will react with countermoves, and the first mover will attempt to defend and enhance the competitive advantage (Figure 6.10). Thus, the race to integrate the value chain began.

Figure 6.10 The competitive advantage model.

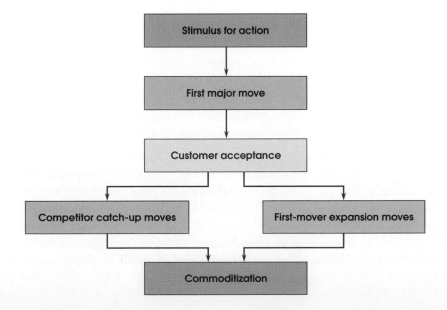

The sudden, unanticipated, competitive need to communicate and share information among the processes that formed the internal value chain caught many companies off guard. Catch-up moves to integrate islands of automation and smooth internal communications were complicated by hardware, software, and data incompatibilities and by the political inertia of the established way of doing business. New companies and those with limited investments in existing **legacy applications** developed for an old platform enjoyed an advantage over established competitors. The new focus was to integrate both existing and new applications, replacing the passing of paper reports with centralized, corporatewide data management.

Hardware, Software, and Data Incompatibilities

The immediate problem faced by early attempts to integrate a company's value chain was incompatible hardware, software, and data. For example, it was not unusual for one functional group to adopt an IBM platform, another to choose Digital Equipment Corporation (DEC), and yet another to go with Burroughs or Sperry UNIVAC. Programs were written in COBOL, PL/1, FORTRAN, and a variety of other languages, including each platform's assembler language. IBM's default character code was EBCDIC, but most other platforms used ASCII. Even peripheral devices were proprietary. Most competitive computer systems could not read an IBM disk, and often, even the physical plugs were incompatible.

Data redundancy, a condition that occurs when the same data values are stored on several different files, was a major impediment to solving the islands of automation problem. For example, accounts receivable, sales, billing, and customer service all require customer information. Because of the single-function orientation of the early applications, each functional area developed its own information system and stored its own version of that customer information. As a result, the organization had multiple independent files, all of which held customer information, and because the files were maintained separately, they contained inconsistencies. For example, if the sales function received an address change or a name change for a customer and failed to share the new information, the accounts receivable, billing, and customer service files contained incorrect data.

To complicate matters, the format of apparently equivalent data values varied significantly from file to file, making integrating the redundant data difficult. The sales file might store the customer name as a single 40-character field, the billing file might contain three separate fifteen-character fields for (respectively) the customer's first, middle, and last names, and another file might store first and last name but only the middle initial.

The solution to the data redundancy problem was to require all the former islands of automation to conform to the standards defined by a centralized corporate database. Because many of those functional groups had invested a great deal of time and effort to develop their own incompatible local databases, the transition was both technically and politically painful. The first databases were hierarchical, which mirrored the organization's top-down management structure and allowed each functional group to retain a certain level of independence. Compared to modern relational databases and shared object-oriented information repositories, those first databases were rather primitive, but they did allow some information sharing and set the stage for value chain integration.

New Approaches to Developing Information Systems

To accomplish the information-sharing objective, organizations had to change their approach to developing information systems. To ensure that individual information technology applications were aligned across functional areas and consistent with long-term corporate strategy, **information systems planning**, the formal process for deciding what systems to implement and how to build them, was elevated to the strategic (corporate) level.

In conjunction with such strategy alignment efforts came a push for standardization and consistency in the use of technology, leading to the evolution of an organizational **information technology infrastructure**, a basic blueprint of how the firm's data processing systems, telecommunication networks, and data would be integrated. To support planning and implementing their information technology infrastructures, companies began to develop **enterprise data models (EDMs)** that integrated the information needs of the entire organization, to define standard computing platforms and an internal network infrastructure, and to establish centralized corporate databases that conformed to the EDM (Figure 6.11).

At the same time, there was a general shift in focus from automating manual tasks to using **business process reengineering** to redesign key processes in a systemwide context. With a well-defined information technology infrastructure and centralized data standards, an organization was able to develop carefully planned systems on established platforms that were driven by and compatible with corporate strategy. As the new enterprise focus began to blur existing functional boundaries, the old single-function islands of automation approach to system development gradually faded away.

These new approaches to information system development did little to solve the legacy application problem, however. The systems that ran on those old islands of automation

Figure 6.11 The evolving information technology infrastructure.

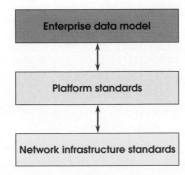

performed useful, often essential tasks, but many of them were technically incompatible with the new standards and had serious data integration issues. Solving those problems meant rewriting the legacy applications or building software bridges to pass data between them and the new corporate infrastructure, and both solutions were expensive.

Integrated Client/Server Applications

Initially, the organization's functional groups used terminals to access the central database over the internal network, but advances in technology soon made it possible to replace the terminals with powerful workstations running user-friendly operating systems with a point-and-click graphic user interface. Concurrently, advances in database technology led to integrated relational databases and de facto standard query languages such as SQL. Combining improved databases and intelligent workstations allowed system developers to distribute the information processing workload and to share the organization's data resources more effectively by implementing client/server applications over local or wide area networks.

On a client/server application, servers communicate with other servers through middleware, and a standard interface greatly simplifies the task of writing a middleware routine. For example, the **common gateway interface** (**CGI**) defines a server-side interface for writing specialized application programs or scripts that are invoked by a client browser, run on a Web server, and access non-Web data. Using CGI allows companies to develop Web-based applications that take advantage of the valuable non-HTML information stored on databases.

Imagine that a user on a client workstation needs customer data stored on a corporate database (Figure 6.12). The user enters (through a browser) a set of parameters that describe the desired data, such as a customer's first and last name, and the browser passes the parameters over a communication line to the Web server. Once the request reaches the

Figure 6.12 Middleware allows two dissimilar programs or applications to interoperate.

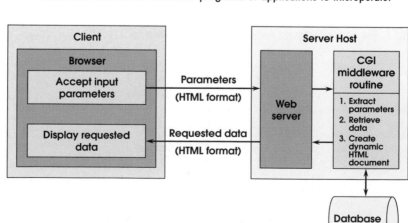

remote host, the Web server invokes the CGI middleware routine and passes the parameters along to it. The CGI routine then uses the parameters to access the database, formats the non-HTML results into a dynamic HTML document, and returns the page back through the Web server to the browser, which displays the results.

Compared to more modern standards such as **Active Server Pages** (**ASP**), CGI is somewhat dated and inefficient. Much like standard HTML documents, ASP pages contain text, tags, and embedded scripts. However, when a client requests an ASP page, the server, rather than the client, executes the scripts (sometimes called servlets) and creates a dynamic HTML page, which is returned to the client. ASP and CGI perform similar functions, but ASP allows Web site developers to work with such familiar tools as VBScript and JavaScript.

Client/Server Application Logic

Most Web information systems utilize the client/server model. Like most application systems, they incorporate three types of logic (Figure 6.13). The **presentation logic** provides a user interface, formats data, and displays the data. The **business logic** enforces the applicable business rules and controls the application. The **information/data logic** handles data storage, access, and retrieval.

Because two computers are involved, a client/server application can be **partitioned** so that some of the logic is implemented on the client and some on the server. For example, consider a Web-based production scheduling system. An order entry clerk (the client) starts the process by interfacing with the browser's presentation logic to enter a customer's order. Additionally, client-side business logic might be needed to ensure that all required information has been entered in the proper format before the order is sent to the server.

Once the completed order form is transmitted to the server, server-side business logic (supported by the appropriate information/data logic) checks the available inventory, schedules a production run, and so on. Other server-side business logic generates such electronic documents as a production schedule, and server-side information/data logic updates the appropriate databases. Finally, an electronic acknowledgement, perhaps a copy of the updated production schedule, and other relevant documents are returned to the client, where the client-side browser's presentation logic displays them.

Figure 6.13 The three types of Web information system logic.

Presentation logic	Formats and displays data Accepts user input
Business logic	Enforces business rules Controls application
Information/data logic	Stores and retrieves data

Partitioning the Workload

The three types of logic can be partitioned in many different ways (Figure 6.14). In one application, the client might perform only a portion of the presentation logic, and in another application, the client might be assigned all the presentation and business logic and some of the data logic. However, because the browser's graphic user interface is so familiar, the presentation logic is typically assigned to the client workstation, and given the need to share and integrate the database's contents, a server-side data server performs the information/data logic. The best place to implement the business logic is not so clear, however, and it is often split across both platforms. Deciding how to partition the application logic is important because many companies have applications that run on thousands of client workstations. The decision is based on trade-offs among such factors as performance, system workload, maintenance concerns, security needs, and the business logic itself.

The partitioning decision for a simple Web surfing application is fairly obvious (Figure 6.15). On the client side, the browser performs the presentation logic, identifying,

Figure 6.14 Options for partitioning client/server application logic.

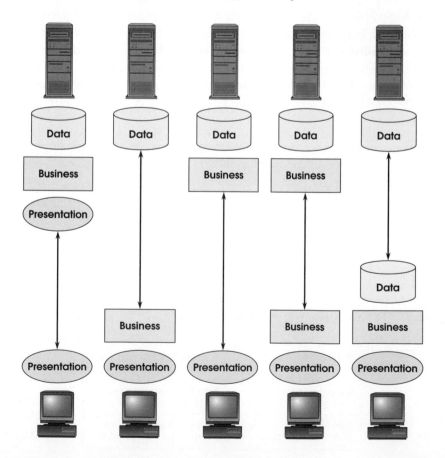

Figure 6.15 The logic necessary to perform two different tasks.

Logic	Surf the Web	Order entry
Presentation	Identify desired page Display page	Display online order form Display order acknowledgment
Business	None	Error-check form data Validate product stock Calculate taxes and total Check customer credit
Information/data	Retrieve and return desired page	Record order Read quantity on hand Access accounts receivable

requesting, and displaying the desired page. On the server side, the Web server performs the information/data logic, retrieving and returning the requested page. There is no business logic.

The partitioning decision is often much more complex, however. For example, on an order entry application (Figure 6.15), the client will almost certainly display the order form and the order acknowledgment, and the server will almost certainly perform the information/data logic, but the business logic can be partitioned in several different ways. All four tasks could be performed on the server. However, if a server-side error-checking routine discovers a missing field on a submitted form, the server must request corrected information from the client, adding at least two more message exchanges to the process. An alternative is to implement client-side business logic to perform simple error checking (for example, a social security number must contain exactly nine digits, an e-mail address must contain an @ symbol, and a required field must not be blank) on the order entry form data before the form is transmitted to the server. Client-side error checking avoids unnecessary network traffic by eliminating the transmission of incomplete or incorrect data.

The final order entry business task in Figure 6.15, check customer credit, is different. It makes no sense to send the customer's entire financial history to the client so the client machine can check the customer's credit. Doing so would create unnecessary network traffic and would probably violate privacy and security guidelines. Credit checking is a server-side task, and the client needs the results of the credit check at most. Validate product stock is another server-side task, because the associated database resides there. However, calculate taxes and total could be performed on either the client or the server.

Fat and Thin Client Applications

Clients are considered thin or fat based on how much logic the application's client side performs. On a **thin client application**, the server does most of the work; Web surfing is a good example. On a **fat client application**, in contrast, the client is assigned more of the processing load. Fat client applications often call for more powerful workstations than thin client applications, but because work is shifted from the server to the client, the required server capacity is reduced.

Administration costs are another consideration, however. Fat client applications create an administrative burden because the client-side application code must be installed and maintained on every client machine. For example, on a relatively small network that links twenty-five fat clients, a change to the application logic means that the program must be changed on all twenty-five workstations. Imagine trying to maintain a fat client application on a large network with thousands of client machines.

Another administrative problem associated with fat client applications is developing multiple versions for different platforms. For example, if a network links Windows, Macintosh, Linux, and UNIX workstations, or even a set of Windows workstations that run various Windows operating system releases (95, 98, Me), bridging platform incompatibilities might require different code, and creating and maintaining multiple versions of an application is expensive. In contrast, a thin client application might run in the context of the standard browser on each of the client machines regardless of platform. Generally, fat client applications are appropriate only if the number of users is limited and homogeneous; an engineering application is a good example. Figure 6.16 summarizes several fat versus thin client issues.

Two-Tier Applications

In early client/server applications, all the presentation logic and the bulk of the business logic were assigned to fat clients, and the servers acted primarily as data servers, storing and retrieving information to and from a central database (Figure 6.17). These first-generation client/server applications were developed using such tools as Microsoft's

Figure 6.16 A comparison of fat and thin clients.

Issue	Fat clients	Thin clients
Client size	Large (to handle workload).	Smaller. Often browser only.
Server size	Small. Limited workload. Must be flexible for two-tier.	Larger. Bulk of workload. Specialized servers in n-tier.
Network traffic	Heavy. Pass information to support business logic.	Light. Pass results of business logic.
Application complexity	Light. Canned middleware.	Complex because of additional middleware.
Application maintenance	Heavy. Code installed and maintained on each client.	Limited software on client. Most application code on server.
Ease of use	Difficult. Each application has own user interface.	Better. Common user interface.

Fat and Thin Clients

At the turn of the last century (1900), the electric motor had just begun to capture the attention of the masses. Young people went to school to study electric motors. Experts predicted that some day we would all have a large electric motor in our basement that would enable us to run a variety of household appliances. The drudgery of housework would be automated, and a leisure-based society would evolve.

Today we all own numerous electric motors. For example, an electric motor resides in your electric toothbrush, your hair dryer, your refrigerator, your washing machine, and your clothes dryer; basically, if you plug it in and something moves, it contains an electric motor. What happened? As technology improved, electric motors got smaller and cheaper until, eventually, they disappeared inside the appliances they powered. When we buy batteries for our power screwdriver, we don't even think about the electric motor. When the electric motor fails, we don't consider repairing it. Instead, we buy a new power screwdriver.

Web-based applications are about where electric motors were in 1900. Everyone agrees that such applications will become increasingly important, but will the information processing be performed by a central server controlling a number of thin clients, or will much of the information processing responsibility move away from the center and out to self-contained, fat client information appliances? Time will tell.

Figure 6.17 A two-tier client/server application.

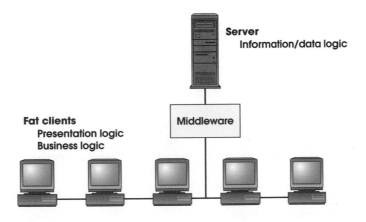

Visual Basic and Sybase's PowerBuilder, both of which incorporated at least some canned middleware. They were called **two-tier** client/server applications because all the clients (the first tier) received services from a single server at the second tier.

Most business users access multiple applications to perform their jobs. Many early applications lacked a standard user interface, so changing from one two-tier application to another meant adjusting to a new interface, a confusing and error-prone task. Often those inconsistent interfaces were remnants of the single-function applications common during the islands of automation era; in effect, the new two-tier system borrowed the presentation logic as well as the business logic from the legacy system. Although shared access to a centralized database helped to integrate the new applications, each application retained an element of independence that caused training, support, and maintenance problems, particularly when fat clients were used.

Three-Tier and N-Tier Applications

In the **n-tier** model, the application logic is partitioned among the clients and multiple specialized servers. In Chapter 3, you learned that a Web server is an application program that runs on a host computer. Similarly, an application server, a data server, an e-mail server, a file server, and other types of servers are implemented in software. Sometimes, multiple servers run on the same host computer; sometimes they are distributed among several hosts. The various server routines communicate with each other through middleware.

The Web information systems you read about in Chapter 4 are **three-tier** (more generally, n-tier) applications with very thin clients (Figure 6.18). The browser, the only software required on the client side, provides a standard user interface for all applications. Sometimes all the business logic resides on the server, but client-side business logic can be implemented by using scripts and applets that run on the browser. The standard World Wide Web architecture allows an application to access such third-tier components as a data server through CGI, ASP, and similar middleware. Three-tier, thin client applications are easier to maintain than fat client applications because, except for a browser and perhaps a few scripts or applets, all the software runs on and is maintained on the server.

Figure 6.18 A three-tier client/server application.

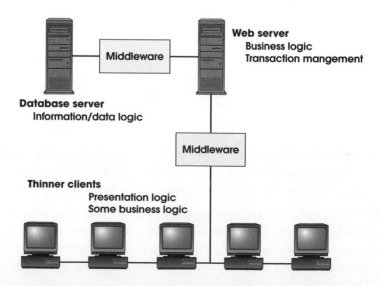

Enterprise Application Integration

The ultimate goal is to develop Web applications to coordinate the operation of *all* the organization's applications, databases, and information technologies so they function as a single efficient, integrated, businesswide system. The term **enterprise application integration (EAI)** is sometimes applied to this underlying principle. EAI incorporates legacy, purchased, Web-based client/server, and traditional client/server applications (Figure 6.19). Building client/server applications integrated around central databases was an initial step down the EAI path. Successfully integrating all applications may make it possible to link electronically all the elements of the value chain.

Given an established corporate database, **enterprise resource planning (ERP)** is one means of achieving the EAI principle. ERP is a business management system that relies on information from an integrated set of applications associated with many of the functional areas (human resources, finance, planning, manufacturing, inventory, sales, marketing) that make up a firm's value chain. It is built around a single centralized corporate database that supports much of the enterprise. For example, numerous integrated solutions are marketed by mySAP.com, and comparable products are available from Baan, J.D. Edwards, Oracle, and PeopleSoft. ERP and other attempts at EAI are appealing because they directly address the functional incompatibilities that once isolated legacy systems on their islands of automation.

The Virtual Value Chain

One objective of EAI is to develop a **virtual value chain (VVC)**, a fully integrated digital picture of a firm's physical value chain. The integrated collection of information that forms the VVC allows management to "see" digitally, often in real time, the company's entire physical value chain from beginning to end, a significant improvement over static paper-based models. The centralized corporate databases provided by integrated client/server applications and ERP systems are integral parts of a VVC.

Figure 6.19 Enterprise application integration (EAI).

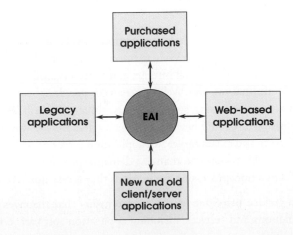

Once visibility is established through the VVC, the electronic sharing of information allows managers to better coordinate the processes that make up the physical value chain to achieve organizational (rather than single-function) efficiency. Often, a desire for improved value chain integration provides the stimulus for action that in turn initiates the first major move, as described in the competitive advantage model you first encountered in Chapter 1.

Many companies use the visibility provided by the VVC to fuel business process reengineering. Imagine, for example, that information gleaned from a soft drink bottler's VVC suggests that more tightly integrating the company's warehouse management and product distribution processes might substantially reduce its order fulfillment costs. Specifically, improving inter-process communication could potentially eliminate the need to inventory the contents of each returning truck manually before loading the product for the next round of deliveries. After careful study, the process engineers design a system that calls for the company's truck drivers to record each delivery electronically as it occurs and transmit the information back to a central network through a handheld wireless communication device. The delivery information is then fed to an order fulfillment application, which integrates order information and determines the precise number of soft drink cases required to restock the truck. Later, when the driver returns to the distribution center, the goods are waiting on the loading dock, saving both time and manpower.

A good VVC can also be used to deliver value in entirely new ways. For example, **data mining** (sometimes called Web mining), the act of ferreting out previously unknown patterns and relationships from a set of data, has been used to analyze integrated information about marketing campaigns and sales to identify how demographical categories respond to different types of advertising. Applying such results promises to make future advertising more effective.

Web Information System Services

A typical Web information system is based on thin client, three-tier client/server applications. Such systems are much more difficult to create and operate than two-tier fat client applications. Thus, it is not surprising that outsourcing, hiring a third party to provide all or part of an organization's information system infrastructure, has become a growing business, and consulting services and system integrators have proliferated.

Other intermediaries offer such tools as **application server software** for building Web-based information systems. The basic Web architecture supports hyperlinked text documents. Within the context of the official Internet and Web standards, few options exist for accessing non-Web information, and Web servers were not designed to handle complex high-volume transaction-processing systems. Thus, three-tier client/server applications require an additional layer of middleware, such as a database gateway, to communicate between the Web server and a data server. An application server provides this middleware and defines a **scalable** (able to adapt to changing demand) platform for integrating numerous high-volume transaction-processing applications that access non-Web information.

An **application service provider** (ASP) is a company that manages and distributes software-based solutions and services, including application software, e-mail, and calendar services, over a TCP/IP network. Many enterprises buy such Web-enabled, off-the-shelf products as ERP software instead of building their own applications, providing another market for ASP intermediaries. Additionally, many ASPs offer, for a fixed monthly fee, software ranging from Microsoft Office to **mission-critical applications** such as ERP systems. For example, IBM's "e-business on demand" initiative features numerous e-commerce application services.

According to Webopedia, a **management** (or **managed**) **service provider** (**MSP**) is "a company that manages information technology services for other companies via the Web." Some MSPs specialize in networking hardware, software, and related services, including security, database management, and appropriate Web applications, and some MSP clients also rely on an ASP to manage their business applications. The services provided by ASPs and MSPs are attractive to business because solutions can be implemented quickly, the client needs no additional skilled personnel, and around-the-clock support is available.

Corporate Intranets and Value Chain Integration

To most companies, the initial focus of the Internet and the World Wide Web was external. For example, a corporate Web site enhances an organization's ability to communicate with its customers, suppliers, business partners, the government, and other players that make up its environment. It wasn't long, however, before business began asking whether the technologies that drove the Internet and the Web could be applied internally, and **intranets**, private corporate networks that use standard Internet protocols and interfaces, were born.

OPINION

Outsourcing

Because outsourcing the responsibility for creating, hosting, and managing an intranet is a popular option, a word of caution is in order. When you outsource a service, you assign responsibility for providing that service to someone else, but you also give up control over that service. What happens when an external service provider, particularly an ASP, decides to discontinue a mission-critical service or goes out of business? How secure is your organization's internal information if the responsibility for maintaining that information is assigned to a subcontractor? Is it reasonable to expect your intranet to support a sustainable competitive advantage when the underlying services are available to your competitors on the open market? The time to answer such questions is before you decide to outsource.

An intranet is essentially a scaled-down, single-organization version of the Internet and World Wide Web. It employs the same technologies (a client/server network, the standard TCP/IP protocols, HTML, HTTP, browsers, Web servers, and so on) and offers the same benefits, including platform independence, widely known and accepted standards, low-cost distribution of current information, and support for Web information systems.

Intranets also help to integrate islands of automation. Because an intranet uses the standard platform-independent Internet protocols, even functional-area systems that run on incompatible computing platforms can communicate over the intranet. Such communication allows the various functional areas to maintain their independence and still take advantage of the benefits resulting from integration. This feature is particularly valuable if the transition to a common computing platform is technically difficult, costly, or politically impossible.

Although they are similar, an intranet differs from the Internet and the Web in two significant ways. First, an intranet is smaller in scope,[1] with access generally limited to a single organization's employees. Second, because the audience is limited, the organization can make information and applications available to its employees that it would not consider releasing to the entire world. Today, many companies spend much more on their intranets than they do on the Internet.

The design, implementation, and maintenance of a corporate intranet might be accomplished using internal skills, consultants, purchased software, or a combination of all three. The same specialized intermediary software and support available to build Web sites aimed at consumers (message boards, chat rooms, Web information systems, and so on) are useful for building internal information-sharing Web sites. Intermediary software also measures site usage and provides input to improve the intranet.

First-Generation Intranets

As with early Web applications, first-generation intranets shared information through static Web pages (Figure 6.20). The goal was to connect employees throughout the organization to important internal information and, at the same time, reduce printing and distribution costs. As mentioned earlier, a Web-based version of the corporate telephone directory accessed through a Web server reduces paper costs and the resources necessary to create and distribute a paper version, and the information available online is virtually guaranteed to be more current than the contents of a printed directory. Early intranets also supported limited interactivity between employees, including e-mail, bulletin boards, and chat rooms. The employee orientation of these first generation intranets is the likely source of the term business-to-employee (B2E) e-commerce.

---

[1] Some intranets are quite large. For example, a major accounting firm's intranet might span the globe. But even the largest intranets are dwarfed by today's Internet.

Figure 6.20 A first-generation intranet.

- **First generation—static content**
  - **Policy and procedure manuals**
  - **Corporate phone directories**
  - **Benefits information**
  - **Corporate newsletters**
  - **Job postings**
  - **Product information**
  - **Corporate expertise**
  - **Meeting minutes**
  - **Project status**

Content Management

An intranet is only as valuable as the information it provides. If the information is not current or not available when needed, the intranet will not be used. Even static documents change over time, and maintaining HTML pages is not a simple task, so new processes are necessary to ensure the value of the intranet's content. Numerous widely dispersed information content providers, many with limited HTML expertise, make maintaining those pages even more difficult.

There are two approaches to **content management**, the process of creating, maintaining, and accessing intranet (and Internet) documents. The centralized approach requires content experts to submit updates through a technical expert who converts the information to HTML. As the amount of content grows, however, the technical expert can become a bottleneck, slowing the information distribution process.

OPINION

Being "Always On"

A well-designed intranet integrates all of an organization's functional areas and allows a given employee to communicate instantly with any other employee. The potential for instant communication can be a powerful business tool, saving time, saving effort, and making everyone more efficient, but often the potential becomes the expectation. Expecting (even implicitly) employees to respond immediately to requests for information can be disruptive, and the feeling of being "always on" can create a high level of stress. Additionally, combining intranet access and wireless communication, such as cellular telephones, effectively allows (or forces) some employees to be on call twenty-four hours per day. Some people thrive in such an environment. Many do not.

The decentralized approach shifts the responsibility for generating the HTML to the content experts. An HTML editor such as Microsoft's FrontPage makes creating a Web page almost as simple as creating a word-processing document. Distributing intranet maintenance responsibility to multiple sources can introduce inconsistencies in the look and feel of each functional area's pages, however, creating problems for users as they navigate the intranet. In an attempt to overcome the disadvantages of both approaches, some organizations use a hybrid approach, allowing the content experts to generate the content in HTML form and assigning a centralized group the responsibility and authority to enforce consistency across the Web site.

Today, a large corporation's intranet might contain more information than the entire Internet did a decade ago. As the amount of information and the number of applications on corporate intranets continues to explode, content management becomes even more difficult. Content management software and service intermediaries are an increasingly important source of intranet (and Internet) support, offering content maintenance services, workflow analysis tools, testing capabilities, and change- and version-control software.

Second-Generation Intranets

The first interactive intranet applications (selecting benefits packages, expense reporting, employee satisfaction surveys, and so on) simply replaced internal paper forms with HTML-based forms. Shifting from moving paper to moving electronic information (the essence of e-commerce) reduced paper costs and streamlined the value chain business processes that administered the forms.

Second-generation intranets (Figure 6.21) go far beyond static Web pages and simple information sharing, combining vast amounts of corporate information into an interactive employee knowledge base. Modern intranets feature more sophisticated Web information systems, many of which reflect the thin client, n-tier client/server architecture discussed earlier in this chapter. For example, existing legacy and other non-Web, corporatewide client/server applications can be linked to the intranet through middleware routines that

Figure 6.21 A second-generation intranet.

- **Second generation—interactive applications**
  - Benefits selection
  - Expense reporting
  - Project administration
  - Inventory levels
  - Production scheduling
  - Online training
  - Groupware (collaborative support)
  - Legacy front ends
  - Database access
  - Customer support
  - Web information systems

translate between the non-Web protocols and data structures and their TCP/IP equivalents by essentially encasing the legacy message in a TCP/IP wrapper (Figure 6.22). New client/server applications are, of course, built to run on the Web architecture.

Many organizations now use their intranets to support high-volume, mission-critical systems such as accounting applications. If a mission-critical application is unavailable for any reason, the loss of access can disrupt normal operations and seriously affect the company's bottom line. Thus, the intranet itself is sometimes deemed mission-critical.

Using Internet and Web technologies for mission-critical applications is potentially dangerous, however. Such applications demand outstanding performance, tight access controls, a high level of security, and fault tolerance. Except for fault tolerance, the Internet and the World Wide Web were not designed with those objectives in mind. New technologies and services, many of them provided by intermediaries, can help, but as you will discover in Chapters 8, 9, and 10, many problems remain.

Intranet support for collaborative work continues to evolve, as well. Software that supports collaborative work is called **groupware** (Figure 6.23); document sharing, e-mail, and appointment scheduling applications are well-known examples. Older, pre-Web groupware products such as e-mail and IBM's Lotus Notes were implemented on traditional fat client architectures, but many newer groupware packages are designed to run on thin, Web-based clients linked to a corporate intranet.

Figure 6.22 Encasing a legacy message in a TCP/IP wrapper allows a legacy application to communicate with the intranet.

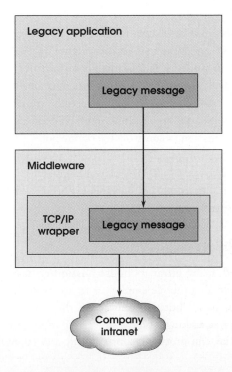

Figure 6.23 Some examples of groupware.

- E-mail
- Scheduling and calendars
- Whiteboarding
- Chat rooms and bulletin boards
- Video conferencing
- Electronic meetings
- Document management
- Workflow management
- Collaborative writing
- Group decision support systems

An intranet provides a platform for enterprise application integration (EAI) by delivering multiple client/server applications to employees through a common browser-based interface. Using an intranet to link thin clients significantly reduces the maintenance burden associated with maintaining multiple sets of redundant applications on multiple workstations, while still allowing each client machine to run all the corporate applications. As a secondary benefit, from the user's perspective, the browser's common interface simplifies learning. Many software vendors, including ERP and groupware providers, have Web-enabled their products to take advantage of intranets.

Enterprise Portals

Many corporate intranets have developed **enterprise portals** to consolidate the available applications, information, expertise, and services (Figure 6.24). Analogous to portal sites on the World Wide Web (such as Yahoo), they help to manage and facilitate end user access to the entire intranet knowledge base and integrate all the company's information systems. Enterprise portals enable personalized access, information filtering, security controls, single sign-on for all applications, and content management. They allow employees to access information (a company telephone book, procedure manuals, and so on), make travel arrangements, manage their expense accounts, order supplies, and collaborate with other employees. Some Web portal companies, including Yahoo, provide middleware tools for implementing an enterprise portal, and Google's search engine powers many intranet front ends.

Security and Recovery Services

As you have discovered, many intranets house mission-critical applications and confidential information. Allowing mobile employees to access such intranets remotely may help them do their jobs better, but it also increases the risk of unauthorized intrusion, both internal and external, making a high level of system security essential. Access control is particularly crucial, and procedures for securing and guaranteeing the integrity of

Management by Exception

In the old paperwork-driven days, gathering current information was difficult, and the lack of good information limited a manager's ability to control and evaluate her employees. The best managers tended to rely on personal observation, which restricted the number of people that a given manager could effectively supervise.

Information technology and e-commerce changed the rules. Today, a sales associate might see his manager once a week or less, and a given manager might be responsible for dozens of employees. On the surface, the employee seems to be more independent, and even relative newcomers are given more decision-making responsibility than was typical a decade ago. Beneath the surface, however, those seemingly independent employees are expected to report on their activities through a corporate intranet, and once the data reaches the company's information infrastructure, it is instantly available. Comparing actual results (sales orders, for example) to targets (such as quotas or sales calls per day) is the key to management by exception. Employees who meet their targets are left alone. Employees who miss their targets are asked to explain why, and unless their performance improves, eventually they are fired. The availability of current information makes management by exception possible.

Some employees, particularly those who can exert control over their activities, like the sense of independence and responsibility that comes from information-based management by exception. Other employees, particularly those who have little or no real control, do not. For example, an intranet that quickly makes sales order data available can also literally count a data entry clerk's keystrokes or time a customer service employee's telephone calls and compare the resulting numbers to standards. Think about it. Would you like to be monitored that closely? You probably will be.

Figure 6.24 Typical enterprise portal services.

- Structured data management
- Unstructured data management
- Content management
- Information filtering
- Search capabilities
- Collaboration
- User administration
- Expense account management
- Ordering supplies
- Security
- Personalization

the information stored on and transmitted over the corporate network must be guaranteed. Security exposures and methods for combating those exposures are discussed in Chapters 8, 9, and 10. Virtual private networks that support secure transmission over public communication facilities are discussed in Chapter 7. Intermediaries often play a major role in providing security services.

Disaster recovery is equally important. Fires, floods, riots, electrical surges, and similar unpredictable events happen, and competitors, critics, and even employees have been known to sabotage a company's information technology resources. Replicating a database at two or more different sites provides a source for recovering lost data and, particularly if the company is geographically disbursed, can make intranet access more efficient by distributing the workload.

Integrating a Geographically Dispersed Value Chain

Integrating the processes that make up the value chain is much more complex if the islands of automation are geographically dispersed, because the value chain itself is more complex. Although each remote location is part of the organization's value chain, each typically has its own mini–value chain. Islands of automation can evolve in the home office, but the likelihood of this problem emerging in a geographically dispersed facility is much higher. For example, imagine the complexity of the value chain for a global manufacturing firm such as Procter & Gamble or an international consulting company such as Accenture.

Geographically disbursed entities can be interconnected in many different ways. A secure private network runs on private or leased bandwidth and limits access to the company's employees and perhaps to its business partners. A value-added network operated by a trusted third party provides shared bandwidth and services to many organizations. Public networks such as the Internet are sometimes used, but security is a potential problem. A virtual private network offers a more secure way to utilize public bandwidth but at a significant cost. These options will be discussed in detail in Chapter 7.

Remote employees, such as mobile sales associates and telecommuters, need access to the corporate intranet to perform their jobs. Usually access is provided through public bandwidth or a direct dial-up connection to the internal network. Whenever critical internal networks are exposed to the outside world, security precautions such as a **firewall**, a combination of hardware and software that protects the corporate network from unauthorized access, are essential. Firewalls and other security measures are discussed in Chapter 9.

mySocrates

Several years ago, General Motors faced a modern version of the old islands of automation problem, with numerous independent departmental and divisional intranets serving subsets of the workforce. Launched in 1997, Socrates was a portal that linked the existing intranets and served as a central directory. Initially, access was limited to salaried employees, but a new enterprise portal called mySocrates, released in late 2001, opened the corporate intranet to all domestic GM employees, salaried and hourly alike. GM's long-term plan is to extend access to all its employees worldwide. In 1999, mySocrates won a CIO Web Business 50/50 award as one of the top fifty corporate intranets.

Employees can access mySocrates from home (through their AOL accounts) or from work. The new enterprise portal's content can be accessed through a search engine, an alphabetized list, or by category. The portal is a primary source of corporate and business news for employees. It provides access to numerous human resources services, including benefit information, benefit management, internal job postings, health information, health plan management, 401(k) transactions, electronic pay stubs, direct paycheck deposit forms, and e-training course enrollment. Using mySocrates, employees can schedule conference rooms and request specialized services such as graphics design. They can also create a personalized Web page to deliver news, weather, stock prices, and even information specific to an employee's family.

Employees seem to like mySocrates, and so does General Motors. For example, the ability of an employee to manage her own benefits, 401(k), and direct deposit applications and to obtain answers to frequently asked questions through mySocrates, rather than visiting the human resources department for a face-to-face meeting, has resulted in significant cost savings. Simply put, intranets and enterprise portals make good business sense.

193

Intra-business (or B2E) e-commerce is rooted in an organization's employees and its value chain. The objective is to reduce operating costs through efficiency gains. Early business application programs reflected the organization's functional orientation by focusing on the individual processes and attempting to optimize those processes. One legacy of that functional focus was a myriad of internal islands of automation, which led to suboptimization. A desire to improve systemwide efficiency prompted several early intra-business e-commerce initiatives.

As hardware and software improved, management began to realize that an organization could add value by sharing information among the various value chain processes. The new focus was to integrate both legacy applications and new applications, replacing inefficient paper reports with corporatewide data management. With this new focus, information systems planning was elevated to the corporate level. In conjunction with such strategy alignment efforts came a push for standardization and consistency in the use of technology, leading to the evolution of an organizational information technology infrastructure, the development of EDM, and the implementation of business process reengineering.

Client/server applications allow a system developer to distribute the information processing workload over multiple computers. A thin client application assigns most of the work to the server, and a fat client application assigns more of the processing load to the client. On an early two-tier client/server application, all the clients received services from a single server at the second tier, but newer client/server applications utilize three tiers and more. In the n-tier model, the application logic is partitioned among the clients and several specialized servers.

The ultimate goal of EAI is to coordinate the operation of all an organization's applications, databases, and information technologies. ERP is one means of achieving that goal. One key objective is to develop a VVC to support such activities as data mining. Intermediaries such as ASPs offer such tools as application servers.

First-generation intranets shared information through static Web pages. Second-generation intranets attempt to combine a great deal of corporate information into an interactive employee knowledge base and often incorporate mission-critical applications and groupware. Because of the size of today's corporate intranets, content management is crucial to success. Many corporate intranets have evolved into enterprise portals.

Integrating the processes that make up the value chain is much more complex if the islands of automation are geographically dispersed, because the value chain itself is more complex. Whenever critical internal networks are exposed to the outside world, good security is essential. A firewall is an important element of any security plan designed to protect an online application.

Active Server Pages (ASP)
application server software
application service provider (ASP)
business logic
business process reengineering
business-to-employee (B2E)
  e-commerce
common gateway interface (CGI)
content management
data mining
enterprise application integration
  (EAI)
enterprise data model (EDM)

enterprise portal
enterprise resource planning (ERP)
fat client
firewall
groupware
information/data logic
information systems planning
information technology infrastructure
intra-business e-commerce
intranet
legacy application
management (or managed) service
  provider (MSP)

mission-critical application
n-tier
optimize
partition or partitioning
presentation logic
scalable
second-generation intranet
suboptimization
thin client
three-tier
two-tier
virtual value chain (VVC)

■■■ Review Questions

1. Explain how intra-business e-commerce can enhance an organization's efficiency and effectiveness.

2. An unintended consequence of early single-function computer applications was the emergence of isolated islands of automation. What problems did those islands create?

3. Explain how integrating the value chain helps to solve the islands of automation problem.

4. What is a legacy application? Why do some legacy applications continue to exist?

5. How did value chain integration lead to new approaches to information system development?

6. What is CGI? What is ASP? How do they contribute to client/server application development?

7. Distinguish among an application's presentation, business, and information/data logic.

8. Explain how partitioning a client/server application's logic distributes the workload between the client and the server.

9. Distinguish between a thin client application and a fat client application.

10. Distinguish among a two-tier, a three-tier, and an n-tier application. Cite at least one example of each.

11. What is enterprise application integration (EAI)?

12. What is a virtual value chain? Why is a virtual value chain useful?

13. What is an intranet?

14. Distinguish between a first-generation intranet and a second-generation intranet.

15. Identify several problems associated with intranet content management.

16. What is the purpose of an enterprise portal?

17. What additional problems are associated with integrating a geographically remote facility into a corporate intranet?

◼◼◼ Exercises

1. Identify several examples of a positive innovation/need feedback loop.

2. Ask fellow students who have changed their name, address, or other personal information in the middle of an academic term to describe their experiences. Their answers might help you understand the problems caused by data redundancy.

3. Compile a list of all your credit cards, magazine and newspaper subscriptions, creditors, bank accounts, correspondents, and any other person or organization you will have to notify when you move. Then estimate how long it would take you to change your address with every one of them.

4. Outsourcing is an excellent way to get things done when internal resources are unavailable. It is difficult to sustain a competitive advantage based on outsourced work, however. Why?

5. How do you feel about people who allow their cell phones or pagers to ring in a movie theater, a restaurant, or at a musical performance? What about people who walk around or drive with a cell phone pressed to their ear? More generally, why do you suppose that some people like being "always on"?

6. A manager's span of control is the number of people he can manage effectively. Traditionally, the management function was performed face-to-face, supported by paperwork. With the advent of corporate intranets, however, it became possible to collect performance data in real time as a byproduct of the primary application. The ability to quickly compare actual results to targets (such as quotas) supported effective management by exception, which in turn allowed companies to increase a manager's span of control.

   For example, imagine that the old span of control was eight subordinates and that information-driven management by exception has made it possible to increase that number to sixteen. Assume the company employs 50,000 operational-level people. Compute the number of managers required at each organizational level using a span of control of 8 and then a span of control of 16. Note the reduction in the total number of managers. How does that change affect corporate efficiency? How does it affect your future job prospects?

■■■ Projects

Current references and supporting resources can be found at this textbook's companion Web site.

Broad-Based Projects

1. Do some preliminary research into corporate intranets; you will find numerous articles in the business literature. Identify one company, research its intranet in more depth, and write a paper describing the applications that run on the intranet and the benefits derived from using an intranet.

2. If possible, arrange for a demonstration of a corporate intranet.

3. Working with one or two other people, conduct some research on an e-commerce topic and jointly write a short paper summarizing your findings. Instead of meeting face to face, however, limit your communications to the exchange of electronic messages.

Building the Case:

4. Working as a team, continue with Chapter 1, Project 6 by carefully reviewing your Web site's employee-oriented content and make sure it supports your strategy. Make changes to your strategy, your implementation plan, and your Web site as necessary.

Business Projects

1. Investigate how intranets have affected the human resources department and write a paper on your findings.

Building the Case:

2. Continue with Chapter 1, Project 2 by creating a flow diagram to show how your client's internal value chain processes produce, maintain, market, sell, and deliver the product. Identify processes that might be improved by implementing an intranet. Investigate options for outsourcing the design, development, and operation of an appropriate intranet and obtain cost estimates. Write a brief report to document your results and add it to the completed flow diagram.

Information Technology Projects

1. Conduct some research on enterprise portals and write a paper on your findings.

Building the Case:

2. Continue with Chapter 1, Project 2 by rethinking your prototype to reflect the contents of Chapter 6. For example, explore the costs and benefits associated with incorporating an intranet in your strategy and identify the elements necessary to support internal, employee-only access to a restricted subset of pages. Be sure to include appropriate security features such as password protection and an independent server. Depending on your background, available time, and your instructor's preference, you might simply identify the need, create static pages to prototype your solution, or actually implement the appropriate access control features on your Web site.

Marketing Projects

1. Investigate how an intranet can be used as an effective medium for conveying key marketing and product information, the corporation's mission and its sense of ethics, a positive corporate image, and similar information to employees, and write a paper on your findings.

Building the Case:

2. Continue with Chapter 1, Project 2 by creating a flow diagram to describe your client's internal value chain. Explain how you will communicate plans and deliver results (such as sales leads) to and solicit suggestions from internal employees over your client's intranet. Write a brief report to document your results, and add information describing intranet communication to the storyboard you started in Chapter 5.

References

Web Sites

Source	URL	Comments
CIO magazine	*www.cio.com/research/intranet/cases.html*	Links to several intranet case studies.

Print and White Papers

Scott, Tony. December 2001/January 2002. "Electronic Wind @ GM." *IHRIM.*

CHAPTER 7

Business-to-Business E-Commerce

When you finish reading this chapter, you should be able to:

- Discuss the relationship between B2B e-commerce and supply chain integration

- Discuss the evolution of interorganizational systems (IOSs)

- Identify and distinguish among several interconnectivity options, including value added networks (VANs) and virtual private networks (VPNs)

- Explain why electronic data interchange (EDI) was necessary

- Define and explain the purpose of an extranet

- Discuss the advantages of XML

- Distinguish between buy-side and sell-side e-procurement

- Discuss the functions performed by payment services, logistics integrators, customer relationship management systems, and supply chain management systems

- Identify the advantages associated with an e-marketplace

The Supply Chain

Intra-business e-commerce (the subject of Chapter 6) has a value chain focus; the objective is to integrate a firm's internal processes. Modern business-to-business (B2B) e-commerce, in contrast, is concerned with *inter*corporate communication, relying on innovative applications of information technology to exchange business information electronically across the supply chain and between numerous trading partners. Improving the efficiency of supply chain transactions is a potential source of significant competitive advantage.

A **supply chain** (Figure 7.1) is the set of business processes that allow multiple independent entities, such as suppliers, manufacturers, and retailers, to function as one virtual organization to develop and deliver products (more generally, economic value) to consumers. Although the basic supply chain model suggests a single path from supplier to customer, the reality is much more complex. For example, as you learned in Chapter 1, Wal-Mart interacts with numerous suppliers, at least some of Wal-Mart's customers buy directly from one or more of Wal-Mart's suppliers, and many of those suppliers interact with each other (Figure 7.2). Plotting a large company's complete supply chain is nearly impossible and not particularly useful, but the basic model is still a useful conceptualization of business-to-business interaction.

A visit to a manufacturing facility is a good way to get a sense of a company's value chain because everything happens in one place, but a large company's supply chain is much more difficult to visualize. Imagine a river (the supply chain) flowing downhill from its source (the raw materials) to its destination (the customer). Along the way, various tributaries (the suppliers) add their contributions (value). That river is a pretty good mental model of a supply chain.

Figure 7.1 The supply chain.

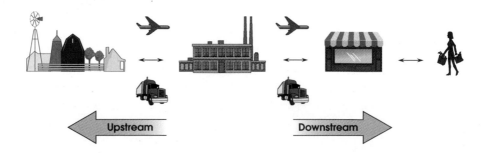

Figure 7.2 A real-world supply chain is very complex.

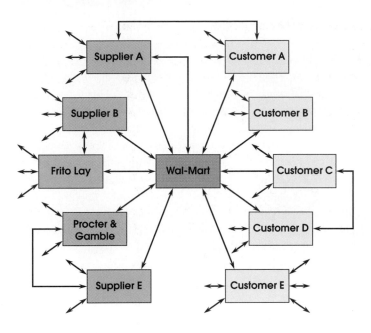

Relate that image to a breakfast cereal producer's supply chain. Numerous farms, grain storage facilities, distributors, packaging suppliers, and transportation services lie upstream. Warehouses, distributors, retail outlets, advertising agencies, delivery services, and, eventually, the retail customers lie downstream. Focus on just one of those components: the retail outlets. How many retailers in your town carry Cheerios and other General Mills products? At the risk of overstating the obvious, a major company's supply chain is incredibly complex.

Now think of the supply chain not as linked entities but as linked processes that perform such tasks as transferring grain from a farm to a local storage facility, then from a local storage facility to a railroad car, and so on. Each process represents the intersection of two entities, and each carries a cost. The islands of automation you read about in Chapter 6 were an unintended consequence of independently optimizing individual processes. The ultimate objective of B2B e-commerce, in contrast, is to optimize the entire supply chain by sharing the information necessary to coordinate all the supply chain's processes.

Intercorporate Collaboration

General Mills produces products such as breakfast cereal and cake mixes at numerous manufacturing facilities and then ships them to warehouses around the country for subsequent distribution to retail outlets. Coordinating all those shipments is a difficult task, and all too often, trucks returned empty to their point of origin after delivering their loads, a problem known as deadheading. Although driving an empty truck yields zero economic value, the driver must still be paid, fuel is still consumed, and vehicle wear-and-tear still accumulates. General Mills wanted to find a way to make use of those wasted resources.

In late 1999, the company hired Nistevo, an e-commerce software development firm, to create a collaborative shipping network. The result was a system that allowed such participating companies as ConAgra Foods, General Mills, Graphic Packaging, Land O' Lakes, Nabisco, Nestle, and Pillsbury,

among others, to coordinate their shipping schedules. For example, the system might arrange for a truck delivering General Mills products from St. Paul to Philadelphia to pick up another participant's shipment near Philadelphia and deliver it to Minneapolis, allowing the truck to travel fully loaded in both directions and saving both companies money.

Nistevo's collaborative shipping network serves multiple companies because more participants mean more opportunities for collaboration. By exchanging and analyzing information using e-commerce tools, the network has reduced the participants' shipping costs by 10 to 15 percent, and *all* the participants have benefited. The success of this B2B venture is demonstrated by the emergence of competitive collaborative shipping networks, such as the National Transportation Exchange, FreightMatrix, Logistics.com, and Transplace.com.

The Evolutionary Nature of B2B E-Commerce

During the dot-com era of the late 1990s, the explosive growth of consumer-based B2C e-commerce seemed to herald a revolution. In contrast, both intra-business and B2B e-commerce evolved steadily over a period of years. Such evolutionary growth, though not as spectacular, tends to be much more sustainable. Today, B2B is by far the most financially successful form of e-commerce, and it is rapidly becoming the way modern business does business. This chapter discusses the ongoing evolution of B2B e-commerce (Figure 7.3).

Interorganizational Systems (IOSs)

An **interorganizational system** (**IOS**) is an information system shared by two or more enterprises. To successfully exchange information electronically, the participants must have compatible information technology and communication infrastructures. Although all the functional groups within a single company report ultimately to the same CEO, as you learned in Chapter 6 integrating the various internal islands of automation that evolved over time was a daunting task. If incompatible computing platforms and network

Figure 7.3 This chapter discusses B2B e-commerce.

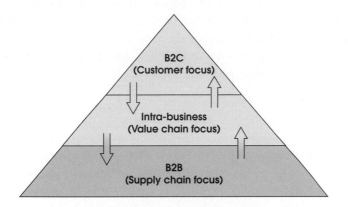

The Growth of B2B E-Commerce

According to eMarketer, in the year 2000, B2B e-commerce generated $124 billion worth of business, accounting for roughly 77 percent of total e-commerce revenues. By 2003, those numbers are expected to increase to $746 billion and 88 percent, respectively. Clearly, B2B is by far the largest e-commerce category.

The data shown below is taken from a year 2000 Juniper Research report on the projected growth of online B2B trading by four major business categories. The numbers do not precisely match eMarketer's projections, but they are the same order of magnitude. Once again, monetary amounts are in billions of dollars.

In five short years, B2B e-commerce is expected to increase from 11 times to 31 times the year 2000 totals. That is growth!

Business category	2000	2005	Change
Computer/ telecommunications	90	1,028	+1100%
Food and beverage	35	863	+2500%
Motor vehicles and parts	21	660	+3100%
Industrial equipment and supplies	20	556	+2700%

protocols made it difficult to link electronically a single company's functional groups, imagine trying to link multiple independent corporate entities. The only way to resolve information infrastructure incompatibilities is for at least one (and probably both) of the parties to make changes, and purchasing new hardware and software, rewriting existing programs, and converting data from one format to another are expensive undertakings. Consequently, getting several companies to agree on whose hardware, software, and data standards should be adopted is a bit like trying to herd cats—difficult, if not impossible.

At one time, creating an interorganizational system required writing custom software to communicate with each participating company. A few decades ago, if companies A, B, and C wanted to exchange information, company A needed two custom middleware routines, one for B and a separate one for C (Figure 7.4). Similarly, company B needed separate routines to communicate with A and C, and company C needed routines to communicate with A and B. Extrapolate the three-company example to many companies, and you can see why early interorganizational systems were limited to large firms and a few of their major trading partners.

Early Examples

As early as the 1970s, such standards and protocols as electronic funds transfer (EFT) and electronic data interchange (EDI) arose to facilitate intercompany exchanges. These standards, which are still in use, effectively bridge application and data problems, but incompatible information technology infrastructures still cause problems. Because implementing information exchanges based on the early standards was quite expensive, B2B applications were limited to large companies. EFT and EDI did, however, demonstrate that exchanging real-time information could yield significant business benefits.

Because the open standards and protocols associated with the Internet and the World Wide Web promote platform independence, interorganizational data communication has moved increasingly to the public infrastructure. Innovative, low-cost applications of newer Web-based technologies, particularly thin client, platform-independent applications, make smaller organizations' participation in B2B e-commerce possible. The result is significant growth. Today, electronically exchanging business information across the supply chain has become an important source of competitive advantage; Figure 7.5 lists several potential benefits associated with interorganizational systems.

Figure 7.4 Creating an interorganizational system (IOS) calls for writing custom software to link each set of two companies.

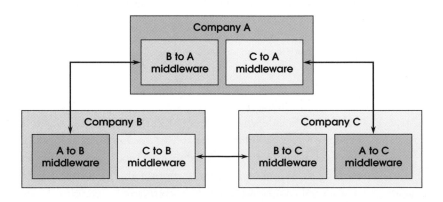

Figure 7.5 Some potential benefits of an interorganizational system.

- Faster transactions
- Lower cost transactions
- Fewer transaction errors
- Reduced cycle time
- Reduced inventory
- Increased information flow
- Increased customer satisfaction
- Improved cash flow

Interconnectivity

As you learned in Chapter 2, electronic communication requires a transmitter, a receiver, a message, a medium, and a set of rules (a protocol) for using that medium. In an interorganizational system, the participating companies' computers serve as transmitters and receivers, and the message consists of the business information they exchange. **Interconnectivity**, the ability of a network, a device, or a software package to communicate with other networks, devices, or software, is provided by the medium and a common protocol. The next few pages discuss the evolution of B2B (and interorganizational) e-commerce interconnectivity options.

Private Leased Networks

In the 1970s, modem-to-modem data transmission over a public telephone line was limited to 300 bps (roughly 37 characters per second), which is much too slow to support e-commerce. In those days, the only viable option for building an interorganizational system was to implement a **private leased network** by leasing relatively expensive, private, high-speed connections from the telephone company. For example, a dedicated T1 line can carry 1.54 Mbps, slow by today's standards, but more than adequate for text-only transmission.

Simply leasing the necessary bandwidth does not guarantee interconnectivity, however. Before communication can take place, the companies involved must agree on a common set of rules or protocols. The odds that both organizations operate compatible information technology and communication infrastructures are (at best) slim, so agreeing on a common set of communication protocols means that at least one company (and often both) must add expensive new hardware or software to convert between its internal protocols and the shared protocols.

The downside to private leased networks is their cost and their lack of **scalability** (the ability to adapt to increasing demand). Remember that such networks are implemented by point-to-point connections between the participating companies. The lack of scalability

[Handwritten margin notes:]
- Expensive
- Not easily scalable
- Highly secure + Reliable

means that adding another company to the network requires another point-to-point connection and another set of protocol conversion routines; look back at Figure 7.2 and imagine how many such connections Wal-Mart would need to communicate with all of its suppliers. Compared with similar public communication services, leasing multiple lines and writing and maintaining separate protocol conversion software for each link is very expensive. That is why only large companies use private leased networks.

In spite of the high cost, private leased networks have advantages, however. The companies sharing the network own exclusive rights and control access to the bandwidth, making it much more difficult for outsiders to intercept transmissions. Private leased networks are also highly reliable. Because the bandwidth is dedicated to the connection between the participating organizations, performance can be monitored, message load can be predicted, and as needs change, additional bandwidth can be purchased.

Value-Added Networks (VANs)

A **value-added network** (**VAN**) is a semiprivate network operated by an intermediary, a trusted third party that offers bandwidth and other value-added services to facilitate interconnectivity among multiple organizations. The VAN eliminates the scalability problem by providing a single network and a single set of communication protocols to which all the interorganizational system's participants must subscribe (Figure 7.6). Typically, a VAN supports connectivity from numerous popular computing infrastructures, accepting information formatted for the sender's protocols and converting it to match the receiver's protocols, thus eliminating the need for additional protocol conversion software.

In addition to bandwidth and protocol conversion, a value-added network provides other services that, as the name implies, add value to the exchange. Information delivery

Figure 7.6 A value-added network (VAN).

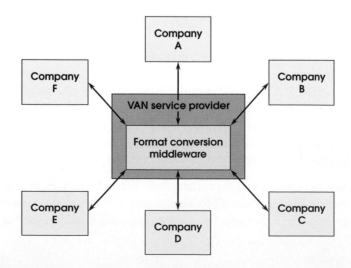

procedures and electronic mail boxes allow individuals and organizations to access accumulated messages at their convenience. The set of common standards defined by the VAN provider simplifies interorganizational data conversion, and most VANs offer security services such as user identification, authentication, and encryption, which will be covered in Chapter 9. Also, because a new trading partner can simply plug into the existing network, a VAN is much more scalable than a private leased network.

VANs are less expensive than secure private networks, but they are still costly. Most charge a subscription fee, plus an additional charge for each transaction. Also, because more organizations have access to the network, a VAN is less secure than a private leased network. Reliability is another concern. All communications go through the VAN service provider, so if the central machine goes down, the network goes down.

Public Bandwidth

Today, many interorganizational systems use the public Internet (Figure 7.7), an option that substantially reduces cost and exponentially increases scalability. A new trading partner can join an Internet-based IOS by simply acquiring an Internet connection and installing the widely available, open standard TCP/IP protocols. Bandwidth is also scalable; a small company might choose a dial-up connection, but a larger firm might prefer one of the broadband options discussed in Chapter 2.

Using public bandwidth has drawbacks, however. Because no single company controls the bandwidth or even the paths followed by its packets, performance can be inconsistent. Also, although the vast number of people with Internet access can be seen as a benefit, multiple users represent a significant security risk. As you will learn in Chapter 8, the Internet can be a dangerous place.

Adv
- Inexpensive
- Highly scalable
P. 5
- inconsistent
- weak security

207

Figure 7.7 Connecting through the Internet.

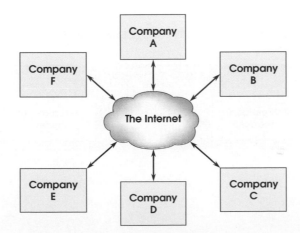

Virtual Private Networks (VPN)

A **virtual private network** (**VPN**) is a pseudoprivate network that uses public bandwidth. For example, imagine an Internet connection linking two firms. To convert that connection to a VPN, an additional layer of software is added at both ends of the connection (Figure 7.8). The VPN software encrypts each outgoing packet and encapsulates it to form a new packet. The new packet includes a header and a trailer for a special protocol understood only by the VPN software (Figure 7.9), a technique called **tunneling**. The new, publicly unrecognizable packet is delivered over the Internet using the standard Internet protocols. The combination of encryption and the special tunneling protocol creates a secure connection (a tunnel) that effectively isolates information flowing over the VPN from the rest of the Internet. At the receiving node, another set of VPN software reverses the process, stripping away the tunneling header and trailer and decrypting the packet. The IP packets then make their way through the receiving company's network as if they had been sent unsecured over the Internet.

A VPN adds effective security to the many benefits of an unsecured public connection. A VPN is less expensive, more accessible, and more scalable than a comparable VAN or a private network. However, relative to unenhanced public bandwidth, the VPN software is expensive and complex, and each trading partner or user must have compatible software. Numerous intermediaries, including many Internet service providers (ISPs), offer VPN software and services, and inexpensive VPN-enabled routers could bring secure connections to even small business enterprises.

Figure 7.8 A VPN utilizes a secure tunnel to cross the Internet.

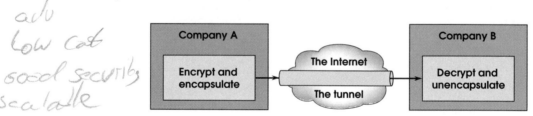

Figure 7.9 On a VPN, each outgoing packet is encapsulated to form a new packet.

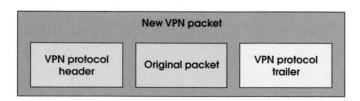

Selecting a Connectivity Option

A secure private network is appropriate for high-volume, very secure information exchanges with a limited number of trading partners, but poor scalability is a problem. A VAN offers comparable, more scalable performance for a larger number of partners at a somewhat lower cost, but with some loss of security. Both options are expensive, however. Consequently, they are used primarily by large organizations and are adopted by small companies only when forced to by a powerful supplier or customer. A **hub and spoke system** is a hybrid of the secure private network and the VAN approaches, implemented by a single powerful trading partner (the hub) that creates its own nationwide network and allows or requires buyers and suppliers (the spokes) to connect to the network.

The public bandwidth options make sense for smaller companies with fewer information exchanges. Connecting to the public infrastructure is inexpensive, but security is a significant concern. A VPN provides reasonable security over the public bandwidth, but extra software adds to the cost and somewhat degrades performance. Some companies implement a hybrid solution, connecting with their larger, high-volume trading partners through a private network or a VAN and using a VPN for smaller, lower-volume connections. Figure 7.10 summarizes several connectivity option selection criteria.

Figure 7.10 Selecting a connectivity option.

Option	Cost	Security need	Scalability	Exchange volume	Company size	Trading partners
Secure private network	****	****	*	****	****	*
Value-added network	***	***	**	***	***	**
Virtual private network	**	**	***	**	**	***
Public network	*	*	****	*	*	****

Legend	Meaning
****	High/large/many
*	Low/small/few

The first computer applications were designed to automate one or more processes within a single functional group. For example, the payroll department developed a payroll system, billing operated a billing system that was incompatible with the payroll system, and so on. The result was a set of islands of automation that emphasized local efficiency at the cost of organizational efficiency.

Each organization on the supply chain can be viewed as a collection of such islands that together form a *continent* of automation. In the real world, there are many options for connecting (or traveling between) two continents. Each continent might build a bridge to each trading partner's continent, an option analogous to leasing a secure private connection. Because only the inhabitants of the two linked continents have access, the bridges are very secure, and they can be built to handle as much traffic as necessary. Building bridges to multiple or distant continents is very expensive, however.

A second option is for a centrally located continent to build bridges to many other continents and then route traffic between them. Assuming the central continent (analogous to a VAN) charges reasonable rates and can be trusted to keep communications private, such an arrangement might provide acceptable service at a somewhat lower cost.

Commercial airlines and shipping companies offer public travel and delivery services, analogous to the Internet, to every continent that has an airport or a shipping port. Unfortunately, traveling in public is neither private nor secure, because information and cargo can be intercepted and competitors can identify the communicating continents. Like commercial transportation services, private aircraft, boats, or (even better) submarines utilize the air and the water, but in a much more private and less obvious way. Like a VPN, private boats and aircraft are more expensive than relying on commercial travel, but much cheaper than building bridges.

Early Systems for Supply Chain Integration

The first interorganizational systems were built decades ago, well before VANs and high-speed public bandwidth were available. Such systems set the stage for today's e-commerce applications.

Sabre

In the 1960s, American Airlines developed the Sabre system to provide online, real-time reservation services to their ticket agents and independent travel agents. Because Sabre gave American Airlines what some considered an unfair competitive advantage, the system was modified to incorporate all major airlines, creating a general-purpose system that is still in use today. The current version of Sabre even supports some reservations made over the World Wide Web.

The success of Sabre encouraged other early B2B applications. For example, Baxter Healthcare built a system to allow hospitals to electronically order supplies directly from Baxter. To encourage hospitals to participate, Baxter even provided the necessary hardware, software, connectivity, and support. The system greatly reduced cycle times and transaction costs. Customers loved it, fueling tremendous growth in the period following implementation.

More recently, Wal-Mart played the first major move role by implementing an inventory management system controlled by information gathered through its point-of-sale registers. Subsequently, Wal-Mart used the information to integrate its supply chain by automatically placing orders with its suppliers. Such point-of-sale systems are now commonplace in retail stores.

Electronic Data Interchange (EDI)

Simply establishing a connection is not enough to build an interorganizational system, because such application problems as data incompatibility must also be addressed. Imagine that Wal-Mart wants to integrate its purchasing process with the order entry processes of all its suppliers. Wal-Mart can accomplish that objective in two ways: by translating its orders into each supplier's order entry format or by requiring each supplier to accept orders in Wal-Mart's format. The first option puts the responsibility for format translation on Wal-Mart. The second option shifts the burden to the suppliers. Wal-Mart is big enough to dictate standards, but suppliers such as Frito-Lay and Procter & Gamble are also big enough to dictate their own standards; imagine trying to negotiate an agreement among those three companies. **Electronic data interchange** (**EDI**), the electronic transmission of business documents directly between trading partners' computers using a standard format, offered a solution.

EDI standards such as ANSI X.12 (the US standard) and EDIFACT (the international standard) define a set of rules, called a syntax, for exchanging the information recorded on certain types of business documents. Adopting a standard EDI document format means that a group of trading partners can implement an interorganizational system by having each participant write two translation routines for each document type, EDI-to-internal and internal-to-EDI (Figure 7.11). Such systems are highly scalable, with each participating company needing only two translation routines for each document type, no matter how many organizations are involved.

To implement an EDI-based interorganizational system, the participating trading partners must first agree on the information to be exchanged, the EDI standard templates to be used, the timing of the information exchanges, and the interconnectivity rules. Each of the trading partners must then implement the appropriate EDI software. Numerous intermediaries provide commercial EDI mapping and translation software.

Figure 7.11 Electronic data interchange (EDI).

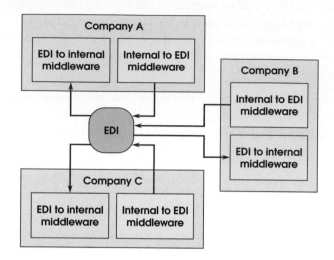

Web-Based Interorganizational Systems

Early interorganizational systems relied on such interconnectivity options as private networks or VANs, making such solutions prohibitively expensive for most companies. Today, however, the Internet and the World Wide Web support numerous options for interorganizational informational exchanges, and using the public communication infrastructure is significantly less expensive than using a private network or a VAN. Additional cost savings result from the widespread availability of Web-compatible hardware and software and of personnel trained to use and program Web-based applications. This section overviews several examples of Web-based interorganizational systems.

Web-Based EDI

EDI standards are often used to exchange business documents over the Internet. Because of the unsecured nature of the public infrastructure, however, Web-based EDI applications require an additional layer of software to encrypt the document, utilize special protocols, or both. Encryption is the subject of Chapter 9.

Extranets

In an effort to expand, optimize, and secure interorganizational information flow, many companies have opened their corporate intranets to selected trading partners and customers by creating an extended intranet, or **extranet** (Figure 7.12), a wide area network (WAN) that typically links two or more intranets. An extranet is built on the standard Internet architecture, including TCP/IP, the client/server model, Web servers, and

Records Retention

B2B e-commerce has significant implications for a company's records retention policy. Securities and Exchange Commission (SEC) requirements and various best management practices determine how long certain types of records must be archived. When the specified time has passed, the records are shredded, burned, or both.

What happens, however, when electronic copies of certain records are left behind? Given the ease of replicating electronic documents, how is it possible to track down every instance of a particular record? The answers to those questions have significant legal and ethical implications. Consider, for example, the video tapes, audio tapes, memos, and other smoking guns that have come back to haunt Enron's executives, former President Nixon, and numerous other alleged wrongdoers, and imagine how much more difficult it is to dispose of the shared, inter-corporate electronic messages that drive e-commerce.

browsers. Think of an extranet as a mini-Internet with access limited to the employees of a given company, its trading partners, and its customers. Many organizations outsource responsibility for building, implementing, hosting, and managing their extranets to intermediaries.

Figure 7.12 An extranet.

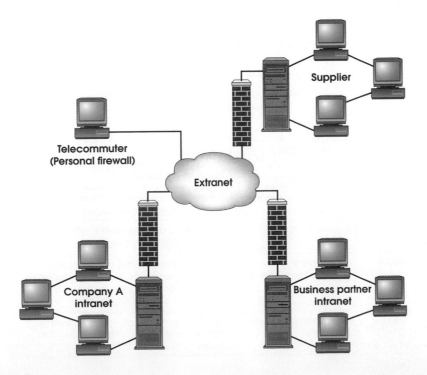

technolgies driving B2B zoday

- XML
- veb services
- shared
  role, processes + portals
- E-marketplaces
- ERP
- CRM
- Enterprise
Application
Integration
(EAI)

Allowing nonemployees to access a company's intranet, even over an extranet, creates significant security exposures. Consequently, most extranets restrict their company's trading partners to a small subset of the intranet by implementing security procedures to authenticate outside users and control the information they can access. Because interconnectivity is often accomplished over public bandwidth, companies utilize firewalls, encryption, and other security techniques covered in Chapter 9 to support exchanging sensitive information.

Extranets offer benefits comparable to intranets (see Chapter 6). They make relatively static information, such as product specifications, training guides, and corporate contacts, more current and more widely available, and they enable thin client Web information systems. For example, by using an extranet, the early interorganizational system that Baxter Healthcare offered to hospitals might have been delivered at a fraction of the cost of the original system. Baxter would not have had to provide customers with proprietary hardware and software, because most modern hospitals have systems capable of accessing the Internet. Additionally, the bulk of the information and business logic could be implemented and maintained on Baxter's Web server, eliminating the cost of maintaining client-side code on all the machines in all the participating hospitals.

Extensible Markup Language (XML)

Over the years, numerous extensions to HTML (Figure 7.13) have been proposed and implemented by the World Wide Web Consortium (W3C), an international organization of companies charged with developing open standards for HTTP and HTML. Of particular interest is **extensible markup language** (**XML**), an extension that enables

Figure 7.13 Some extensions to HTML.

Acronym	Name	Function
CSS	Cascading style sheets	An HTML specification for attaching style sheets that define page layout details.
DHTML	Dynamic HTML	A set of HTML extensions that allow a Web page to respond to user input without involving the server.
VRML	Virtual reality modeling language	A language for creating three-dimensional, interactive graphical images.
XML	Extensible markup language	A proposed replacement for HTML that supports customized tags.
XHTML	Extensible hypertext markup language	A cross between HTML and XML. An XHTML page can be readily displayed on such Web access devices as handheld computers and digital phones.
XSL	Extensible stylesheet language	A language for creating style sheets. A style sheet is a template for laying out a page.

data sharing by providing a formal standard for dynamically defining, validating, interpreting, representing, and transmitting content between applications (spreadsheets, databases, Java applets, Web applications, and so on) and between organizations. Because XML files are text files, applications written in XML are relatively easy to debug using such readily available tools as a word processor or a text editor.

Standard HTML consists of text and tags that tell a browser how to display the contents of a Web page, but an HTML document carries no information about the data. Like HTML, XML is a markup language. However, XML allows an industry or an enterprise to extend the standard by defining special tags to delimit specific data fields (a supplier name, a telephone number, an e-mail address) and to associate such attributes as data structure, syntax, and data typing with those fields. Given the XML tags and associated metadata (the data about the data), a middleware routine can then extract the data values from an XML document and store them in a database, or obtain data values from a database and represent them in XML document form.

For example, Figure 7.14 shows a set of XML tags that describe the data structure of a customer order. The first tag, *<?xml version="2.0"?>*, tells the browser that XML tags follow. The *<order>* tag marks the beginning of a data structure named *order*; look for the matching delimiter, the *</order>* tag, near the bottom of Figure 7.14. The next set of tags reads

```
<salesperson>John Doe</salesperson>.
```

It assigns a value (*John Doe*) to a field named *salesperson*. If you have ever written a computer program, you should recognize the generic data structure to the right of the XML code in Figure 7.14; simply match the field names to the XML tags.

Figure 7.14 The XML code for a set of customer order data.

XML Tags	Equivalent Data Structure
`<?xml version="2.0"?>`	Order
`<order>`	Salesperson
`<salesperson>John Doe</salesperson>`	Item
`<item>Acme rocket engine</item>`	Quantity
`<quantity>4</quantity/>`	Date
`<date>`	Month
`<month>12</month>`	Day
`<day>13</day>`	Year
`<year>2002</year>`	Customer
`</date>`	
`<customer>Harry Potter</customer>`	
`</order>`	

Figure 7.14 shows the *date* fields spread over three lines. An alternative is to nest the XML tags; for example:

```
<date><month>12</month><day>25</day><year>2002</year></date>
```

This version breaks a *date* structure into three fields: *month, day,* and *year.* Figure 7.15 shows another example of an XML-encoded order; note that the *date* is coded as a single field in this data structure. In XML, the meaning of a given tag is defined by the participating organizations, not by an international standards group.

Extensibility is another significant XML advantage. (It is, after all, the *extensible* markup language.) Once they were defined, earlier extensions to HTML were fixed, but it is possible to add new XML schemata to the base markup language to define data structure, content, and semantics appropriate for specific applications and to register those schemata with the W3C so they can be shared. To create an XML-based interorganizational schema, the participating organizations must simply agree on a common set of XML tags defined in a registered schema.

For example, the extensible business reporting language (XBRL) is designed for financial reporting, and XBRL GL is an implementation of XBRL for general ledgers. Other registered schemata include ACORD (insurance), FIX (financial information

Figure 7.15 Another XML example.

XML Tags	Equivalent Data Structure

```<?xml version="2.0"?><order> <date>12/13/2002</date> <customer>Acme Company</customer> <item> <part-number>T3214B</part-number> <description>Mounting bracket</description> <quantity>12</quantity> </item></order>```	Order
	    Date
	    Customer
	    Item
	        Part number
	        Description
	        Quantity

exchange), FIXML (FIX for security transactions), GML (geography markup language), LOGML (log markup language), and XGMML (extensible graph markup and modeling language). Additionally, consortiums such as Covisint (automobiles) and RosettaNet (electronics) are defining new industry-specific schemata.

Extracting data values from an HTML or EDI document is a tedious process. XML, in contrast, resembles a programming language that supports referencing data fields by name, effectively defining a programmer-friendly platform or infrastructure for creating Web applications. Many experts believe that XML will eventually replace EDI as the preferred solution for bridging trading partners' application and data inconsistencies, but EDI is still widely used. The next few years should determine whether EDI and XML will coexist or one of those standards will come to dominate.

TECHNOLOGY

J2EE and .NET

J2EE, the Java 2 Enterprise Edition platform, is an open standard developed by Sun Microsystems, IBM, and others to support server-side enterprise application development. Java, J2EE's native language, is a standard, widely accepted, platform-independent programming language, which makes J2EE available to everyone.

In contrast, .NET, Microsoft's enterprise application development platform, is a family of Microsoft products, not a standard, although those products are integrated by XML, which is a standard. The .NET strategy appears in Microsoft system software products such as Application Server 2000 (load balancing), Internet Security and Acceleration (firewalls, Web caching), Active Directory Server (directory services), and Host Integration Server (legacy system access). Several programming tools are supported, including Active Server Pages (ASP), C#, Visual Basic, Visual C, Visual C++, and Visual FoxPro. Microsoft's Visual Studio brings together multiple software development tools to create an integrated developer environment. The .NET strategy even extends to Microsoft's end-user software, with XML compatibility built into such well-known Office applications as Access, Excel, and Word.

At present, J2EE is an established standard, while .NET is still evolving. Driven in part by Microsoft's dominant market position, however, .NET is winning converts and promises to play a major role in future e-commerce application development. Will both J2EE and .NET survive, or will one win the lion's share of the enterprise application development business? Time will tell.

B2B E-Commerce Software and Services

Numerous intermediary service providers have arisen to support supply chain integration, offering solutions and services comparable to the intra-business enterprise systems and enterprise application integration efforts discussed in the previous chapter. Some intermediaries specialize in such supply chain activities as purchasing or logistics. Others take a much broader approach. The involvement of an intermediary is not always obvious; sometimes a service provided on one site is actually fulfilled on a different, intermediary site. Note that many B2B e-commerce services are implemented as three-tier client/server applications, as discussed in Chapter 6.

E-Procurement

Most organizations purchase raw materials, components, and subassemblies from their suppliers, add value by performing a series of processes, and then pass the resulting products on to other companies further down the supply chain. Individual transactions range from simple commodity exchanges to deeply entrenched, carefully negotiated, long-term buyer/seller relationships. A purchase might be highly customized, off the shelf, or something in-between. A supplier might offer different products, prices, and financing terms to different customers. Internally, most organizations have complex purchasing processes that identify authorized negotiators, assign responsibilities, place limits on how much a given purchasing agent can spend, spell out the approval process, and so on. In other words, procurement is complex.

E-procurement applications and services, often supplied by application service providers, e-marketplaces, and similar intermediaries, facilitate the exchange of information between trading partners by integrating the buyer's purchasing process with the seller's order entry process. With a **buy-side** solution, the e-procurement application on the buyer's system controls both access (who can place orders) and the approval process, perhaps limiting purchases to preapproved supplier products at previously negotiated rates. The supplier provides the product and pricing information, perhaps in the form of a customized electronic catalog that resides on the buyer's or the supplier's system. **Sell-side** solutions, in contrast, allow trading partners to connect and place orders directly on the supplier's system, a process analogous to Web-based business-to-consumer (B2C) e-commerce. Sell-side solutions are often implemented as extranets with controlled access to electronic catalogs customized for the buying organization. Note that both buy-side and sell-side e-procurement applications call for exchanging information electronically.

Electronic Invoice Presentment and Payment (EIPP)

Based on the Internet bill presentment and payment (IBPP) systems introduced in Chapter 5, **electronic invoice presentment and payment** (**EIPP**) is a rapidly developing service that supports B2B e-commerce. EIPP coordinates the electronic exchange of invoices and payments (often in the form of electronic funds transfers) between trading partners. Similar to the standard IBPP models, invoices can be sent directly from the billing enterprise to the customer (the direct model), or the billing company can outsource all phases of the process to an intermediary (the consolidation model). Financial institutions provide EFT services, and sometimes serve as EIPP service consolidators.

EIPP solutions contribute directly to the bottom line by reducing bill generation costs and by reducing billing cycle float, thus enhancing cash flow. Because of their cost, legacy EDI-based electronic payment systems were limited to large trading partners, but EIPP is Web-based and thus accessible to smaller customers. Customer access to a user-friendly, convenient EIPP system supports a company's customer relationship management (CRM) efforts as well, providing payment history details on demand, serving as a forum for disputes and questions, and supporting personalized relationship-marketing efforts. Some companies and financial institutions have converted their EIPP services into revenue sources by hosting other companies' invoice presentment and payment systems.

Logistics Integrators

According to the Council of Logistics Management, **logistics**, a key supply chain element, is "the process of planning, implementing, and controlling the efficient, effective flow and storage of goods, services, and related information from point of origin to point of consumption for the purpose of conforming to customer requirements." Modern business relationships are increasingly based on just-in-time inventory, production, and shipping, giving a significant competitive advantage to firms that can deliver products exactly when and where they are needed. Logistics integrators provide software and services to support such activities. For example, United Parcel Service and Federal Express allow their customers to schedule and track deliveries electronically, and other logistics integrators, such as Logistics.com, offer solutions for integrating both manufacturing firms and shipping companies.

Customer Relationship Management (CRM)

Whether the customer is a retail consumer or another company, demand-based business models significantly increase the value of good customer relationships. **Customer relationship management** (**CRM**) relies on data analysis and supply chain integration software to increase customer satisfaction and loyalty.

Many CRM applications are designed to gather information about interactions with past, current, and potential customers and to concentrate that information in a central repository, such as a data warehouse. Decision support systems and such tools as data mining are employed to analyze the data in an effort to extract ideas, trends, customer likes and dislikes, and similar information that might prove useful.

CRM overlaps with other forms of supply chain integration, such as e-procurement and logistics. Dynamic, customized customer catalogs based on information about past purchases help to improve the selling process, and that same information can be used to personalize after-sales service. Also, access to logistics information provides the real-time order tracking information desired by some customers.

Supply Chain Management

According to Stanford professor Warren Hausman, "Competition is not really company versus company but supply chain versus supply chain."[1] The objective of **supply chain management** (**SCM**) is to manage effectively the flow of products, information, and finances between multiple trading partners, delivering the right product at the right time in the right amount to the right place in the supply chain. Key goals include reducing time to market, costs, and inventory without compromising quality. Accomplishing those goals requires making relevant, timely, accurate supply and demand information available to every upstream and downstream supply chain participant at high speed and low cost.

Supply chain management implies more than simply interfacing between related applications in multiple organizations, however. Making supply and demand information accessible across the supply chain means that each participating organization's internal data must be visible to its suppliers and its customers. Maximizing the efficiency of the entire supply chain requires a high level of cooperation and collaboration among the trading partners who, in effect, create a virtual organization of organizations. The payoff is a competitive advantage shared by all the participants.

Supply chain management begins with software-aided planning. Sales information is captured in real time and used to generate a customer demand forecast. That forecast, in turn, drives such activities as purchasing supplies, components, and raw materials; factory or production scheduling; order tracking; market research; and product design. As those activities take place, more real-time data is captured and used to fine-tune the forecast. Figure 7.16 identifies several supply chain management intermediaries and their products.

B2B E-Marketplaces

An **e-marketplace** is a type of intermediary that offers supply chain integration services by providing a Web site and a set of applications that allow many organizations to exchange information, goods, and services in one place using a common technology platform. E-marketplaces are analogous to enterprise portals and consumer-based Web portals such as Yahoo. An e-marketplace generates revenue by charging subscription fees, listing fees, and transaction fees and by selling services to integrate a customer's internal systems with the e-marketplace.

Most e-marketplaces fall into one of three categories. As the name implies, a commodity e-marketplace deals in commodities, including financial instruments such as futures contracts. A business service e-marketplace performs financial services and supports such processes as logistics, e-procurement, order fulfillment, and MRO (maintenance, repair, and operation) procurement. An integration services e-marketplace specializes in facilitating process-to-process integration. Within the context of its category, a vertical or industry portal, such as Covisint, provides support for a particular

---

[1] Mount, Ian and Caulfield, Brian. May 2001. "The Missing Link. What You Need to Know About Supply Chain Technology." *Business* 2.0: 82–88.

Figure 7.16 Supply chain management intermediaries.

Category	Supplier	Product
Planning and forecasting	I2 Technologies Manugistics SAP	TradeMatrix NetWorks APO
Purchasing	Ariba Commerce One Oracle RightWorks	Ariba Sourcing MarketSet Supply Chain Exchange eProcurement
Factory scheduling	Baan Oracle QAD SAP	Baan SCS Discrete Manufacturing Supply Chain Optimizer APO
Order tracking	EXE Technologies Manhattan Associates Optum	eFulfillment MA Fulfill TradeStream
Market research and product design	Agile Software MatrixOne PTC SAP	Agile Anywhere eMatrix Windchill MySAP PLM

Source: Thompson Financial and E Business 2.0, May 2001, page 85.

industry (the automobile industry), and horizontal e-marketplaces such as FreeMarkets offer services for companies in numerous industries.

In addition to aggregating trading partners, e-marketplaces offer services to support interaction among those trading partners, both real and potential. Collaboration software makes supply and demand information visible, which supports CRM and facilitates planning, forecasting, inventory control, and even joint product design. Product catalog and Web information system services, traditional auctions, and reverse auctions are other common features.

The dmoz Open Directory Project (*http://dmoz.org*), an international effort to create a definitive catalog of the Web (Figure 7.17), lists many, many e-marketplaces. The survival of all of those marketplaces is unlikely, and some experts anticipate a dot-com-like shakeout in the near future. Perhaps, as is so often the case, a few highly successful giants will dominate the e-marketplace playing field, with numerous niche specialists filling in the gaps.

Figure 7.17 The Open Directory Project's e-marketplaces screen.

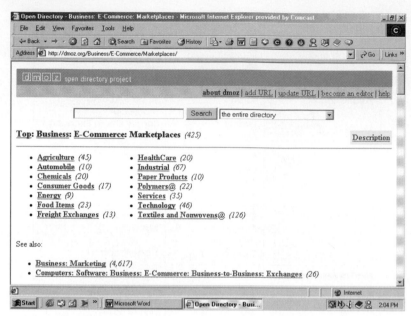

Source: The Open Directory Project, *http://dmoz.org.*

Enterprise Resource Planning (ERP)

Enterprise resource planning (ERP) was introduced in Chapter 6. It is mentioned here because the principles embodied in ERP are every bit as essential to B2B e-commerce as they are to intra-business e-commerce. In fact, the intra-business and B2B categories share at least as many similarities as differences, which, given the relationship between a company's value chain and its supply chain, should not be surprising.

Cisco's $2.2 Billion Inventory Write-Off

Cisco Systems, Inc. is the world's best-known supplier of routers, switches, and similar e-commerce infrastructure hardware. You may be surprised, however, to learn that the company subcontracts production responsibility for virtually all of its products to a handful of manufacturing firms. Cisco focuses on marketing and product development and relies on a highly respected supply chain integration system to ship routers and switches on demand directly from the manufacturer to the customer. The system seemed to work perfectly until May 2001, when Cisco announced a one-time $2.2 billion inventory write-off, an expense that significantly affected the company's financial statements and stock price. According to a March 2002 *Business 2.0* article, a primary cause of Cisco's inventory glut was a failure of that very same supply chain integration system.[2]

Apparently, the problem started when Cisco's customers, anticipating high demand and possible shortages, placed duplicate orders for routers and switches with both Cisco and Cisco's competitors with the intent of buying from the supplier offering the earliest delivery date and canceling the other orders. Unaware of the duplicate orders, Cisco's supply chain integration system generated what turned out to be an overly optimistic demand forecast.

Cisco's manufacturing partners, fearing shortages, reacted to that forecast by placing duplicate orders for components and subassemblies with their subtier suppliers. Because those subtier suppliers were unable to see Cisco's initial forecast, they had no knowledge of the duplicate orders and thus developed plans to manufacture components to meet what they thought was the real demand. The result was to take an already optimistic forecast and further inflate it. When the recession hit, Cisco was left holding roughly three times as many routers and switches as its customers were willing to buy.

Cisco's supply chain failure is an excellent illustration of an old principle: garbage in, garbage out. Supply chain integration starts with an accurate forecast of likely demand, and if that forecast is flawed, subsequent computations and decisions will almost certainly compound the initial error. Rather than rejecting e-commerce, however, Cisco responded by improving its supply chain integration system by implementing eHub, a new exchange that makes relevant information visible to supply chain participants at all levels. Run by Viacore, a supply chain intermediary, eHub promises to dampen future bidding wars before they start.

---

2 Kaihla, Paul. March 2002. "Inside Cisco's $2 Billion Blunder." *Business 2.0*: 88–90.

Summary

B2B e-commerce is concerned with intercorporate communication, relying on innovative applications of information technology to exchange business information electronically across the supply chain. An interorganizational system is an information system shared by two or more firms. Because the open standards and protocols associated with the Internet and the World Wide Web promote platform independence, interorganizational data communication has increasingly moved to the public infrastructure.

Some large organizations use a private leased network to implement an interorganizational system. A VAN is a semiprivate network operated by a trusted intermediary. The public Internet offers a third option. A VPN uses the Internet but adds security by creating a secure connection called a tunnel. A hub and spoke system is a hybrid, borrowing features from the secure private network and VAN approaches.

The Sabre air reservation service was one of the first successful interorganizational systems. EDI was an early solution to incompatibility problems but was prohibitively expensive for most companies. EDI standards are still used to exchange business documents over the Internet, however. In an effort to expand the flow of interorganizational information, many companies have opened their corporate intranets to outsiders by creating an extranet. XML, an extension to HTML that offers a new option for sharing information both inside and outside a company, is growing in popularity. A key advantage of XML is its extensibility.

Numerous intermediary service providers have arisen to support supply chain integration. E-procurement applications and services facilitate the exchange of information between trading partners by integrating the buyer's purchasing process with the seller's order entry process. EIPP services support exchanging invoices and payments. Logistics is concerned with planning, implementing, and controlling the flow of goods, services, and information through the supply chain. CRM focuses on improving customer satisfaction and loyalty. The objective of supply chain management is to deliver the right product at the right time in the right amount to the right place in the supply chain. An e-marketplace offers supply chain integration services by providing a Web site and a set of applications that allow organizations to exchange information, goods, and services in one place using a common technology platform.

Key Words

buy-side

customer relationship management (CRM)

electronic data interchange (EDI)

electronic invoice presentment and payment (EIPP)

e-marketplace

e-procurement

extensible markup language (XML)

extranet

hub and spoke system

interconnectivity

interorganizational system (IOS)

logistics

private leased network

scalability

sell-side

supply chain

supply chain management (SCM)

tunneling

value-added network (VAN)

virtual private network (VPN)

XML (extensible markup language)

Review Questions

1. Discuss the relationship between B2B e-commerce and supply chain integration.

2. What is an interorganizational system? Why are interorganizational systems so difficult to create?

3. What is a private leased network? Cite several advantages and disadvantages associated with a private leased network.

4. What is a value-added network? Cite several advantages and disadvantages associated with a value-added network.

5. What is a virtual private network? Cite several advantages and disadvantages associated with a virtual private network.

6. Explain why electronic data interchange (or something like it) was necessary.

7. Define and explain the purpose of an extranet.

8. What is tunneling? Why is tunneling used?

9. What is XML? Discuss the advantages of XML over traditional HTML and EDI.

10. Distinguish between buy-side and sell-side e-procurement.

11. Discuss the functions performed by electronic invoice presentment and payment (EIPP) services.

12. Discuss the functions performed by a logistics integrator.

13. Discuss the functions performed by a customer relationship management (CRM) system.

14. Discuss the functions performed by a supply chain management system.

15. What is the purpose of an e-marketplace? Describe several varieties of e-marketplaces.

Exercises

1. A chapter sidebar discussed an intercorporate collaboration aimed at reducing deadheading. Explain how the system worked. Identify other examples of B2B processes and discuss how efficiency improvements made possible by collaboration and information sharing can generate a competitive advantage for all the participating companies.

2. Although B2B is by far the largest e-commerce category, B2C is more widely known. Why?

3. Explain how the design of Cisco's supply chain management system contributed to the company's recent inventory glut and $2.2 billion inventory write-off.

4. In your opinion, do B2B applications violate the federal government's antitrust laws? Explain your answer.

▪▪ Projects

Current references and supporting resources can be found at this textbook's companion Web site.

Broad-Based Projects

1. There have been many examples of apparently destroyed electronic documents and e-mail messages coming back to haunt their originators. Do some research and find several examples. Then write a short paper discussing how electronic communication affects records retention.

2. To gain a better sense of how difficult it really is to delete information from your computer, send a test e-mail message to yourself. When it arrives in your inbox, delete it. Then open your e-mailer's Deleted Items or Trash folder and you'll find a recoverable copy of the message you just deleted. Delete it again, and watch the message disappear. Then minimize your mail program, go back to your desktop, and double-click on the Trash icon. After a brief delay, you will see a list of recently deleted files. Find your test e-mail message, highlight it, click on the Recover button, and follow directions. Maximize your mail program, and you'll find the twice-deleted test message has reappeared in the Deleted Items folder.

3. Only if you "empty the trash" does a deleted file become unrecoverable, but not even deleting the contents of the Trash folder completely removes all traces of the file from your computer. When you delete a file, your computer's operating system deletes the link to the file from the system directory, but the file's contents remain on the disk. Only when the disk space allocated to the file is overwritten with new information does the file become truly unrecoverable, and even then a skilled data recovery expert might be able find at least traces of the file. Relate the file deletion process to a company's records retention policy.

Building the Case:

4. Working as a team, continue with Chapter 1, Project 6 by carefully reviewing your Web site's supply chain links and make sure they support your strategy. Make changes to your strategy, your implementation plan, and your Web site as necessary.

Business Projects

1. Research Cisco's $2.2 billion inventory write-off and write a paper explaining exactly what happened.

Building the Case:

2. Continue with Chapter 1, Project 2 by creating a flow diagram to document your client's supply chain. Identify upstream and downstream links that might be improved by implementing an extranet. Investigate options for outsourcing the design, development, and operation of an appropriate extranet and obtain cost estimates. Write a brief report to document your results and add it to the completed flow diagram.

Information Technology Projects

1. Write a paper comparing the J2EE standard to Microsoft's .NET strategy.

Building the Case:

2. Continue with Chapter 1, Project 2 by rethinking your prototype to reflect the contents of Chapter 7. For example, add elements to allow authorized employees of your client's business partners to access the restricted subset of pages available on the company's extranet. Be sure to include appropriate security features such as password protection and an independent server. Depending on your background, available time, and your instructor's preference, you might simply identify the need, create static pages to prototype your solution, or actually implement the appropriate access control features on your Web site.

Marketing Projects

Building the Case:

1. Continue with Chapter 1, Project 2 by creating flow diagrams to document your client's supply chain and extranet. Explain when and how you will communicate with external entities over the extranet. Write a brief report to document your results, and add information describing extranet communication to the storyboard you started in Chapter 5.

References

Web Sites

Source	URL	Comments
The Open Directory Project	*www.dmoz.org*	The Open Directory Project home page. The definitive directory of the Web.
W3C	*www.w3.org/TR/xmlschema-0/*	XML Schema Part 0: Primer.
Web Developer's Virtual Library	*www.wdvl.com/Authoring*	Introductions to a variety of Web development tools, including Flash, HTML, Java, JavaScript, and XML.

Print and White Papers

iPlanet, A Sun|Netscape Alliance. 2000. "Internet Bill Presentment and Payment, a Business White Paper." *www.iplanet.com*.

Kaihla, Paul. March 2002. "Inside Cisco's $2 Billion Blunder." *Business 2.0*: 88–90.

Mount, Ian and Caulfield, Brian. May 2001. "The Missing Link. What You Need to Know About Supply Chain Technology." *Business 2.0*: 82–88.

PART 4
Growing Pains

The Internet and the World Wide Web were not designed with business in mind. As a result, layering an e-commerce application on top of the infrastructure defined by the Internet and the World Wide Web is a bit like building a rectangular house on an oval foundation. A casual inspection might suggest a good fit, but a closer look reveals the inevitable incompatibilities, cracks, overhangs, and patches.

Chapter 8 focuses on cybercrime, cyberterrorism, and cyberwarfare, three topics that have become significantly more relevant since September 11, 2001. To some, the ultimate solution to e-commerce's growing pains is effective security, the subject of Chapter 9. As you will discover, however, implementing effective security involves numerous trade-offs that widen one set of vulnerabilities as they narrow another. Chapter 10 explores such issues as privacy, identity theft, and online fraud. These less technical issues are particularly important because they contribute to the fear, uncertainty, and doubt that shape the popular perception of cyberspace as a dangerous place.

CHAPTER 8
Cybercrime, Cyberterrorism, and Cyberwarfare

When you finish reading this chapter, you should be able to:

- Define cybercrime and distinguish among hackers, crackers, phreakers, and script kiddies

- Explain several techniques a hacker might use to obtain a password

- Explain how a packet sniffer works

- Identify several hacker software tools, including time bombs, logic bombs, rabbits, Trojan horses, backdoors, viruses, and worms

- Describe several techniques a hacker might use to identify a vulnerable system

- Distinguish between a denial of service attack and a distributed denial of service attack

- Explain DNS spoofing, IP spoofing, and smurf attacks

- Distinguish among information warfare, cyberwarfare, and cyberterrorism

- Explain why the Internet is an attractive cyberwarfare and cyberterrorism target

The Internet Worm

At approximately 6:00 p.m. on Wednesday, November 2, 1988, Robert Tappan Morris, Jr., a 23-year-old Cornell University graduate student, released an experimental Internet worm that exploited some well-known flaws in the UNIX operating system. The worm was designed to spread slowly across the Internet by e-mail. However, a programming error caused the rogue program to proliferate uncontrollably, infecting about 10 percent of the fledgling Internet in a matter of hours and effectively shutting down the network for three days.

Fortunately, the Internet worm, also known as the Morris worm, was relatively benign. It did no tangible damage beyond stealing machine cycles and wasting the time of thousands of system operators and computer scientists who, for the most part, enjoyed the challenge. In 1988, the Internet linked roughly 60,000 hosts, and the worm disabled about 6,000 of them. Today's Internet links more than 100 million hosts, and a comparable rogue worm might shut down 10 million. Imagine the chaos if that ever happened.

Morris, ironically the son of a National Security Agency (NSA) computer security expert, paid a price for his experiment gone wrong. He was the first person tried for violating the Computer Fraud and Abuse Act of 1986, and following his conviction he was ordered to pay a $10,000 fine, perform 400 hours of community service, and serve three years probation. His name lives on because his worm clearly and unambiguously demonstrated the Internet's vulnerability to external attack and presaged today's cybercrime, cyberterrorism, and cyberwarfare.

Cybercrime

Academics and researchers created the Internet and the World Wide Web to support research. One key research principle, free and open access to information, is integral to the Internet's underlying design. To a researcher, the Internet's users are implicitly assumed to be honest and trustworthy, withholding or hoarding information is almost sinful, and secrecy and security are viewed as immoral because they disrupt the free flow of information.

The idea that information should be free and accessible to all is a wonderful principle, unless you happen to run a business. How is it possible to establish and maintain a competitive advantage without secrecy? And how can a business organization guarantee the integrity of essential operating and financial data if anyone can access and (potentially) modify that data?

Such questions would be irrelevant if all the Internet's users really were honest and trustworthy. Unfortunately, some aren't. **Cybercrime** is a general term for illegal or unethical activities performed in **cyberspace**, the nonphysical space created by networked computers that contains such digital objects as files, messages, and so on.

Sometimes a computer is the target of cybercrime; sometimes a computer is a tool. The perpetrators are called hackers, crackers, phreakers, script kiddies, and a variety of other names, not all printable.

Hackers, Crackers, Phreakers, and Script Kiddies

Back in the 1970s, to be called a **hacker** was a compliment. In those days, a hacker was an expert programmer with a knack for quickly creating elegant solutions to difficult problems. Today, however, the term is more commonly applied to someone who breaks into computer systems.

True hackers (in the expert programmer sense) resent that characterization. They divide themselves into white-hat and black-hat categories. The **white-hat hackers** follow an unwritten code of ethics. They believe that a hacker should cause no harm and should not profit financially from her hacking activities. They believe that software and data are intellectual property that should be shared. Secrecy is the ultimate sin because it retards intellectual growth and forces people to rediscover what is already known. To a hacker, any activity that liberates information is good, almost by definition.

Consistent with that philosophy, white-hat hackers willingly share their knowledge. Both hackers and security personnel attend Def Con, a hackers' convention held annually in Las Vegas, and hackers frequently post information on numerous Web sites and newsgroups. For example, Figure 8.1 shows a recent list of postings on a chat room–like hacker newsgroup forum, and Figure 8.2 shows the contents of a typical posting, which could have come from a hacker or a system administrator.

White-hat hackers tend to be anticorporation, antigovernment, anticopyright, and antipatent, positions consistent with their philosophy, but they do not intentionally cause harm. In fact, many white-hat hackers argue that they perform a valuable public service by exposing and publicizing security flaws in the systems they attack. Although the practice seems inconsistent with the "do not profit financially" principle, it is not

Figure 8.1 A list of postings on a hacker newsgroup.

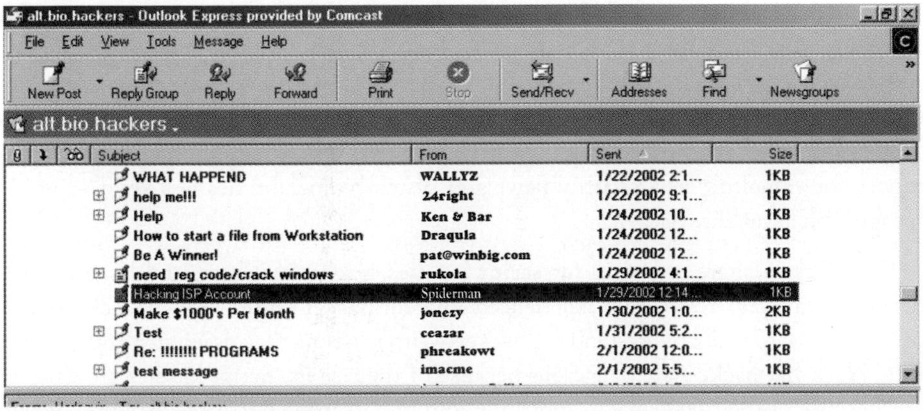

Source: *alt.bio.hackers* newsgroup

Figure 8.2 A typical posting.

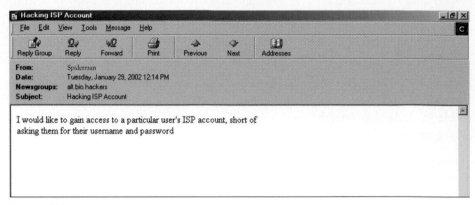

Source: *alt.bio.hackers* newsgroup

uncommon for an elite white-hat hacker to be hired by a corporate data center as a security consultant. A hacker (good or bad) for hire is called a **samurai**.

Black-hat or **dark-side hackers**, on the other hand, break into computers with malicious intent; they are the Internet's cyberterrorists, industrial espionage agents, freelance spies, and troublemakers. Some white-hat hackers view the black-hats as a bit immature because they have not yet outgrown the need to break security just to prove they can. (White-hat hackers sometimes break security, too, but only for what they consider benign reasons.) To distinguish themselves from their somewhat unsavory contemporaries, the white-hats sometimes call the black-hats crackers. The term *cracker* is also applied to a person who cracks (or breaks) codes, however, and code crackers sometimes use a password cracker program, which suggests that computers are hacked and codes are cracked. As activities approach the edge of legality, definitions sometimes lose precision.

Elite hackers, both white-hat and black-hat, possess significant technical skills that allow them to hack undetected in the background, and most are expert programmers. Their most important attribute is probably persistence, however; the good ones stay with a problem until they solve it, no matter how long it takes. They often write routines or scripts to support their **exploits** (software vulnerabilities they have identified and successfully attacked) and publish them on both public and password-protected Web sites (Figure 8.3), an activity called trophy gathering. In fact, discovering and publicizing techniques for exploiting new security flaws and system vulnerabilities is a key to gaining recognition as an elite hacker.

True hackers share a disdain for **script kiddies**, packet monkeys, and lamerz (pronounced lame-ers), relatively inexperienced amateur hacker wanna-bes who lack the skill or knowledge to really understand the hacker-written scripts they download and execute. Elite black-hat hackers are dangerous because of their skills. Script kiddies are dangerous because of their tendency to attack random targets using borrowed exploits they do not fully understand.

Figure 8.3 Elite hackers often publish their exploits.

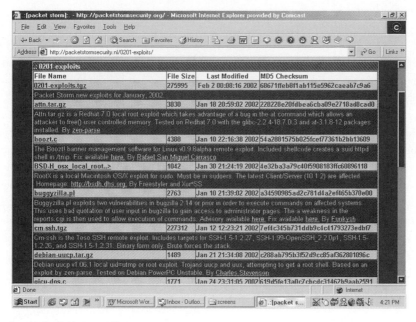

Source: *Packetstormsecurity.org*

Accessing a distant computer can be expensive, so many hackers (both white-hat and black-hat) are also phreakers. A **phreaker** (pronounced *freaker*) is a person who cracks (or breaks into) the telephone network. The objective is often to make free calls, but some phreakers go a bit further. For example, one urban legend claims that a phreaker in California won several area radio station contests by cracking the telephone network and blocking calls to the station from all telephones but his own.

Some cybercriminals (such as traditional hackers) work from outside the organization and enter a target system over the Internet. Others, ranging from disgruntled employees to undercover imposters, are insiders. In a business setting, an **insider** is a trusted employee with legitimate rights to access the organization's network and sufficient knowledge to find important or sensitive information. Often, the insider *requires* such access to do his job. Outsiders, in contrast, must sneak into the system and look around to find what they want, giving the observant system manager an opportunity to spot them. That is why inside jobs represent a greater risk.

Motivation

Why do hackers hack? The reasons vary. Some white-hat hackers feel they have a duty to expose and publicize vulnerabilities and security holes. Others simply explore cyberspace for the same reasons spelunkers explore caves—curiosity and the thrill of the challenge. Samurai hack for money. To a black-hat hacker, hacking is a source of pirated software and personal information that can be used to support identity theft, a topic to be explored in Chapter 10. Disgruntled former employees turned black-hat hackers seek

Insider Sabotage

In July 1996, Omega Engineering Corporation demoted a chief programmer named Tim Lloyd, allegedly for his inability to get along with his coworkers. The company's bread-and-butter products, electronic measurement and control instruments, were built by robots, and three weeks after Lloyd's demotion, a software time bomb detonated, erasing the mission-critical software that guided those robots. That single act of sabotage cost Omega roughly $12 million in damages, and eighty employees lost their jobs. Lloyd was convicted of computer fraud in May 2000, but his conviction was later overturned. The prosecutor appealed, however, and on February 27, 2002, Lloyd began serving a three-year sentence. While in prison, he'll have plenty of time to think about the $2 million in restitution he was ordered to pay his former employer.

Disgruntled current and former employees bent on sabotage or revenge are extremely dangerous because of what they know. Tim Lloyd was able to launch such a devastating attack because his insider position gave him access to Omega's information technology infrastructure and the knowledge to identify the programs that were most crucial to the company's survival. A motivated insider has the ability to do significantly more damage than virtually any external hacker.

revenge for real or imagined mistreatment. Hacker wanna-bes try to add to their list of exploits in an effort to gain the respect of elite hackers, and script kiddies are sometimes guilty of mindless vandalism, such as defacing a Web site. Cyberwarriors and cyberterrorists hack for a political cause, an ideal, or something they believe in passionately. The objective of an espionage agent (government, military, or industrial) might be to steal sensitive data, to destroy or modify data, or to undermine a system's integrity.

Whatever their motivation, most hackers enjoy hacking. In fact, it is not unusual for a hacker to become so focused that he slips into "hack mode," a Zen-like state of total concentration. Perhaps that is why hackers have an often-undeserved reputation for social ineptitude.

Password Theft

How do hackers gain access to an unauthorized computer? The easiest strategy is to log in or to establish a telnet connection using the ID and password of someone who has the appropriate rights. The first step is obtaining a valid user ID and password.

The hacker's most common source of passwords is carelessness. Many users fail to give their choice of passwords much thought, and obvious passwords, though easy to remember, are also easy to guess. In the lab, a hacker might watch a student (particularly an unskilled, one-finger typist) and steal a password by reading the keyboard, a technique called shoulder surfing. Often a user writes down and then throws away a password. Hackers do not hesitate to hunt through the paper trash, an activity they call **dumpster diving**, trashing, or phishing (pronounced *fishing*).

Most people implicitly believe that their office or cubicle is secure. They may be right with respect to external threats, but insiders can be far more dangerous. Some users write their password on a sticky-back note and paste it to their display screen, visible to anyone who might walk by. Many users are surprised to learn that deleting a file does not necessarily remove it from the computer. Hackers call those supposedly deleted files leftovers, and such electronic garbage is also susceptible to insider attack.

Standard patterns give the cracker another potential source of passwords. For example, at Miami University, all students are assigned a user ID derived from their name and a default password that follows another standard algorithm. Knowing the pattern, hackers find it relatively easy to guess valid user IDs and the matching passwords. The first time a student accesses the system, he is expected to change the password to something more difficult to guess, but not everyone does. Also, some students never access the university system and thus never know that someone has hijacked their password.

Password crackers, software designed to crack passwords, can be downloaded over the Internet. Some password crackers try the words or phrases in a word list or a dictionary until they find the correct password. Others rely on brute force, trying every possible combination of characters until they find a hit. The brute force approach is less efficient, but it can find passwords that are not in a dictionary. One popular password cracker named *lOphtcrack* is a hybrid that uses both techniques. Although they are best known as cracker tools, system administrators sometimes rely on password crackers to recover lost or forgotten passwords.

When you log on to most systems, your password is input to an algorithm, which encodes it and compares it to an encoded version of your password that is stored on the computer (Figure 8.4). Unless the two encoded passwords (one computed, one stored) match, you are denied access. The stored passwords are encoded for security reasons. (You will learn more about security in Chapter 9.) If a hacker gains access to a system and steals a copy of the password file (a relatively easy task, particularly for an insider), the encoded passwords are not particularly useful, because to log on to the system successfully, the *un*encoded password must be entered. A good password-cracking program can clear that hurdle, however.

Social Engineering

It is surprising how many people simply tell others their password. According to *The Jargon Dictionary*, **social engineering**, also known as **human engineering**, is a "term used among crackers and samurai for techniques that rely on weaknesses in wetware [people] rather than software,"[1] an informal definition that captures the essence of the practice.

---

[1] See *http://astrian.net/jargon/terms*.

Figure 8.4 For security reasons, passwords are stored in encoded form.

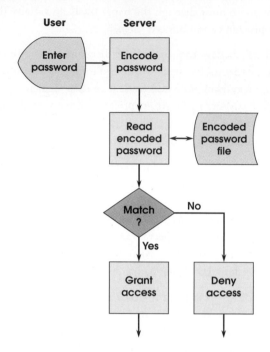

The act of convincing someone to voluntarily divulge her password by taking advantage of the target's apathy, courtesy, curiosity, good nature, greed, gullibility, or ignorance is a form of social engineering. For example, phreakers sometimes impersonate a linesman on a telephone pole and request a "forgotten" access code from a helpful operator, and hackers have been known to impersonate a traveling sales associate who can't remember his new password.

Packet Sniffers

Another way to capture passwords and other information is to use a **packet sniffer**, a software wiretap that captures and analyzes packets. A packet sniffer must have access to the physical line over which the target packets travel, but the sniffer software can be installed on any intermediate workstation, proxy server, Web server, host, router, or Internet service provider's (ISP) server. Typically, however, a sniffer is placed on the client side of the target's ISP because predicting the path a particular packet will follow once it reaches the Internet is difficult.

For example, many local area networks (LANs) rely on Ethernet technology. Ethernet is a broadcasting protocol, so every workstation connected to the LAN receives a copy of every message. Normally, each workstation is set to filter out packets with the wrong media access control (MAC) address and to accept only packets addressed to it, but there is a way to turn off the filter and reset a given workstation to promiscuous mode, allowing

Good Passwords

Your password is your first line of defense against hackers, crackers, and script kiddies, so pick a good one. A good password is easy to remember and difficult to guess. Longer is better—six to nine characters is a good target. Mix different types of characters (letters, digits, special characters) to increase the number of possibilities a cracking program must test. Give your password a challenging meaning by using an acronym formed from a phrase; for example, "my first dog's name was Spot" becomes *m1dnws*, where the second character is the digit 1. To thwart password-cracking programs, avoid dictionary words, proper nouns, and foreign words; if you can find it in a dictionary, don't use it. Incidentally, stick-

ing a digit or two at the beginning or the end of a dictionary word or substituting ph for f will not confuse a good password cracker. Stay away from personal information, too; a determined cracker can easily locate your telephone number, your mother's maiden name, your significant other's name, your pet's name, the last four digits of your social security number, and similar information. To limit the damage caused by a cracked password, avoid using the same password on multiple accounts. Finally, changing your password only takes a few minutes, so change it regularly. Quarterly is reasonable for most users, but people with access to sensitive information should change their passwords more frequently.

it to accept all the messages (Figure 8.5). A packet sniffer located on the promiscuous-mode workstation can then analyze the packets, identify the ones that contain a logon ID and password (or other targeted information), and extract the ID and password for later use.

Note that all Ethernet connections and virtually all the standard Internet protocols (including telnet, HTTP, SNMP, POP, and FTP) are vulnerable to packet sniffing. Once an intercepted packet has been analyzed and categorized based on criteria programmed

Figure 8.5 A packet sniffer.

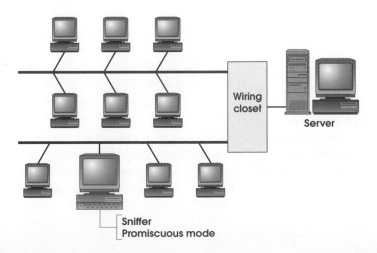

into the sniffer, the contents of the packet (a user ID and password, a portion of an e-mail message) are available to the hacker. If the packets are aggregated based on such criteria as the source IP address, a complete message can be reassembled and its contents read.

Packet sniffers are not strictly hacker tools. Network managers use them to analyze network performance, perform certain types of network fault analysis, analyze network traffic (perhaps by logging packet volume by protocol), and detect certain types of **intrusions** (attempts to break into or misuse a computer system). Management uses sniffers to monitor employees' online activities, an issue to be discussed in depth in Chapter 10. Numerous sniffing programs are commercially available, including Ethereal (UNIX), WinNT Server, BlackICE Pro, Analyzer, EtherPeek (Macintosh), and tcpdump (UNIX).

Carnivore/DCS 1000 and TEMPEST

Better known by its original name, Carnivore, the FBI's DCS 1000 (the new, more politically correct official name) is a packet sniffer designed to monitor e-mail. The acronym DCS stands for data collection system, which is an accurate description of Carnivore's purpose. The process begins with a court order authorizing a wiretap on an alleged criminal's e-mail. The criteria for screening messages are programmed into Carnivore, and the DCS is installed on the target's ISP server. All packets that flow through the server also flow through Carnivore, where messages that match the filtering criteria are stored for later analysis. Because packet flow is not disrupted in any way, the Carnivore wiretap is completely transparent to the ISP's customers.

TEMPEST (Transient Electromagnetic Pulse Standard) is an acronym for technology designed to intercept the van Eck radiation generated by virtually all electronic devices, including processors, monitors, keyboards, and communication lines. Given the right equipment (basically, a quality receiver and a high-quality recording device), a signal can be intercepted from a water pipe, a heating duct, or a wire that passes through the room in which the target electronic device is operating. For example, a government agent might rent a hotel room one or two floors above the target's room. Once the TEMPEST equipment is activated, the agent can then capture all of the target's computer activity by tapping a water pipe common to the two rooms and tuning a receiver to the frequency of the van Eck radiation. TEMPEST can even monitor van Eck radiation through the air by using a directional microphone.

The most effective way to shield against TEMPEST is to create a secure room with copper sheeting on the walls, floor, and ceiling, no windows, airlock-style doors, an isolated power supply, and no communication lines coming in or going out. To further reduce the risk, a possible target can generate random white noise to jam the van Eck radiation detection devices. Think of the secure rooms you've seen on television or in the movies. They really do exist.

Time Bombs, Logic Bombs, Rabbits, and Trojan Horses

Once they gain access, hackers, crackers, and script kiddies sometimes introduce destructive software (or malware) into a computer system. A **logic bomb** is a program that symbolically blows up in memory, often taking the contents of a hard disk, selected data, or selected software with it. A variation called a **time bomb** executes on a particular date or when a particular condition is met. Other logic bombs are triggered by externally generated signals and similar apparently random events, making the cause of the system disruption difficult to trace. Note that a logic bomb or time bomb need not "explode" catastrophically. Some do their damage in slow motion, destroying or changing small amounts of data over a period of time. Such slow-motion logic bombs are difficult to detect and, consequently, can do a great deal of damage before corrective action is taken.

A **rabbit** is a program that replicates itself until no memory is left and no other programs can run. One well-known rabbit copies itself twice and then launches the copies. A few nanoseconds later, four rabbits are running. Then eight, then sixteen, then... By the time the operator realizes what is happening, the rabbit is out of control. Few rabbits destroy data. Instead, they deny legitimate users access to the affected system.

A **Trojan horse** is a seemingly harmless program that invites an unsuspecting user to try it. Typically entering a system in the guise of a computer game or a cool graphic attached to an e-mail message or available for free download from a mysterious Web site, a Trojan horse is often used as a delivery vehicle for a payload that might hold a sniffer, a logic bomb, a time bomb, a rabbit, a backdoor, or a similar piece of destructive software.

Backdoors

A **backdoor** is an undocumented software routine (less frequently, a hardware trap), that is deliberately inserted by a system's designers or a hacker. Once activated, the backdoor allows undetected access to the system. Sometimes called a trapdoor or a wormhole, a backdoor is a legitimate programming, testing, and debugging tool. For example, have you ever played an interactive computer game in which you work your way through a series of levels as you accumulate points? Imagine trying to debug level 5 by first playing through levels 1, 2, 3, and 4, discovering a bug, inserting a possible fix, and then starting over again at level 1 to see if the level 5 fix worked. It is much more efficient to insert into the code a backdoor that jumps directly to level 5 when the debugger presses an unusual key combination. Backdoors are also valuable system management and remote system administrative tools. A system administrator might use a backdoor to enter a remote system, check on system status, reset key parameters, and update software without disrupting normal operations.

Sometimes programmers and system administrators forget to close a backdoor properly after they finish using it. Perhaps you have discovered an undocumented backdoor in a computer game that allows you to jump ahead and accumulate points quickly. Game programmers sometimes intentionally hide a backdoor or two in the finished version of the game as a gift (called a cheat or an easter egg) for skilled players. Hackers and crackers use such backdoors to gain access to a system, and they sometimes leave behind a backdoor for future use following an initial intrusion by some other means. For example, an elite hacker group known as the Cult of the Dead Cow created a well-known backdoor called Back Orifice, a pun on Microsoft's BackOffice server software.

Viruses and Worms

Perhaps the biggest fear among Internet users and corporate network managers alike is the uncontrolled spread of a virus or a worm. A **virus** is a program that is capable of replicating and spreading between computers by attaching itself to another program. Viruses typically spread through infected diskettes, downloaded copies of infected programs, or e-mail attachments. They are parasites that require a host program to reproduce and survive.

Viruses are not particularly difficult to create; if you know how to program, you can probably write one. A typical virus consists of three primary components: a routine that allows the virus to reproduce by attaching itself to another program, logic that helps the virus avoid detection, and a payload (Figure 8.6). Often the payload is trivial, but it can also carry such destructive code as a time bomb, a logic bomb, a rabbit, a sniffer, or a backdoor. Viruses have been known to erase disks, crash programs, and modify data, but the most effective (and most insidious) viruses do their dirty work quietly, in the background, and never announce their presence.

A **worm** is a viruslike program that is capable of spreading under its own power. A source computer often starts the delivery process by broadcasting a small "scout" routine to numerous targets. Once the scout establishes itself on a target computer, it transmits a message asking the source computer to send the rest of the worm. Although worms can carry the same destructive payloads as viruses, they are often used to collect information and report back to their source. In the late 1960s, worms were used to monitor remote terminals electronically and to report status information to the server so necessary maintenance could be scheduled. Today, hackers use worms to collect and return such information as passwords.

At best, viruses and worms are an annoyance. At worst, they can do real damage. Three well-known viruses, Love Bug (or Loveletter), Melissa, and Hi (or Goner), enter a system as e-mail attachments and are activated when the recipient opens the attachment. Once launched, the viruses access the recipient's Outlook address book and send copies of themselves to the recipient's contacts. In some large organizations, the amount of meaningless e-mail traffic generated by these virus attacks literally shuts down the

Figure 8.6 The structure of a typical virus.

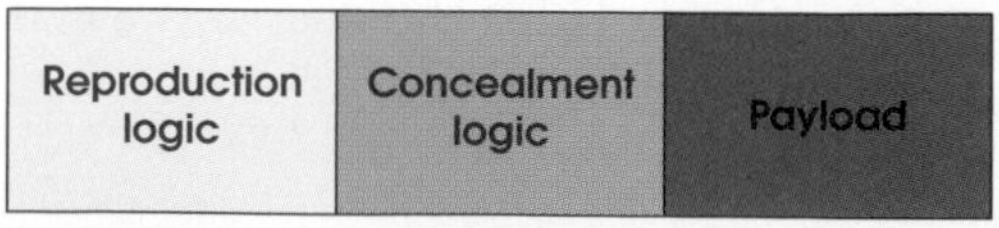

| Reproduction logic | Concealment logic | Payload |

internal e-mail system, and cleanup costs can easily reach millions of dollars. Nimda is an example of a worm that spreads via e-mail and other means. Many security service providers post virus descriptions and downloadable recovery software on their Web sites; for example, Figure 8.7 shows the Web page that describes the Sircam virus (*http://www.europe.f-secure.com/v-descs/sircam.shtml*).

Viruses can be difficult to detect or remove, so the best defense is prevention. Start by installing up-to-date **antivirus software**, and do not access an unknown diskette, download "free" software, or open unanticipated e-mail attachments without first screening them for viruses, worms, and Trojan horses.

A good antivirus program protects a system in three ways. First, it scans incoming and outgoing messages and files (and files stored on disk) for code patterns called **virus signatures** that uniquely identify a given virus. When a virus is detected, the software sounds an alarm, and many antivirus programs can isolate and destroy the virus before it even enters the system. The software also incorporates heuristic logic that continuously monitors the system for abnormal activity, such as an attempt to modify the Windows registry. Finally, most virus programs include facilities that help a system manager to recover from a virus attack.

Perhaps the most effective approach is to implement virus protection in layers (Figure 8.8). Placing a router between the host server and the Internet and running a firewall on that router provides a measure of networkwide protection. A firewall plus antivirus software running on the host server represents a second layer of protection.

Figure 8.7 An online description of the Sircam virus.

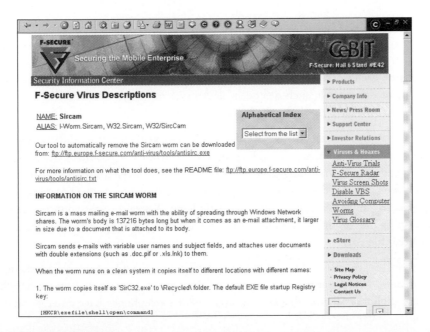

Courtesy of F-Secure Inc.

Figure 8.8 System security and virus protection are often implemented in layers.

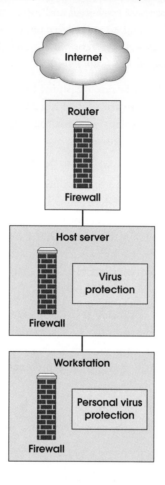

Running on each workstation, personal firewalls and personal antivirus software form a third line of defense. On such defend-in-depth systems, the lower-level filters trap any malware that manages to slip by the higher layers.

Serious virus writers incorporate various tricks to make their viruses difficult to detect. A polymorphic virus mutates, changing slightly each time it reproduces and making its virus signature a moving target. When a virus attaches itself to another program, it changes the program's file size, so a change in the length of a file is one parameter that is monitored by an antivirus program's heuristic logic. A stealth virus counters heuristic detection by intercepting certain file scans and returning what appears to be the correct (virus free) file size.

New viruses are created almost daily, so updating antivirus software by regularly downloading new virus signatures and heuristics is important. Viruses that attack handheld personal digital assistants (PDAs) and even cellular telephones have emerged and are expected to become common over the next several years. A new type of virus (Bubbleboy and Kak are examples) is embedded in an e-mail message and activates when the recipient reads the message, even if she does not open the attachment. In theory, it may be possible to create a virus that is launched when a user opens a mail reader and downloads new messages even before those messages are read. Cluster viruses that spawn vast numbers of miniviruses represent a possible near-future threat. An undetectable, highly destructive supervirus has yet to emerge, but it could happen.

To date, most viruses have been relatively harmless. Even a harmless virus can be disruptive, however, and business organizations spend billions of dollars each year purchasing or leasing antivirus software, monitoring for virus intrusions, and cleaning up after virus attacks. Add to those expenditures such difficult-to-quantify costs as lost productivity, lost information, compromised data integrity, and lost business, and the numbers are substantial. For example, Computer Economics, an independent research organization, estimates that the three most expensive viruses/worms of 2001, Code Red, Sircam, and Nimda, cost the worldwide business community $2.62 billion, $1.15 billion, and $635 million respectively.[2]

Virus hoaxes are a troubling new phenomenon. A typical hoax starts as an e-mail message that warns the recipient about a "newly discovered" nonexistent virus and relies on basic social engineering techniques to trick the recipient into spreading the message. These hoaxes are often circulated like chain letters, with each recipient forwarding multiple copies to colleagues and friends, warning them about the phony risk. The resulting message clutter can clog communication channels as effectively as a real virus.

Viruses

Viruses are not particularly new. A man named Fred Cohen coined the term *virus* to describe a type of computer program in 1983, but the concept of self-replicating software has been around since the late 1960s. Widespread access to the Internet and the World Wide Web has made it much easier for viruses to propagate, however, and the numbers have exploded. In 1993, there were roughly 3,000 known viruses in the entire world. By the year 2000, the number had increased to roughly 40,000. Macro viruses account for about 75 percent of that total; they typically run when the recipient opens an e-mail attachment that contains a Word, Excel, or similar document. Approximately six to twelve new viruses appear every day, and the speed of propagation has also increased. For example, in 1999, an e-mail virus named Melissa infected roughly 250,000 computers before it was brought under control. A year later, a similar virus named Love Bug infected in excess of 2.5 *million* computers.

---

2 See *http://computereconomics.com*.

System Vulnerabilities

Not all attacks rely on hacker-created malware, however. Most Internet and Web-based systems contain well-known **vulnerabilities** that allow a hacker to gain access. For example, computers are typically shipped with default passwords (such as *system*, *setup*, *startup*, *sysop*, and so on) that are used by the system operator to initialize the operating system. Once the system is properly initialized and ready to use, the system operator is expected to assign new passwords and disable the defaults, but sometimes the operator forgets, creating a form of backdoor. Once a hacker discovers a vulnerable system, he can simply log on using the default password and gain system operator (sysop) or root status (a common hacker objective), giving the hacker the ability to access and change virtually anything on the system. Like lists of exploits, lists of default passwords for various operating systems are posted on hacker Web sites.

Computer systems are particularly vulnerable at interface points where input and output data enter and leave the system. For example, the TCP/IP protocol supports up to 65,535 ports, and each of those ports is a potential point of access. **Port scanning** is the act of systematically scanning a system for open ports with exploitable weaknesses. For example, hackers often attempt to log on to a system using the telnet protocol following a scan for a telnet-ready port. Note that port scanning is not illegal. Like so many hacker tools, it is a legitimate system management tool that is sometimes misused.

Other system vulnerabilities result from software bugs or logical inconsistencies, within both application and system software routines and at the software interfaces between layers. Like good system managers, good hackers read published security alerts and download recommended vendor patches. Many system managers are slow to respond to such alerts, so the hacker probes for known vulnerabilities and attacks unprotected systems.

How does a hacker find a vulnerable computer? Some rely on published lists created by other hackers. A **war dialer** is a program that dials all the telephones in a single exchange (for example, all the telephone numbers starting with 123), looking for the tell-tale tone that identifies a modem. Each time it reaches a modem, the war dialer logs the matching telephone number for the hacker's later perusal. Various types of scanners are used to probe automatically a block of IP addresses, looking for systems that exhibit potential vulnerabilities. To cite just one particularly attractive target, the U.S. Department of Defense systems are probed roughly 250,000 times a year.

Denial of Service Attacks

Hacker attacks exploit system vulnerabilities. For example, a **denial of service (DoS) attack** is the cyberspace equivalent of spray-painting graffiti or throwing bricks through windows—an act of pure vandalism that gains the perpetrator little but denies the victim the use of a resource. The idea is to overwhelm a target computer by sending it so many packets in a brief period of time that the rate of arriving packets exceeds the target server's ability to respond. One of the first DoS exploits, the **ping o' death**, used a slightly different strategy, crashing the target computer by transmitting oversize packets that overflowed the TCP/IP stacks you read about in Chapter 2. The vulnerability that

Software Security

OPINION

Why are so many software products vulnerable to security attacks? Complexity is one answer. For example, a popular software suite such as Microsoft Office integrates several programs, and each of those programs is huge. (The minimum requirement for installing Microsoft Office XP Standard Edition is 210 MB of hard disk space). It is simply impossible for any programmer or team of programmers to test so much code fully, particularly when the suite's multiple components interact in ways no one could predict. Excessively tight deadlines, perhaps imposed for financial or marketing reasons, are another cause. Generally, the system developer's first priority is to create software that works, and such criteria as adequate testing, documentation, and security are all too often secondary considerations. Until security

becomes a priority, software will continue to be vulnerable to security attacks.

Given the nature of software, bugs and vulnerabilities are probably inevitable, but why are so many hacker attacks directed against Microsoft products such as Windows, Outlook, Outlook Express, Word, and Excel? Are Microsoft's products significantly more buggy and vulnerable than competitive software? Some would argue that they are, but the reason Microsoft is disproportionately targeted is probably Microsoft's dominance in the marketplace. For example, knowing that the vast majority of potential targets use Microsoft Word, a hacker looking for maximum impact is much more likely to write a Word macro virus than a WordPerfect macro virus.

enabled the ping o' death no longer exists, but the term lives on. Today, a ping o' death refers to any hacker attack that works by overwhelming the target computer or to a legitimate system change that triggers unforeseen problems.

An interesting set of jargon has grown up around modern DoS attacks. The intentionally flawed packet that starts an attack might be called a Chernobyl packet, a Christmas tree packet, a Godzillagram, a kamikaze packet, or a nastygram. The result might be a broadcast storm that leads to a network meltdown. Hacker humor is an acquired taste.

A DoS attack, a favorite tool of script kiddies, can be launched by writing a simple script that contains a loop with an embedded command; for example, the script might send a page request to the target computer and then repeat the request again, and again, and again. A **distributed denial of service (DDoS) attack** (Figure 8.9), a more sophisticated version, is launched simultaneously from a number of computers, making it difficult to identify the attacker. Hackers have been known to take over personal computers and use them as platforms for a DDoS attack. Usually the hijacked computer's owner is unaware that her machine has been used as a DDoS launching pad.

Spoofing

Spoofing exploits known system vulnerabilities by faking key system parameters. For example, with **DNS spoofing**, a hacker alters a DNS entry on a server and consequently redirects a browser's page request to an alternate site, such as the hacker's site. Once the

Figure 8.9 A distributed denial of service (DDoS) attack.

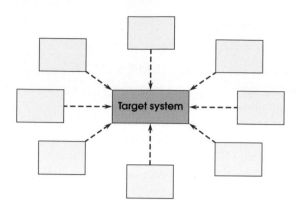

hacker intercepts a message, he can extract any information it holds. After caching a copy or extracting the desired information, a clever hacker might forward the message to the real target site, leaving the user with no evidence of the hijacking. DNS spoofing is sometimes used as an identity theft tool, a topic to be discussed in Chapter 10.

As the name implies, **IP spoofing** relies on altered IP addresses. For example, many organizations run an IP broadcast server that sends system messages (such as "The network is going down in 15 minutes") to everyone on the network. A **smurf attack** is a distributed denial of service attack that exploits the broadcast server. Three parties are involved: the attacker, a broadcast server, and the victim. The attacker creates a ping packet with a forged source address, substituting the victim's IP address for her own. The forged packet is then sent to the intermediary, which broadcasts the packet to all the nodes on its network. Each node then sends a ping response to the victim. The resulting ping flood overwhelms the target network, and the attacker's identity remains hidden. If the forged ping packet is sent to multiple intermediaries, the outcome is even more disruptive.

To improve system efficiency, servers often establish trust relationships with their clients and with other servers. Within Miami University, the servers that control access to the various divisions' networks maintain trust relationships with each other, thus allowing a School of Business user to access the library's network without going through a second password check. A more complex form of an IP spoofing attack exploits those trust relationships to bypass security. A hacker starts the attack by probing the target network (often far in advance) to identify its trust relationships. Assume, for example, that a series of initial probes shows that the target server, Alpha, maintains trust relationships with servers Beta, Gamma, and Epsilon.

Once the groundwork is laid, the hacker launches a denial of service attack by flooding one of the trusted servers (Beta) with bogus messages. The hacker then sends a message purporting to come from server Beta to the *target* computer, server Alpha (Figure 8.10, step 1). The transport layer protocol on Alpha attempts to establish a communication link with Beta by sending an acknowledgement (step 2), but Beta cannot reply because it is flooded. After a suitable interval, the hacker sends a counterfeit version of the trusted

Figure 8.10 IP spoofing.

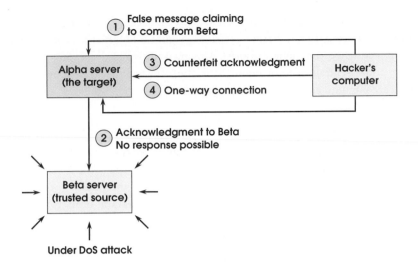

source computer's acknowledgement (step 3) to the target system (Alpha). As a result (step 4), a one-way communication path is established between the hacker's computer and Alpha, allowing the attacker to transmit commands to Alpha and establish a back-door, insert a Trojan horse, install a sniffer, or provide some other means of future access.

The Microsoft Attack

Over the course of several days in October 2000, a sophisticated hacker attack was launched against Microsoft Corporation. Posing as internal workers, the hackers apparently either exploited a well-known Trojan horse, took advantage of a backdoor, or both to gain access to the system. Returning again and again, they were able to view (at the very least) the source code for an unnamed future software product, and they may have done additional damage before Microsoft detected the intrusions and plugged the security holes.

The attack raised several questions. If hackers were able to penetrate Microsoft, how safe are the rest of us? When Microsoft eventually releases that unnamed software product, can we expect counterfeit versions to flood the market? Can we really be sure Microsoft software is safe, or did the hackers insert a backdoor or a Trojan horse into the code? Microsoft could answer such questions by publishing the source code for the affected software, but Microsoft does not, as a matter of policy, publish its source code. Perhaps we will never know what really happened, until it's too late.

Information Warfare

In the mid-1990s, Col. John Warren of the United States Air Force proposed a five-ring model to depict key national defense priorities (Figure 8.11). At the center, the nation's leadership is assigned the highest priority. Moving outward in decreasing priority order are the organic essentials (electric power, fuel), the infrastructure (transportation, industry, finance, communications), and the population. The nation's military acts as a shield protecting the four inner rings.

The essence of **information warfare** is to bypass the military and directly attack the inner rings. In the introduction to a book by Winn Schwartau, John I. Algar, the Dean of the School of Information Warfare and Strategy at the U.S. National Defense University, defines information warfare as "…those actions intended to protect, exploit, corrupt, deny, or destroy information or information resources in order to achieve a significant advantage, objective, or victory over an adversary."[3] Algar's definition incorporates a number of tactics, ranging from propaganda and disinformation to disabling the enemy's power plants, to disrupting or jamming the enemy's communication networks, to brutal acts of terror designed to intimidate the population.

Figure 8.11 The Warden defense model.

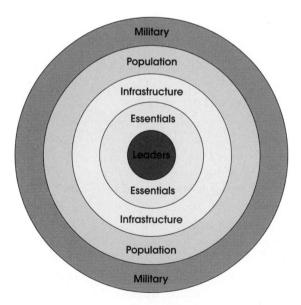

---

[3] Winn Schwartau, *Information Warfare—Cyberterrorism: Protecting Your Personal Security in the Electronic Age*, 2nd ed. (New York: Thunder's Mouth Press, 1994), 12.

Selecting Targets

The most attractive targets concentrate value, where the attacker defines how value is measured. For example, the World Trade Center's twin towers concentrated large numbers of people in a restricted space, making them tempting targets for terrorists bent on killing Americans. In contrast, an isolated farmhouse in the middle of Kansas is not a very attractive target, unless the attacker has a personal grudge against the occupants. Similarly, a hydroelectric dam makes a better target than a windmill farm, a network access point (NAP) makes a tempting target if the objective is to disrupt Internet communications, and a terrorist attack on a nuclear power plant is a nightmare scenario.

Concentration of value is not the only criterion, however; cost is a factor, too. The attack on the World Trade Center was devastating, killing roughly 3,000 people and costing billions of dollars in property loss and economic dislocation, but the attackers paid a high price, too. The hijackers are dead, and America's response stripped the Taliban of political power and disrupted al-Qaida's effectiveness, at least temporarily.

The best target is the one that delivers "the most bang for the buck," in other words, the one for which the expected gain exceeds the expected cost by the greatest margin. For

TECHNOLOGY

EMP Weapons

An electromagnetic pulse (EMP) weapon is an information warfare tool that disables or destroys electronic devices. The potential for EMP weapons was first recognized during the 1950s when the EMP generated by an atmospheric nuclear test disabled virtually all communication devices in the vicinity. Today, anyone with the appropriate electronic skills and a few hundred dollars can build an EMP gun or an EMP bomb small enough to fit in the back of a van and powerful enough to do considerable damage.

A simple EMP bomb consists of a copper coil surrounded by an explosives-lined outer shell. A power source, such as an array of automobile batteries, places a high-voltage electrical charge on the coil. Once the charge reaches a critical level, the ring of explosives is detonated, instantly compressing the copper coil into a tiny, dense ball. The resulting rapid change in the electrical field generates a powerful electromagnetic pulse.

In many high-rise buildings, electric wires, communication lines, and plumbing run from floor to floor through the central elevator shaft. If an EMP bomb is placed in the back of a panel truck, and the truck is parked against the elevator shaft, those wires and lines will channel the electromagnetic pulse generated by the bomb's detonation, destroying the integrated circuits in literally every electronic device on every floor in the building. In microseconds, every computer, telephone, office copier, personal digital assistant, printer, monitor, projector, sound system, video device, coffee maker, vending machine, electronic lock, light bulb, and any other electronic device you can imagine will die. The "good news" is that the EMP does not kill people, unless they are wearing a pacemaker or a similar medical device that relies on integrated circuitry.

example, blowing up Hoover Dam might cause a power blackout in Las Vegas and a disastrous flood in the lower Colorado River flood plain, but the dam is an imposing, difficult to destroy target. Using the Internet to insert a destructive virus into a power distribution software routine is an alternative that's far less expensive, less risky, and more likely to succeed, and it might disrupt power to Las Vegas just as effectively.

Cyberwarfare

Cyberwarfare, a form of information warfare conducted in cyberspace, uses several well-known hacker tools as weapons. Sophisticated probes and sniffers monitor and intercept enemy communications. A well-executed denial of service attack can disable communication and computer networks. Backdoors and cracking techniques allow an attacker to penetrate an enemy's computer systems and deny the enemy the use of its own intelligence information, compromise the integrity of that information, plant false or misleading information, or insert logic bombs, time bombs, rabbits, viruses, and worms. Other cyberwarfare attacks focus on the enemy's civilian infrastructure, crippling or compromising the computers that control government operations, communications, transportation, power distribution, financial transactions, and so on.

A few years ago, an interesting variation of a distributed denial of service attack disrupted Web sites operated by former Mexican president Zedillo, the White House, the Pentagon, the Frankfurt Stock Exchange, and the Mexican Stock Exchange. The attack, a virtual sit-in, was launched by New York's Electronic Disturbance Theater in support of the Zapatista National Liberation Army, a group representing Native Americans in the state of Chiapas in southern Mexico in their fight against the Mexican government. The attackers flooded the target Web sites with requests for service, often by establishing a link and then simply clicking on their browser's Refresh button repeatedly.

Cyberwarfare is not limited to hacking, of course. For example, a technique called **chipping** involves replacing selected integrated circuit chips with functionally equivalent but modified chips that broadcast a detectable signal, enable a hardware-based virus or backdoor, or fail on command. Such chips might pinpoint a bombing target, enable a hacker to penetrate security, or launch a denial of service attack. For example, in the early 1990s, it was widely rumored that a cyberwarfare attack utilized both chipping and hacking to disrupt Iraq's air defense systems just before Desert Storm was launched.

Cyberwarfare is effective, inexpensive, difficult to defend against, and relatively anonymous. Given global access to the Internet and the World Wide Web, a cyberattack can be launched from virtually anywhere in the world by a handful of skilled people (even a single individual) using standard, commercially available equipment, making the source of an attack very difficult to trace.

Cyberterrorism

Cyberwarfare is a legitimate military tool that supports a broader national strategy by launching coordinated electronic attacks on multiple targets. **Cyberterrorism**, an online form of terrorism that relies on various cyberwarfare tools and tactics, tends to be more hit-and-run in nature, with a limited number of targets selected as much for their symbolic value as their strategic importance. Inexpensive and anonymous, cyberterrorism delivers considerable "bang for the buck."

The Internet is a particularly attractive cyberterrorist target because it is publicly accessible, built on open standards, defines a crucial infrastructure, and represents an important symbol of the evolving global economy. Because of its dispersed design, the Internet would seem to be almost immune to successful attack, but there are numerous vulnerabilities and chokepoints that a cyberterrorist can exploit. Disabling an NAP can shut down significant parts of the Internet, attacking a regional service provider can black out a state or two, and as the Morris worm clearly demonstrated, a well-designed virus or worm can cripple the Internet.

The same infrastructure that spreads malware so efficiently also supports denial of service attacks. For example, in the United States, DoS attacks have been used to shut down or manipulate the contents of Web sites operated by Yahoo, Starbucks, and the World Trade Organization, and shortly after September 11, 2001 (to the chagrin of the U.S. government), some American hackers took it upon themselves to launch their own retaliatory attacks against several Middle Eastern countries, defacing at least 200 government-sponsored Web sites.

Recently, for the same reasons business enterprises replaced their electronic data interchange (EDI) networks with Internet connections, electric power distributors and telecommunication providers have implemented TCP/IP links with remote facilities and substations to support performance monitoring, maintenance, and similar activities. Using the public infrastructure reduces operating costs, but it also gives a cyberterrorist an access point for disrupting the power grid by inserting a destructive virus into a software patch or taking some other action. B2B supply chain integration (Chapter 7) is another good example of how open standard networks increase risk. Broader access, particularly Internet access, may be good for business, but it significantly increases the number of potential attack points.

Adding to the Internet's vulnerability is the dominant status of the Microsoft Windows operating system. Most Internet workstations and many hosts run Windows software, and like a biological virus attacking an insufficiently diverse ecosystem, a powerful Windows virus could literally shut down the Web. Recognizing the Internet's vulnerability, the Pentagon and the NSA have developed the Joint Worldwide Intelligence Communications System (JWICS), a separate-but-better Internet with no connection to the public infrastructure to carry highly secure messages, and a similar independent network has been proposed for the U.S. government.

Vulnerability

In 1951, science fiction writer Arthur C. Clarke wrote a short story entitled "Superiority." Set far in the future, the story concerned an intergalactic war between two civilizations, one of which possessed vastly superior technology. Unfortunately, their "superior" technology required significant logistical support, which presented the enemy with numerous targets of opportunity, and the civilization with the "inferior" technology won the war.

On September 11, 2001, terrorists destroyed New York's World Trade Center and damaged the Pentagon, and suddenly many of the just-in-time delivery, inventory, and production systems made possible by B2B e-commerce lost a great deal of their effectiveness. Almost immediately, communications through New York City, an important financial hub, were disrupted. Soon enhanced security caused trucks and aircraft to back up at airports, bridges,

tunnels, and border crossings, delaying shipments that no longer arrived "just in time." Many companies responded by maintaining a level of safety stock in their (recently thought obsolete) work-in-process inventories. Others suffered severe disruptions to their production and distribution facilities. Many firms lost a great deal of money, which they may never recover.

Does the United States rely too heavily on technology? Is it possible that, like the society depicted in Arthur C. Clarke's story, our modern technology-driven global economy might ultimately lose the battle to a technologically inferior opponent? More to the point, what happens to a company if an intermediary who supplies a mission-critical service goes out of business? Is it possible that a technologically inferior competitor might win a significant slice of the affected company's business? Interesting questions.

Cybercrime is a general term for illegal or unethical activities performed in cyberspace. A hacker is a person who illegally breaks into computer systems. White-hat hackers claim to do no harm; black-hat hackers, sometimes called crackers, are the Internet's cyberterrorists, industrial espionage agents, and freelance spies. Elite hackers share a disdain for script kiddies. A phreaker is a person who cracks (or breaks into) the telephone network. Hackers can work from inside or outside an organization, but insiders represent the bigger threat.

The easiest way to gain access to an unauthorized computer is to log in with the user ID and password of someone who has the appropriate rights. A hacker's most common source of passwords is carelessness. Hackers do not hesitate to hunt through the paper trash, an activity they call dumpster diving. The act of convincing someone to voluntarily divulge her password is called social engineering. For security reasons, passwords are normally stored in encoded form. A packet sniffer is a software wiretap that captures and analyzes packets and is sometimes used to capture passwords.

A logic bomb is a program that symbolically blows up in memory. A variation called a time bomb executes on a particular date or when a particular condition is met. A rabbit is a program that replicates itself until no memory is left and no other programs can run. A Trojan horse is a seemingly harmless program that invites an unsuspecting user to try it. An undocumented software routine or hardware trap that allows undetected access to a system is called a backdoor. A virus is a program that is capable of replicating and spreading between computers by attaching itself to another program, and a worm is a viruslike program that is capable of spreading under its own power. Antivirus software scans files for virus signatures, monitors a system continuously for abnormal activity, and helps a system manager recover from a virus attack.

Many Internet and Web-based systems contain vulnerabilities that allow a hacker to gain access. Port scanning is the act of systematically scanning a system for open ports with exploitable weaknesses. A war dialer is a program that dials all the telephone numbers in a block looking for a modem tone.

The objective of a DoS attack is to overwhelm a target computer by sending it multiple messages or multiple commands in a brief period of time so that the rate of arriving messages exceeds the target server's ability to respond. A DDoS attack is launched simultaneously from a number of computers. Spoofing exploits known system vulnerabilities by faking key system parameters. With DNS spoofing, a hacker alters a DNS entry on a server and redirects a browser's page request to an alternate site, such as the hacker's site. A smurf attack is a DDoS attack that exploits a broadcast server. An interesting application of IP spoofing exploits network trust relationships to bypass password checks and similar security features.

The essence of information warfare is to bypass the military and to attack directly an enemy's population, infrastructure, and leadership. The best information warfare targets deliver the most value for the lowest cost. Cyberwarfare, a form of information warfare conducted in cyberspace, uses several well-known hacker tools as weapons. Cyberterrorism is an online form of terrorism that relies on cyberwarfare's tools and tactics. The Internet is a particularly attractive cyberterrorist target.

■ ■ ■ Key Words

antivirus software	hacker	smurf attack
backdoor	human engineering	social engineering
black-hat hacker, or dark-side hacker	information warfare	spoofing
chipping	insider	time bomb
cybercrime	intrusion	Trojan horse
cyberspace	IP spoofing	virus
cyberterrorism	logic bomb	virus hoax
cyberwarfare	packet sniffer	virus signature
denial of service (DoS) attack	phreaker	vulnerability
distributed denial of service (DDoS) attack	ping o' death	war dialer
DNS spoofing	port scanning	white-hat hacker
dumpster diving	rabbit	worm
exploits	samurai	
	script kiddie	

■ ■ ■ Review Questions

1. Distinguish between a white-hat hacker and a black-hat hacker (or cracker).

2. What is a phreaker? Many hackers are also phreakers. Why?

3. What is a script kiddie? Why do elite hackers and crackers disdain script kiddies?

4. Why do hackers hack?

5. Describe several techniques a hacker might use to obtain a password.

6. What is a packet sniffer? How does a packet sniffer work?

7. What are time bombs, logic bombs, and rabbits?

8. What is a Trojan horse? Why are Trojan horses dangerous?

9. What is a backdoor? Identify several legitimate uses of backdoors.

10. What is a virus? What is a worm?

11. Describe several techniques a hacker might use to identify a vulnerable system.

12. What is a denial of service attack? What is a distributed denial of service attack?

13. What is spoofing? Explain DNS spoofing, smurf attacks, and IP spoofing.

14. What is information warfare? What is cyberwarfare? What is cyberterrorism?

15. What makes a potential target attractive to a cyberwarrior or a cyberterrorist?

16. Explain why the Internet is an attractive cyberwarfare and cyberterrorism target.

▪▪▪ Exercises

1. In your opinion, do a white-hat hacker's good intentions justify his actions?

2. Many experts believe that insiders are potentially more dangerous than external hackers. Do you agree or disagree? Why?

3. A significant number of viruses are written to exploit vulnerabilities in Microsoft products. Why do you suppose this is so?

4. In your opinion, why do people write viruses?

5. Why do you suppose the attack on Microsoft described in a chapter sidebar was significant?

▪▪▪ Projects

Current references and supporting resources can be found at this textbook's companion Web site.

Broad-Based Projects

1. Given what you have learned about password security, change the passwords on your computer accounts.

2. Investigate Carnivore and TEMPEST technologies and write a report on your findings.

3. Search the Web and find a few sites that describe software vulnerabilities.

4. Read Arthur C. Clarke's "Superiority." You will find the story in numerous science fiction anthologies, including *The Collected Stories of Arthur C. Clarke*. After you read the story, write a paper discussing its relevance to current technology.

5. Research the size and the growth rate of the computer security industry. Write a paper that summarizes your findings and discusses the career implications of security services.

6. Write a page or two summarizing how you feel about hackers and viruses. Then research the economic impact of viruses and hacking and summarize your findings. Did your research change your opinion? Why or why not?

Building the Case:

7. Working as a team, continue with Chapter 1, Project 6 by discussing your proposed Web site's potential exposure to hackers and other external attacks and to internal misuse.

Business Projects

Building the Case:

1. Continue with Chapter 1, Project 2 by identifying risks that arise from weak points or holes in your solution that might allow a hacker, a disgruntled employee, or some other unauthorized user to damage your system. For each risk you identify, describe the possible damage (lost or corrupted information, user downtime, and so on) resulting from a successful intrusion and roughly estimate the cost of fixing that damage. Write a report to document your results.

Information Technology Projects

1. Issue the following commands from the MS-DOS or line prompt:
   a. To test access to a given URL, code *ping url*. For example, try *ping muohio.edu*.
   b. To report the IP address of your computer, code *ipconfig/all*.
   c. To report an IP address given a domain name, code *nslookup url*. For example, code *nslookup muohio.edu* and *nslookup microsoft.com*.
   d. To report the path a packet travels over the Internet, code *tracert url*. For example, try *tracert muohio.edu*. Then issue a *tracert* to a URL located across the country and another *tracert* to a URL in a foreign country.

   Explain how a hacker might use these tools to gain illegal access to a system. (Note: You may have conducted a similar exercise in Chapter 2.)

Building the Case:

2. Continue with Chapter 1, Project 2 by identifying possible weak points or holes in your solution that might allow a hacker or some other unauthorized outsider to gain access to your system. Then identify possible weak points or holes that might allow an internal hacker, a disgruntled employee, or an improperly trained user to misuse the system. For each scenario, identify the possible damage (lost or corrupted information, user downtime, and so on) resulting from a successful intrusion and roughly estimate the cost of fixing that damage.

Marketing Projects

Building the Case:

1. Continue with Chapter 1, Project 2 by identifying risks that arise from weak points or holes in your client's system that might allow a hacker, a disgruntled employee, or some other unauthorized user to compromise security or privacy, and describe each of those risks from a customer's perspective. Write a report to document your results.

◼◻◼◻◼ References

Web Sites

Source	URL	Comments
F-Secure	*www.datafellows.fi/virus-info/*	An excellent source of information about viruses.
FBI	*www.fbi.gov/hq/lab//carnivore/ carnivore2.htm*	Information on Carnivore.
The Jargon Dictionary	*http://astrian.net/jargon/terms*	Definitions of computer jargon.
Robert Graham	*www.robertgraham.com/pubs/ sniffing-faq.html*	Packet sniffer FAQs.
TechTV	*www.techtv.com/cybercrime/*	Definitions of cybercrime terminology.

Print and White Papers

Clarke, Arthur C. 2002. *The Collected Stories of Arthur C. Clarke*. New York: Tom Doherty Associates, LLC.

Denning, Dorothy E. 1999. *Information Warfare and Security*. Boston: Addison-Wesley.

Schwartau, Winn. 1994. *Information Warfare—Cyberterrorism: Protecting Your Personal Security in the Electronic Age*. New York: Thunder's Mouth Press.

Slatalla, Michelle and Quittner, Joshua. 1995. *Masters of Deception: The Gang That Ruled Cyberspace*. New York: HarperCollins.

Zetter, Kim. December 2000. "Viruses, the Next Generation." *PC World*: 191–203.

CHAPTER 9

Security

When you finish reading this chapter, you should be able to:

- Define security and explain how implementing security requires making trade-offs between conflicting objectives

- Discuss the significance of access, authentication, integrity, privacy, non-repudiation, recovery, and auditability

- Relate the use of networks to increased system vulnerability

- Relate the placement of a firewall to the resources it protects

- Define cryptanalysis and relate key length to the strength of an encryption algorithm

- Distinguish between secret-key and public-key cryptography

- Explain how a digital envelope overcomes the key exchange problem

- Explain how digital signatures and digital certificates help to ensure authentication and nonrepudiation

- Define steganography and cite several examples

- Discuss the secure sockets layer (SSL)

Why Security?

Have you ever wondered whether your Visa card number is really safe when you send it over the Internet? If so, you are not alone. In fact, the fear of a credit card number being stolen, intercepted, or misused is a major factor limiting the growth of B2C e-commerce.

The problem is even more significant in B2B e-commerce. Imagine that a supplier has just sent a truckload of subassemblies to a manufacturer. The associated paperwork (a purchase order, shipping documents, a bill, and so on) moves electronically between the two firms. Such information is not intended for the general public, so both parties expect a reasonable level of privacy. Eventually, an electronic funds transfer pays the bill. The funds transfer represents a flow of money, and intercepting, modifying, or redirecting those funds is theft, little different than armed robbery. Clearly, those funds transfers must be protected.

The problem of protecting information resources from theft, modification, or disruption is not limited to data transfers, of course. Increasingly, business organizations view their information technology infrastructure as a strategic resource and a platform for mission-critical applications. Consequently, the infrastructure, including computer centers, access sites, workstations, and networks, must be protected. In the world of e-commerce, the key to protecting information is implementing effective security.

What Is Security?

According to Merriam-Webster's Collegiate Dictionary (the online version), **security** is "the quality or state of being secure," which includes "freedom from danger" and "freedom from fear or anxiety." Security also means "something that secures," including "measures taken to guard against espionage or sabotage, crime, attack, or escape." In an information technology context, security is a set of procedures, techniques, and safeguards designed to protect the hardware, software, data, and other system resources from unauthorized access, use, modification, or theft.

Conflicting Objectives

Those definitions seem straightforward, but there are complications. Consider, for example, a deceptively simple question: How much security is appropriate? The emotional answer is to keep all intruders off the system and protect everything, but implementing and supporting security is expensive and security costs have a direct impact on the bottom line. In contrast, the cost of not implementing security is indirect—somebody *might* compromise the system. It is not surprising that management is often tempted to choose the low-cost, low-security option.

Security is a series of trade-offs between conflicting objectives. Users want convenience and ease of use and seem to believe that avoiding downtime is information technology's responsibility, not theirs. System administrators are under constant pressure from management and users to keep the system up and running, and security is essential to achieving that objective. But security adds an extra layer of overhead that makes system access more difficult and less convenient. The key to effective security is balancing those conflicting objectives.

Balancing Conflicting Objectives

To an attacker, a system is worth penetrating only if the value of the protected resources exceeds the cost of breaking security. Key costs (to the attacker) include training, tools, time, and the risk of getting caught, all of which can be estimated. For example, at one time the banking industry could choose from three levels of safe doors. A two-hour door guaranteed that a skilled safecracker equipped with the proper tools would need at least two hours to break in. A four-hour door increased break-in time to four hours, and an eight-hour door, the highest level of security, increased break-in time to eight hours. Why did the eight-hour door provide the highest level of security? The longer the safecracker was on the job, the greater the probability that she would be caught, an important component of the bank robber's perceived cost. Increase the risk, and the crook is likely to seek an easier target.

One problem with balancing cost and value is determining value. Willie Sutton robbed banks because "That's where the money is." Crooks rob retail stores to get money or merchandise. But what is the value of information? How valuable is a copy of your business competitor's pricing strategy? How much is knowledge of a pending initial public offering worth to an investor? How much is an enemy's battle plan worth to a military commander? If the value is sufficiently high, the cost is irrelevant.

Shift to the defender's perspective. The cost of implementing security includes purchasing and maintaining the appropriate hardware, software, and data components and (because security precautions take time) lowering the efficiency of the system's legitimate users. Inadequate security, on the other hand, increases the risk of an intrusion that can divulge confidential plans and trade secrets, compromise the integrity of key operating data, disrupt internal and external communications, cripple normal operations, and put a company effectively out of business for a time. In other words, the cost of inadequate security can be devastating.

To further complicate matters, an organization's view of security changes with time or experience. Consider, for example, border security. The bridge that links Detroit, Michigan, and Windsor, Canada, is one of the busiest border crossings in the world. Until recently, average crossing time for a fully loaded truck was perhaps twenty minutes. Then came the terrorist attacks of September 11, 2001, and suddenly the need for enhanced security increased crossing time to several hours.

The automobile industry has been a leader in implementing B2B e-commerce links, and many of those links connected a U.S. assembly plant with a Canadian supplier (and vice versa). Before September 11, such business relationships were able to support just-in-time delivery, but border-crossing delays make time-critical delivery impossible. In at least one case, the unavailability of essential subassemblies forced an assembly plant to shut down. In other cases, assembly plant managers responded by maintaining a safety stock, an inefficiency that B2B supply chain integration was supposed to cure. Add the costs of lost production and inefficiency, and you begin to get a feel for the cost of security.

Airport Security

In the 1960s, airports in the United States essentially ignored security. Passengers, accompanied by their nonflying friends and family members, went straight from the ticketing counter to the gate without passing through so much as a metal detector. A series of hijackings led to security enhancements, including metal detectors, carry-on baggage scanners, and air marshals, and the hijackings pretty much stopped. After a few years, the air marshals slowly faded away, leaving only the familiar security checkpoint staffed (all too often) by inexperienced, undertrained, underpaid private employees subcontracted by the airlines. The flying public wanted convenience, not delays. Real security was expensive and could lead to a loss of business. So the traveling public got what it wanted—just enough security to support the illusion of safety.

Everything changed on September 11, 2001, when hijacked airplanes crashed into the World Trade Center's twin towers and the Pentagon. Suddenly, airport security became essential. Security checkpoints were tightened. Baggage was checked more carefully. National Guard troops patrolled key access points. The air marshal program was reinstated. Cockpit doors were strengthened. And passengers were advised to get to the airport two (sometimes three) hours before flight time to allow for the long lines that resulted from increased security.

Consider the cost of the new security precautions. Ignore, for a moment, the fear that kept so many people from flying and economically crippled many airlines, and focus instead on time. Driving from Oxford, Ohio, to Columbus takes two hours. Flying used to take three hours: one hour to drive to the Cincinnati airport, one hour waiting at the airport, and roughly one hour of flying time. No one flew from Oxford to Columbus because driving was more convenient. Cleveland, in contrast, is a five-hour drive and, before September 11, only a three-plus hour flight (including drive time, wait time, and flight time), so some Oxford residents did fly to Cleveland. September 11 changed the rules, however. It still takes five hours to drive to Cleveland, but the need to arrive at the airport two hours early increases total travel time to at least four hours. Few Oxford residents fly to Cleveland anymore.

Finding the correct level of security means trading off conflicting objectives. If you tighten security to keep terrorists out, you inconvenience legitimate travelers. If you loosen security for passenger convenience, you make it easier for a terrorist to slip through. The same thing happens with e-commerce security. Loose security lets customers in, but it also encourages hackers. Tight security helps to control hackers, but it inconveniences customers. Picture a seesaw. When one end goes down, the other end goes up. That's a good way to visualize the task of balancing conflicting security objectives.

Security Planning

The only way to achieve perfect security is to disassemble your network, lock your computers in a safe, and not allow anyone to access them. Clearly that solution is unrealistic; if you want to communicate with the outside world, you must accept some risk. The question is, how much? The answer lies in balancing cost and risk across the entire network, not just the individual components or layers. The key to balancing conflicting objectives systemwide is to make security planning and risk assessment key elements of the company's information technology strategy.

Risk Assessment

One way for a company to select the appropriate level of security is to view the decision as an insurance problem. Start by estimating the value of the information resources to be protected using such criteria as recovery cost, the cost of lost business if the resource is compromised, the company's pain threshold (its maximum tolerable loss for each resource), and so on. The estimated value of a resource defines an upper limit on security cost, because it makes little sense to insure anything for more than it is worth.

Next, assess the risks; the help of intermediary security consultants can be invaluable at this stage. List the ways an attacker might penetrate security and gain access to each of the resources. Assess an attacker's probability of success for each of those risks and compute the expected cost of a successful attack by multiplying each resource's value by its risk factor and adding the products. Repeat the process using several different security levels, and pick the level that best balances security cost and risk.

Assessing value and risk is complicated by social and political considerations. For example, a functional group within a company might lobby for tight security to protect information it considers critical. If, subsequently, a politically powerful manager within that functional group is denied access to important information because of enhanced security, that same group might insist security be loosened. Loose security makes it easy for legitimate users to access the system but also increases the risk that attackers will succeed. Tight security reduces the risk of a successful attack but increases the risk that a legitimate user will be denied access. Once again, the problem is balancing risk, security cost, and resource value.

Customers and businesses view risks differently. To a bank, a certain level of credit card fraud might represent an acceptable risk, a legitimate cost of doing business. To a consumer, however, the slight risk that a hacker might steal his credit card number is often enough to dissuade that individual from purchasing products online. One way banks attempt to deal with consumer fear is to assume the risk by absolving the customer of all fraudulent transaction costs.

Security Threats

An important prerequisite to accurate risk assessment is to know your potential attackers and your system's vulnerabilities. Banks rely on locks, safe doors, vaults, security cameras, security guards, customer identification, and other operating procedures to counter bank robbers. Since the attack on the World Trade Center, we have all become more aware of the need for airport security and more tolerant of the costs and delays associated with enhanced security.

Modern Internet-accessible information systems have added new wrinkles to the traditional security threats. Unauthorized access (such as breaking and entering) is an old problem, but today's cybercriminals, both insiders and outsiders, can follow a difficult-to-trace electronic path into a system from literally anywhere in the world. Once in, they can steal, alter, destroy, or copy private files or modify Web site content by inserting offensive material and misinformation. A denial of service (DoS) attack directed against a mission-critical application or system could literally put a company out of business for a time. Viruses can be destructive or simply disruptive. Packet sniffers can capture private data en route from its source to its destination. Such information attacks can be difficult to detect, much less to prosecute successfully.

Perhaps the most pervasive information infrastructure security threats arise from poor system administration and apathy on the part of both system administrators and users. The first step in achieving a secure system is to take security seriously. See Chapter 8 for an in-depth discussion of security threats.

Security Criteria

Figure 9.1 summarizes several key security criteria, including access, authentication, integrity, privacy, nonrepudiation, recovery, and auditability. Each criterion must be addressed in a company's security plan.

Access

The first criterion, **access**, focuses on the user. The principle is simple: Security must not interfere with the company's primary business activities. As a minimum, each employee must have reasonable access to all the system resources required to do her job. The other criteria must be balanced against the need for access.

Authentication

The purpose of **authentication**, the act of verifying a user's credentials and confirming that the user is who he claims to be, is to ensure that only authorized people are allowed access to a network, a service, a system, or a facility. Several criteria are used, including personal characteristics, knowledge of a secret, possession of a physical object, and physical location (Figure 9.2). Unless a person is properly authenticated, she should not be granted access to a system.

Figure 9.1 Key security criteria.

Criterion	Achieved if:
Access	Each employee has reasonable access to all the system resources required to do her job.
Authentication	Only authorized users are allowed access to a network, a service, a system, or a facility.
Integrity	The message was not modified during transmission.
Privacy	The contents of the message are known only to the sender and the recipient.
Nonrepudiation	The sender cannot deny that he sent the message.
Recovery	Procedures are in place to get the system back online quickly after a security breach has occurred.
Auditability	The security procedures can be audited.

Figure 9.2 Authentication criteria.

Criterion	Examples
Personal characteristics	Height, weight Hair and eye color Picture Biometrics
Knowledge of a secret	Password PIN Combination to a safe
Possession of an object	ID card Badge Credit card
Physical location	Physically secure site Callback GPS coordinates

On most networks, the de facto standard authorization tool is the combination of a user ID and a password. When a user logs on to a server, the user ID serves as a key to look up the associated password. If the password entered matches the one stored on the system, the user is authenticated, because he has demonstrated knowledge of a secret. Although passwords are universally understood and easy to use, they are also easily stolen or guessed, so knowing the right password does not necessarily prove that the person requesting access is the person authorized to use that password. By itself, a valid password is a relatively weak form of authentication.

The best authentication techniques combine two or more criteria, such as linking knowledge of a secret (a password, a PIN, or a logical key such as the combination to a safe) to possession of a physical object (an identification card, an access token, a credit card, or a physical key). The physical object becomes even more effective if it incorporates such personal characteristics as a description, a picture, or other appearance attributes. For example, your driver's license has an expiration date, shows your photograph, and lists such physical characteristics as your hair color, your eye color, and your date of birth. When you present your license as identification (possession of an object), security can verify that the license is current and, by comparing you to the picture and the other listed criteria (personal characteristics), that the bearer is the person described on the license.

Physical location offers additional options. For example, on a system equipped with callback, after a user logs on from a remote workstation, the host computer verifies the user ID and password, reads the workstation's hardware address, breaks the connection (hangs up), and uses the hardware address to get the workstation's assigned telephone number. If there is no number on file, access is denied. If there is a valid number, the host reestablishes the connection. Assuming that an approved workstation resides in a physically secure location that requires an additional security screen (personal characteristics, possession of an object) to gain admission, it is reasonable to assume that a user with a valid password (knowledge of a secret) logging in from that workstation is authorized to use the system. Other location-based techniques rely on the user's GPS coordinates to ensure that she is accessing the system from a secure or approved location.

To cite another example, an ATM transaction involves multiple authentication criteria: possession of an object (the ATM card), knowledge of a secret (a PIN), and location (each ATM machine has a unique ID). Additionally, every transaction is logged, and a camera records the user's picture (personal characteristics).

Integrity

The purpose of the **integrity** criterion is to ensure that the message was not modified during transmission. If the transmitter, the receiver, or any intermediate node has been compromised, integrity cannot be guaranteed. Security tools for ensuring integrity include encryption, digital signatures, and digital certificates (to be covered later in this chapter) and integrity checksums, also known as authentication codes or digital fingerprints, that are computed from the message data using some form of hashing function. For example, a hashing algorithm on the sending node might add together the contents of all even-numbered bytes (the data, remember, is binary), separately add all odd-numbered bytes, and then divide the first sum by the second. The quotient is then attached to the message. At the receiving node, the same algorithm is applied to the message, and the computed quotient is compared to the transmitted quotient. If they do not match, the message received is not the message sent.

Privacy

The purpose of the **privacy** criterion is to ensure that only the sender and the receiver know the contents of a transaction. Perhaps the best way to protect privacy during transmission is to encrypt the message using one or more of the encryption techniques that will be discussed later in this chapter. The problem is not limited to message transmission, however. The data that makes up a transaction must remain private before it is sent and after it is received, so some firms store key information in encrypted form. If a Trojan horse, a virus, a backdoor, a sniffer, or some other intrusion technique has been used to compromise either the transmitter or the receiver, privacy cannot be guaranteed.

Nonrepudiation

Nonrepudiation prevents the sender from denying that he sent the message. If the message can be repudiated, the sender or someone posing as the sender can commit fraud and later deny any involvement. Nonrepudiation is achieved by using digital signatures and digital certificates, two more topics to be discussed later in this chapter.

Recovery

Because accepting some risk is necessary, even a well-secured system will eventually be penetrated; the question is when, not if. The **recovery** criterion calls for effective backup and recovery procedures to get the system back online quickly after a security breach has occurred. Networks support this objective by providing such services as off-site backup and workload sharing.

Auditability

An audit is an examination of an organization's records intended to determine how well the organization is following its approved operating procedures. As the name implies, a security audit is an audit of a set of security procedures. Authentication, integrity protection, privacy protection, and nonrepudiation are all real-time tasks that must be performed concurrently with a transaction. A security audit, in contrast, occurs after the fact, and thus cannot prevent a security violation from happening. A properly conducted audit can, however, detect previously unrecognized or unreported security violations and highlight weak points in the system.

Auditability, a measure of the extent to which a set of procedures can be audited, is an essential element of any security plan. The key to auditability is consistent, accurate data collection. **Logging** (or recording) each transaction on a difficult-to-change medium is an important source of that data. For example, accurate logs might allow an auditor to select an individual employee and a date randomly and determine the precise times when that individual entered and left a physical facility. An online log might show the precise sequence of events that occurred when a particular customer's invoice payment was posted. Logging attempted security intrusions can help to identify potential weak points and provide essential documentation in the event that security is penetrated. Checking the logs can determine whether the appropriate procedures were followed and, in some cases, provide evidence to support or undermine a legal claim.

Countering Security Attacks

Physically secure information systems, networks, and access points are essential to system security. Even the most physically secure system can be successfully attacked, however. A well-designed security plan recognizes that attacks will occur and incorporates tools for countering them.

Access Control

As the term implies, the objective of access control is to ensure a physically secure location. Doors, locks, and guards are the traditional tools. The idea is to prevent unauthorized users from gaining access to the system and to its workstations, work areas, and other entry points by using screening techniques such as identification cards to authenticate legitimate users. If access to an intranet or an extranet is breached, it is difficult if not impossible to guarantee authentication, integrity, privacy, nonrepudiation, and even auditability.

One problem with traditional authentication tools, such as a driver's license or a similar identification card, is that the documents can be altered or even counterfeited. **Biometrics** offers a possible solution. Biometrics devices authenticate individuals based on such difficult-to-fake personal criteria as voiceprints, fingerprints, hand geometry, retinal scans, iris scans, signature recognition, and facial appearance. For example, a company might implement a biometrics authorization system by issuing each employee a smart card with a digitized copy of her fingerprint (or some other biometrics criterion) stored on the embedded chip (Figure 9.3). To gain access to a facility, the employee inserts the smart card into a secured, trusted reading device and then inserts her finger into a fingerprint scanner (Figure 9.4). The employee is authenticated only if the fingerprint on the card and the scanned fingerprint match. Such authentication techniques combine possession of an object (the card) and personal characteristics (the fingerprint).

Many highly sensitive facilities use mantraps to prevent unauthorized access. An individual starts the process by presenting a traditional form of identification, such as an ID card, to get through the first door, which is then locked. A biometrics screen, such as a fingerprint or retinal scan, is required to pass through the second door. Those who fail the second screen are trapped until the police or security guards arrive. Mantraps are effective because they increase the intruder's risk of getting caught.

Even laptop computers can be protected by biometrics. For example, if a laptop is equipped with a thumbprint scanner, the authorized user's digitized thumbprint can be

Figure 9.3 A smart card.

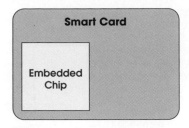

Figure 9.4 Biometric authentication.

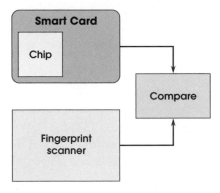

used just like a password to enable such tasks as launching the operating system and accessing the hard disk, making the laptop virtually useless to anyone who might find or steal it.

Because computers are binary devices, biometrics parameters must be digitized, and a digitized fingerprint is nothing more than a string of bits comparable to a long password. Passwords can be cracked, and a skilled hacker might be able to record his own digital fingerprint on a stolen smart card and then use the card to gain access to a secure facility. A partial solution is to compare a fingerprint (or some other biometrics parameter) read by a trusted scanner to a digitized version stored on a database (Figure 9.5). The employee ID card provides a search key for accessing the database. The stored fingerprint is then compared to the scanned fingerprint, and if they match, the employee is authenticated—assuming, of course, that the database has not been compromised.

Biometrics techniques are not particularly effective on the Internet, especially when the source of the input data is unknown and unsecured. A digitized fingerprint or retinal scan is, after all, nothing more than a long password, and passwords, even long ones, can be faked. The real danger of such a scenario is that an individual who gains access by using compromised biometrics data is unlikely to be challenged, because people tend to trust biometrics screening more than their own good judgment.

Figure 9.5 Adding a database increases the accuracy of biometric testing.

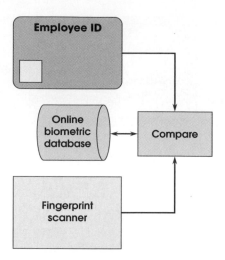

One significant biometrics problem is the risk of false negatives. A slight misalignment of the finger, a cut, or a burn can cause a fingerprint to be misread, denying access to a legitimate employee, and a head cold can affect an individual's voiceprint. One solution is to loosen the test criteria, but loosening the criteria increases the risk of a false positive—authenticating an imposter. As you know, security is a series of trade-offs.

Network Vulnerabilities

Utilizing a network, particularly a public network such as the Internet, significantly increases system vulnerability. Because both legitimate users and cybercriminals can access the Internet from virtually any computer located anywhere in the world, there is no way to physically secure all possible access points. Also, because the Internet's public lines and channels are outside a corporate system's control, they are vulnerable to packet sniffing. Network software often contains security holes. User computers, particularly dial-up workstations, represent yet another security exposure. To most companies, the advantages of using the Internet outweigh the risk, but it is dangerous to ignore that risk.

E-mail is a major security hole. In most companies, e-mail has become an accepted way of communicating and conducting business, so the access point must remain open. Knowing that, hackers rely on e-mail attachments to insert Trojan horses, backdoors, viruses, and worms into a system, making some form of e-mail screening essential. One solution is to block individual e-mail messages based on such criteria as subject, key words, source, and so on. Additionally, many organizations have implemented software to block the distribution of spam by rejecting messages with too many recipients.

Instant messaging is a growing problem. The technology relies on presence detection and buddy lists to identify friends, colleagues, and business contacts who are currently online and allows a user to send instant messages to them. Instant messaging eliminates

The National Transportation System Smart Card

Following September 11, 2001, one suggestion for enhancing security while reducing wait time, at least for frequent flyers, was to implement a national transportation system smart card. The proposal, called SkyD, called for storing a passenger's flight history and such biometric information as a fingerprint or retinal pattern on the smart card's embedded chip. When the passenger confirmed the flight, the appropriate personal information would be transferred to the airline's active database. When the passenger arrived at the airport and inserted the smart card (possession of an object) into a reading device, the personal information stored on the card would be compared against the database. A subsequent fingerprint or retinal scan would further confirm the passenger's identification.

Proponents argued that SkyD would allow frequent flyers (the airlines' best customers) to move quickly from curb to gate while the screeners focused their time and attention on unregistered passengers. A key element of the proposal was shifting from screening things (such as carry-on bags) to screening people, a strategy that seems to make sense.

Opposition was based primarily on privacy and discrimination concerns. Opponents argued that the SkyD card could easily evolve into a form of national ID, allowing the government or a business concern to track the cardholder's movements. Also, because only frequent flyers would be eligible for a SkyD card, the program would discriminate against occasional flyers and anyone who could not afford to or chose not to obtain a card, effectively profiling them. Imagine an 80-year-old woman in a wheelchair being randomly selected for a physical search while a well-dressed terrorist who had established his credentials over a period of years walked right through the security checkpoint. Absurd? Ask *Newsweek* columnist Anna Quindlen, who reported in the March 18, 2002, issue that she was randomly selected for a pat down and a wand check three times in an eight-hour period, even though there has never been an incident in which a woman has hijacked an airplane.

phone tag and crossing e-mail messages and makes possible an effective, ad hoc form of data conferencing. Users like instant messaging because it improves efficiency and makes their jobs easier. However, the popular instant messaging services are provided by public domain service providers such as AOL, Microsoft Network, and Yahoo, so the supporting software is outside the organization's control. As a result, the instant messages must leave the corporation's secured network and travel over the public Internet, making it difficult, if not impossible, to physically control a message's source, destination, or data path. That lack of control exposes the message to sniffing, interception, and modification and jeopardizes integrity and privacy.

Once again, the company faces a trade-off. If the convenience and efficiency gained from instant messaging exceeds the risk, integrating the necessary technology into the corporation's information technology infrastructure makes sense. For example, instant messaging software might be installed on an intranet or an extranet, limiting the available communication links to fellow employees and business partners who share a secure network.

Intrusion Detection

It has been said that Internet security is an oxymoron. The Internet was not designed with electronic commerce in mind; its creators were academics and researchers dedicated to the free and open interchange of information. Consequently, you would be wise to assume that a corporate system attached to the Internet will be attacked and that at least some attacks will succeed. Intrusions can be countered by preventing, deterring, or deflecting them or by taking countermeasures, such as conducting preemptive strikes. The first step, however, is intrusion detection.

As the term implies, the objective of **intrusion detection** is to detect an intrusion when it occurs or as soon thereafter as possible. The idea is to limit damage and to simplify recovery. Intrusions can sometimes be detected as they occur by using anomaly detection techniques to monitor for unusual usage patterns or activities, such as repeated unsuccessful logons, an attempt to modify the Windows registry, or an attempt to modify the contents of a database without proper authority. Often, however, detection takes place after the fact, as the result of a security audit.

Logging is a useful deterrent. If such information as user login attempts and changes to a database are recorded on a write-only medium such as magnetic tape, various detection procedures can be used to analyze the log, looking for intrusion signatures, traffic patterns, anomalies, or use patterns associated with break-ins. Following a break-in, the log documents the hacker's activities, which can simplify recovery and serve as evidence for possible prosecution, increasing the intruder's risk. Additionally, such logs provide valuable audit trails.

Logging is passive. A honey pot (sometimes called a honey net or a phishing line), in contrast, is an active countermeasure that resembles a reverse Trojan horse. The idea is to lure an attacker into a confined space controlled by the system operator and then to monitor the hacker's activities. Using a honey pot allows the defender to identify system vulnerabilities by watching what the hacker attacks and also yields all the benefits of logging.

The principle of confinement is another important security concept. The idea is to restrict an authenticated user's access to a system's resources based on her need to know. Often, each user is assigned (individually or by job classification) a set of rights, privilege levels, and permissions that define and limit the resources she is authorized to access. Authentication procedures allow a user to gain access to the system. Privilege levels and permissions define what the user can do once she has gained access. Attempts to bypass restrictions are flagged as possible security violations.

Firewalls

Typically supplied by an intermediary, a **firewall** isolates a private network from a public network by controlling how clients from outside can access the organization's internal servers. A good firewall can block many intrusion attempts before they happen. Often, the firewall runs on a router or a bastion host, a host computer that is directly linked to the Internet and thus fully exposed to attack. Such firewalls sit between the host server and the Internet and block potentially dangerous or questionable transactions from getting in or out (Figure 9.6). Another common configuration allows unrestricted access to Web servers, FTP servers, and similar public services but restricts access to the corporate intranet or a local area network (Figure 9.7). Proxy servers are often firewall-protected, too.

Firewalls are also used to isolate internal subnetworks from each other. For example, payroll personnel have a legitimate need to access salary data, but most other employees do not, so key payroll applications often run on a firewall-protected subnet. Similarly, the only way to access key strategic planning information is through the executive suite's firewall-protected subnet. In large corporations, the number of firewalls protecting internal subnets often exceeds the number protecting against external intrusion.

Figure 9.6 A basic firewall configuration.

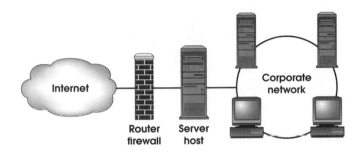

Figure 9.7 This firewall configuration allows unrestricted access to public services but limits access to private services.

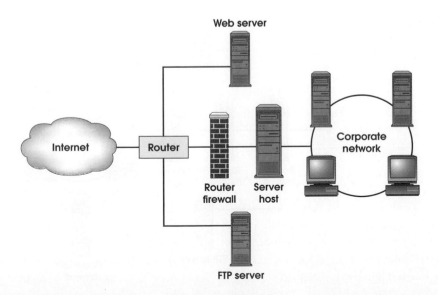

Corporate systems increasingly implement the defend-in-depth principle, with a relatively open firewall protecting all servers, a tighter firewall protecting the intranet or LAN, and personal firewall software protecting the individual workstations (Figure 9.8). Servers in particular must be protected because they typically control access to a number of clients. An unprotected server is a valid reason for assigning a failing security audit grade to a network.

A packet-filtering firewall works by screening incoming and outgoing packets at the TCP/IP Internet level. It accepts or rejects packets based on criteria stored in the message headers, such as protocol (reject all telnet transactions), sending IP address, outgoing IP address, and incoming port (reject all packets that do not come through port 80, the HTTP port). Packet-filtering firewalls are common on DSL and Ethernet routers. Like the Internet, most packet-filtering firewalls are stateless; in other words, they treat each packet as an independent entity and accept or reject it without considering related packets.

Other firewalls run at the application level and function as content filters, perhaps enforcing the organization's acceptable use policies. Sometimes called stateful firewalls, they rely on a proxy server to cache related packets, reconstruct the original message, and inspect the message content. Stateful firewalls tend to make better, more intelligent accept/reject decisions. For example, by screening content, a stateful firewall can reject messages or pages with a possible sexual content by looking for such key words as *breast* and *sex*. One problem with such screens, however, is that they can reject legitimate information, such as articles about breast cancer or biographical information about John Sexton, and they do cause some performance degradation. Once again, security is a series of trade-offs.

Figure 9.8 Defend in depth.

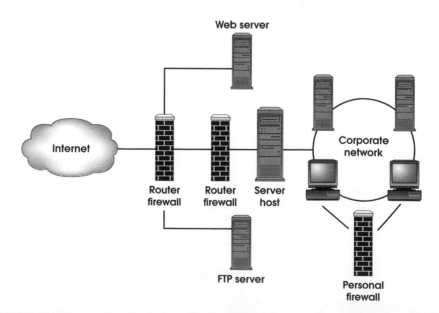

A good firewall significantly improves security, but even a good firewall has weaknesses. Firewalls are particularly vulnerable to inside attack, such as a Trojan horse planted by an internal hacker that lets an outsider bypass the firewall. Carelessness is perhaps the most serious internal risk, however, with system operators failing to remove default passwords, users choosing easy-to-guess passwords or writing their passwords on paper, users failing to disable Windows printer and file sharing, and users failing to update their antivirus software. A solution to many of these problems is to take responsibility away from the user and to automate such tasks as software updates and regular password changes, but some tasks require human involvement.

Not all security holes are inside the organization, of course. E-mail is a huge hole in the firewall, particularly when it is used to transfer attached files. The standard World Wide Web (HTTP) access port represents another significant leak. Users demand e-mail and Web access, but such applications introduce security risks.

Other leaks are created by business applications (such as instant messaging and groupware) that users download from a noncorporate source and install themselves, thus bypassing the information technology department. The responsible technical professionals see such applications as potential carriers of destructive software and, because they are not officially approved, consider them inconsistent with the organization's information strategy.

The users see the information technology department as a roadblock that prevents them from implementing a new, useful tool, however, an opinion supported by at least an element of truth. The information technology department is rewarded based on such negative outcomes as a lack of crashes and is penalized for system disruptions, even if the department's intent is to improve efficiency. However, if users take control of the network's configuration and contents, the results can be disastrous. Users focus on their own application—a single layer. Security is a systemwide problem, and in most organizations, the information technology department is the only group charged with protecting the entire system.

Cryptography

No matter how well a network is protected, some intrusion attempts will succeed. An effective security plan must include provisions for protecting the integrity of internal databases and applications even if security is breeched. When you send an e-mail message or transmit information on the Internet, you assume, often implicitly, that the contents are private (known only to you and the intended recipient) and that the integrity of the message has not been compromised. In a business context, where key operating and decision-making information is routinely communicated over an e-commerce network, privacy and integrity are not merely desirable, but essential. Unfortunately, there are ways (both legal and illegal) to intercept and even modify a message in transit. Cryptography offers a possible solution to both problems.

Cryptography is the science of encrypting or otherwise concealing the meaning of a message to ensure the privacy and integrity of the information transfer. An unencrypted message is called **plain text**. The originator uses a secret code or cipher to **encrypt** the message into encoded or ciphered form. A code replaces one word or phrase with another; for example, the Secret Service assigns a code name to the president. A cipher replaces each letter or digit with another, for example, substituting Q for A. On the other end of the line, the recipient reverses the process, **decrypting** the message by converting it back into plain text. Cryptographic techniques can also be used to protect the contents of a database from an intruder.

Cryptography has its limits, of course. For example, if a hacker gains access to the sending or receiving node, he can read the message before it is encrypted, after it is decrypted, or while the message contents are being processed, and keystroke monitoring software can capture a plain text message as it is being composed. Like any security tool, a cryptographic process is no stronger than its weakest link, because hackers will exploit any weakness they find.

Caesar-Shift Substitution Ciphers

One of the easiest encryption techniques to understand is a **Caesar-shift substitution cipher**. This technique is named after Julius Caesar, an early user and perhaps the originator. The idea is simple (Figure 9.9). Start with the plain text: ATTACK AT DAWN. Next, shift the alphabet; for example, Figure 9.9 shows a one-letter shift, so *A* becomes *B*, *B* becomes *C*, *C* becomes *D*, and so on. The resulting encrypted text, BUUBDL BU EBXO, is meaningless unless you know the rule (the encryption algorithm) that was used to generate it.

The Caesar-shift technique is not limited to a one-letter shift, of course. Try shifting the plain text message by two letters, then three, then four, and so on. Each shift yields a different encoded message. An encryption **key** converts a general encryption algorithm (the Caesar-shift) into a specific rule for encrypting and decrypting a particular message. In this example, the key is the number of letters that the plain text message is shifted. For Caesar-shift encryption to work, both the sender and the recipient must use the same algorithm and the same key.

Figure 9.9 A simple Caesar-shift substitution cipher.

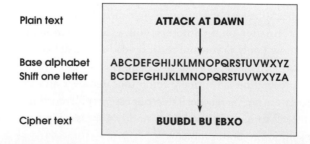

Symmetric Secret-Key Cryptography

Modern encryption has moved well beyond simple Caesar-shift substitution. Symmetric encryption uses a single key that must be known by both parties. Asymmetric encryption, in contrast, uses different keys to encrypt and decrypt a message. Both symmetric and asymmetric encryption techniques rely on complex algorithms and long keys and are extremely difficult to crack.

Secret-key cryptography is a symmetric technique that uses the same key to both encrypt and decrypt a message (Figure 9.10); Caesar-shift substitution ciphers fall into this category. Secret-key algorithms can be almost unbreakable, and both the encryption and decryption processes are relatively fast. However, both the sender and the receiver must know the key, and the key exchange process (getting the right key to both parties) represents a significant security risk.

Data encryption standard (DES) is a well-known 128-bit secret key algorithm developed in the 1970s. It was subsequently adopted as a standard by the National Security Agency (NSA) and was used by banks for electronic funds transfers until **advanced encryption standard (AES)**, a new algorithm with a key length ranging from 128 to 256 bits, replaced it in October 2000. Like all secret key (single key) techniques, however, both DES and AES require the sender and the receiver to use the same key, and key exchange is a problem.

Asymmetric Public-Key Encryption

Public-key encryption (Figure 9.11), an alternative to secret-key encryption, is asymmetric because different keys are used to encrypt and decrypt a message. The keys are distributed in related pairs. The receiver keeps one, the **private key**, and publishes the other, the **public key**. A message is encrypted using the *receiver's public* key and decrypted using the *receiver's private* key. The process works both ways: If a message is encrypted

Figure 9.10 With secret-key cryptography, there is only one key.

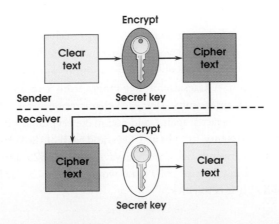

Figure 9.11 Asymmetric public-key encryption.

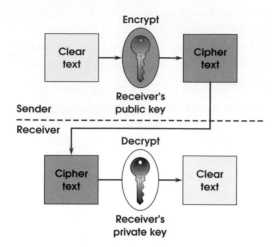

with Bert's public key, it can be decrypted only with his private key. If Bert uses his private key to encrypt a message, it can be decrypted only with his public key.

Public-key algorithms are more complex and use longer keys than secret-key algorithms. Consequently, they are much slower (perhaps thousands of times slower) than secret-key algorithms, making them unsuitable for encrypting real-time or lengthy messages. Public-key algorithms are more secure than secret-key algorithms, however, primarily because there is no need to exchange keys. Another trade-off.

Cryptanalysis

Cryptanalysis is the process of decrypting a message without knowing the key. For example, a simple Caesar-shift substitution cipher is very easy to crack. Because there are only twenty-six letters in the Roman alphabet, there are only twenty-five possible shifts. (*A* can be replaced by *B, C, D, E, F*, and so on, but if you replace *A* with *A* you get the plain text version.) Try each possible shift, and you will crack the code, probably in fifteen minutes or less.

Given enough time, trial-and-error **brute-force cryptanalysis**, trying all possible keys until the right one emerges, always works. That is why the length of the key, which defines the maximum number of possible keys, is an important measure of the strength of an encryption algorithm. A Caesar-shift key ranges from 1 to 25, yielding very weak encryption. Perform two Caesar-shifts (shift each character once, take the encrypted text, and shift each encrypted character again), and you make cryptanalysis much more difficult. The first shift yields twenty-five possible keys, and each of those twenty-five encryptions can be re-encrypted twenty-five different ways, yielding 625 different possibilities. Instead of minutes, cracking the cipher by hand would take hours (at least). The longer the key, the more difficult it is to crack.

Public-Key Encryption

In 1975, three British cryptanalysts named James Ellis, Clifford Cocks, and Malcolm Williamson developed the first public-key encryption algorithm, but it remained a military secret until the British government declassified it in 1997. The idea was subsequently rediscovered and published in 1976 by three computer scientists, Whitfield Diffie, Martin Hellman, and Ralph Merkle. A year later, Ronald Rivest, Adi Shamir, and Leonard Adleman created the RSA (Rivest-Shamir-Adleman) algorithm, an elegant implementation of the DHM (Diffie-Hellman-Merkle) principle.

Initially, the NSA blocked release of RSA in the name of national security. In 1991, Phil Zimmerman—in spite of heavy pressure from the NSA, which threatened him with arrest for violating national security—released a product to the Internet that combined RSA with a secret-key algorithm similar to DES. He called it PGP (Pretty Good Privacy), and suddenly, government-quality encryption was available to everyone.

Why did the NSA object so strongly to the release of public-key encryption? The RSA algorithm provided such strong encryption that cracking the cipher was almost impossible. Domestically, law enforcement considers wiretapping one of its most effective crime-fighting tools, and the CIA and the NSA gather much of their international intelligence by intercepting electronic transmissions. If the bad guys (domestic and foreign) started using strong encryption, those sources of information could dry up. What do you prefer, effective law enforcement or personal privacy?

There are alternatives to brute-force cryptanalysis. If you have ever watched *Wheel of Fortune*, you know that certain letters (*n*, *l*, *r*, *s*, *t*, and the vowels) occur more frequently than others, so a simple frequency distribution of the symbols in a message can often provide clues about the plain text values of certain characters. Guess a few letters correctly, and the message begins to make sense. Other techniques start with snippets of stolen, intercepted, or guessed plain text and use that wedge to attack the message. For example, in World War II, the Germans often started certain messages (such as weather reports) with a predictable string of characters (such as the weather station and the date), and such information proved crucial in breaking their Enigma cipher.

Key Length

Modern cryptographic techniques are computer-based. They use binary keys to encrypt binary data, and the efficiency of brute-force cryptanalysis depends on processing speed and **key length** (Figure 9.12). Note that using year 2002 technology to test a 128-bit key's 10^{38} possible values would take something like 10^{24} years, while a 32-bit key can be broken in minutes. Moore's Law suggests that processing speed doubles roughly every eighteen months, and when speed doubles, decryption time is cut in half. Consequently, as processing speed increases, the minimum acceptable key length increases with it.

Clearly, expecting anyone to memorize a secret 128-bit key is unreasonable, and the keys used by public-key algorithms are even longer (Figure 9.13). Such lengthy keys are

Figure 9.12 The relationship between key length and brute-force decryption time.

Key length	Possible keys	Decryption time
32 bits	10^9	Minutes
56 bits	10^{16}	10^3 years
128 bits	10^{38}	10^{24} years
168 bits	10^{50}	10^{36} years

Figure 9.13 A public key.

```
00:96:f8:ea:aa:de:bc:33:74:ce:02:54:ef:1a:c7:
9d:0b:93:28:f3:59:e5:36:9b:a4:05:df:79:fd:99:
71:66:2c:90:1d:9c:d9:44:df:b9:ca:d9:e5:dd:f1:
69:03:dc:4a:e3:ba:ea:7d:68:84:7a:78:e8:b6:b7:
8e:94:ac:af:93:1e:05:81:0b:25:a0:72:ff:9e:0c:
24:9f:e3:bb:95:d4:40:82:c0:ff:d6:80:f2:ff:a4:
d6:20:be:09:bd:ec:44:59:74:ff:6f:5d:7a:69:3d:
d0:38:1e:33:17:be:d2:f7:ec:a7:e8:a9:05:ae:ba:
0b:98:85:3e:25:7e:92:e0:6f:25:32:a1:05:1f:7b:
54:01:3c:28:09:58:d8:7a:83:ed:aa:18:33:5a:14:
df:da:d5:d0:fe:d8:c2:17:16:fc:a7:16:af:de:c7:
06:f0:07:62:de:26:7b:bb:44:c8:02:ad:99:e4:d7:
f4:ff:1a:9f:51:d2:cd:9f:91:82:88:ae:f5:93:18:
5e:ec:37:1a:06:5c:62:1e:cf:9c:dd:5a:3f:23:8e:
e8:c3:59:05:5a:09:0e:9c:8c:08:c5:ad:55:fc:13:
b3:bb:38:08:45:f2:36:8e:f8:5a:3c:ba:96:45:38:
82:da:95:87:35:f8:2a:9a:75:1f:de:34:3d:27:0c:
6c:39
```

Courtesy of the Corporation for Research and Educational Networking, from *http://www.cren.net.*

stored on a computer and accessed only by the encryption and decryption software, but storing a key on a computer makes it susceptible to hacking and cracking. Yet another trade-off.

Given the difficulty of cracking a lengthy key, what happens if a legitimate user loses his private key, perhaps as the result of a computer failure? The answer is key recovery. Important keys are archived. To prevent theft from the archive, the key is typically split into two or more pieces and the pieces are stored separately, but archiving represents yet another potential security exposure.

At a 1998 data security conference, the Electronic Frontier Foundation (EFF), a nonprofit organization, won the DES Challenge II contest by cracking a 56-bit key to a DES-encoded message in three days. A year later, EFF teamed up with distributed.net, a coalition of computer experts, to win DES Challenge III in a mere twenty-two hours. As processing speed continues to increase exponentially, that number will shrink exponentially. The results of the DES Challenge forced the government to increase the DES key length from 56 to 128 bits and accelerated work on AES, the new national standard that supports 256-bit keys.

Digital Envelopes

Secret-key cryptography is much faster than public-key cryptography, but the key exchange problem is a significant security risk. The solution is to use a secret key to encrypt the message and then use public-key encryption to create a **digital envelope** that holds the secret key. Generally, the message is much larger than the secret key, so using the more efficient secret-key algorithm to encrypt the message makes sense, and using a public-key algorithm to encrypt the secret key has only a minor impact on efficiency. Because the secret key is transmitted in encrypted form, there is no key exchange problem.

Imagine, for example, that Bert wants to send an encrypted message to Ernie. He starts by using a secret key and a synchronous algorithm such as DES to convert the plain text message to cipher text (Figure 9.14). Next, he uses Ernie's public key to encrypt the secret key, creating a digital envelope. Finally, he sends the encrypted message and the digital envelope to Ernie. At the other end of the line (Figure 9.15), Ernie receives the message and the digital envelope, uses his private key to decrypt the secret key (in effect, opening the digital envelope), and then uses the secret key to decrypt the message.

Digital Signatures

Imagine that Bert has just received a message from Ernie encrypted with Bert's posted public key. How can Bert be sure that Ernie actually sent the message? Anyone could have signed Ernie's name, accessed the key registration site, obtained Bert's public key, and encrypted the message. A password does not adequately authenticate Ernie as the sender, nor does his name at the bottom of the message, or even a digitized version of his written signature. Such constants are too easy to steal. Physical location is no help either, because a skilled hacker can simply spoof Ernie's IP address (see Chapter 8).

One solution is for Ernie to attach a **digital signature** to the message. To create his digital signature, a program on Ernie's computer prepares a digest (a meaningless bit string derived from the message contents) by using a hashing algorithm. The digest is then encrypted using Ernie's *private* key to create his digital signature, which is attached to the

Figure 9.14 Sending a digital envelope.

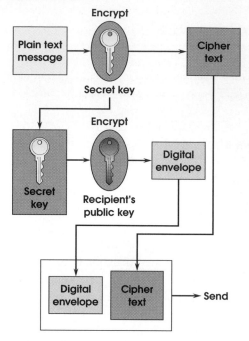

Figure 9.15 Receiving a digital envelope.

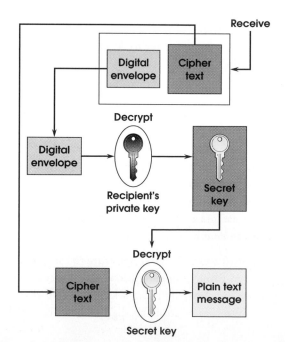

message (Figure 9.16). The message with the attached digital signature is then encrypted using Bert's public key. Subsequently, Bert uses his private key to decrypt the message plus the digest and Ernie's *public* key to decrypt the digest (Figure 9.17). Bert then creates a new digest by running the decrypted message through the same hashing algorithm Ernie used. If Bert's digest matches Ernie's digest, Bert knows the sender is Ernie, because only Ernie's public key can decrypt a message encrypted using Ernie's private key. Thus, a digital signature supports authentication and nonrepudiation.

The digest is a meaningless bit string derived from the message contents. It is unique to the message, however—changing the message changes the digest. Because the sender uses her private key to encrypt the digest, it is unique to both the sender and the message content. If the sender's and receiver's digests do not match, the message was likely either modified in transit or did not originate with the apparent sender. Digital signature standard (DSS) and MD5 (an algorithm) are two open standards for creating digital signatures.

Although it is difficult, a skilled hacker can work around a digital signature. If a Trojan horse, a virus, a backdoor, or a hacker attack has compromised a system's security, the perpetrator can steal an individual's private key from her hard drive and use the key to create a counterfeit digital signature. Other potential problems arise from the commercialization of cryptography. For example, PGP is now a commercial product that incorporates numerous business options. One option is sending an automatic blind "carbon copy" of each encrypted message to the company's security officer, allowing the company to scan and, if necessary, read all an employee's messages. The blind copy is encrypted using the security officer's public key, so the employee cannot decrypt it even if she knows the copy exists. Under certain conditions, a skilled hacker might be able to activate this option and send encrypted copies of the victim's e-mail to himself.

Figure 9.16 Creating a digital signature.

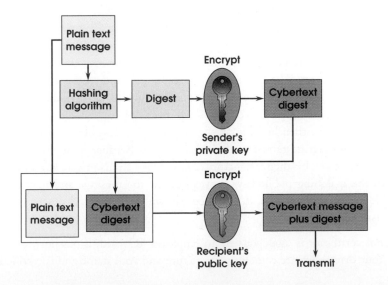

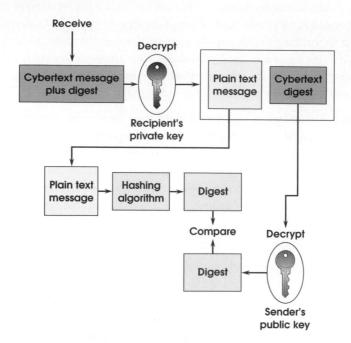

Figure 9.17 Verifying a digital signature.

Digital Certificates

A digital signature is an excellent authentication tool, but it is possible to fake one. Imagine that a hacker has created a set of encryption keys and registered the public key in Ernie's name. When Bert receives a message ostensibly from Ernie, the posted public key will correctly decrypt the digital signature, apparently authenticating Ernie as the sender even though Ernie did not send the message.

One way to overcome the digital signature forgery problem is for Ernie to obtain a **digital certificate** (Figure 9.18), an electronic document issued by a trusted third party called a **certificate authority** (**CA**). To apply for one (Figure 9.19), Ernie first contacts a registration authority (RA), which authenticates Ernie's identity and passes his request to a certificate authority. The CA assigns him a key pair and creates a digital certificate that incorporates a serial number plus Ernie's name, e-mail address, public key, and similar personal information. The CA's digital signature completes the digital certificate. Valid digital certificates are then listed in an online publicly accessible repository, so anyone can access Ernie's certificate and verify his public key. Because he is the only one who knows his private key, his digital signature (encrypted with his private key and decrypted only with the matching public key) proves he sent the message and makes it almost impossible for him to repudiate it. The steps shown in Figure 9.19 describe the **public key infrastructure** (**PKI**).

A digital certificate is analogous to an employee ID card, a passport, or a driver's license. Your driver's license contains your picture and your name and is certified by the

Figure 9.18 The contents of a digital certificate.

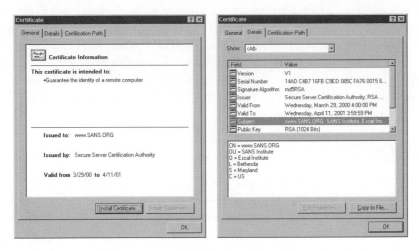

Figure 9.19 The public key infrastructure (PKI).

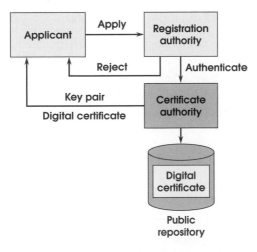

state. When you show your license to cash a check or to pass through an airport security checkpoint, the bank teller or the security guard matches your picture to your face and (implicitly) trusts the state that the picture shows the person whose name is on the license. Similarly, a digital certificate represents the certificate authority's word that a given public key is associated with a particular name. By checking Ernie's public key against the certificate issued by the certifying authority and then validating the CA's digital signature, you can be confident that you are communicating with Ernie.

Asynchronous Encryption Vulnerabilities

If Ernie is careless and loses his private key, whoever finds or steals it can easily impersonate him electronically. If Ernie's CA fails to properly verify his identity, an imposter might create a fake digital certificate in Ernie's name and subsequently impersonate him. If an employer fails to repudiate Ernie's digital certificate after he resigns or is fired, he might use his no-longer-valid access rights to gain revenge. If a CA's private key is compromised, every digital certificate listed on that CA's repository is suspect. Note that all those vulnerabilities involve human error.

Steganography

Cryptography is the science of encrypting or otherwise concealing the meaning of a message. One problem with cryptography is that an encrypted message is still recognizably a message. Furthermore, because someone took the time to encrypt it, the message probably contains important information. To a cryptanalyst, the act of encrypting a message is a bit like waving a red flag that says, "Decrypt me!"

The objective of **steganography** (from the Greek for "covered writing") is to hide the message to make it invisible and undetectable. In ancient times, a king or a general sometimes shaved a courier's head and tattooed a message on his scalp. After the hair grew back, the courier traveled to the recipient, where his head was once again shaved and the message revealed. (Things moved much more slowly in those days.) If, by chance, the courier was stopped in transit, the message was invisible.

Consider the rather transparent example of steganography shown in Figure 9.20. Imagine the passage purports to be a satire on our tendency to invent new diseases and conditions to explain the obvious. Select only the uppercase characters, insert blanks to separate words, and the hidden message emerges. Figure 9.21 shows a somewhat more realistic example. Extract the first letter of each word, insert spaces to separate the words,

Lost Digital Certificates

BUSINESS

On January 29 and 30, 2001, VeriSign issued two digital certificates to one or more imposters who fraudulently claimed to represent Microsoft. VeriSign attributed the error to the failure of the responsible personnel to confirm adequately each applicant's identity—in other words, to human error. Because Microsoft uses digital certificates to authenticate software and other content it distributes online, the stolen documents could have been used to trick an unwary user into downloading and running malicious software she assumed came from Microsoft. To date, there has been no evidence of such malware, and both VeriSign and Microsoft have formally repudiated the fraudulent digital certificates, so apparently no harm was done. However, this incident clearly shows that as long as human beings are part of the process, there is no such thing as perfect security.

Figure 9.20 A simple example of steganography.

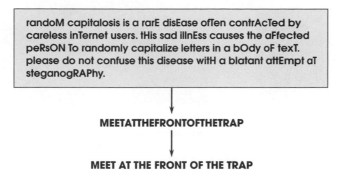

randoM capitalosis is a rarE disEase ofTen contrAcTed by careless inTernet users. tHis sad illnEss causes the aFfected peRsON To randomly capitalize letters in a bOdy oF texT. please do not confuse this disease witH a blatant attEmpt aT steganogRAPhy.

MEETATTHEFRONTOFTHETRAP

MEET AT THE FRONT OF THE TRAP

Source: Donovan Artz, "Digital Steganography: Hidding Data within Data," *IEEE Internet Computing,* May/June 2001: 75–80.

Figure 9.21 A somewhat more realistic example of steganography.

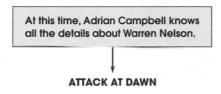

At this time, Adrian Campbell knows all the details about Warren Nelson.

ATTACK AT DAWN

and read the message. Other examples might use the second letter of each word or write the message between the lines using invisible ink.

Digital data stored on a computer can be used to create hidden messages that are much more difficult to detect. For example, imagine a color digital image that uses 24 bits (3 bytes) to represent each pixel: one byte for red, one for green, and one for blue. The least significant bit in each byte has a very small effect on the image, so replacing those bits with bits from the hidden message yields a stegoimage that reveals little more than subtle color shifts when displayed (Figure 9.22). Given side-by-side access to both the original bit-mapped cover image and the stegoimage, you might be able to spot those color shifts, but you will almost certainly see only the stegoimage. Similar results can be achieved by hiding a message in an audio or video file. Note that because only one of every eight bits is used for the hidden message, the inserted image must be smaller than the cover image.

Terrorists have allegedly used steganography to hide maps, photos, and other information, but steganography has legitimate applications, too. For example, steganographic techniques can be used to insert a hidden watermark into a graphic image (Figure 9.23), an audio file, or even a text file, and the watermark can be used to prove the source or ownership of intellectual property or to discourage reproduction of the property.

Figure 9.22 A stegoimage.

Cover image	Inserted image	Stegoimage

Source: *http://chacs.nrl.navy.mil/publications/CHACS/2000/2000moskowitz-stego.pdf*

Figure 9.23 A steganographic watermark.

A visible watermark proves ownership and makes the image unusable.	The image with the watermark removed or hidden.

Digital Watermarking: Courtesy of Karl Frank.

Remember, however, that watermarking is effective only as long as the algorithm remains a secret. There is no such thing as a crack-proof digital distribution system.

Perhaps the most effective use of steganography is to supplement cryptography, not to replace it. Inserting an encrypted message into a steganographic image provides a very high level of security, because the message is not only encrypted but also hidden, so the cryptanalyst is not even aware that the message exists.

The Secure Sockets Layer (SSL)

The **secure sockets layer** (**SSL**) is a protocol that runs in the context of the standard TCP/IP protocols. It uses public-key encryption, a digital envelope, a digital signature, and digital certificates to authenticate and establish a secure, symmetric secret-key connection between a client and a server for the duration of a session, thus ensuring the integrity and privacy of the messages. Rather than assuming that users have the necessary public, private, and secret (for the digital envelope) keys, SSL randomly generates the appropriate keys for each transaction. The next time you pay for an e-commerce purchase by submitting your credit card number over the Internet, look for a closed lock icon near the bottom of your screen. It indicates that SSL is active. Check the protocol field in the URL, too; it should read *https*. Some security experts tout the Secure Electronic Transaction (SET) protocol as a replacement for SSL. SET is more comprehensive, but it is also more complex, which may account for its limited success.

Internet protocol security (**IPSec**), commonly used on a virtual private network (Chapter 7), is a set of protocols that supports secure packet exchange at the IP level. IPSec provides authentication and encapsulation services and uses public-key encryption. In transport mode, only the message is encrypted. In tunnel mode, encrypting both the headers and the message enhances security. In both modes, a digital certificate is used to authenticate the sender.

BUSINESS

Visa's Security Standards

Credit card fraud costs the banking industry about $1 billion a year. Compare the loss to an order-of-magnitude $2 *trillion* a year in sales volume, however, and the potential profit clearly justifies the loss. Granting credit is inherently risky. Theft and fraud are recognized costs of doing business, and the objective is to control, not to eliminate, those costs. Intelligent risk management and good security standards are crucial to achieving that objective.

Visa's security begins with the card itself. Access to the card manufacturing plant is very tight, featuring pre-employment screening, electronic badges, biometrics checks, and mantraps. The card itself features a difficult-to-counterfeit hologram of a bird in flight. The cards are individually embossed and encoded for each customer, and a unique card verification value (computed by a secret algorithm) is stored on each card's magnetic stripe. By computing a new value for the algorithm and comparing the result to the value stored on the card, the bank can verify that the card is legitimate.

Security also extends to the transactions. Although the actual transactions take place between a customer and a merchant and do not directly involve the bank, Visa International requires that its merchants implement the SSL as a minimum, and Visa has endorsed the more secure, digital certificate-based SET standard. Finally, VisaNet, Visa International's global electronic payments system, incorporates neural network technology, a form of artificial intelligence that identifies possibly fraudulent transactions or transaction patterns. All this security is invisible to the customer, and invisible security tends to be the most effective type.

Summary

Security is a series of trade-offs between conflicting objectives. One way for a company to identify the appropriate level of security is to view the decision as an insurance problem. Key security objectives include access, authentication, integrity, privacy, nonrepudiation, recovery, and auditability. The objective of access control is to ensure a physically secure location. Biometrics devices can identify and authenticate individuals based on such personal physical criteria as fingerprints. Utilizing a public network significantly increases system vulnerability, and e-mail and instant messaging are major security holes. Intrusion detection techniques are designed to detect an intrusion when it occurs or as soon as possible thereafter. The principle of confinement restricts a user's access to a system's resources based on the user's need to know.

A firewall is a set of hardware and software that isolates a private network from a public network. A packet filtering firewall accepts or rejects packets based on criteria stored in the packet headers. Other firewalls function as content filterers. A stateful or session-level firewall relies on a proxy server to cache the packets generated during a single session and inspects those packets in context.

Cryptography is the science of encrypting or otherwise concealing the meaning of a message. An unencrypted message is called plain text. The originator uses a secret code or cipher to encrypt the message, and the recipient reverses the process to decrypt the message by converting it back into plain text. A Caesar-shift substitution cipher is a simple encryption algorithm. An encryption key converts a general encryption algorithm into a specific rule for encrypting and decrypting a particular message. With secret-key cryptography there is only one key; DES is a well-known secret-key algorithm. With public-key encryption, keys are distributed in related pairs, a secret private key and a published public key. Cryptanalysis is the process of decrypting a message without knowing the key. The length of the key is an important measure of an encryption algorithm's strength.

Secret-key cryptography is much faster than public-key cryptography, but the key exchange problem is a significant security risk. One solution is to create a digital envelope to exchange the secret key. A digital signature supports authentication and nonrepudiation. A trusted third party called a certificate authority (CA) issues a digital certificate to authenticate an individual's digital signature. The objective of steganography is to hide a message to make it invisible and undetectable.

The SSL is a protocol that runs in the context of the standard TCP/IP protocols. IPSec is a set of protocols that supports secure packet exchange at the IP level.

Key Words

Chapter 9 Security

access
advanced encryption standard (AES)
auditability
authentication
biometrics
brute-force cryptanalysis
Caesar-shift substitution cipher
certificate authority (CA)

cryptanalysis
cryptography
data encryption standard (DES)
decrypt
digital certificate
digital envelope
digital signature
encrypt

firewall
integrity
Internet protocol security (IPSec)
intrusion detection
key
key length
logging
nonrepudiation

plain text
privacy
private key
public key

public-key encryption
public key infrastructure (PKI)
recovery
secret-key cryptography

secure sockets layer (SSL)
security
steganography

▪▪▪ Review Questions

1. Define security. Explain why security is necessary.

2. Explain how implementing security requires trade-offs between conflicting objectives.

3. One key to determining the appropriate level of security is risk assessment. What exactly does that mean?

4. Discuss the significance of such security objectives as access, authentication, integrity, privacy, nonrepudiation, and recovery.

5. Identify several physical access security tools and procedures. How does using a network increase system vulnerability?

6. What is a firewall? Relate the placement of a firewall to the resources to be protected.

7. Explain how a Caesar-shift substitution cipher works.

8. Distinguish between secret-key and public-key cryptography.

9. What is cryptanalysis?

10. Key length is an important measure of the strength of an encryption algorithm. Why?

11. Explain how a digital envelope works and how it helps to overcome the key exchange problem.

12. Explain how digital signatures and digital certificates work.

13. Define steganography and cite several examples.

14. What is the secure sockets layer (SSL)?

▪▪▪ Exercises

1. Discuss the changes in airport security in the six months after September 11, 2001. How did those changes affect the way business is conducted? Why? Do you agree with the changes? Why or why not?

2. Discuss the changes in border security in the six months after September 11, 2001. How did those changes affect the way business is conducted? Why? Do you agree with the changes? Why or why not?

3. Do you think a national identification card is a good idea? How about a national transportation system smart card designed to help improve airport security?

4. When Phil Zimmerman released Pretty Good Privacy (PGP), his public-key encryption system, to the Internet, the National Security Agency (NSA) threatened him with criminal prosecution. Do you agree with Phil or with the NSA? Why?

5. Invisible security tends to be the most effective type. Do you agree or disagree? Why?

Projects

Current references and supporting resources can be found on this textbook's companion Web site.

Broad-Based Projects

1. Investigate how you might add the secure sockets layer (SSL) to your Web site.

2. Investigate how you might add biometrics authentication to your network.

Building the Case:

3. Working as a team, continue with Chapter 1, Project 6 by discussing the security features needed to protect against the potential exposures you identified in Chapter 8. Make changes to your strategy and your Web site as necessary. Remember that your Web site is a prototype, so simply describing the recommended security features should be enough.

Business Projects

1. Investigate how the added cost of border security has affected B2B e-commerce in the automobile industry.

2. Develop a set of security standards for your company. Include physical security, authentication, integrity, privacy, and nonrepudiation in your plan.

Building the Case:

3. Continue with Chapter 1, Project 2 by creating a preliminary security plan to counter each of the risks identified in Chapter 8. Then go online, investigate the products offered by various security service providers, identify a security suite or set of applications that fits your needs, and obtain the price of that security solution. Write a report to document your results.

Information Technology Projects

1. Research the RSA algorithm and explain (basically) how it works.

2. Research steganography and write a paper explaining how at least one steganography technique not described in this book works.

Building the Case:

3. Continue with Chapter 1, Project 2 by creating a preliminary security plan to counter each of the intrusion scenarios identified in Chapter 8. Depending on your background, available time, and your instructor's preference, you might simply describe your security strategy on paper or actually implement the security safeguards in your prototype.

Marketing Projects

1. Research how security can be used to achieve a competitive advantage.

2. Prepare a draft advertising campaign designed to get consumers over their fear of sending their credit card number over the Internet. Focus on your company's transaction security procedures.

Building the Case:

3. Continue with Chapter 1, Project 2 by including elements in your advertising strategy to counter potential customers' security concerns, including currently installed security features and new security features your client should consider. Estimate the cost of implementing and operating each security feature and the potential revenue loss (due to customer concerns) if the feature is not installed. Write a report to document your results, and add information describing security features to the storyboard you started in Chapter 5.

References

Web Sites

Source	URL	Comments
CREN	*www.cren.net/ca/new_root.html*	CREN is a certificate authority.
SANS Institute	*http://rr.sans.org/index.php*	The SANS Information Security Reading Room, an impressive collection of articles.

Print and White Papers

Artz, Donovan. May/June 2001. "Digital Steganography: Hiding Data Within Data." *IEEE Internet Computing*: 75–80.

Conry-Murray, Andrew. November 5, 2001. "Strategies & Issues: Public Key Infrastructure Nuts and Bolts." *Network Magazine: http://networkmagazine.com/ article/NMG20011102S0008.*

National Institute of Standards and Technology. 1994. FIPS Publication 186, Digital Signature Standard (DSS). Washington, D.C.: Federal Information Processing Standards Publications.

Johnson, Neil F. and Jajodia, Sushil. February 1998. "Exploring Steganography: Seeing the Unseen," *Computer*: 26–34.

Savage, David E. January 25, 2001. "A Digital Certificate Introduction." SANS Institute: *http://rr.sans.org/encryption/certificate.php.*

Singh, Simon. 1999. *The Code Book: The Science of Secrecy from Ancient Egypt to Quantum Cryptography*. New York: Anchor Books.

CHAPTER 10

Privacy and Other Social Issues

**When you finish reading this chapter,
you should be able to:**

- Explain how knowledge can help off-set the fear, uncertainty, and doubt that shape the popular perception of information technology

- Explain how an individual's or a group's viewpoint affects the definition of privacy

- Distinguish between opt-in and opt-out privacy policies

- Explain why personal information is valuable and identify several legal sources of personal information

- Describe how tracking techniques are used to capture clickstream data

- Discuss several modern surveillance and monitoring tools and techniques

- Describe several ways in which technology can be misused

- Discuss several examples of online fraud

- Identify steps you might take to protect your online privacy and avoid falling victim to online scams and fraud

Gators and Gator Food

Southwest Florida's Upper Myakka Lake is about as close to paradise as an alligator can get. The shallow, rain-fed waters, stained nearly black by subtropical vegetation, are home to roughly 1,000 gators, plus countless fish, amphibians, reptiles, aquatic birds, and other tasty prey. On its east side, the lake's shore disappears into an impenetrable swamp that is perfect for nesting. Paradise.

Take an airboat ride on the lake and you are likely to see hundreds of large gators sunning themselves in the shallow water. You are also likely to see numerous canoes and bass-fishing boats sharing the lake with all those gators. You might even see a few brave fishermen standing waist deep in the murky water, nonchalantly casting their lines. You might be inclined to question their sanity. Then again, you might secretly envy them. Unless you know a great deal about alligators, however, the good old FUD (fear, uncertainty, and doubt) factor will probably keep you from joining them.

Consider a few facts: According to the Florida Museum of Natural History, between 1948 and 1995 (forty-seven years), slightly more than 200 people were attacked by alligators, and only 7 of those attacks were fatal. In Florida, lightning kills roughly seven people each *year*. Florida residents have learned to live with gators by following three simple rules: Don't feed them, leave them alone, and stay out of the water after dark. Gators are night feeders. "Only two things in the water after dark," goes an old Florida saying, "gators and gator food." Unless they deliberately provoke a big old gator, those canoeists and bass fishermen have little to fear. It takes only a little knowledge to overcome the FUD factor.

To many Web users, cyberspace resembles a gator-infested lake. You glide across the Web's surface, riding your nice, safe browser, even though you suspect that lurking beneath the surface lie hackers, crackers, con artists, identity thieves, spammers, and various forms of surveillance, monitoring, tracking, and snooping just waiting to get you. If you use a little common sense, the risk of falling prey to cybercrime is minimal, but unless you really understand what is going on beneath the surface, you feel a little bit like gator food.

Even experienced computer users suffer from fear, uncertainty, and doubt. Consider for example the (absolutely legitimate) process of changing Internet service providers (ISPs). In February 2002, following the failure of broadband ISP Excite@Home, Comcast Cable inherited the defunct company's former customers, forcing all of them to change their e-mail addresses. The process seemed straightforward: *handle@home.com* became *handle@comcast.net*. To Comcast's surprise, however, a significant number of customers encountered difficulty, and more than a few responded by switching to DSL.

We will focus on a gentleman we'll call Dave, a recently retired office manager. Dave had used computers for several years and was quite proficient with accounting and office management applications, but electronically downloading new software and modifying his online e-mail account stymied him. After several hours of fruitless work, he gave up and phoned a technically proficient friend for help. We'll call his friend the Wizard. In an hour-long telephone conversation, the Wizard talked him through the process, and the new connection worked without a hitch. When they finished, however, Dave readily admitted he had absolutely no idea what he had done and did not believe he could repeat the process on his own.

Technically skilled people understand the context in which applications run because they understand what happens beneath the surface in the lower layers. Dave's wizard friend knew that an e-mail message is sent to the recipient's mailbox using the SMTP protocol and is subsequently transferred to his mail program by a POP3 protocol. He knew that several network parameters had to be reset from Excite@Home's values to Comcast.net's values and that Dave's e-mail account had to be edited to reflect his new e-mail address. He assumed (correctly) that Comcast's software would make the broad changes affecting all users, and he knew how to download that software. He understood that Dave would have to make any changes that affected only his account, and he knew how to make those changes.

Expecting most users, even relatively skilled users, to possess such knowledge is unreasonable. You don't have to be an auto mechanic to drive a car. You can enjoy television without the slightest understanding of signal transmission and electron beam scanning. Because of information technology's layered design, you can use such applications as a word processor, a spreadsheet program, or an e-mail program without understanding how a computer works. And users like Dave should be able to change their ISPs even if they have no idea what happens in the underlying layers.

Science fiction author Arthur C. Clarke once said, "Any sufficiently advanced technology is indistinguishable from magic." In ancient Egypt, the temple priests zealously guarded the knowledge that allowed them to predict when the Nile would flood. Like an ancient temple priest, Dave's wizard friend knew the proper incantations, and to Dave, what his friend did seemed magical. The inability to complete such tasks as changing e-mail accounts and switching to a new ISP without help confirms the user's feelings of technical illiteracy and contributes to the fear, uncertainty, and doubt that shape the popular perception of information technology and the Web.

Knowing at least a little about the Web's seamy side is important, however. On the Web, what you do not know can hurt you. Like the gators in Upper Myakka Lake, the hackers, con artists, identity thieves, and other lowlifes are out there, lurking beneath the surface. Their scams existed long before the Internet came into being, of course, but online access has opened new opportunities for ripping people off. A little knowledge is your best defense. We begin by examining online privacy.

Privacy

In January 1999, Intel, bowing to intense pressure from privacy advocates, agreed to disable features that would have added a unique identification code to each Pentium III chip. Critics argued that a Pentium chip's unique ID could be linked to an individual user, allowing that user's online activities to be monitored and violating her privacy. That evening, Scott McNealy, the CEO of Sun Microsystems, Inc., told a group of reporters, "You have zero privacy anyway. Get over it." There are many ways to interpret McNealy's remarks, but one is particularly troublesome, because at least in cyberspace, it just might be true. Perhaps Intel's decision to disable chip identification really wasn't all that significant, because the type of monitoring condemned by Intel's opponents already exists.

What Is Privacy?

Privacy means different things to different people. According to the 2001 edition of the Microsoft Encarta World English Dictionary, **privacy** means freedom from the observation, intrusion, or attention of others. To an individual, that definition implies a right to be left alone and to be free of unreasonable intrusions, but society's view is different. Sometimes law enforcement, antiterrorism, and national defense take precedence over individual privacy rights, and businesses need customer information to support relationship management strategies.

Clearly, privacy rights are not absolute. Balancing individual rights with society's needs is tricky at best, because the sense of where to draw that line properly is influenced by cultural, generational, and even individual viewpoints. To cite a simple example, today's university students do not hesitate to tell friends, professors, and the school's career placement office how much they will be paid on their first post-graduation job. Those students' grandparents would have found such behavior appalling, however, because two generations ago, an individual's salary was considered private and personal, not to be divulged. If two generations in the same family cannot agree on what should and should not be kept private, how is it possible to reach universal agreement on exactly what privacy means?

Privacy and the Law

Many U.S. citizens sincerely believe that they have a constitutional right to privacy. They might be surprised, however, to learn that the word *privacy* does not even appear in the Constitution. Although the Third Amendment prohibits the government from quartering soldiers in a private home in times of peace, it allows for exceptions in times of war or national emergency. The Fourth Amendment bans unreasonable searches and seizures, but the word *unreasonable* is subject to interpretation. Some jurists argue that the Fourteenth Amendment, which prohibits state governments from abridging the rights of any U.S. citizen, implies a right to privacy, but that right is not specifically defined anywhere in the Constitution.

Because digital information is so easy to collect and aggregate, an individual's online privacy rights have become a particularly thorny issue. Over the past decades, the U.S. Congress has passed numerous laws intended to clarify privacy rights (Figure 10.1). Congress is a deliberative body, however, and by the time a proposed new law is written, debated, and voted upon, a very good chance exists that technological change will have rendered it moot, at least in cyberspace. Some laws actually tip the balance away from personal privacy. For example, the Patriot Act passed in October 2001 in response to the September 11 terrorist attacks is aimed at apprehending terrorists at some cost to individual privacy rights. Even the bankruptcy laws seem to work against individual privacy rights, as several dot-coms learned when they were forced to sell personal data to the highest bidder even though their stated policy was never to sell such data.

Several informal guiding principles have emerged, however, and are beginning to influence both the law and policy (Figure 10.2). You must be told when and why personal information is being collected. You must be given a choice to **opt in** (agree to participate) or **opt out** (choose not to participate) of any activity that involves sharing or selling your personal information. You must have access to your personal information and must be given an opportunity to correct errors. The party that collects the personal information is responsible for guaranteeing its integrity and ensuring that access is limited to authorized personnel performing authorized activities. Finally, if any of these principles are violated, you have a right to seek legal remedies.

Figure 10.1 Some U.S. privacy laws.

Year	Title	Intent
1970	Fair Credit Reporting Act	Limits the distribution of credit reports to those who need to know
1974	Privacy Act	Establishes the right to be informed about personal information on government databases
1978	Right to Financial Privacy Act	Prohibits the federal government from examining personal financial accounts without due cause
1986	Electronic Communications Privacy Act	Prohibits the federal government from monitoring personal e-mail without a subpoena
1988	Video Privacy Protection Act	Prohibits disclosing video rental records without customer consent or a court order
2001	Patriot Act	Streamlines federal surveillance guidelines to simplify tracking possible terrorists

Figure 10.2 Emerging privacy principles.

Principle	Meaning
Notice/awareness	You must be told when and why personal information is collected.
Choice/consent	You must be given an opportunity to opt in or opt out.
Access/participation	You must have access to your personal information and an opportunity to correct errors.
Integrity/security	The collecting party is responsible for the integrity of personal data.
Enforcement/redress	If one or more of these principles are violated, you have a right to seek a legal remedy.

U.S. government guidelines suggest (but do not require) that business Web sites post a privacy policy; for example, Figure 10.3 shows a portion of Amazon.com's policy. Most enterprises follow the guidelines outlined in Figure 10.2 and stress how they protect their customers' privacy, but some are a bit less politically correct. For example, Go!Zilla's Privacy Policy states:

The Demographic and Personally Identifiable information collected by Go!Zilla, and/or the user profiles, may be used by Go!Zilla, its licensees, agents, and assigns, and/or its client software companies and developers, as well as shared, rented, leased, sold, or otherwise made available to third-party marketing entities, advertisers, and other parties at the sole discretion of Go!Zilla.[1]

Figure 10.3 A portion of Amazon.com's privacy policy.

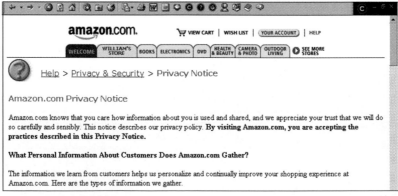

Courtesy of Amazon.com, Inc.

[1] *www.gozilla.com*, Privacy Policy.

Give them credit for honesty.

To further complicate the legal picture, different countries and cultures have a very different view of privacy, a significant problem given the global nature of the Internet and e-commerce. Some cultures and governments do not consider individual privacy a priority. In many European and Asian countries, however, privacy laws are much stricter than they are in the United States. In fact, there is concern that European privacy laws could become the world's de facto standard, forcing the United States and other countries to conform or risk losing access to the European market. For example, the European Parliament recently voted to forbid Web sites from downloading cookies without prior permission. Imagine how such a regulation would impact a company like Amazon.com that relies on cookies to maintain state during a transaction.

The Seal of Approval

Well-known brand names like Amazon.com, Sears, and Visa convey a sense of trust, but how can a smaller online business overcome a potential customer's privacy concerns? One answer is to display a recognized seal of approval that certifies that the company meets a set of online standards. Figure 10.4 shows the Better Business Bureau's reliability certificate as it appears on Dell's Web site. TRUSTe offers a similar service, and the accountant-run WebTrust service takes certification a bit farther by conducting online security audits of its client Web sites. Posting a seal of approval from a well-known, trusted source significantly enhances an unknown Web site's credibility.

Customer rating programs are also effective. For example, eBay allows buyers and sellers to rate each other, and BizRate, a shopping portal, posts customer evaluations of online merchants. A pattern of negative ratings should raise a red flag, telling potential customers to avoid doing business with a low-rated online company or trader.

Collecting Personal Information

To most people, the idea that such information as their name, e-mail address, and telephone number is valuable seems a bit absurd. Offer us a handful of coupons, a super-shopper card, or a chance to win a prize in exchange for answering a few questions, and we answer the questions. Offer us a free e-mail account or free access to some other online service, and we eagerly complete the online application form. We get something of value in exchange for what appears to be little or nothing. What's the harm? What are they going to do with my name, e-mail address, and telephone number anyway?

Figure 10.4 Dell displays the BBB seal.

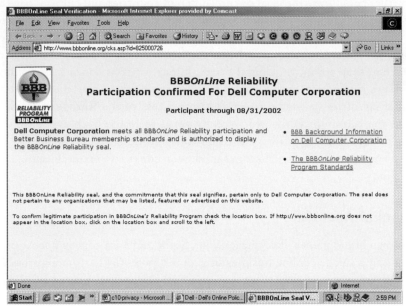

Reprinted with permission of the Council of Better Business Bureaus, Inc., Copyright 2002.
The BBBOnline Reliability Seal is a trademark of the Council of Better Business Bureaus, Inc.

Plenty. Companies collect personal information because it is valuable. Typically, they input the personal data extracted from an application form or an interview to a customer relationship management (CRM) database. Subsequently, they incorporate information gleaned from a customer's shopping patterns to build and enhance a profile to support relationship marketing, targeted ads, and customization. By aggregating such data, they get the demographic information they need to understand their customers, to set advertising rates, and to anticipate trends. Unfortunately, the technology that allows a CRM application to target specific customers can, in the wrong hands, allow a wrongdoer to target a specific victim.

Some Legal Sources

Customers who perform such tasks as filling out a form, requesting information, or registering for a prize voluntarily provide much of the personal information stored on a company's CRM database. Other perfectly legal personal information sources are a bit less obvious, however, because they do not require the subject's direct participation.

The availability of online, publicly accessible personal and demographic information is mind-boggling. Change of address information can be obtained from the post office. Telephone numbers are listed in telephone books and online databases, and anyone (or any company) with caller ID knows your telephone number as soon as you call his 800 number. Your e-mail address is probably listed on one or more Internet directories, and a determined person with reasonable computer skills can probably track you down. Government records, including criminal records, directories, tax information, and public

Harrah's Total Rewards Program

A decade ago, Harrah's was just another casino chain fighting to keep its share of the coveted high rollers who drove the gaming industry in those days. Today, Harrah's operates more than twenty casinos in twelve states and ranks number two domestically behind only MGM Entertainment. It still covets the high rollers, of course, but in today's gaming industry, the slot machines, not the high stakes tables, generate the bulk of a casino's operating profit.

The key to Harrah's recent success is the company's Total Rewards program. Visitors are encouraged to sign up for a personal magnetic stripe card as soon as they walk through the casino door, and most willingly provide such seemingly innocuous information as their name, home address, gender, and age. A player inserts his card into a slot machine before starting to play, and the system credits points to the player's account based primarily on the number and size of his wagers. In return, the player gets complementary or discounted travel, rooms, meals, and shows based on accumulated points. Behind the scenes, however, Harrah's uses the information generated by the Total Rewards program to create a detailed profile of each player's gambling habits.

The immediate benefit derived from the Total Rewards program is enhanced customer loyalty. A player is less likely to casino-hop if playing only at Harrah's delivers better perks than splitting the action over multiple casinos. Other casinos offer similar programs, so the long-term potential of single-casino cards is limited, but Harrah's network links more than 40,000 gaming machines in twelve states, allowing a player who lives in New Jersey to combine points earned at Harrah's casinos in Atlantic City and Las Vegas.

CRM opportunities represent the real value of the Total Rewards program, however. Harrah's groups the personal profiles into demographic segments based on such revenue predictors as proximity to a casino, frequency of visits, amount wagered per bet, and number of wagers per visit. (Note that the amount bet, not the amount won or lost, is the key; a casino knows the odds.) An elderly retiree living in Philadelphia who catches a bus for a monthly day trip to Atlantic City and wagers a few hundred dollars per trip is much more attractive than a once-a-year vacationer.

To lure a player back, the casino mails its Total Rewards program participants incentive opportunities based on the player's demographic group. The local retiree might get free meals and free entertainment. The vacationer might get a coupon good for a discount on the breakfast buffet. Typically, the incentives expire quickly, perhaps enticing the retiree to return in three weeks instead of four and potentially increasing her number of visits per year.

Clearly, CRM based on detailed personal information works. Less clear, however, are the ethical, moral, and privacy implications of using CRM tools to encourage gambling.

305

employees' salaries, are available on publicly accessible databases, and popular search engines make it relatively easy to find information about a specific individual. Even social security numbers and, in many states, department of motor vehicle records are available online, and the U.S. Census Bureau and other government Web sites are incredibly rich sources of demographic information. For example, Figure 10.5 shows a single page from an online information broker's Web site.

Figure 10.5 A single page from the Database Bureau's list of online information assets.

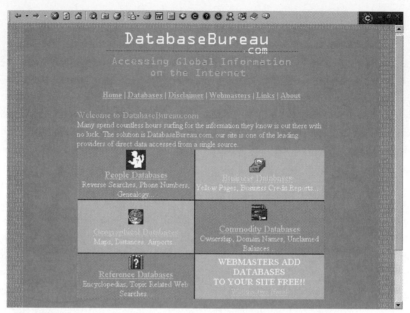

Database Bureau: A division of InfoBureau.net. From *http://www.databasebureau.com*.

Aggregation

Fortunately (or unfortunately, depending on your point of view), those disparate information sources are difficult to **aggregate** or combine, which complicates the task of compiling a complete dossier on any single individual. In fact, one reason why privacy advocates consistently oppose proposals for a national ID card is the risk that it might simplify aggregating all that personal information.

The privacy advocates' worst fears might be realized anyway, because information technology offers numerous data aggregation tools. Various peripherals facilitate collecting raw data, and inexpensive high-speed computers simplify interpreting, screening, and collating the data. The Web allows data from multiple sources to be combined, and cheap data storage makes keeping all that data economically feasible. Additionally, databases, indexing tools, and data mining techniques allow a company to extract meaning from the aggregated data, creating a very real potential for privacy violations.

Finding Missing Pieces

Even the best data aggregation tools cannot supply missing data. If a CRM application calls for specific personal information that is not readily available, filling in the missing pieces might be necessary before the new application can be used effectively.

Although the task can be difficult, it is often possible to find missing information using other legal (or at least not illegal) tools and techniques. For example, when you request a Web page, your browser reveals a great deal about your system, including your operating

A National ID Card

Over the years, proposals for implementing a national ID card have come and gone, but the events of September 11, 2001, added a sense of urgency to the debate. Recently, Larry Ellison, the CEO of Oracle Corporation, offered to provide the software required to operate a national ID card system free of charge, and several members of Congress supported the idea. Proponents argue that the time has come to reexamine the balance between freedom and security. A national ID card, they suggest, is an essential first step in controlling America's borders and identifying potential terrorists. However, opponents, including the Bush administration, counter that personal freedom is one of the core principles that define the United States of America and that sacrificing any of those principles means the enemy has won.

One option is to use a smart card that displays an individual's photograph and holds a digitized version of her thumbprint. Individuals would be authenticated by inserting their smart card and their thumb into a biometric device, which scans the thumbprint and compares the result to the digitized version stored on the card. Issuing cards to every U.S. citizen is a daunting and extremely expensive task, however, with many unanswered questions. Who collects the data? Who ensures the integrity of that data? What happens to an American citizen who forgets her card? Under what circumstances can an official demand to see "your papers"? Until those questions are thoroughly debated and adequately answered, implementing a national ID system may be premature.

system, your browser, your IP address, your computer's startup sequence, and the contents of your clipboard, even if your system is protected by a firewall. Public forums are another potential source of information. Conversation tracking services actively market focus-group-like intelligence extracted by data mining software from newsgroups, listservs, chat rooms, and message boards.

As you learned in Chapter 8, elite hackers, crackers, and samurai (hackers for hire) are adept at cracking passwords and using other techniques, such as social engineering, to gain access to a computer system or to obtain personal information directly. Hackers have been known to impersonate a small business owner or a human resources manager and to purchase current credit reports for a nominal fee. Such reports typically include the subject's social security number, date of birth, and credit history, plus links to driving records and other personal information. Another option is to hire an online investigative service to locate the missing data.

Capturing Clickstream Data

Most Internet transactions leave an electronic trace. A **clickstream** is a collection of such traces that forms a record of an individual's Internet activity, including Web sites visited, pages downloaded, newsgroups frequented, and the addresses of both incoming and out-going e-mail messages. Such information is extremely valuable to those who market and advertise on the Web. The act of secretly collecting information about a person's surfing patterns is called **tracking**.

Your ISP is in a position to capture your complete clickstream by simply logging your transactions, with or without your knowledge. When you visit a Web site, the host server can track everything you do on that site, again with or without your knowledge. Additionally, several techniques for gathering clickstream data, including cookies and Web bugs, require neither your ISP's cooperation nor a voluntary visit to a Web site.

Tracking with Cookies

In Chapter 3, you learned how cookies are used to maintain state. The first time a user visits a Web site, the server writes a cookie on the client's hard disk. The next time the user visits the site, the cookie is returned to the server, where the server software extracts the user's database key and accesses his record. Unless the system is set to a sufficiently high level of security, the cookie exchange is completely transparent to the user. You should not be surprised to learn that cookies are sometimes used secretly to collect click-stream data.

Imagine, for example, that Gotcha, an information service provider, has created an infrastructure for capturing clickstream data by establishing a network of associated companies, one of which is Acme. Embedded in Acme's home page HTML is a reference to a banner ad that resides on Gotcha's computer, not Acme's (Figure 10.6). When you link to Acme, your browser displays Acme's home page and requests the embedded ban-ner ad from Gotcha, which returns the image file and surreptitiously places a cookie on

Figure 10.6 Tracking with cookies.

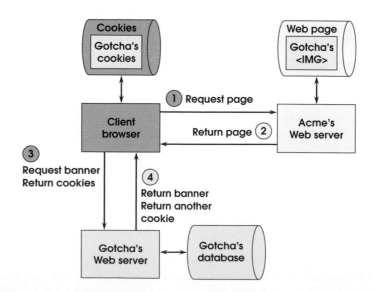

your hard drive. In the future, whenever you return to Acme's Web site, the cookie is returned to Gotcha. Because every company in Gotcha's network does exactly the same thing, your computer might hold multiple Gotcha cookies, and a visit to any affiliated Web site returns all those cookies to Gotcha. Check the cookies file on your computer. If you are a frequent Web surfer, you will probably find at least one entry for DoubleClick, a well-known personal information provider, even if you never visited DoubleClick's Web site (Figure 10.7).

What do third-party information services like DoubleClick do with the information they collect? Simply put, they aggregate it and sell it, which is perfectly legal because there is no law against gathering and selling information. The information that services such as DoubleClick provides is quite valuable to business—check DoubleClick's weekly newsletter at *www.iconocast.com* for examples. From a personal privacy perspective, however, hidden data collection is troubling.

Tracking with Web Bugs

Web bugs are even more troubling than cookies. A **Web bug** is a virtually invisible, single-pixel clear gif. A reference to the bug image is buried in a Web page's HTML stream. When a Web server returns a requested Web page to your browser, the browser scans the HTML, extracts the file reference for the embedded single-pixel image, and requests the Web bug. Embedded in your browser's request is such information as your IP address, the URLs of the page you are viewing and the Web bug, the current time, browser information, and any cookies previously placed on your computer by the Web bug. Marketing organizations, information brokers, and CRM applications use the tracking data to enrich your personal profile.

When the Web bug's server—which may or may not be the server on which the initial HTML stream resides—receives the request, it extracts the tracking data and returns the Web bug, plus a new cookie. When your browser receives the file, it inserts the Web bug into the screen image; Figure 10.8 shows a demonstration page that contains an over-sized, visible Web bug. Normally, a single blank pixel is hardly noticeable on a display screen, few people are willing to scan a Web page's HTML on the chance that they might find a suspect IMG tag, and no software can effectively distinguish a Web bug from a

Figure 10.7 Even your author's cookie file contains a cookie from DoubleClick.

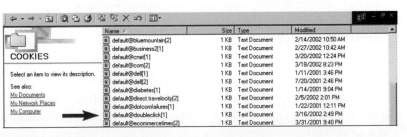

Figure 10.8 A demonstration Web bug.

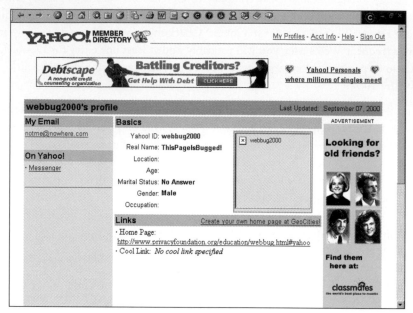

spacer gif, which is used to align elements on a Web page. In other words, it's tough to spot a Web bug.

A Web bug can also be buried in an HTML e-mail message, where it serves as a hidden return receipt, secretly alerting the sender the instant the recipient opens the message. Normally you cannot see them, but Figure 10.9 shows a demonstration e-mail that contains an oversized, visible Web bug.

Surveillance and Monitoring

Surveillance and monitoring represent very real threats to personal privacy. Consider, for example, the high-tech surveillance equipment featured in popular spy thrillers. Satellites look down from above. Thermal imaging technologies peer through walls. Scanners see through clothing. Hidden cameras and microphones capture every move and utterance. There is no escape.

Much of the high-tech surveillance gear you see in spy movies really exists, but it is not available to the average person. You can, however, purchase similar technology, including recording devices for your cell phone, tiny digital cameras, video cameras small enough to hide in a knickknack, tiny microphones, directional microphones for eavesdropping

Figure 10.9 A Web bug buried in an e-mail message.

Dear friend,
This message was sent to you by a request made at http://www.mackraz.com/trickybit/readreceipt.

If you can see the following image, then your reading this message has been logged.

⬚

Watch your inbox for an automatically-generated read-receipt message from our logging-server, which will contain the information we were able to glean automatically as you read this message.

Source: Jim Mackraz, *www.mackraz.com*.

from a distance, night-vision scopes, and even electronic devices that jam nearby cell phones, making them inoperative.[2]

Surveillance (continual observation) and **monitoring** (the act of watching someone or something) are facts of modern life. For example, the city of Tampa, Florida, implemented a battery of video cameras to scan the crowds going to and from the January 28, 2001, Super Bowl. Closed-circuit cables linked the cameras to a computer running an experimental biometric face-scanning program. As a camera picked a face from the crowd, the computer quickly created a digital pattern and compared it to a file of digitized face prints of known criminals and terrorists. No one was arrested or even stopped as a result of Tampa's facial profiling, but the experiment raised a firestorm of protest. That was before September 11, 2001, however, and attitudes may have changed.

The e-commerce infrastructure enables new forms of surveillance and monitoring. For example, **spyware** is software that employs a background or back channel Internet connection to transmit information secretly from a target computer to a receiver. A suspicious employer, parent, spouse, or significant other might use **snoopware**, PC monitoring software that secretly records everything the target does online. Some spyware and snoopware programs collect samples of online activity by capturing screen shots, while others log more detailed data. Incidentally, don't confuse spyware and snoopware with the packet sniffers you read about in Chapter 8. A packet sniffer usually resides on a network server or an ISP host. Spyware and snoopware run directly on the computer being monitored.

You might be surprised to learn that workplace monitoring is perfectly legal. Your employer has a right to protect his information technology investment by ensuring that employees use the equipment only for approved, productive purposes. He has a right to install a Trojan horse or a back door on "your" computer to capture your keystrokes and your files for analysis. He also has a right to install a chip or a software routine that monitors your clickstream. And he is not required to ask your permission or even tell you about it. In other words, don't put anything in a business e-mail message that you wouldn't write on a postcard.

Even vehicles can be monitored. For example, OnStar, the online automotive service, relies on GPS tracking to locate a subscriber's vehicle. Recently, several carjacked automobiles have been tracked by OnStar and recovered by the police. In at least one case, as

---

[2] No, we're not going to tell you where to find such devices.

a carjacking victim watched her car speed away, she calmly called 911 and then called OnStar to authorize the release of tracking data. The car was recovered and the perpetrator arrested several minutes later, just a few blocks from the scene of the crime.

New York's E-ZPass system provides another example of vehicular monitoring. Systems like E-ZPass read a chip or a bar code affixed to a side window as a vehicle drives through a freeway, bridge, or tunnel tollbooth and charges the toll to the driver's account. Recently, the data collected by the E-ZPass system has been used to check the alibis of people charged with a crime, confirming some and rejecting others. It is difficult to argue with an electronic device that automatically records the exact time you passed through a specific tollbooth. Even if you never use a tollbooth, many communities have installed cameras to snap pictures of the license plates of cars that run red lights. Those pictures are time- and date-stamped, and the camera's physical location documents precisely where you were when you ran the light.

On a more personal level, everyday transactions such as telephone calls, cell phone calls, and credit card purchases are very effective at tracking an individual's movements. Communication lines are particularly easy to monitor, with inexpensive wiretapping devices available online and at many electronics stores. Cell phones broadcast their transmissions, and anyone with a frequency scanner can eavesdrop on a conversation, as Republicans Newt Gingrich and John Boehner discovered on December 21, 1996, when a politically embarrassing cell phone call was intercepted and secretly recorded by a Florida couple using a (possibly modified) police scanner. Not even the technically skilled are immune. A few years ago, a notorious hacker named Kevin Mitnick was located and arrested when federal agents and a computer security expert named Tsutomu Shimomura joined forces to track Mitnick's cell phone signals.

The Internet is highly susceptible to surveillance and monitoring. As you learned in Chapter 8, packet sniffing is a technique for intercepting selected packets as they move across the Internet, and the e-mail Web bugs described earlier in this chapter can be used as a form of hidden electronic return receipt. More disquieting are e-mail messages that contain embedded logic, which notifies the sender each time the message is forwarded by transmitting to the sender a copy of the message, including any added notes. Imagine a subcontractor using such techniques to monitor a potential client's comments about a bid as the electronic documents work their way through the approval process. Imagine a mailing list provider capturing yet another e-mail address each time a message is forwarded. You may have encountered e-mail messages that urge you to send a virus alert or some other bit of news to several friends. The best response is usually to hit the Delete key.

The real problem with surveillance and monitoring is not gathering personal information, but separating the wheat from the chaff. Any form of automated or electronic surveillance or monitoring tends to collect a great deal of data, most of which is useless, and unless the relevant nuggets can be isolated quickly and easily, they tend to get buried. Today, however, such digital criteria as watch lists, key words, serial numbers, IP addresses, and media access control (MAC) addresses are commonly used to identify potentially significant messages and packets. Various data mining tools do an incredibly good job of digging out those relevant nuggets, too.

Misusing Technology

Everything you do on the Internet leaves a trace. Exposing your Web surfing preferences to those who collect and aggregate personal information is part of the price you pay to participate in e-commerce. The apparent deception that enables third-party cookies and Web bugs is a concern, however, and knowing that you must actively opt out to prevent an online organization from sharing your personal information with whomever they please is annoying at best. But personalized Web pages, properly targeted ads, and other visible evidence of effective CRM have value, and for most e-commerce participants, the benefits outweigh the costs. Not always, though.

Spam

Spam is electronic junk mail sent indiscriminately to every e-mail address on a mailing list. Roughly 40 percent of the mail delivered by the U.S. Postal Service is junk mail, so the problem is hardly unique to cyberspace. But because it costs about the same to send one copy or several million copies of a digital message, spam is economically very efficient.

To an active e-mail user who wades through hundreds of unwanted junk messages a day, spam is at least as offensive as those telemarketing phone calls that seem to arrive the instant you sit down to dinner. The hacker community considers spam so offensive that a known spammer is likely to be subjected to a **flame attack**, a barrage of nasty e-mail messages that overwhelms the spammer's in-box. That is why most spammers distribute their electronic junk mail through an **anonymous remailer**, a service that accepts outgoing e-mail and remails it, thus hiding the identity of the original source.

TECHNOLOGY

Magic Lantern

In recent years, criminals, drug dealers, and terrorists have turned increasingly to encryption to defeat law enforcement wiretaps. The FBI's Magic Lantern program is designed to bypass encryption by capturing information before it is encrypted.

Magic Lantern is a Trojan horse implanted in the target computer by a viruslike program. Once installed, Magic Lantern logs the user's keystrokes and transmits them back to the FBI. Picture a criminal typing a message, encrypting it, and sending it, secure in the knowledge that even if the authorities intercept it, they won't be able to read it. Imagine the criminal's surprise when a complete transcript compiled from her preencryption keystrokes is produced at trial. Because Magic Lantern captures keystrokes, the authorities can even intercept information that was typed but never sent.

Why do privacy advocates object to such technology? Wiretaps are, after all, legitimate law enforcement tools. Some people mistrust the government, but that argument carries less weight than it did before September 11, 2001. The problem is that keystroke-logging software is readily available to anyone who wants it. Put yourself in the target's shoes and imagine that everything you type through your keyboard will be read by someone else. Even if you have nothing to hide, you might find that violation of your privacy upsetting.

To a network manager, incoming spam can clog a mail server. Outgoing spam is even worse, because no self-respecting ISP or network administrator wants to be known as a spammer. To control spamming, many ISPs restrict outgoing e-mail messages to a limited number of copies. Should a spammer figure out how to get around the limit, Web sites such as *www.spamcop.net* allow a recipient to alert the spammer's ISP. Not surprisingly, proposals have been made to make spam illegal, but the term *spam* is difficult to define (one person's spam is another person's treasure). Like junk mail, spam is considered a form of free speech protected by the U.S. Constitution. The Federal Trade Commission (FTC) has, however, gone after spammers who peddle illegal pyramid and Ponzi schemes.

Why do spammers do it? The answer is simple: It pays. Sales from telemarketing cold calls total hundreds of billions of dollars a year even though only a tiny handful of people respond favorably to such calls. Similarly, although most recipients screen spam or delete spam messages without even reading them, a few do respond. Once the initial sales pitch is written, it costs the spammer no more to send the message to a million people on a mailing list than it does to send it to a single recipient. If only 0.1 percent of those million recipients respond, the spammer has reached 1,000 potential customers at very little cost.

Often, spammers buy their e-mail addresses from a personal information service or a B2C Web site that sells the personal data it collects. Software is available to harvest e-mail addresses from newsgroup postings, ISP member directories, and other online directories. Dictionary attack software works by generating a set of all possible user handles for a given e-mail domain (*JoeA@isp.com, JoeB@isp.com, JoeC@isp.com...*). Such software is a likely explanation for the millions of e-mail messages rejected daily by most large ISPs because the username is invalid. Incidentally, that is why you should not respond in any way to a spam message, even if a hyperlink prompts you to "click here to unsubscribe." There is a very good chance that the message was sent by a dictionary attack program, and the act of clicking on the unsubscribe link confirms your e-mail address to the spammer. In other words, "unsubscribe" really means "send me lots of spam."

What can you do to limit the amount of spam in your in-box? First, as mentioned earlier, do not respond to spam in any way—just hit the Delete key. The spam filters available on many e-mail programs and spam blocking software like Yahoo's SpamGuard can be effective, but they let some spam through and sometimes trash legitimate mail. The best strategy is to avoid getting on a spammer's mailing list in the first place. Do not divulge your e-mail address to an unknown party or Web site. If you absolutely must provide your address, "munge" it by inserting a few extra characters— *mynameNOSPAM@isp.com*, for example. A spammer's e-mail extraction software will add an undeliverable address to its evolving mailing list, but a legitimate contact working with a limited number of responses will know exactly what you mean. Another option is to create a junk e-mail account (perhaps with one of the free e-mail services) and give out only that address to unknown parties. Access your junk account perhaps weekly, forward the legitimate messages to your regular account, and delete the rest.

Really Annoying Ads

Online advertising is a fact of cyberspace life. Although banner ads, pop-up ads, pop-under ads, and pop-off ads can be annoying, most Web surfers should realize that the incredible variety of free content available on today's Web probably could not exist without the advertising-generated revenues that pay the sponsor's personnel, hardware, software, and bandwidth bills. Like newspaper, magazine, and television advertising, no one forces you to read or respond to online ads, so you can look at the ones that interest you and ignore the rest. It's a small price to pay for access to so much information.

Some online ads go too far, though. For example, have you ever seen a banner ad that mimics a dialog box announcing a "Message Alert" or a "Security Lapse" (Figure 10.10)? They are banner ads. If you click anywhere but on the close box (the little X-marked square at the upper right), you will hyperlink to the unknown advertiser's Web site. Even worse, you might start a spiral of ads, perhaps for porn or other offensive Web sites, that doesn't stop until you close your browser.

A **spawner** is a piece of malware (harmful software) that enters a computer much like a Trojan horse, through downloaded shareware or freeware or as an attachment to an e-mail message, particularly a spam message. Once established, the software spawns its own pop-up ads that replace or compete with legitimate ads as you surf. Some high-speed spawners open new pop-up windows faster than you can delete them. A **mouse-trapper** is a type of ad that turns off the browser's Back button, disables the pop-up window's close box, or both, leaving you with no way to escape the ad short of closing your browser or rebooting your system. Spam is a common source of spawners and mouse-trappers, so it's a good idea to avoid clicking the links in a spam message. People have also been known to pick up such malware during a visit to a porn site—sort of an electronic version of a sexually transmitted disease. The Web can be a dangerous place if you're careless.

Figure 10.10 This banner ad mimics a dialog box. Do not click OK.

Fraud

According to the 2001 edition of the Microsoft Encarta World English Dictionary, **fraud** is the "crime of obtaining money or some other benefit by deliberate deception." People who commit fraud take advantage of the good nature, greed, or gullibility of other people. Fraud has existed since the first human beings began walking the planet, so the problem certainly cannot be blamed on the Internet. However, the same infrastructure that supports e-commerce also provides opportunities for deception.

For example, in 1994, a Russian named Vladimir Levin was imprisoned for using a personal computer to steal $10 million from a U.S. bank. More recently, a Russian hacker who called himself Maxus tried to extort a large sum of money from an online e-retailer by threatening to release 300,000 stolen credit card numbers. Those two criminals were caught, but many others are not. How do they get away with it? Anonymity is one key: On the Internet, the person on the other end of a transaction can be anyone she claims to be and can work from literally anywhere on the globe, making prosecution difficult, if not impossible.

Identity Theft

Identity theft, the act of using another person's identity to surf the Web, purchase merchandise, and so on, is a growing problem. Identity theft can (and does) exist without the Internet. For example, dumpster divers often search the trash for those preapproved credit card offers that arrive in the mail so they can change the address and apply for the card in the original recipient's name. (If you receive such offers, and who doesn't, destroy them

Ad Blockers

TECHNOLOGY

If you like to surf the Web but you find all the online ads annoying, you might consider installing an ad blocker. For a fee, software products such as AdSubtract Pro, Norton Internet Security, and WebWasher can zap banners, pop-ups, Flash ads, and even cookies. One of these products, Guidescope (*www.guidescope.com*) even offers a free service. Online ads are not about to go away, but a good ad blocker can still give you relatively ad-free Web surfing.

If everyone used ad blocker software, you might not like the outcome, however. According to Harry McCracken, a *PC World* executive editor, "A Web in which every user erased every ad would be a Web that no rational advertiser would subsidize."[3] Those ads, remember, pay for valuable "free" Web services, much as TV and radio advertising pays for "free" programming. Without advertising, Web service providers would be forced to charge a user fee or stop offering those services; in other words, you might still be able to find what you want on the Web, but it's going to cost you. Perhaps the occasional banner or pop-up ad isn't so bad after all.

---

[3] Harry McCracken, "Ads, Ad Blockers, Us, and You," *PC World*, May 2002: 13.

before throwing them away.) The perpetrator's ability to access personal information anonymously over the Web makes the job much easier. As you learned in Chapter 8, skilled hackers sometimes use DNS spoofing to steal personal information by altering a DNS entry on a server and redirecting a browser's response to a request for information (such as an application form) to an alternate site (the hacker's).

Often, the perpetrator starts with a few bits of information about the target individual and uses the Web to build a surprisingly complete dossier that includes the victim's name, address, telephone number, e-mail address, social security number, credit card numbers, and so on. In the early 1990s, a man named Steven M. Shaw used a terminal at his employer's Orlando, Florida used car dealership to search for the credit reports of people with similar names. A freelance writer named Stephen J. Shaw from Washington, D.C., stood out because of his clean record and high level of available credit, so Steven M. became Stephen J. The Orlando used car salesman obtained copies of the freelance writer's credit cards, opened new bank accounts, and took out loans in the writer's name, running up unpaid debts exceeding $100,000 before he was caught. Steven M., the bad guy, was convicted of a felony and spent three years in jail. Stephen J., the victim, spent a few years trying to straighten out his tangled finances. That was a decade ago. Identity theft tools have improved since then.

Credit Card Fraud

Credit card fraud is as old as credit cards. The only way to eliminate the practice is to stop issuing cards, but the blizzard of junk mail touting preapproved credit cards shows that the banking industry has no intention of cutting back. To a major bank, credit card fraud is a cost of doing business, and as long as the level of fraud is kept under reasonable

TECHNOLOGY

High-Profile Identity Theft

In March 2001, a New York restaurant busboy was arrested and charged with multiple counts of criminal impersonation, forgery, and fraud. Allegedly, the accused 32-year-old man used the Internet and a *Forbes* magazine list of the richest people in America to compile personal information on such luminaries as Steven Spielberg, Warren Buffet, Oprah Winfrey, and Martha Stewart with the intent of hijacking their identities to steal money. When arrested, he was allegedly picking up equipment for making phony credit cards. In his possession were the names, addresses, birth dates, and social security numbers of 217 wealthy people, and the police also found roughly 400 stolen credit card numbers, some of which had been used to purchase merchandise. Apparently, the busboy's attempt to transfer $10 million from an account owned by Thomas Siebel tipped the authorities that something was wrong.

Why did he go after such high-profile people? Probably because wealthy people make attractive targets. The real story, however, is that a 32-year-old high school dropout working as a busboy and using public access computers at the library to access the Internet was able to gather enough personal information on more than 200 powerful people to create a realistic threat of identity theft. That's a little scary.

control, the benefits derived from increasing the number of card holders outweighs the cost of fraud. If you are the person whose credit card account has been fraudulently misused, however, the results can be devastating.

Criminals don't need a computer or a network to commit credit card fraud. Credit cards can be lost or stolen. Unscrupulous waiters and sales clerks have been known to run duplicate copies of receipts and sell the credit card numbers. A surprising number of people discard their credit card receipts, and a dumpster diving expedition through the paper trash at the local mall can prove lucrative to a crook.

Although submitting a credit card number online to a known and trusted merchant who uses the secure sockets layer (SSL) protocols described in Chapter 9 is much less risky than handing that same credit card to your waiter in an unfamiliar restaurant, people are more likely to trust the waiter than the online merchant. The reason is probably the FUD factor described earlier in this chapter. When you give your card to a waiter, you can imagine exactly what happens, even though the waiter and the card disappear for a time. Unless you know how the Internet and SSL work, however, you don't have a clue about what happens to your credit card number after you click Submit.

Stealing a credit card number in transit is, at best, very difficult, and a single number does not make a very attractive target. Your credit card number is probably at greater risk when it resides on a merchant's database, particularly if the merchant is a bit too casual about security. Successful attacks are rare, but they do happen, even to companies without a B2C presence.

Scammers and Con Artists

Some con artists use their social engineering skills to leverage such horror stories and take advantage of people. In one common scam, the con artist, posing as an official of some kind, calls or e-mails the potential victim to report a possible online theft involving the victim's credit card. He then asks the victim for his credit card number so it can be checked against a list of allegedly stolen cards. It is surprising how many people respond by handing over their credit card number.

Pyramid schemes are common, too. Often, the con artist starts a chain e-mail that invites recipients to send her a sum of money and then forward the letter to fifty friends. Those fifty friends, in turn, are asked to send a sum of money to the mark and forward the letter to fifty of their friends, and so on. Inevitably, the chain dies, and only the people near the top get rich. Like most scams and cons, pyramid schemes are not new, but the Internet allows a chain letter to circulate much more quickly than was ever possible with snail mail.

Dialer programs are a particularly nasty scam. Here's how they work. The victim starts the process by clicking on a banner ad, often for a porn site. The scam Web site then terminates the victim's ISP connection and dials a long distance number, often in a foreign country. Access to the foreign Web site is usually "free," but the call is billed at an exorbitant rate, perhaps exceeding $7 per minute. Dialer program scams are frequently linked to porn sites, perhaps because the victim is unlikely to report being ripped off.

Rogue Web sites are also distressingly common. Some are virtual clones of other well-known sites; a black-hat hacker might create a page that looks almost exactly like Amazon.com's customer support page and ask the target to enter a credit card number for "verification." Misspelled URLs are another common scam. A Web site called PayPai recently impersonated PayPal, an online payment service, and may have tricked a few people into sending it money before it was quickly shut down.

Shill bidding (using a planted accomplice to bid up the price) and similar scams are as old as auctions, but online sites like eBay create new opportunities for auction fraud. Failure to deliver is a common problem, particularly on hard-to-get items, and not all bidders pay for the items they purchase. The buyer/seller ratings on eBay make it difficult for repeat scammers to continue pulling the same con, but the company does not guarantee either delivery or payment. An escrow service is a good option when dealing with an unknown party, particularly when the item being auctioned is expensive.

Financial Swindles

Between August 1999 and February 2000, a New Jersey teenager named Jonathan Lebed operated a classic **pump-and-dump** scheme. First, he purchased large blocks of low-priced stocks and hyped them on several Internet financial message boards. Quite a few people responded to Lebed's "tips" and bought the hyped stocks, pushing the price up. After a few days, Lebed sold (or dumped) his stock and pocketed a nice profit, perhaps as much as $1 million. The Security and Exchange Commission eventually brought civil fraud charges against him, and Lebed agreed to return $285,000 without admitting guilt. He was not the first to commit Internet stock fraud, and he will almost certainly not be the last. For example, pump-and-dump tactics on questionable initial public offerings are allegedly a popular organized crime tool.

Some financial swindles prey on the poor. A person with a bad credit rating might be offered a guaranteed credit card or expedited loan application processing in exchange for an upfront fee. All too often, after paying the fee, the mark gets absolutely nothing. Other scams combine social engineering with the implied legitimacy of a well-known e-commerce Web site. As mentioned earlier, a scammer might simulate Amazon.com's customer services Web page and ask a victim (who may have responded to a spam message sometime before) to complete a form to "verify" his social security or credit card number. Such requests are not legitimate and should not be answered. Legitimate Web sites will *not* request your social security number or your credit card number unless *you* initiate the transaction.

Pornography and Gambling

Someone once said that selling Internet pornography is a lot like owning your own money machine, but the reality does not quite match the hype. Although a few porn sites dominate the industry and make a great deal of money, most are marginally profitable. Still, online pornography is a thriving worldwide business. Some forms of pornography are protected by the First Amendment to the U.S. Constitution, making prosecution difficult. There is, however, widespread agreement that child pornography is wrong.

Some porn sites use spawners, mouse-trappers, and other questionable advertising tactics, and **porn napping**, the act of taking over innocent-sounding lapsed URLs or using a variation of a legitimate URL, is common. Consider an imaginary federal Web site named *www.fedsite.gov*. Imagine further that a porn site owns the URL *www.fedsite.com*. Most popular URLs end with .com, so an inexperienced user or a child is likely to type the wrong address and visit the porn site by accident. Scams, cons, and fraud are common, too, perhaps because many porn sites operate under the belief that people may think twice before reporting them. Who do you call if a porn site rips you off? The police?

Online gambling (or gaming, as the industry prefers to be called) is another potential money machine. For a relatively small investment in gaming software, hosting hardware, and connectivity, an online gambling site can operate worldwide. Most require a prepaid account or a credit card number before allowing a player to place bets, so the online gaming parlor faces little risk. Although many question the morality of gambling, it is difficult to argue against it successfully when thirty-eight of our fifty states have lotteries, and even a successful prosecution does little more than force the gambling operation offshore.

Countering the Bad Guys

Fortunately, you can do several things to protect yourself. Start by implementing appropriate security measures by installing up-to-date virus protection and a personal firewall on your computer. Change your passwords and clean out your cookies folder regularly. Also, use an outside service like Anonymizer (*www.anonymizer.com*) to analyze your system's vulnerabilities and take steps to plug them. If your computer uses Windows 98 or Me, run the system configuration utility (Start/Run/MSCONFIG/Startup tab) to check the programs that run when you boot your computer, and question any you don't recognize.

Visit *www.idfraud.org* to learn more about identity theft. The law allows you to obtain an annual copy of your credit report from the three major credit reporting services: Equifax, Experian, and Trans Union. Get them, read them, and challenge any errors.

Limit your e-mail address to people and organizations you trust. Sign up for a junk e-mail account from one of the many available free services and use it whenever an unknown individual or online service asks for your e-mail address. If you don't want your e-mail traced, consider using an anonymous remailer. If you are really concerned about being tracked, consider a **stealth surfing** service that accepts your page requests, fills them through its own proxy server, and returns them to you from the proxy.

Finally, use common sense. Deal only with recognized, trusted e-retailers. Do not divulge your social security number, credit card number, password, or e-mail address unless you initiated the transaction and have reason to trust the other party. Make sure your passwords are difficult to guess, and change them frequently. If an online offer sounds too good to be true, it probably is. If your computer begins acting strangely, find out why. Will such steps guarantee your online security and privacy? No. But they certainly help.

■■■ Summary

Privacy means different things to different people, and balancing individual rights with society's needs is tricky. People are often surprised to learn that the word *privacy* does not appear in the Constitution. Because digital information is so easy to collect and aggregate, an individual's online privacy rights have become a particularly thorny issue. To further complicate the legal picture, different countries and cultures have very different views of privacy.

Companies collect personal information because it is valuable. Customers voluntarily provide much of the personal information stored on a company's CRM database. A great deal of personal and demographic information is available online, and information technology offers numerous data aggregation tools. The act of secretly collecting a person's clickstream is called tracking. Cookies and Web bugs are used to support tracking.

The Internet is highly susceptible to surveillance and monitoring, and spyware and snoopware support monitoring at the workstation level. Spam is a common source of spawners and mouse-trappers. Identity theft is a growing problem. Stealing a credit card number in transit is difficult, and your credit card number is probably at greater risk when it resides on a merchant's database. Some con artists use their social engineering skills to take advantage of people. Some financial swindles, such as pump-and-dump, target investors, while others prey on the poor. Online pornography and gambling are readily available to anyone who wants them.

Though scams and fraud exist on the Internet, there are things you can do to protect yourself from online criminals.

■■■ Key Words

aggregate	mouse-trapper	snoopware
anonymous remailer	opt in	spam
clickstream	opt out	spawner
dialer program	porn napping	spyware
flame attack	privacy	stealth surfing
fraud	pump-and-dump	surveillance
identity theft	pyramid scheme	tracking
monitoring	rogue Web site	Web bug

☰ Review Questions

1. Explain how technical complexity contributes to the fear, uncertainty, and doubt that shape the popular perception of information technology. Explain how knowledge can offset that fear, uncertainty, and doubt.

2. Explain how an individual's or a group's viewpoint affects the definition of privacy.

3. Distinguish between opt-in and opt-out privacy policies.

4. Identify several legal sources of personal information and explain why personal information is valuable to a company.

5. Why is clickstream data valuable?

6. Describe how tracking techniques are used to capture clickstream data.

7. Discuss several common surveillance and monitoring tools and techniques.

8. What is spam? Why do spammers distribute their spam? Why is spam so difficult to control?

9. What is a spawner? What is a mouse-trapper?

10. What is identity theft?

11. Explain how the Internet can be used to support credit card fraud.

12. How do pyramid schemes, dialer programs, and rogue Web sites work?

13. What is auction fraud? What is shill bidding? Why are these crimes considered a serious online auction problem?

14. Explain how a pump-and-dump financial swindle works.

15. Why is it important to be cautious when visiting a morally questionable Web site?

16. Identify several steps you might take to protect your online privacy and avoid falling victim to online scams and fraud.

☰ Exercises

1. What advantages does Harrah's gain from its Total Rewards program? What are the downsides of such programs?

2. In your opinion, is a national ID card a good idea? Why or why not?

3. The FBI's Magic Lantern software allows the agency to capture a suspect's keystrokes and reconstruct messages before they are encrypted. Discuss the advantages and risks associated with such software.

4. Would you consider installing an ad blocker on your computer? Why or why not?

5. How does the ability of an individual hacker to steal the identities of such well-known people as Oprah Winfrey and Steven Spielberg affect you?

6. Do you think porn nappers should be subjected to stiff penalties for their crime? Why or why not?

Projects

Current references and supporting resources can be found on this textbook's companion Web site.

Broad-Based Projects

1. Write a paper explaining why spammers do what they do. Include some examples of spam that you have encountered over the past few days.

Building the Case:

2. Working as a team, continue with Chapter 1, Project 6 by discussing your proposed Web site's potential exposure to privacy violations and suggesting possible solutions.

Business Projects

1. Write a paper on the benefits that a supermarket and its customers derive from a frequent shopper card program.

Building the Case:

2. Continue with Chapter 1, Project 2 by identifying possible threats to the privacy of your customers, your business partners, and your employees. Suggest strategies to counter those threats and estimate the cost of each strategy. Write a report to document your results.

Information Technology Projects

1. If you have a personal firewall installed on your computer, experiment by varying the security level from low to medium to high. After resetting the level, visit a few Web sites and note how your firewall monitors the process. When you finish, select the right level of security for your system.

Building the Case:

2. Continue with Chapter 1, Project 2 by creating a plan to ensure the privacy of your customers, your business partners, and your employees. Depending on your background, available time, and your instructor's preference, you might simply describe your privacy strategy on paper or actually implement appropriate privacy safeguards on your Web site.

Marketing Projects

1. Write a paper on the potentially annoying ads described in this chapter. Why do advertisers use them?

Building the Case:

2. Continue with Chapter 1, Project 2 by identifying possible threats to the privacy of your customers, your business partners, and your employees. Suggest strategies to counter those threats and estimate the cost of each strategy. Write a report to document your results, and add information describing privacy features to the storyboard you started in Chapter 5.

References

Web Sites

Source	URL	Comments
Andre Bacard	*www.andrebacard.com/remail.html*	Anonymous remailer FAQ.
Anonymizer.com	*www.anonymizer.com*	An anonymous remailer and stealth surfing service.
Cookie Central	*www.cookiecentral.com*	Everything you want to know about cookies.
Junkbusters	*www.junkbusters.com*	Tips and tools for countering spam and telemarketing calls.
Privacy Foundation	*www.privacyfoundation.org/ resources/webbug.asp*	FAQs on Web bugs.
Privacy.net	*http://privacy.net/track*	Illustration of how a company can track you.

Print and White Papers

Lane, Carole A. 1997. *Naked in Cyberspace: How to Find Personal Information Online.* Medford, NJ: CyberAge Books.

PART 5
The Future of
E-Commerce

Chapter 11 introduces a methodology for evaluating possible futures and then uses the methodology to explore tiered Internet services, e-books, Web services, and biometrics authentication. The chapter ends with a brief discussion of how e-commerce and related technologies might affect your future.

CHAPTER 11

Where Do We Go from Here?

When you finish reading this chapter, you should be able to:

- Define technical, economic, and political feasibility and explain how feasibility analysis can be used to evaluate alternative possible futures

- Explain how wild cards such as unanticipated technical breakthroughs can affect a forecast

- Discuss the feasibility of tiered Internet services

- Discuss the feasibility of e-books and explain how evolving video game platforms and intellectual property rights might affect the future of e-books

- Explain Web services and discuss their feasibility

- Explain how biometrics authentication works and identify its strengths and weaknesses

- Discuss the feasibility of biometrics authentication

- Discuss how e-commerce is likely to affect *your* future

Assessing the Future

Baseball great Yogi Berra once said, "Predictions are very difficult, especially when they are about the future." Once you stop chuckling, you realize he was absolutely right. No one, not Nostradamus, not even Miss Cleo, can predict the future with precision beyond perhaps a few days.

Technological change is particularly difficult to forecast because major breakthroughs are almost impossible to anticipate. Very few blacksmiths saw the automobile as a threat to their profession. The railroads ignored trucks, interstate highways, and cargo planes until after they had lost a substantial part of their customer base. Mainframe manufacturers missed the microcomputer revolution. A decade ago, almost no one predicted CDs, CD-Rs, CD-RWs, or DVDs, including the companies that manufactured cassettes and diskettes.

Although the underlying principles and concepts tend to be relatively stable, everything you know about how e-commerce works is likely to change, and change quickly over the next several years. The best way to deal with change is to anticipate it. This course and this textbook have given you solid base for understanding e-commerce as it is today. Faced with a possible change, you can build on that base to assess its odds of occurring and its likely impact. To help you get started, we'll consider four possible changes that might affect e-commerce in the near future. The specific innovations we consider are less important than the concept. Our intent is not to predict the future, but to get you thinking about the future.

Identifying Possible Futures

The essence of the process is to identify several possible futures and estimate when (or if) they are likely to come to pass. The first step is to identify the possible futures. Consider, for example, an interface that allows you to talk directly to a computer. We already have limited voice recognition hardware and software, but are such interfaces likely to become widespread?

Without going into details, we can imagine at least three possible futures for such an interface:

1. Slow, steady improvement of the current technology, but no major breakthroughs by 2020.

2. Significant improvements in voice recognition technology that lead to acceptance by a sizable but specialized market niche by 2020.

3. A dramatic breakthrough that makes voice recognition the new standard mass-market user interface by 2020.

Note that much like a long-range weather forecast, we have identified low, median, and high-range possible futures.

Feasibility Analysis

The next step is to study those possible futures and determine their relative likelihood of occurring. **Feasibility analysis**, a traditional systems analysis tool for evaluating the odds that a project will be successfully completed, is an effective tool for studying possible futures (Figure 11.1). Conducting a real feasibility study is a major undertaking, but it is possible to borrow the underlying principles to support a preliminary assessment.

Feasibility analysis forces you to look at the future from three different perspectives. **Technical feasibility** asks if the necessary technology exists or if it is likely to exist in time to affect the outcome. **Economic feasibility** focuses on cost/benefit analysis. **Political feasibility** asks if the task can be done in the context of the existing or expected social and political environment; in other words, it asks if the innovation enjoys the support of the right people.

The strength of feasibility analysis is its multiple perspectives. Becoming enamored with a new technology and predicting great things for it is easy; perhaps that is why forecasts tend to be overly optimistic in the short run. Thinking about economic and political feasibility helps to dampen the "this stuff is totally cool" factor by introducing some real-world constraints.

Consider the voice recognition scenario outlined in the previous section. The first possible future is simply an extension of the current reality. Voice recognition is clearly technically feasible because the necessary hardware and software already exist, and if voice recognition were not economically or politically feasible, it is reasonable to assume that the products would not be on the market. Without a technological breakthrough, the first possible future is where that state-of-the-art is likely to be in 2020.

Because current technology is not up to the task, the mass-market voice recognition envisioned in the third possible future is not yet technically feasible. How long is it likely to take for the necessary technology to emerge? Five years? Ten years? Twenty years? Technical feasibility does not guarantee economic feasibility. Like an automobile that gets 100 miles per gallon, the revenue potential of a mass-market voice interface is incredible, but cost is a different matter. Unless an effective product can be delivered at a reasonable cost, mass-market voice recognition will not be economically feasible by 2020.

Figure 11.1 Feasibility analysis.

Feasibility type	Question to be answered
Technical	Does the necessary technology exist or is likely to exist in time to affect the outcome?
Economic	Does the outcome promise a reasonable return on investment?
Political	Can the task be done in the context of the existing or expected social and political environment?

An excellent way to evaluate political feasibility is to identify the likely winners and losers. Who wins if voice becomes the new standard interface? First in line are the suppliers of voice recognition hardware and software. A simplified interface is likely to make computers accessible to a new cadre of potential users, including many physically disabled people, and new customers mean growth, so computer manufacturers, software suppliers, and related businesses are likely to benefit, too.

Who loses? The companies that supply mice, keyboards, and other related products could see their revenues drop. People with speech impediments and those who do not speak the language supported by a voice interface might lose accessibility, and the government will almost certainly react if that happens. Once you have identified the potential winners and losers, ask a simple question: Which group has more clout? The answer will give you a pretty good sense of political feasibility.

Wild Cards

A wild card is an impossible-to-anticipate technological breakthrough that makes all hypothetical futures irrelevant. For example, in his classic four-volume science fiction "trilogy" *The Hitchhiker's Guide to the Galaxy*, Douglas Adams describes a small yellow creature called a Babel fish. When you insert a Babel fish into your ear, it instantly translates words spoken in any language into your own language, no matter how alien that other language might be. Imagine how a Babel fish capable of translating between a human being and a computer would change the dynamics of voice recognition and voice response. The example may seem a bit silly, but it's a nice illustration of a wild card.

The point of feasibility analysis is to evaluate several possible futures to give you a sense of their relative likelihood of occurring. Much as a weather forecast helps you plan your activities, a feasibility analysis helps you plan for the future. The bulk of this chapter will examine the feasibility of four potentially significant e-commerce trends.

Tiered Internet Services

At several points in this book, the authors allude to the possibility of **tiered Internet services** evolving in response to increasing demand, economic pressures, or security and social needs. The television industry offers an excellent example of tiered services. If you live in or near most cities, you can receive four or five broadcast channels free of charge through an antenna. Reception can be spotty, selection is limited, and except for PBS (when it is not conducting a membership drive), there is no way to avoid advertising, but the service is free. For perhaps $20 per month, you can get basic cable service, more choices, and better reception. Another $10 moves you up to a preferred tier with many more choices. Add another $10 and you can get an ad-free premium channel like HBO or Showtime. The top tier is pay-per-view with current movies, sporting events, concerts, and similar specials, all commercial-free.

A near-future tiered Internet service might resemble Figure 11.2. The basic tier will probably resemble today's free access, advertising-supported Internet. Content will likely be limited, with full access limited to unfiltered, unedited information and corporate press releases. Like snail mail, the basic tier will be relatively slow, with no priority, security, or privacy guarantees. It will be adequate for standard e-mail and casual Web surfing, however.

Passwords and fees will restrict access to the higher tiers, with both price and content increasing as you move up. Each tier will incorporate everything in the lower tiers and add new services. For example, tier 3 will be fully supported by fees and private investments, and all ads will be blocked unless the user chooses to view them. The entire network will be broadband, so response will be very fast, and accessing most remote sites will seem much like accessing a local disk. To further guarantee speed, tier 3 packets will be given priority as they flow across the Internet; in other words, no tier 2 packet will move unless there are no tier 3 packets in line. To help ensure security and privacy, the tier 3 network is likely to resemble a virtual private network (VPN). Such services will be expensive, but many corporate and B2B applications will require the services offered only at a higher tier.

The premium tier will almost certainly not use the public infrastructure, relying instead on independent physical networks featuring the highest possible levels of speed, priority, security, and privacy. Exactly how they will be supported, what they will contain, and how they will be used will probably be none of your business (NOYB), but the military, the government, and corporate executives will clearly be potential customers.

Possible Futures

The tiered services described in the previous section are hypothetical, a figment of the authors' imaginations. If such services do evolve, they might take thousands of different

Figure 11.2 A tiered Internet services model.

Tier	Cost	Supported by	Speed	Priority	Security/ privacy	Content	Applications
Basic	Free	Advertising Sponsors	Slow	Low	None	Limited Unedited	E-mail Surfing
1	$	Advertising (Opt-in) Fees	Medium	Medium	Web	Broad Monitored Quality	Research B2C
2	$$	Fees	High	High	VPN	Business	Business Intra-business
3	$$$	Fees Private	Very fast	Very high	VPN	Corporate	Corporate B2B
Premium	$$$$	NOYB	Max.	Max.	Max.	NOYB	NOYB

forms, but we will adopt this model as representative and consider three possible futures for tiered services:

1. Tiered services will go the way of the late, lamented dot-bombs and slowly fade away, becoming little more than a niche phenomenon by 2020.

2. Tiered services will be independently implemented site by site, application by application, and enterprise by enterprise, with no obvious trend emerging by 2020.

3. A tiered Internet services model similar to the one outlined in Figure 11.2 will become the accepted standard by 2020.

That third possible future is intriguing. Is it likely?

Technical Feasibility

Is a tiered Internet services model technically feasible? Current technology suggests that it is. Today's public access Internet could easily become the basic tier. Many Web sites already charge a fee for accessing premium services, so we have a model for tiers 1, 2, and 3. Existing private, independent, highly secure networks run by the military, the government, and many corporations represent the premium tier. In other words, there is no technical reason why tiered Internet services cannot evolve by 2020.

Economic Feasibility

The economic feasibility of tiered services is not yet clear, however. At the basic level, free services are already beginning to disappear, and the evolution of a tiered, fee-based system could leave the free tier with very little useful content. Once again, television broadcasting provides a parallel. Most new television sets are sold cable-ready, and it is increasingly difficult to find one that comes with an old-fashioned antenna in the box. Consequently, the customer is faced with a choice: Buy an antenna, sign up for cable, or install a satellite dish. Basic Internet users are likely to face a similar choice: Sign up for at least tier 1 service or take what you get.

The first fee-based tier is likely to be reasonably priced, but potential customers and service providers will probably face a classic chicken-or-egg dilemma as they consider moving to a higher tier: Few customers are likely to sign on if the price is too high, and prices are likely to remain high until a critical mass of customers sign on. Depending on how many price points are able to achieve critical mass, anywhere from one to dozens of fee-based tiers might evolve, but no compelling reason can be argued that tiered Internet services are not economically feasible.

Political Feasibility

A tiered Internet services model appears to be technically and economically feasible, but is it politically feasible? The answer is unclear because tiered services represent a change in the very nature of the Internet and the World Wide Web.

On today's public Internet, every packet is treated pretty much the same, whether it originates with Bill Gates or some twelve-year-old kid in a middle-school computer lab. A tiered model would scrap all pretense of equality, however. A top-tier subscriber's packets would get preferential treatment, jumping to the beginning of any queues and moving securely over the fastest available connections. In contrast, that middle-school kid's packets would get whatever connection was left after all the higher-tier packets were transmitted. Picture a political ad pointing out the unfairness of such a system. "This is the USA," it might say. "All Web surfers are created equal! Down with favoritism!"

Compared to the hacker community, however, the politicians' response is likely to seem muted. Many hackers believe fervently that information should be free and that the very idea of tiered access to the Internet approaches blasphemy. The activists will respond with denial of service attacks, flame attacks, and various other forms of cyberterrorism. Ironically, such attacks could accelerate a move away from the public infrastructure to private infrastructures, further widening the gap between the middle-school kid and the corporate professional.

Who wins if tiered Internet services become the new norm? Some form of free Internet will almost certainly survive, so people who just exchange e-mail and do a limited amount of surfing probably won't notice much difference. Higher-tier academics, researchers, business people, and others affiliated with large organizations will be able to access information free of advertising and similar distractions, and the content they find is likely to be of higher quality because filters and editors will screen out much of the junk that pollutes the free Internet. Service providers will be big winners too, because the high-tier access fees will generate a dependable cash flow. At the organizational level, tiered services could replace intranets and extranets, providing comparable service at a significantly reduced cost. Streaming audio and video could boom, too, because the speed and priority routing guaranteed by a high-level tier would virtually eliminate delayed and out-of-order packets, yielding playback quality comparable to radio and television.

Who loses? Serious independent Web surfers will be forced to choose between the basic tier's limitations and a higher tier's cost. Small business owners and telecommuters who rely on the Internet to exchange information with coworkers will be forced to move up to a higher tier and pay a higher cost. With the most desirable consumers choosing the higher tiers, basic tier advertising is likely to decline, generating less revenue and further eroding content. Less useful content at the basic level could, in turn, worsen the digital divide, pushing even the technically proficient poor into the information have-not category. Which brings us back to the politicians and the hackers.

Tiered Internet services are technically feasible, and they make sense economically. They do face some politically powerful foes, however. What politician can resist taking the side of the little people against the elitists? And what hacker, white- or black-hat, can resist a little politically correct hacking in the name of the hacker's creed?

Consider the other side of the equation, however. Big corporations, research centers, and similar organizations stand to gain speed, content, and quality. If tiered services eventually replace private intranets and extranets, the new public infrastructure could actually reduce total connectivity costs. Money talks. If the public infrastructure does not provide tiered services, a parallel, independent, private "Internet" is likely to evolve. If such a private infrastructure manages to skim off the organizations that pay for today's free Internet (a not unlikely outcome), the impact on the public infrastructure could be significant.

Will tiered Internet services become the accepted standard by 2020? The odds look pretty good, but that's just our opinion. What's yours?

E-Books

As you learned in Chapter 5, a digitized product such as an **e-book** can potentially be distributed an unlimited number of times at little or no incremental cost. Also, because there is no physical book, such costs as printing, binding, delivering, warehousing, handling, and returns processing disappear. Given the potential for almost infinite revenue at little or no incremental cost, it is easy to see why e-books have caught the publishing industry's attention.

Imagine that you work for a publisher and have been assigned to a task force charged with recommending whether or not the company should begin marketing e-books. If digital distribution becomes the new standard, publishers with a strong e-book presence will do very well, but those who wait too long could find their very survival at risk. On the other hand, if e-books bomb, the first movers stand to lose a great deal of money.

Possible Futures

Your initial reaction might be to take a chance and bet on the future, but that strategy is little better than rolling dice. Your task force will be in a position to make a much more informed decision if the members have a good sense of several possible futures. Although thousands of outcomes are possible, we will focus on three:

1. By 2020, e-books will remain a relatively insignificant niche product accounting for less than 10 percent of publisher revenues.

2. By 2020, e-books will carve out a significant niche, accounting for roughly 20 to 25 percent of publisher revenues.

3. By 2020, e-books will become the dominant medium, accounting for at least 50 percent of publisher revenues.

The first outcome is an extension of the status quo, requiring no change in corporate strategy. The second outcome's revenue potential may or may not justify a first-mover risk. The publisher will have time to react to relatively slow development in niche markets, so there is no need to rush. Possible future number three is significant, however. If e-books really do account for 50 percent of publisher revenues by 2020, the first movers are likely to make a great deal of money. That one is worth studying.

Technical Feasibility

There is no question that e-books are technically feasible, because successful e-books already exist. For example, encyclopedias, dictionaries, atlases, and similar reference books are sold on CD-ROM, most word processing programs incorporate a spelling dictionary and a thesaurus, and as you learned in Chapter 4, most of today's books are created digitally (Figure 11.3).

If e-books are to become the dominant medium, they must be able to compete effectively with paperbacks, however. People buy paperbacks because they are inexpensive, convenient, and easy to read. You can stick a paperback book in your pocket and read it almost anywhere, even on a sunny beach. Until you can do the same with an e-book, paperbacks will probably continue to be the dominant medium.

The big problem with today's e-books is the lack of a convenient reader. You can read an e-book on a computer monitor or a tiny PDA screen (if you don't mind eyestrain),

Print-on-Demand

TECHNOLOGY

This discussion of e-books implicitly assumes that digitized books will be downloaded electronically over the Internet and read on some type of display device. It might not happen that way, however. Many experts believe that print-on-demand is a more viable strategy for marketing digitized books.

The key to print-on-demand is a new type of technology that prints one to a handful of copies of a book at a reasonable cost and at a level of quality comparable to a product purchased off the shelf. When a customer places an order, a digital copy of the book is downloaded over the Internet from a central source, the content and the cover are printed, the pages are bound, and the finished book is ready for pickup or shipping within a matter of minutes. Such equipment might be located in a bookstore, a print center, a distribution center, or even a kiosk in a shopping mall, and the big online services with their virtual warehouses are almost certain to buy the technology.

Print-on-demand makes it economically feasible for publishers to retain books that were once declared out-of-print, giving customers access to a much larger selection of low-demand, backlist, and niche books. It does not appear to be a viable mass market tool, however. A few minutes to print a book might not seem like much, but the time delay begins to accumulate when fifty people are standing in line to purchase the latest Harry Potter novel. However, combined with a limited-access tiered Internet service and strong security to protect publishers' and authors' intellectual property rights, print-on-demand just might prove to be technically, economically, and politically feasible long before e-books.

Figure 11.3 Most books are created digitally.

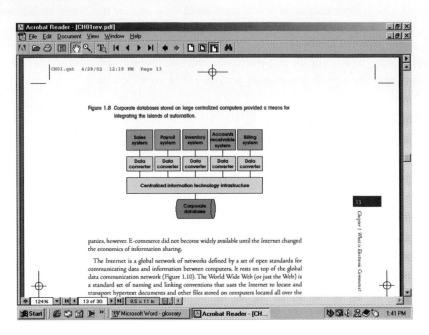

but would you seriously consider hauling your desktop or even your laptop to the beach? Even if you could, have you ever tried reading a display screen in full sun? Until a more convenient, higher quality, reasonably priced reading device emerges, e-books are likely to remain a niche product.

Is such a reading device even possible? Use a popular search engine like Google to search on "e-book reader" and you quickly discover that specialized hardware is already available from companies like Microsoft, Adobe, and Gemstar (Figure 11.4). Search on "digital paper," and you are likely to find references to Anoto, a Swedish firm that recently began marketing a form of digitized paper that can sense pen movements and capture a bitmap. Although neither technology is the answer, they do suggest that a small, inexpensive digital reading device is at least plausible. It probably won't happen in five years, but it might happen in ten, and if sufficient demand develops, you can probably count on such a device in twenty years.

Economic Feasibility

Imagine that a small, inexpensive digital reading device exists. Unless a critical mass of e-books is available, few people are likely to buy a reader. Unless enough people buy a reader, publishers are not going to market large numbers of compatible e-books. Who takes the first step, the publisher or the manufacturer of the digital reader? Predicting when a critical mass is likely to emerge is difficult at best.

To the publisher, e-books promise to deliver significantly lower incremental production costs, warehousing costs, and distribution costs; eliminate overstock, returns, and shortages; reduce risk; and generate Microsoft-like profit margins. Given such incentives, if the established publishers do not move into e-books quickly, someone else will.

Customers see things a bit differently, however. They need an incentive to switch, and publisher profit just isn't very compelling. Reference books make sense; they are easier to use, provide additional features like search tools, and cost less than their dead tree predecessors. But reference books are niche products. How can customers be convinced to switch from mass-market paperbacks to e-books? Paperbacks do an excellent job of delivering inexpensive, acceptable-quality reading material in a convenient, easy-to-use form, and the old, familiar ways of doing things tend to hang around until *all* of their functions are rendered obsolete.

The mass market for digital novels is unlikely to explode until some innovator releases a compact, easy-to-use e-book reader that is as convenient as a paperback and sells for less than $100. Is such technology an impossible dream? The next time you visit the beach, note the number of radios, CD players, PDAs, cellular telephones, television sets, digital cameras, and even laptop computers being used by your fellow sun worshipers. Not too long ago, exposing a sensitive electronic device to wind, sand, and water was unthinkable. Today it is commonplace. That e-book reader is coming; it's just a matter of time.

Even an inexpensive e-book reader will probably cost about $100, however, and customers are reluctant to make such investments without incentives. Availability is one key. Because most books exist in digital form before they are printed, that problem will almost certainly be solved. Price is another key. People are unlikely to buy a digital reader

Figure 11.4 An e-book reader.

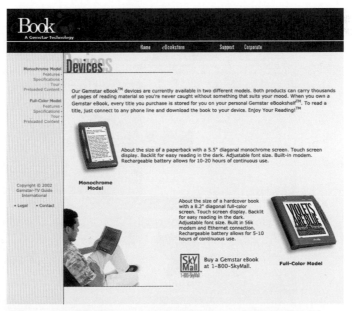

if e-books cost more than paperbacks. If e-books are priced at half the cost of a paper-back, however, even a $100 reader looks like a bargain if you read enough books.

Political Feasibility

Who wins if e-books become the dominant distribution medium for written words? At the top of the list are the publishers who will enjoy higher profits and reduced risk. Authors will benefit because their books will stay in print longer, and lower publisher risk may lead to more publishing outlets. Readers will no longer find the current best-seller out of stock, niche market and formerly out-of-print books will be available, and prices are likely to drop.

Who loses? Publishers who fail to adapt to the new reality head the list; they will either find a niche or go out of business. Distributors, shipping firms, warehouses, retail book-sellers, university bookstores, and other intermediaries will see their profits shrink. Shopping malls will lose tenants. Even librarians will have to adjust from cataloging and managing physical books to maintaining electronic collections.

The Video Game Wild Card

If you want to see the state of the art in information technology, check out such video game platforms as PlayStation 2, Sega Genesis, Super Nintendo, Microsoft's Xbox, and even the handheld Game Boy (Figure 11.5). Their screen resolution, graphics, 3-D effects, sound, processing speed, interactivity, and other parameters are much more

Figure 11.5 Video game platforms are the state of the art.

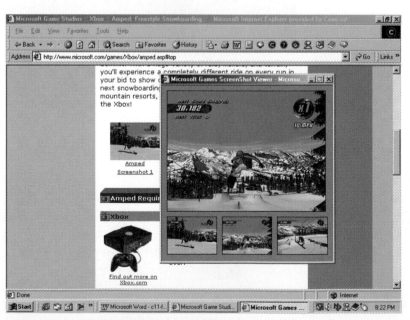

Screen shot reprinted by permission from Microsoft Corporation.

advanced than the technology available on a general purpose PC. If you have never tried a modern video game platform, you should. Be careful, though—they're addictive.

Those video game platforms represent a major e-book wild card because they just might be a near-future source of a compact, portable, easy-to-use, convenient, inexpensive e-book reader. Consider a handheld platform like Game Boy, for example. Game Boys sell well because they are highly portable, but the screen is so small that the games themselves pale in comparison to their big-screen counterparts. Imagine if some company announced an inexpensive, portable, big-screen game-playing platform that could be folded to fit in a pocket and used almost anywhere. How would you like to own stock in that company? Video gamers alone would create an immediate critical mass.

If such a video game platform existed, adopting it to serve as an e-book reader would be trivial. With a critical mass, publishers would rush to release digital titles. Given interesting choices, nongamers would snap up e-book readers, and a self-perpetuating cycle would begin. Is such a video game platform likely to evolve in the near future? Don't be surprised if it does, because a successful first move could generate an incredible amount of revenue.

Remember, however, that a new video game platform is likely to be designed with video games, not e-books, in mind. Because of the sophisticated sound, video, and processing capability of such a device, using one to read a book is a bit like using a Porsche to deliver a pizza. It works, but so does a Yugo. One possibility is a stripped-down e-book platform, but we're already talking about an inexpensive device. A more likely outcome is enhanced e-books. Enter audio mode and you have the equivalent of a book on tape. Activate the Babel fish feature and you can read a book written in any language. Touch a character's name and you see a picture of that character. Switch into animation mode and the story unfolds like a live performance.

If such features exist, authors (or whatever we decide to call the new class of content creators) will learn to exploit them. Perhaps in that brave new world, the only way you'll be able to read a good, old-fashioned book and rely on your own imagination to fill in the details will be to get your hands on a bound version printed on paper.

Intellectual Property Rights

Intellectual property rights are guaranteed by the U.S. Constitution, which reads: "To promote the Progress of Science and Useful Arts by securing for limited Times to Authors and Inventors the exclusive Right to their respective Writings and Discoveries" (art. 1, sec. 8). Unfortunately, we do not yet know how to protect intellectual property rights online.

Those rights take the form of copyrights, trademarks, and patents, and perhaps trade secrets and domain names. The copyright law includes a fair use provision that allows an individual to make a single copy of a copyrighted document for personal use. For example, it is perfectly legal to make a photocopy of a journal article to support your personal research, but it is illegal to make multiple copies of the same article for distribution to a class without permission from the copyright holder. Otherwise, the law gives authors exclusive rights to their creations.

Existing copyright laws work reasonably well with print media, but they are not very effective in cyberspace. Digital documents are so easy to copy that the act of storing one on the Internet effectively places it in the public domain, and digital piracy is a serious problem. For example, a key word search recently uncovered a (since removed) digital version of at least one chapter from this book on a faculty member's Web site. Anyone who found that document could have copied it, much as they have copied posted works by Harlan Ellison, Stephen King, and other well-known authors from various free access Web sites (Figure 11.6).

Digital watermarks can be used to prove ownership of a stolen document, but no antitheft system is immune to hacking and cracking. Digital rights management (DRM) software can help a company or a library conform to the law, but such software is designed to protect the company or the library, not the copyright holder. Legislation is not very effective, either. Congress is a deliberative body, and the Internet does not wait for politicians to make up their collective mind. Until someone finds a way to preserve the author's and the publisher's intellectual property rights without so inconveniencing the customer as to discourage sales, e-books are likely to remain a secondary or underground distribution medium.

Figure 11.6 Existing copyright laws are not very effective in cyberspace.

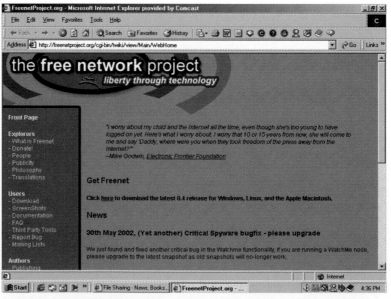

Source: *www.freenetproject.org.*

The Future of E-Books

If a product or a service can be reduced to a string of numbers, the incremental cost of transmitting those numbers over a communication line is essentially zero, and like water seeking its own level, business will, sooner or later, gravitate to the most efficient distribution channel. It will take time, of course, and no product, digital or physical, will be distributed in any form if it is not worth distributing. But it will happen. Digital products will be distributed electronically, and e-books will become the dominant distribution medium for books and booklike material. The question is when, not if. In other words, the odds that e-books will become the dominant medium, accounting for at least 50 percent of publisher revenues by 2020, look pretty good.

Web Services

The long-range goal of many companies is complete enterprise application integration, with all applications, including legacy, custom-developed, and off-the-shelf applications, working seamlessly together, a vision that sometimes extends to interorganizational systems as well. As you learned in Chapters 6 and 7, integrating applications to share information freely is extremely difficult, however.

Web services are intermediary-supplied e-utilities that allow incompatible application programs to interact and share information over the Internet. They resemble the less-than-successful proprietary applications marketed by application service providers (ASPs), such as enterprise resource planning software. Web services take a more iterative approach, however, providing specialized utilities that, like software building blocks, can be assembled to support numerous applications.

For example, business transactions that cross international boundaries often require currency conversion. The computations are straightforward, but maintaining up-to-date exchange rates is a tedious process. For most companies, paying for access to a currency conversion Web service is significantly less expensive. Think of such Web services as remote subroutines (Figure 11.7). If Acme receives an invoice from a European supplier, the company's accounts payable Web application calls the currency conversion Web service, passes it the amount due in euros, gets back the equivalent amount in dollars, and records the transaction.

Unlike many ASP applications that were written for another platform and ported to the Internet, the newer Web services are designed specifically for the Web, exchanging open-standard XML messages and relying on several other standard Internet protocols. In the ASP world, a company that relied on a failed conversion service was out of luck. Because Web services are based on open standards, however, if one currency conversion service fails, its former customers can simply plug into another one.

Figure 11.7 Think of a Web service as a remote subroutine.

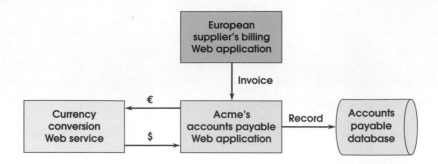

Currency conversion is not the only Web services application, of course. Other conversion services, such as Microsoft Word to PDF, MP3 to WAV, and even German to English, are naturals. An existing Web service application links Dollar Car Rental's reservation Web site to the Southwest Airlines reservation site, allowing Southwest's customers to book a rental car as they book a flight. Because the Web service relies on open standards, Dollar will find it relatively easy to establish similar links to other potential business partners in the future. A similar Web service might allow a company's customers to access its order tracking data no matter what computing platforms they use.

Possible Futures

Your company is about to launch a major value chain integration effort. Should you invest in Web services to link your internal systems, or is customized software a better choice? Looking further into the future, are Web services a viable option for integrating your company's supply chain?

To answer those questions, you need a sense of how Web services are likely to evolve. Three possible futures include:

1. Like the dot-coms, Web services will experience a hype-driven growth spurt and then fade into the background when they fail to live up to expectations. By 2020, they will be just a memory.

2. Web services will prove highly successful. By 2020, numerous competing and incompatible standards will be in use, with no one standard dominating.

3. Web services will prove highly successful. Much like Microsoft Windows, however, one set of Web services (or perhaps two or three) will achieve a dominant position and become the accepted standard for application integration by 2020.

If the first possible future is the most likely outcome, creating a custom solution is probably a better option than relying on Web services. Possible future number two suggests a long-range risk that supply chain integration will be complicated by trading partners who are committed to incompatible proprietary Web services. The third possible future offers the greatest promise for true supply chain integration, making it the most attractive outcome for a company that is thinking about eventually integrating its entire supply chain.

Microsoft's .NET My Services

If you have ever changed Internet service providers, you know how frustrating it is to try to update your e-mail address and other personal data with every B2C Web site and every online service you visit regularly. It seems that each site has its own rules and its own data structures to which you must conform. Some Web sites are almost arrogant, implying by their actions that they own the personal information you gave them. Check their privacy policy. Chances are they do.

Microsoft's .NET My Services promises to change that model. For a fee, subscribers record such personal information as their name, address, telephone numbers, e-mail addresses, passwords, credit card numbers, preferences, and contacts with Microsoft's .NET Passport service. Microsoft guarantees the security, privacy, and integrity of the data. My Services follows an affirmative consent or opt-in model that allows each individual subscriber to control access to his record. Anyone who wants to access a subscriber's data must request the user's permission, and consent is valid only for a limited purpose and a limited time.

Imagine that you are a subscriber. Rather than filling out a Web form to order merchandise, you simply authorize the e-retailer to obtain the necessary information from Microsoft. Record your user IDs and passwords with My Services and you don't have to look them up every time you log on to a Web site. If you move, recording the new address with My Services changes it with everyone. If security is a concern, My Services can mask your credit card number with a one-time random code so only three parties know the real number: you, the bank, and Microsoft. Make an airline reservation and My Services can automatically provide your seating preferences and credit card information. Assuming the fees are reasonable and you trust Microsoft to safeguard your personal information, .NET My Services looks promising.

Technical Feasibility

Web services are clearly technically feasible because intermediary XML-based applications are already common. The definition of Web services is still evolving, however, with competing organizations offering solutions based on incompatible methodologies, technologies, and platforms. Years ago, a single-function focus led to the evolution of islands of automation. Value chain integration helped to solve the islands problem, but incompatible internal systems meant that trading partners with incompatible platforms operated as continents of automation. To continue the metaphor, unless one or two of those evolving Web services emerges as an effective standard, clusters of companies committed to incompatible approaches will form planets of automation.

Perhaps a set of industry standards will evolve, allowing companies with compatible product lines to integrate their applications seamlessly. Maybe an international standards body will step in and define a set of standards. Survival of the fittest is the more likely outcome, however. Some Web service providers will fail. Others will be absorbed by bigger, more successful rivals. If history is a guide, a few dominant Web services providers are likely to emerge by 2020, assuming, of course, that the Web services approach is more than just hype and proves economically and politically feasible.

Economic Feasibility

From an economic perspective, Web services seem to make sense. If software and infrastructure vendors can offer a semistandard way of solving application integration problems at a reasonable price, demand should be high, and that's exactly what appears to be happening. *CIO Insight* magazine predicts that Web services revenue will explode from a mere $380 million in 2001 to $15.5 billion by 2005.[1]

If that forecast is even close to accurate, it is easy to understand why so many intermediaries are marketing propriety Web services. If your proprietary scheme becomes the standard, that $15 billion could be yours. Expect vendors to compete fiercely for market share, and expect a great deal of hype, too. Competition might postpone or even block the emergence of a dominant supplier and a widely accepted standard. And if marketing hype gets too far ahead of the technology, the whole Web services movement could become another example of **vaporware**, software that is announced and hyped long before it is released (if it is ever released).

Political Feasibility

If a dominant proprietary Web services standard evolves, the clear winner will be the vendor that owns the standard. Most of the major vendors are already touting their solutions, including Microsoft's .NET platform, Sun Microsystem's J2EE, IBM's Tivoli software portfolio, Lotus's Sametime collaboration suite, and BEA's WebLogic Server that supports Web services development in Java. Companies trying to integrate incompatible applications are also likely to win, unless the dominant standard becomes a monopoly that discourages future Web services innovation.

Other political and legal issues threaten to muddy the waters a bit, however. For example, the emergence of a successful Web services standard would make it much easier for companies to integrate their supply chain processes, but at what point does integration become collusion? And at what point does the market share held by a dominant standard become a monopoly? Based on the recent Microsoft antitrust case, Congress and the courts should have fun with Web services and supply chain integration. Perhaps the legal and political climate will force some official group to develop a set of Web services standards, but that might take decades. Unless the politicians and the lawyers intervene, however, the marketplace will pick a winner.

As was the case with the overhyped dot-coms, if Web services fail to catch on as expected, anyone who invests her time or her money or commits her company's e-commerce infrastructure to such services stands to lose. In the late 1990s, ASPs were hyped as the next big thing, but the ASP business model has been slow to catch on, costing many investors and venture capitalists a great deal of money and many technically skilled people their jobs. In other words, caution is in order.

---

[1] Stephen Lawton, "Custom Services: Putting Web Services to Work," *CIO Insight* (April 15, 2002): *www.cioinsight.com/print_article/0,3668,a=25691,00.asp*. See the Web services fact sheet near the end of the article.

Web Services

Look at the companies that are investing in Web services. IBM, Microsoft, and Sun Microsystems do not enter new markets blindly; clearly, they see real potential, and their track records are generally good. In Chapter 4, you learned how the accelerating pace of innovation is forcing companies to operate as efficiently as possible and to react quickly to the marketplace. Because they serve as a new layer of technological building blocks, Web services promise quick, easy efficiency gains, and that promise is what makes them appealing. It is unlikely that Web services will fade away.

Is a single dominant vendor's proprietary approach likely to emerge as a Windows-like voluntary standard? Perhaps, but a variety of industry-based standards supported by different vendors and consortiums seems more likely. Those planets of automation will be causing problems in 2020.

Finally, remember that Web services are provided by intermediaries, and an intermediary service used by your company is also available to your competitors. Is it possible to achieve a competitive advantage by leveraging the efficiency gains made possible by Web services when those services are available to everyone? If the answer is no, Web services may join the ASP business model and the dot-coms as overhyped technological shooting stars that burn brightly and then fade from view.

Biometrics Authentication

Today's authentication tools leave a great deal to be desired. Passwords are easily lost, stolen, guessed, or forgotten. Badges and other identification tokens can be counterfeited and rely too heavily on humans to match the object to the person. Knowing a password proves that the access seeker knows a secret, and presenting a badge proves that he possesses an object, but neither technique proves that the individual is really who he claims to be.

Rather than relying on what you know or what you have, biometrics authentication is based on who you are. A biometrics trait cannot be lost, stolen, or recreated. Biometrics tests are conducted objectively by a machine, not an easily distracted, error-prone human being. At first glance, biometrics technology looks like an ideal solution for both local and remote authentication. But is it?

Possible Futures

We will start trying to answer that question by identifying three possible futures for biometrics authentication:

1. By 2020, biometrics technology will be used primarily for local physical access control and rarely for remote authentication.

2. By 2020, improvements in biometrics will support both local physical access control and remote authentication from a physically secure location.

3. By 2020, biometrics technology will become the new standard for both local and online authentication.

All three could happen, but which of those possible futures is the most likely?

Evaluating Biometrics

Biometrics authentication is based on the results of a comparison. Imagine that you have a smart card and that your fingerprint has previously been scanned and stored on the embedded chip. As you approach a fingerprint scanner, you insert the card into one slot and your index finger into another. Your fingerprint is scanned and the result is compared to the version stored on your smart card. If they match, you pass.

Behind the scenes, the comparison is performed by a computer. Computers work only with binary data, so digitized fingerprints, not real fingerprints, are compared. Imagine laying a fine net on top of a fingerprint. Each hole in the net corresponds to a single point, and the characteristics of the swirls at that point (in, out, up, down, left, right) can be recorded as a series of numbers. Those digitized points are called **minutiae**, and increasing the number of minutiae increases accuracy. Note, however, that the minutiae are captured and stored as a pattern of bits, and that a mathematical representation of a fingerprint is not exactly a fingerprint.

When a scanned fingerprint is compared to a stored fingerprint, the computer generates a score based on how well the two sets of minutiae match. If every point matches, the score is 1.0; if only a few don't match, the score might be 0.9; if no points match, the score is 0.0. The computed score is then compared to a **threshold** value. If the score exceeds the threshold, the subject is authenticated. If the score falls below the threshold, the subject is rejected. Why not set the threshold at 1.0 and authenticate only perfect matches? Because little things like a cut, a burn, a speck of dirt, or a slight misalignment of the finger in the scanner can affect the accuracy of the scan, and a threshold of 1.0 virtually guarantees that almost no one will pass.

Look at the three blocks pictured in Figure 11.8. If an individual's score falls inside the left box, she is clearly an impostor. If the score falls inside the right box, he is clearly authorized and should be approved. A score that falls between points A and B is questionable, however. It might represent an authorized individual, and it might represent an impostor.

Setting the threshold at point A guarantees that all authorized personnel will be approved, but so will any impostors in that middle range. Setting the threshold at point B keeps the impostors out, but it also denies access to many authorized users. Approving an impostor is called a false positive. Rejecting an authorized subject is called a false negative. False positives and false negatives are related: If you move the threshold to reduce one type of error, you inevitably increase the other. The challenge is to define a threshold

Figure 11.8 Biometrics testing generates false negatives and false positives.

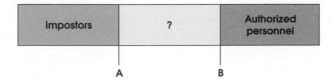

point that balances false positives and false negatives, letting most of the good guys in and keeping most of the bad guys out. Like virtually all security tools, biometrics authentication implies a trade-off.

The nature of the system is another significant biometrics variable. Biometrics screening is most effective when the system is closed, in other words, when a computed score is compared against a limited database that holds data for a restricted subset of the population, such as a company's employees, a university's students, or air travelers known to be departing today. Biometrics screening is least effective when the system is open and the subject can be anyone in the general population. Basically, as the number of people in the database goes up, the accuracy of biometrics screening goes down. Consequently, currently available biometrics technology is best used to confirm, not to establish, an identity.

Biometrics Criteria

A standard law enforcement tool for decades, fingerprint scanning appears to be the most likely biometrics criterion to succeed by 2020. Fingerprints are data-rich (thirty to forty minutiae per print), about 98 percent accurate, and generate less than 1 percent false positives. Of all the available biometrics criteria, fingerprints have the lowest data collection error rate, are the most difficult to fool, and are the least expensive. Some people are uncomfortable having their fingerprints taken, perhaps because popular culture equates the act with criminal activity, but that attitude is changing.

A retinal scan measures the pattern of blood vessels in the retina of the eye. The accuracy of a retinal scan is affected by the operator's skill, however, and retinal scans are relatively expensive. Still in the prototype stage, an iris scan is similar to a retinal scan. DNA analysis is the most accurate biometrics criterion, but it requires highly trained technicians, is much too expensive, and takes too long to serve as a real-time authentication tool. Hand geometry screening is considerably less effective than fingerprinting. Facial recognition is appealing because that is how human beings recognize each other, but the technology is not quite ready for everyday use. People also identify each other through voice dynamics, but voice prints are inaccurate and can be faked. Signature recognition is an established identification criterion, but the technology tends to generate unacceptably high levels of false negatives and false positives. In other words, none of the alternative criteria looks as attractive as fingerprint scanning, so it makes sense to focus on fingerprinting.

Some Negatives

Although fingerprint scanning has a long history of success, particularly in law enforcement, using it as a real-time authentication tool may not be as successful. Fingerprints are normally collected under carefully controlled conditions. When your prints are taken, a technician guides and rolls one finger at a time to ensure a clean impression. When latent prints are lifted at the scene of a crime, the police follow very precise procedures to ensure accuracy.

Such controls are effective if the number of prints to be collected and analyzed is small, but they begin to break down as volume increases. Without tight controls, precision drops, variability soars, and the rate of false negatives and false positives goes up. Today, a biometrics parameter captured in real time is typically compared to a restricted list of preselected individuals (employees, customers, known criminals), and the subject is considered authenticated or identified if a match is found. Increase the size of the population, however, and accuracy goes down.

Remote authentication adds yet another variable. A computer, remember, compares digitized images of fingerprints, not real fingerprints. A digitized fingerprint is just a string of bits, in effect a long password, and passwords can be hacked, cracked, or modified. What happens if a digitized fingerprint is hijacked as it is transmitted? Encryption might help to overcome that problem, but what if a hacker penetrates the sending computer on the scanner side and modifies the binary string before it is sent? To minimize the system's vulnerability to hacking, physically securing both the sending and receiving computers and encrypting all transactions might be necessary. If such restrictions are imposed, fingerprint scanning is unlikely to become the new standard for online authentication, because no way to physically secure every possible network access point exists.

Perhaps the biggest concern, however, is the way people view biometrics. We read about how the guilty are imprisoned and the innocent are freed based on fingerprints, DNA, and similar biometrics tests, and we begin to believe that such tests are foolproof. If a DNA test says the little old lady in room 714 is Robert Redford, she becomes Robert Redford in spite of abundant physical evidence to the contrary. That's an exaggeration, of course, but at the very least someone would have to document why that little old lady cannot possibly be Robert Redford, because the biometrics test is assumed to be right until it is proven to be wrong.

How does an inflated faith in the precision of biometrics affect authentication? There is no question that biometrics screening is more accurate and more difficult to fool than passwords, smart cards, and other traditional forms of authentication, but errors can happen and hackers are remarkably persistent. Because people tend to trust biometrics, once you penetrate the system, you are in, and no one is likely to question your credentials, because you passed a biometrics test and biometrics never lie. Like a fox in the hen house, a successful intruder is free to roam and pillage at will.

The Future of Biometrics

Is biometrics screening likely to become the new standard for online authentication by 2020? Probably not, because the potential damage resulting from a false positive is much too high. Biometrics authentication from a physically secure remote site is much more likely, particularly if the sending and receiving computers are linked by a secure line and use a high-tier Internet service. In other words, possible future number two is the most likely outcome: Improvements in biometrics will support both local physical access control and remote authentication from a physically secure location by 2020.

E-Commerce and Your Future

E-commerce is incredibly complex. Fortunately, the underlying infrastructure and e-commerce applications consist of layers that can be independently studied and understood. Those components are not really independent, however, and one danger of the layered approach is missing the interrelationships. Attempting to forecast the future by analyzing one component at a time carries a similar risk. Tiered Internet services, e-books, Web services, and biometrics authentication are not really independent. They, and every other e-commerce layer and application, are interrelated, and ignoring the possible ripple effects can be dangerous.

You should also consider unintended side effects. If e-books succeed, what happens to traditional publishers, distributors, and bookstores? If tiered Internet services become the new norm, what services will remain on the free content Web? If the top tiers get significantly better service, will the information haves enjoy a significant competitive advantage over the information have-nots? Interesting questions without clear answers.

Rather than analyzing the possible futures of yet another promising technology, it makes more sense to end this book by examining those interrelationships and unintended side effects. Specifically, consider how e-commerce might affect *your* future.

Technology

Technology forms the underlying infrastructure, making it a good place to start. In addition to the possibility of a tiered Internet service discussed earlier in this chapter, wireless communication seems to be on the brink of exploding. The dizzying array of cellular plans available today is confusing, but if you look beyond the hype, the advertising, and the fine print, a clear trend begins to emerge. Little by little, calling areas are expanding, fewer and fewer calls are charged by the minute, and the base charge is dropping. Eventually, you will be able to purchase, for a fixed monthly fee, a calling plan that really lets you call anywhere in the United States at no extra charge and with no roaming fees.

If such a fixed-cost wireless service emerges, one likely outcome is a significant increase in the number of people who abandon their traditional wired telephone service and adopt wireless as their everyday communication medium. A nationwide wireless telephone service means that you carry your telephone number with you when you move or travel, and you are always within easy reach of 911 in the event of an emergency. In fact, there is an active proposal to equip cell phones with GPS sensors so the 911 operator can locate you within a few square yards and inform the emergency personnel of your precise whereabouts.

Short-range wireless communication shows promise, too. As technologies like Bluetooth and WiFi continue to improve, personal LANs will become common. Initially, you might connect your desktop, your laptop, and your PDA and allow them to exchange information. Next, you might get rid of the tangle of wires behind your desk by integrating your monitor, your mouse, your keyboard, your printer, and your scanner into your wireless network. Eventually, your TV, your VCR, your DVD, and your sound system might join the network, allowing you to control your entire home entertainment system centrally.

Be careful, though. Some evidence suggests that constant exposure to the radiation generated by a cell phone can be harmful. Also, wireless signals are relatively easy to intercept, which compromises privacy and security. Even the signals that tell 911 where you are can be potentially intercepted. Imagine that you are walking through a mall. Every time you pass a storefront, your cell phone rings, and you hear a personalized message generated by the store's customer relationship management system inviting you to come in and shop. You hang up, move on to the next storefront, and it happens again. Won't that be fun.

Finally, there is a downside to being "always on." The Internet is a global phenomenon, and business is always being conducted somewhere, twenty-four hours a day. Do you really want to be accessible all the time? Do you really want to conduct business on your cell phone and your laptop while you are on vacation? To some people, the answer is yes. With no time off, however, burnout could come quickly.

Business

As more and more companies successfully integrate their value chains and supply chains, automatic, instant reporting up and down the supply chain will enable applications that begin to approach the ideal of frictionless e-commerce. Lower costs will almost certainly lead to lower prices as companies fight for competitive advantage. In such an environment, only the most efficient will survive, possibly leading to consolidation rather than competition. Such an outcome could have significant political, legal, and social consequences. Also, instant reporting over communication lines is extremely risky without dependable security. The need for in-transit security could accelerate acceptance of tiered Internet services and biometrics screening and could slow the transition to wireless communication.

One of the most effective ways to improve physical security is to disburse potential targets. In the aftermath of September 11, 2001, we might begin to see a trend away from large, centralized offices and campuses and toward smaller offices in smaller population centers. Telecommuting could become more common, too, because employees who work at home are about as disbursed as they can possibly be. In addition to better security, a more disbursed workforce will probably mean lower physical facility costs, although the expense of creating and maintaining a secure extranet to link those remote offices and telecommuters to each other could wipe out much of the savings. Web services could blossom in such an environment, because they offer low-cost options for supporting an extranet.

Efficient, high-speed communication also enables real-time employee monitoring. Telecommuters, traveling sales associates, and remote office employees may feel independent, but the company will be able to track their activities in real time. The "always on" syndrome is another likely consequence. An ambitious executive in an East Coast office might find working a very long day necessary, arriving before 8:00 a.m. to greet her employees and leaving after 8:00 p.m. when the West Coast office closes. Some people already do that, of course, but disbursed offices and an "always on" extranet will further encourage such work patterns.

Where We Live

Most of America's oldest cities, including Boston, New York, Philadelphia, Baltimore, Charleston, Savannah, and New Orleans, were located on a harbor or a navigable river, because when they were founded, water served as the transportation infrastructure. The railroads broke that pattern by creating a new layer based on steel rails, and population centers began springing up at major rail junctions (Atlanta, Kansas City, Denver) and around refueling stations. Eventually, the interstate highway system supplanted the railroads, and population centers began following the new infrastructure, with suburbs and subdivisions lining circle freeways and clustering around interchanges.

The Internet (or its successor) could evolve into a new base infrastructure and have a similar impact on living patterns. For example, more and more companies, responding perhaps to the threat of terrorist attacks, could decide to disburse their operations and tie the pieces together with a high-speed extranet. If that happens, expect new business centers to develop near the best access points to backbone connections, top-tier services, and broadband services, and expect new access points to emerge in places where people want to live. Do you like cities? A seaside resort? The desert? The mountains? Fly-fishing? White-water rafting? Europe? Asia? Chances are that you'll have a choice, because if the Internet becomes the new base infrastructure, it really doesn't matter where you live.

Watch for unintended consequences, too. Think of the vast support infrastructure that has grown up around the interstate highway system. What happens to all those subdivisions, roads, shopping centers, parking lots, gas stations, and entertainment complexes if the population they evolved to serve moves elsewhere? It won't be pretty.

Education

Education seems like an appropriate closing topic, and there is a link to e-commerce. As you know, the pace of technological change is accelerating. One implication of rapid change is a decline in the half-life of what you know. Lifetime learning is not just a slogan. The underlying principles change slowly, but tools and techniques quickly become obsolete, and after you graduate, you're going to need continuous retraining just to keep up. That's why graduation is called commencement—it marks the beginning, not the end.

There is a significant difference between a traditional 18- to 22-year-old college student and an adult learner, however. After you graduate, you begin to take on responsibilities and obligations—a car loan, a mortgage, a spouse, children—that make it impossible for you to even consider taking sixteen weeks off work to go back to school for a semester. New educational models are needed, and they are beginning to emerge. Schools like the University of Phoenix and ITT offer evening, weekend, and self-paced academic programs both online and at branch campuses located in places like shopping centers, and those two schools are already among the top institutions of higher education in the country in terms of number of degrees granted. Even high schools are offering online course work. For example, in Sarasota, Florida, the county school district supports a virtual school that has all but replaced summer school. Corporate courses and training programs represent another growing market for online education. Online tutorials can be quite effective. If you have never used one, try one of the tutorials referenced at the end of Appendix C.

Over the next few decades, alternative education and training is likely to grow much faster than traditional K–12, undergraduate, and graduate education. Does that mean traditional education will fade away? Of course not; in spite of some well-known problems, the existing system works too well to scrap it. Traditional schools are likely to become a smaller piece of the total education and training pie, however (Figure 11.9). Assume that our existing schools account for two-thirds of the dollars spent on education today. By 2020, that share might drop to one-third, with nontraditional options grabbing the lion's share. Note, however, that the total amount spent on traditional education is unlikely to shrink and will probably rise. What will change is the size of the pie.

The quality of those nontraditional courses is a concern, however. Traditional schools are subject to a rigorous accreditation process, and losing accreditation has serious consequences. Although organizations that accredit online schools exist, none has developed sufficient credibility to guarantee quality. More often than not, a nontraditional profit-making school's perceived quality is based on the success of its graduates. If employers keep hiring its graduates, a school must be doing something right.

Society's tendency to focus on credentials rather than knowledge or ability is a related concern. As any non-college graduate can tell you, certain jobs are simply unavailable

Figure 11.9 Traditional education is likely to become a smaller piece of the total education and training pie.

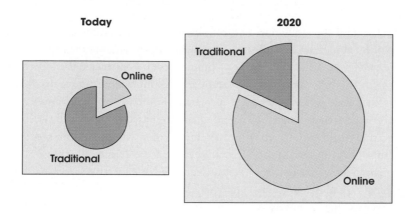

without a degree. In many public school systems, teachers move up the salary scale by earning graduate school credits without much regard for quality of the course or the school. Successful business managers who lack an MBA find promotions difficult to obtain. Content experts who lack a Ph.D. rarely become university professors.

In most cases, requiring a certain set of credentials is justified because earning those credentials implies successfully mastering a body of knowledge. The occasional false negative (rejecting an otherwise qualified candidate) is more than offset by a reduction in false positives (accepting an unqualified candidate). As the number of online schools and courses begins to proliferate, however, judging academic quality will become increasingly difficult. Already certain credentials can be purchased, and others can be "earned" by simply attending a few classes. Unless we find a way to distinguish between quality and junk, the credentials could become meaningless.

Influencing the Future

Although most predictions are speculative, informed people can influence the future. The first step is understanding what might happen. The future evolves from the present, so a firm foundation in the current state of the art is a necessary prerequisite, and we sincerely hope that this book has helped you establish such a foundation. Identifying the possible futures that could evolve from that base gives you a sense of your options and helps you decide where you want to take your life. Perhaps you will identify the most likely future and take steps to prepare yourself for it. Perhaps you will focus on your preferred future and work to influence its likelihood of occurring. The future belongs to those who prepare for it.

Summary

Feasibility analysis is an effective tool for evaluating possible futures. Three types of feasibility are considered: technical, economic, and political. Tiered Internet services appear to be technically and economically feasible. Political feasibility is less clear, however, because tiered services represent a change in the nature of the Internet and the World Wide Web.

Given the potential for almost infinite revenue at little or no incremental cost, it is easy to see why e-books have caught the publishing industry's attention. However, the mass market for digital novels is unlikely to explode until some innovator releases a compact, easy-to-use e-book reader that is as convenient as a paperback and sells for less than $100. Video game platforms represent a major e-book wild card because they might be a near-future source of such an e-book reader. Our inability to protect intellectual property rights online is another wild card.

Web services are technically feasible and seem to make economic sense. The definition of Web services is still evolving, however, with competing organizations offering solutions based on incompatible methodologies, technologies, and platforms.

Biometrics authentication is another possible future standard. A biometrics trait cannot be lost, stolen, or recreated. Biometrics authentication works by generating a score based on how well two sets of minutiae match and then comparing the score to a threshold value. If the score exceeds the threshold, the subject is authenticated. Biometrics screening is most effective when the system is closed. Of the available biometrics criteria, fingerprint scanning seems to be the most likely to succeed by 2020. Wireless communication appears to be on the brink of exploding, and short-range wireless communication shows promise, too.

E-commerce will also affect your personal future. Potential technological advances that could change your life include frictionless e-commerce, Web-influenced living patterns, and the need for continuous retraining. Informed people can influence future directions by the choices they make.

Key Words

e-book	political feasibility	vaporware
economic feasibility	technical feasibility	Web services
feasibility analysis	threshold	
minutiae	tiered Internet services	

Review Questions

1. Identify the basic questions that must be answered to demonstrate technical, economic, and political feasibility.

2. Explain how feasibility analysis can be used to evaluate the relative likelihood of alternative possible futures.

3. Explain how wild cards, such as unanticipated technical breakthroughs, can affect a forecast.

4. Discuss the feasibility of tiered Internet services.

5. Discuss the feasibility of e-books.

6. Explain how evolving video game platforms might affect the future of e-books.

7. Explain how intellectual property rights might affect the future of e-books.

8. What are Web services?

9. Discuss the feasibility of Web services.

10. Explain how biometrics authentication works.

11. Distinguish between a false negative and a false positive.

12. Although biometrics authentication is considerably more effective than passwords and tokens, it does have weaknesses that can be exploited. Identify some.

13. Discuss the feasibility of biometrics authentication.

14. Discuss how e-commerce is likely to affect your future.

Exercises

1. The precision of a forecast varies with time. Explain why.

2. Do you think tiered Internet services are a good idea or a bad idea? Why?

3. Do you think e-books will ever become the dominant medium for distributing traditionally printed materials? Why or why not?

4. Do you think digital textbooks are a good idea? Why or why not?

5. Which technology do you think is more likely to enjoy widespread success by 2020, digital books or print-on-demand? Why?

6. Would you consider signing up for Microsoft's .NET My Services? Why or why not?

7. Are you at all concerned that biometrics authentication will lead to increased monitoring and surveillance? Why or why not?

8. Identify the type of profession you would like to practice in 2020 and evaluate how e-commerce and related technologies are likely to affect that profession.

▣ Projects

Current references and supporting resources can be found on this textbook's companion Web site.

Broad-Based Projects

1. Complete one of the tutorials referenced at the end of Appendix C and note your impressions.

Building the Case:

2. Working as a team, continue with Chapter 1, Project 6 by presenting your recommended strategy and demonstrating your prototype Web site to the class. Then prepare an executive summary (no more than three pages, double-spaced) of the proposed strategy and submit to your instructor the summary, a printed copy of your recommended strategy and implementation plan, a copy of your slides or other presentation materials, the URL or a printed copy of selected pages from your Web site, and other relevant documentation.

Business Projects

Building the Case:

1. Continue with Chapter 1, Project 2 by compiling the various reports you wrote throughout the term. Reread the individual reports in context and make the corrections necessary to ensure accuracy, consistency, clarity, and continuity. Collect revenue and cost information from the various reports.

Prepare a design and development budget and a summary of anticipated annual revenues, operating costs, and net cash flows for five years. Use the financial data to compute the project's return on investment. Prepare a financial information page that documents the development budget, cash flow data, and the return on investment. Add a cover page, a table of contents, and a one- to two-page executive summary to complete the business plan, and submit it to your instructor for evaluation.

Information Technology Projects

Building the Case:

1. After putting the finishing touches on your Web site, present it either in class or online. As part of your presentation, identify and discuss the extra features you might add if you had more time.

Marketing Projects

Building the Case:

1. Continue with Chapter 1, Project 2 by completing the story board you started in Chapter 5. Make necessary corrections to ensure accuracy, consistency, clarity, and continuity, and make sure the individual elements of the plan are consistent with your marketing strategy. Present your marketing strategy and your story board in class.

▣ References

See this textbook's companion Web site for late-breaking news.

APPENDIX A

Digitization

Numbers and Text

Inside a computer, all data is stored in digital form as a pattern of 0s and 1s. A binary number consists of a series of binary digits. Many computers can store and manipulate binary approximations of scientific numbers called real or floating-point numbers. Some business applications require decimal numbers, so many computers support a form of binary-coded decimal data.

Computers are not limited to storing and manipulating numbers. For example, many applications call for such character data (or text data) as names, addresses, and product descriptions. Each character is represented by a binary code, such as ASCII or EBCDIC (Figure A.1), and occupies 1 byte. A text file is a string of characters.

Imagine a string of fifty consecutive uppercase letter As stored in a sending computer's memory. Rather than transmitting a 50-byte string containing fifty identical characters, it makes more sense to compress the string to a single A followed by a 1-byte count, a total of only two characters, and to transmit the compressed string. Assuming the receiving computer knows the compression rule, it can easily reconstruct the data. Compression reduces the amount of space required to store a file. Text files can be compressed into such formats as ARC and ZIP.

Figure A.1 The ASCII and EBCDIC codes for digits and uppercase letters.

Character	ASCII	EBCDIC	Character	ASCII	EBCDIC
0	0011 0000	1111 0000	I	0100 1001	1100 1001
1	0011 0001	1111 0001	J	0100 1010	1101 0001
2	0011 0010	1111 0010	K	0100 1011	1101 0010
3	0011 0011	1111 0011	L	0100 1100	1101 0011
4	0011 0100	1111 0100	M	0100 1101	1101 0100
5	0011 0101	1111 0101	N	0100 1110	1101 0101
6	0011 0110	1111 0110	O	0100 1111	1101 0110
7	0011 0111	1111 0111	P	0101 0000	1101 0111
8	0011 1000	1111 1000	Q	0101 0001	1101 1000
9	0011 1001	1111 1001	R	0101 0010	1101 1001
A	0100 0001	1100 0001	S	0101 0011	1110 0010
B	0100 0010	1100 0010	T	0101 0100	1110 0011
C	0100 0011	1100 0011	U	0101 0101	1110 0100
D	0100 0100	1100 0100	V	0101 0110	1110 0101
E	0100 0101	1100 0101	W	0101 0111	1110 0110
F	0100 0110	1100 0110	X	0101 1000	1110 0111
G	0100 0111	1100 0111	Y	0101 1001	1110 1000
H	0100 1000	1100 1000	Z	0101 1010	1110 1001

Images

Imagine laying a fine screen over a line drawing, a chart, a graph, a photograph, or a similar image. Each hole in the screen is one dot, or pixel, and numbers can be used to record each pixel's brightness, color, and other appearance parameters. For example, visualize an electronic scoreboard that displays the score by turning on and off selected light bulbs to form a pattern. Represent each unlit bulb as a 0 and each lit bulb as a 1, string those bits together, and you have a good mental model of a digital image.

A bitmap or raster image is a digital version of that dot pattern stored in memory. Bitmaps can be very large. For example, at 1 byte per pixel, a high-resolution, 1,024-by-768-pixel bitmap occupies 786,432 bytes of memory. Such large files can quickly fill a hard drive and slow the download process.

To save space, bitmaps are usually compressed. Some compression algorithms, such as GIF (graphics interchange format) are lossless; in other words, following compression, they retain every bit in the original bitmap. Others, such as JPEG (Joint Photographic Experts Group) are lossy—they lose some content during the compression process. Generally, lossy algorithms yield smaller files.

Rather than storing bitmaps, vector graphics rely on geometric formulas to represent images; Macromedia's Flash (SFW) format is an example. Before displaying or printing an image, the necessary pixel or dot values are computed from the formulas. Because the formulas require less space than an equivalent bitmap, a vector graphics file requires less memory and downloads faster than an equivalent raster graphics image. Defining a set of formulas for a complex image such as a photograph is difficult, however, so vector graphics are used primarily for lines and geometric shapes. Figure A.2 lists several common graphics formats.

Sounds

The idea of representing a visual image as a pattern of dots makes sense to most people, but sounds are different. By their very nature, sound waves are continuous (analog), not discrete (digital). How can sound be digitized?

Sound is digitized through a sampling process. Imagine turning a microphone on and off thousands of times per second. During the time the microphone is on, it captures a

Figure A.2 Some common graphics formats.

Extension	Description
AVI	Microsoft's Audio Video Interleave format. Used for movies and videos with sound track. Access through Windows Media Player.
BMP	Microsoft Windows bitmap. No compression.
GIF	Graphics interchange format. A de facto Web standard developed by CompuServe for compressing bitmapped graphics and pictures. Lossless. Limited to 256 colors.
JPG or JPEG	Joint Photographic Experts Group. A de facto Web standard for compressing bitmapped still images and photographs. Lossy.
MOV	QuickTime movie file. The Apple Macintosh video format, now supported by Windows.
MPG or MPEG	Moving Picture Experts Group. A highly compressed format for storing movies.
PDF	Portable Document Format. Adobe Acrobat's page definition format. Download Acrobat Reader to view a PDF file.
PNG	Portable network graphics. A proposed replacement for GIF. Lossless, with better compression than GIF.
QTW	QuickTime for Windows. Movie files.
SVG	Scalable vector graphics. An open, XML-based vector graphics standard.
SWF	Macromedia Shockwave Flash file. Flash is a proprietary, scalable, vector graphics file format. Requires a downloadable plug-in.
TIF or TIFF	Tagged image (or information) file format. A bitmap format popular in desktop publishing applications. No compression.

brief pulse of sound, and for each sound pulse, such parameters as tone, pitch, frequency, and so on are represented as numbers. Later, playing back the sound pulses in the proper order reproduces the original samples, and as long as the time between samples is sufficiently short, a human listener hears continuous sound.

Audio files can be huge. For example, to create an audio CD, the sound is sampled 44,100 times per second. Two bytes are used to store the information generated by each sample, so one second of sound consumes 88.2 KB and each minute fills 5.292 MB (that's mega*bytes*) of storage. Consequently, audio files are almost always compressed. Figure A.3 lists several common audio formats.

Figure A.3 Some common audio formats. Note that AVI, MPEG, and QTW (in Figure A.2) incorporate a sound track.

Extension	Description
AIFF	Audio Interchange File Format. An Apple Macintosh format.
AU	Audio file. An early Internet sound format.
MID or MIDI	Musical instrument digital interface. Access through Windows Media Player.
MP3	MPEG, audio layer 3. MP3 uses a compression algorithm that shrinks CD-level sound files by a factor of 12 with no loss in sound quality. A popular format for swapping audio files.
RA or RAM	RealAudio file. Used for Internet streamed audio and video.
WAV	Waveform. Sound file for Windows. Access through Windows Media Player and Sound Recorder.

APPENDIX B

TCP/IP Headers

Header Contents

On a typical Internet-based system, numerous application programs are supported by numerous application layer protocols. The precise format of the message header and the application layer protocol header vary with the application and the protocol.

The transport layer is responsible for ensuring successful end-to-end transmission of the entire message between an application program (a port) on the source node and an equivalent application program (a port) on the destination node. Not surprisingly, the TCP header contains the message's source and destination port numbers (Figure B.1). Each of the message's packets is assigned a sequence number, which is stored in header bytes 04 through 07. The sequence numbers are used to reconstruct the message when all the packets have been received and to identify missing packets.

The Internet layer's IP protocol routes packets from node to node and, ultimately, from the source to the destination. Thus, the source and destination IP addresses are found in an IP header (Figure B.2).

For the last hop to the destination node, the address resolution protocol (ARP) maps the node's IP address to a physical media access control (MAC) address (which is hard-coded into the network adapter card) and passes the MAC address to the network access layer. The network access layer is responsible for routing a packet to the next node on its own network. A given local area network (LAN) might use Ethernet, token ring, or some other transmission protocol, and the format of the network access header is a function of the protocol used.

Figure B.1 The format of a TCP header.

Byte	Contents
00 01	Source port number
02 03	Destination port number
04 05 06 07	Sequence number
08 09 10 11	Acknowledgment number
12	Header length
13	Control bits
14 15	Window size
16 17	TCP checksum
18 19	Pointer

Figure B.2 The format of an IP header.

Byte	Contents
00	Version/header length
01	Type of service
02 03	Length (bytes)
04 05	Identification
06	Flags/offset address
07	Offset address
08	Time to live
09	Protocol
10 11	Header checksum
12 13 14 15	Source IP address
16 17 18 19	Destination IP address

APPENDIX C
Implementing an E-Commerce Solution: Building a Web Site

The Problem

Imagine that you are a Web services consultant conducting your first interview with a potential client. BC Promotions (BCP) is a small fictitious company that specializes in customizing objects for various types of promotions. The company does not manufacture those objects. Instead, it purchases the products from various manufacturers and adds value by arranging to have them imprinted or embossed with a corporate logo, an individual's name, or whatever the customer wants. BCP's logo says it all: "We'll customize anything."

BCP's office is located in southern Indiana. The business started as a husband and wife team. Chuck did the marketing, designed the logos, and coordinated the customization process with various subcontractors. Brenda handled the finances and the bookwork. They now have two part-time sales associates who work on a commission basis and a full-time administrator who works in the company office.

The promotions industry is very competitive, but because of BCP's personal approach and solid reputation for delivering a quality product on time, the company has done very well. BCP has been in business for fifteen years and has developed a national reputation. The company has customized literally hundreds of products, ranging from large quantity orders for coffee mugs and beverage holders to high-end one-of-a-kind products like customized rifles, boats, retirement gifts, and special awards. For example, in one well-received promotion sponsored by a baby food manufacturer, BCP embossed and delivered a free personalized baby blanket to each customer who mailed in enough proofs of purchase. Although most contracts are for one-time promotions, BCP does have a few large, continuing corporate accounts, including a line of corporate logo clothing for a major automobile manufacturer and a variety of personalized items to support Acme, Inc.'s corporate employee awards program.

Much of BCP's business is based on word of mouth and recommendations from past customers. The company typically has as much business as it can handle, but Brenda and Chuck do call on potential clients and follow leads from numerous sources, such as industry conferences, to find additional work, particularly during slow periods. Recently, the owners attended a national sporting goods convention in Dallas and rented a booth to promote a new product, high-quality pocketknives with a corporate logo inlaid on the simulated bone handle. The resulting flood of new orders more than justified the cost of the trip.

BCP has taken very little advantage of e-commerce to this point, in part because the company prides itself on the personal nature of its business. The owners fear that the impersonal nature of the Internet might damage that image. Chuck and the two sales associates have established ongoing relationships with numerous customers and with the manufacturers whose products they customize, in part by initiating business face-to-face or over the telephone and then following up with frequent e-mail communications and phone calls. A few years ago, BCP joined a national association of promotion companies, primarily to gain access to its industry portal. The portal lists catalogs for many of the manufacturers who produce the products BCP customizes, and Chuck uses the Web to search for products he can't find in a catalog.

Brenda and Chuck are concerned that they might be missing opportunities by not taking advantage of e-commerce, but they have no idea what might work for them. Their decision to contact your consulting firm was prompted by a proposal from one of BCP's continuing customers, Acme, Inc. In the past, BCP met annually with several people at Acme's corporate headquarters to create a catalog of approved corporate logo items. The catalog was then distributed to Acme's many divisions, and throughout the year, Acme's central purchasing department consolidated internal orders and forwarded them to BCP. Acme's new proposal is for BCP to build a Web site, post the corporate-approved catalog, and allow Acme's divisions to place orders directly with BCP. Acme is still very pleased with BCP's service and has not threatened to go elsewhere for products, but BCP is concerned that they might.

BCP's owners and employees are not technically savvy. There are three workstations in the central office. All have Internet access, but because the office consists of only three rooms, the owners have seen no need to network them. Everyone uses e-mail, but BCP does not have a Web site. The office administrator and Brenda are skilled users of accounting and financial software. Although Brenda and Chuck recognize that not building a Web site could cost them Acme's business, they are hesitant to risk their company's image on a technology they do not fully understand. That is why they need your help.

Initial Reactions

For most students (and unfortunately, too many Web service professionals), the immediate solution that comes to mind is to build a Web site. Remember, however, that the client is not technically savvy. BCP approached your firm for help because they do not know what to do. The owners are looking to you for more than just a Web site. They want your advice.

Does the client even need a Web site? If the only application is posting Acme's catalog, easier ways can achieve that objective, including a simple hosting agreement with an established Web site or an ISP. Are there other e-commerce applications that might be implemented on a Web site created for BCP? Do the benefits derived from those potential applications justify building a Web site? Would it make sense for BCP to connect electronically with other customers down their supply chain and with their suppliers and subcontractors up their supply chain? Building a simple Web site might address the immediate need, but an effective consultant's job is to help a client think about tomorrow while addressing the problems of today.

Because the process of analyzing BCP's problem and designing a long-term e-commerce strategy is beyond the scope of this appendix, we will assume that a Web site will be at least part of the ultimate solution. Thus, the balance of this appendix will focus on the process of defining, designing, and implementing BCP's Web site.

Developing a Web Site

Web site development requires careful planning, and adherence to a well-defined methodology, such as the traditional system development life cycle, helps to ensure that nothing is overlooked. Because Web-based applications are so interactive, prototyping is a particularly effective tool for creating them. A prototype is a working model of a system, an application, or an object. The basic idea is to create a simple prototype, allow the user to interact with it, improve the prototype, allow the user to interact with it again, and continue the iterative improve/test cycle until the user is satisfied.

Problem Definition

The goal of problem definition is to clearly define the problem (or the opportunity) so that everyone understands exactly what a solution is expected to accomplish. Attempting to solve a problem you don't understand is a bit like taking a trip without knowing where you are going. You can't get "there" if you don't know where "there" is, and if you do, how will you know you've arrived? There is simply no substitute for a good problem definition.

BCP is reacting to Acme's proposal. You can reasonably assume that Acme expects to benefit if BCP implements a Web site, but how will BCP benefit? Not creating a Web site might mean losing Acme's business, and there is a cost associated with that risk. A second option is building a Web site specifically for Acme. A third option is building a more general Web site that appeals to additional customers and might bring in new business. The drawback is that Brenda and Chuck might decide that the relatively impersonal nature of e-commerce is inconsistent with the company's long-range strategy of emphasizing high-end customized products and might prefer the no-Web-site option.

Any one of those three general directions might be the right way to go, but picking the wrong direction has consequences. Not building a Web site risks losing Acme's business. Building a sophisticated Web site to support e-commerce might change the nature of the company, and the expense of maintaining such a site could bankrupt a small firm like BCP. Choosing the middle route might seem safe, but a Web site designed for a single customer puts BCP at the mercy of that customer. As a consultant, your responsibility is to define the options clearly and to spell out the advantages and disadvantages of each one so that Brenda and Chuck can make an informed decision.

We will assume that BCP has chosen the third option. The objective is to create a Web site that will meet Acme's request and will allow BCP to move into the brave new world of e-commerce.

Analysis

Once the problem is defined, the analysis stage begins. The objective of analysis is to understand exactly what the proposed system must do by documenting the system's requirements. To ensure success, the end users must be involved in the analysis process, but Chuck and Brenda are not technically savvy. Prototyping can help to close the gap in user understanding.

The first step is to create a preliminary prototype, a nonfunctional mock-up of the proposed solution. Often, an initial prototype consists of static mock-ups of the Web site's pages. The prototype serves as a vehicle for discussing and clarifying the system's requirements, because it allows the users to actually see what the proposed pages will look like and how people will interact with them. User suggestions are incorporated into an improved prototype, which is subjected to a second round of user review. The process continues through a series of iterations until the users and the site developers agree on a version that meets the requirements.

As the responsible consultant, you might begin by showing Brenda and Chuck a number of relevant B2C and B2B Web sites to give them a sense of what e-commerce might do for them and to gauge their likes and dislikes. Based on that information, you might use an HTML editor to create simple static Web pages to display a possible BCP home page, a mock-up of Acme's online catalog, and a mock-up of the order entry subpage. These preliminary pages include little or no business or information/data logic. Instead, they focus on the presentation logic and demonstrate how the user interface will look. After several iterations, when Brenda and Chuck agree with the prototype, the static pages might be shared with representatives from Acme. After incorporating Acme's suggestions, the prototype might be shared with other current and potential customers, suppliers, and subcontractors to ascertain their possible interest, obtain their suggestions, and incorporate those suggestions in a new iteration.

The key question to be answered during the analysis stage is, *What* must the system do? At the end of the analysis stage, the prototype consists of independent static pages supported by almost no business or information/data logic, because until you know what to do, it makes little sense to worry about how to do it. During the next stage, design, you will begin planning the Web site's physical implementation details.

Design

As you enter the design stage, the key question changes from *what* to *how*. During this stage, your focus shifts from general, logical, conceptual possibilities to a specific physical implementation. The objective is to define the system's infrastructure, its components, and precisely how those components will interact.

Assume that a Web-based information system is the desired alternative. That means you'll be developing a browser-based thin client application. One key design issue is determining the best way to partition the application's presentation, business, and information/data logic between the client and the server. What logic should be executed client side? What logic should be executed server side? What functions are best performed by middleware? Nonsoftware components must be considered during the design stage, too. The interfaces that link BCP's internal processes to each other and to the outside world, the data to be stored, the physical data storage devices, and the interface with the data server must all be defined.

The preliminary prototype built during the analysis stage provides an excellent starting point for designing a physical solution. As the design stage begins, the prototype consists of several static Web pages that show content and imply flow but lack the underlying business logic. If BCP decides that Acme's catalog pages will remain static, simply linking the catalog page and the order entry page might be sufficient. To test that strategy, add the necessary hyperlinks to the prototype pages and let Brenda, Chuck, and others try to place a test order. If BCP doesn't like the result, try another approach, such as generating catalogs dynamically from product and customer information stored in a database. The database option requires several test data records (ten is plenty) and server side logic (a CGI script or a database gateway such as ASP). Once again, the necessary code can be added to the prototype and the prototype can be tested. Another key decision is whether the order entry form data should be validated on the client side (Java or JavaScript) or on the server side. To find out, add the appropriate code to the prototype and see which option the client prefers.

Development, Implementation, and Maintenance

The system is built or created during the development stage. Often, the responsibility for the individual components is assigned to different people or even outsourced to different intermediaries. If the interfaces that link the components have been well designed, integrating those independent components tends to go smoothly, but careful testing is essential. Sometimes a good prototype evolves into a working prototype that eventually becomes the working system.

Some Useful Resources

The following Web sites feature excellent tutorials and reference materials on a variety of Web application development tools and methodologies.

HTML Goodies: *www.htmlgoodies.com*

> *Primers:* HTML, Ad Banners, JavaScript, Perl/CGI

> *Tutorials:* Getting Started, Tables, Forms, Frames, Image Maps, Images, Colors, Buttons, HTML 4.0

> *Advanced:* Style Sheets, JavaScripting, Java Applets, CGI Scripting, DHTML/Layers, ASP, XML

Webmonkey, The Web Developer's Resource: *http://hotwired.lycos.com/webmonkey*

> *Authoring:* HTML Basic, Tables, Frames, Browsers, Tools, Stylesheets, DHTML, XML

> *Design:* Site Building, Graphics, Fonts

> *Multimedia:* Audio/MP3, Shockwave/Flash, Video, Animation

> *E-business:* Building, Marketing, Tracking

> *Programming:* JavaScript, Java, ASP, PHP, ColdFusion, Perl/CGI

> *Backend:* Databases, Apache/XSSI, UNIX, Security, Networks, Protocols

A few more useful resources:

> EarthWeb's Developer.com: *http://softwaredev.earthweb.com*. Tools and tips for developing Web sites.

> Kevin Werbach, The Barebones Guide to HTML: *http://werbach.com/barebones/barebones.txt*. A good HTML reference.

> The Willcam Group, Willcam's Comprehensive HTML Cross Reference: *www.willcam.com/cmat/html/crossref.html*. A compact index of HTML tags. A complete index is available at *www.willcam.com/cmat/html/crossname.html*.

Glossary

Accelerating pace of innovation The tendency of technological innovations to appear at an ever-increasing rate.

Access A security criterion intended to ensure that each employee has reasonable access to all the system resources required to do a job.

Access network The facilities that connect a customer to the Internet.

Active Server Pages (**ASP**) HTML documents that contain text, tags, and embedded scripts (sometimes called servlets) that are executed on the server side to create a dynamic HTML page.

Address resolution protocol (**ARP**) An Internet layer TCP/IP protocol that matches an IP address to a MAC address.

Advanced encryption standard (**AES**) A proposed replacement for the Data Encryption Standard (DES) algorithm with a key length ranging from 128 to 256 bits.

Agent A software routine on a workstation that handles communication between the workstation's operating system and the network operating system.

Aggregation The act of combining data from multiple sources.

Angel A wealthy individual who provides seed money to business startups in exchange for equity or stock options.

Anonymous remailer A service that accepts outgoing e-mail and remails it, thus hiding the identity of the original source.

Antivirus software Software that is used to screen foreign disks, downloaded files, software, and other digital assets for viruses, worms, and Trojan horses.

Applet A small program that is executed from within another program.

Application layer The top TCP/IP layer that holds a number of protocols that directly support application programs.

Application server software Software for building Web-based information systems.

Application service provider (ASP) A company that manages and distributes software-based solutions and services over a TCP/IP network. An intermediary that manages and distributes software-based services and solutions.

Auditability A measure of the extent to which a set of procedures can be audited.

Authentication The process of confirming that a user is who he claims to be.

Backbone A network of high-speed communication lines that carries the bulk of the traffic between major segments of the Internet.

Backdoor An undocumented software routine (less frequently, a hardware trap) that allows undetected access to a system. Also known as a trapdoor.

Bandwidth A measure of the amount of data a communication line can transmit in a given period of time.

Banner A common form of online advertisement.

Baseband A line on which the entire bandwidth is used to transmit one high-speed signal at a time.

Base station An intermediate signal reception/transmission device in a wireless network.

Biometrics Authentication based on such difficult-to-fake personal criteria as voiceprints, fingerprints, hand geometry, retinal scans, iris scans, signature recognition, and facial appearance.

Black box A module that accepts a set of well-defined input parameters, performs a single function, and outputs a set of well-defined output parameters. How the black box performs its function is hidden.

Black-hat hacker A hacker who breaks into computers with malicious intent.

Bot Short for *robot*. A program that uses artificial intelligence to perform a specific task, usually in the background. Also known as an intelligent agent.

Bricks-and-clicks A marketing strategy in which a company combines a physical bricks-and-mortar presence with an online presence.

Bricks-and-mortar An adjective that describes a traditional physical retail presence.

Bridge A computer that links two or more similar networks.

Broadband A line on which the available bandwidth is divided into distinct channels that act much like independent wires and can carry simultaneous messages in parallel. A high-speed communication line.

Broadcast A method of data communication in which every message is sent to every node on the network.

Browser An application program that provides a user-friendly interface for accessing the Internet over the World Wide Web.

Brute force cryptanalysis Trying all possible keys until the right one emerges.

Business logic Web application logic that enforces the applicable business rules and controls the application.

Business model An architecture for a business's product, service, and information flows that includes a description of the various business actors and their roles, the potential benefits that might accrue to those actors, and the sources of revenue.

Business plan A document that clearly describes (as a minimum) a business, its product, its customers, its sales and marketing plans, appropriate financial information, and the qualifications of its management team.

Business planning The act of creating a business plan or strategy.

Business process reengineering The act of redesigning key processes in a systemwide context.

Business strategy A description of a firm's high-level, long-term vision or direction.

Business-to-business (B2B) e-commerce The electronic exchange of information, digital goods, and services between companies and across the supply chain. The most significant form of e-commerce.

Business-to-consumer (B2C) e-commerce The electronic marketing of goods and services directly to the retail customer. The best-known form of e-commerce.

Business-to-employee (B2E) e-commerce A form of e-commerce that applies the basic information-sharing principles of B2B e-commerce to an organization's internal value chain. Also known as intra-business e-commerce.

Buy-side The e-procurement application on the buyer's system that controls both access and the approval process.

Cable A physical connection, such as a twisted pair of wires, a coaxial cable, a fiber optic cable, and so on.

Cache To save data for subsequent reuse. For example, Web pages are sometimes cached to save time if a given page is requested again.

Caesar-shift substitution cipher An encryption technique named after Julius Caesar.

Central office A telephone service provider's local switching center.

Certificate authority (CA) A trusted third party that issues, certifies, and manages digital certificates.

Channel The physical path over which a message flows.

Chipping Replacing selected integrated circuit chips with functionally equivalent but modified chips that broadcast a detectable signal, enable a hardware-based virus or backdoor, fail on command, or perform some other undesirable function.

Click ratio The percentage of visitors to a page who click on an advertisement.

Clickstream A record of an individual's Internet activity, including Web sites visited, pages downloaded, newsgroups frequented, and the addresses of both incoming and outgoing e-mail messages.

Client A computer that requests a resource or a service from a server.

Client/server model A computing model in which one computer, the server, controls access to a resource needed by the other computer, the client. In order to access that resource, the client must ask the server for help.

Client/server network A network structure in which a server controls access to the network's shared resources and services, and the various workstations or hosts act as clients.

Collision An event that occurs when two or more nodes try to transmit data simultaneously over the same line.

Collision detection A network management technique that allows each node to transmit whenever it chooses. If a collision is detected, the messages are retransmitted.

Common carrier A company that provides public communication services.

Common gateway interface (CGI) A set of standards that defines a server-side application programming interface for specialized programs that run on a Web server, are invoked by a client browser, and access non-Web data. A set of specifications for writing middleware.

Competitive advantage A business advantage derived from something a company does or has that its customers want and its competitors cannot (or choose not to) match.

Compression Removing repetitive or unnecessary bits from data to save storage space and/or to reduce the number of bits that must be transmitted over a communication line.

Conflicting objectives A set of objectives that conflict with each other. Business decision making often involves choosing between or balancing conflicting objectives.

Connection An agreement to communicate. A channel for communication.

Connectivity The ability of a device or a software package to work with other devices or software over a network connection. Often, the term is used to describe the ease with which a particular device can be connected to communication media, with more options implying greater connectivity.

Consumer-to-consumer (C2C) e-commerce The direct, one-to-one exchange of electronic information between consumers.

Content management The act of creating and maintaining the content of a Web site or an intranet.

Content management services A set of tools and techniques for maintaining and accessing Web site and intranet content.

Cookie A small text file that holds information about the user and/or the state of the application.

Cracker A person who breaks into computers with malicious intent. Also, a person who cracks (or breaks) codes. See *black-hat hacker*.

Cryptanalysis The process of decrypting a message without knowing the key.

Cryptography The science of encrypting or otherwise concealing the meaning of a message to ensure the privacy and integrity of the information transfer.

Customer relationship management (**CRM**) A powerful customer acquisition and retention tool that incorporates numerous technologies and applications to support sales and marketing.

Customization The act of modifying a product or service to fit a given user's requirements.

Cybercrime A general term for illegal and/or unethical activities performed in cyberspace.

Cyberspace The nonphysical space created by networked computers that contains such digital objects as files and messages.

Cyberterrorism An online form of terrorism that relies on various cyberwarfare tools and tactics.

Cyberwarfare A form of information warfare conducted in cyberspace.

Cycle time The elapsed time from idea to implementation.

Dark-side hacker See *black-hat hacker*.

Data communication The process of transferring data, information, or commands between two computers or between a computer and a terminal.

Data encryption standard (**DES**) A secret key algorithm developed in the 1970s and subsequently adopted as a standard by the National Security Agency (NSA).

Data mining The act of ferreting out previously unknown patterns and relationships from a set of data.

Data services layer The Web application layer that determines what data to retrieve, how to access it, how to store it, and so on. Also known as the information layer or information/data layer.

Decrypt To convert a message from encrypted form to plain text.

Denial of service attack (**DoS**) A hacker attack that overwhelms a target computer by sending it multiple messages or multiple commands in a brief period of time so that the rate of arriving messages exceeds the target server's ability to respond.

Dialer program An online scam that terminates the victim's ISP connection and dials an expensive long-distance number, often in a foreign country.

Digital Data that is represented as discrete numbers.

Digital cash A payment service used to pay for microtransactions.

Digital certificate An electronic document issued by a certificate authority (CA) that authenticates a digital signature.

Digital envelope An attachment to a message that holds a secret key encrypted using a public-key algorithm.

Digital signature An attachment to a message that authenticates the sender.

Digital subscriber line (DSL) A technology that enables high-speed data communication on standard telephone lines.

Diminishing returns The tendency of unit cost to increase as sales quantity increases.

Disintermediation Eliminating the middleman (an intermediary), a common byproduct of e-commerce.

Distributed denial of service attack (DDoS) A denial of service attack launched simultaneously from a number of computers, making it difficult to identify the attacker.

DNS spoofing A form of spoofing in which a hacker alters a DNS entry on a server and consequently redirects a browser's page request to an alternate site, such as the hacker's site.

Domain A set of nodes that are administered as a unit.

Domain name Two to four words separated by dots that uniquely identify a node on the Internet.

Domain name system (DNS) The TCP/IP system responsible for converting domain names to IP addresses.

Dumpster diving The act of hunting through paper trash in search of passwords and other information that might prove useful to a hacker.

Dynamic page A Web page created in real time in response to user input.

E-book A digitized book that can be distributed and read electronically.

E-business, or electronic business Electronically buying, selling, servicing customers, and interacting with business partners and intermediaries over the Internet.

E-cash A payment service used to pay for microtransactions.

E-commerce, or electronic commerce (1) Transactions conducted over the Internet, either by consumers purchasing goods and services or directly between businesses. (2) Conducting business online.

Economic feasibility A condition that occurs when a project or a possible future promises a reasonable return on investment.

Electronic data interchange (EDI) A set of procedures for exchanging business documents between a company's information technology infrastructure and the information technology infrastructures of its suppliers and distributors.

Electronic invoice presentment and payment (EIPP) A standard that coordinates the electronic exchange of invoices and payments between trading partners.

E-marketplace A type of intermediary that offers supply chain integration services by providing a Web site and a set of applications that allow many organizations to exchange information, goods, and services in one place using a common technology platform.

Encapsulation The process of wrapping an upper layer's output in a new message complete with a new header.

Encrypt To convert a message into encoded or ciphered form.

Encryption key See *Key, encryption.*

Enterprise application integration (EAI) The principle of coordinating the operation of all of an organization's applications, databases, and information technologies so they function as a single efficient, integrated, businesswide application.

Enterprise data model (EDM) A model that integrates the information needs of the entire organization.

Enterprise portal A portal that consolidates all the applications, information, expertise, and services available on an intranet.

Enterprise resource planning (ERP) A business management system that relies on information from an integrated set of applications associated with each of the functional areas that make up a firm's value chain.

E-procurement Applications and services that facilitate the exchange of information between trading partners by integrating the buyer's purchasing process with the seller's order entry process.

E-retailer, or **e-tailer** A company that sells retail products online.

Escrow service A payment service that reduces risk by accepting a payment from a buyer, holding it, and releasing the payment to the seller after the buyer receives the shipment.

Ethernet A popular, inexpensive, high-speed, collision detection, local area network protocol.

Exploit A software vulnerability that has been identified and successfully attacked by a hacker.

Extensible markup language (XML) An extension to HTML that enables data sharing by providing a formal standard for dynamically defining, validating, interpreting, representing, and transmitting content between applications and between organizations.

Extranet An extension to an intranet that allows selected outsiders to access the private network over the public Internet.

Fat client A client/server application in which the client does most of the information processing.

Fault tolerant Able to preserve data integrity and continue operating when one or more components malfunction.

Feasibility analysis A traditional systems analysis tool for evaluating the odds that a project will be successfully completed.

File transfer protocol (FTP) An application level protocol that enables the transfer of files between two computers.

Firewall Hardware and/or software that protects the corporate network from unauthorized access.

Flame attack A barrage of nasty e-mail messages that overwhelms the target's in-box.

Fraud The crime of obtaining money or some other benefit by deliberate deception.

Gateway A computer that links two or more dissimilar networks.

Global competition Competition that can come from anywhere on the globe. A byproduct of electronic commerce.

Groupware Software that supports collaborative work.

Hacker Originally, an expert programmer with a knack for creating elegant solutions to difficult problems. Today, the term is more commonly applied to someone who illegally breaks into computer systems.

Header A prefix to a message that carries information for delivering the message, such as the transmitter's address and the receiver's address.

Hit A request for an HTML document or an embedded file.

Home page A starting point for Web browsing that serves as a table of contents or index to the other pages on the site.

Hook A means of attracting potential customers to a retail outlet.

Host A computer that is accessed by and provides services to a remote user but does not link networks. A computer attached to the Internet that runs (or hosts) application programs. A domain's gateway to the Internet is usually a host. Also known as an end system.

HTML (hypertext markup language) A markup language for creating Web pages using tags.

HTTP (hypertext transfer protocol) An application level protocol that supports the World Wide Web by defining the format of requests from a browser and replies by a server.

Hub A common connection point that contains several ports.

Hub and spoke system A hybrid of the secure private network and value added network approaches implemented by a single powerful trading partner (the hub) that creates its own nationwide network and allows or requires buyers and suppliers (the spokes) to connect to the network.

Human engineering A term used among crackers and samurai for techniques that rely on weaknesses in wetware (people) rather than software.

Hyperlink A logical pointer to another page on the same Web site or on a remote site.

Hypertext Blocks of text linked by logical associations, such as key words.

Identity theft The act of using another person's identity to surf the Web, purchase merchandise, and so on.

Impression The appearance of an advertisement on a Web page.

Information/data logic Web application logic that determines what data to retrieve, how to access the data, how to store the data, and so on. Also known as the data services layer.

Information systems planning The formal process for deciding what systems to implement and how to build them.

Information technology infrastructure A basic blueprint of how a firm's data processing systems, telecommunication networks, and data will be integrated.

Information warfare Those actions intended to protect, exploit, corrupt, deny, or destroy information or information resources in order to achieve a significant advantage, objective, or victory over an adversary.

Insider A trusted employee with legitimate rights to access the organization's network and sufficient knowledge to find important or sensitive information.

Integrity A security criterion intended to ensure that the message was not modified during transmission.

Intelligent agent A software routine that performs such tasks as retrieving and delivering information and provides automated support for repetitive tasks.

Interconnection A measure of the extent to which one company's product is linked to another company's product. A potentially risky form of specialization.

Interconnectivity The ability of a network, a device, or a software package to communicate with other networks, devices, or software.

Intermediary A company that assists or adds value to the exchange of products and/or information across the value and supply chains.

Intermediary service A support service provided by an intermediary. A profitable form of e-commerce.

Internet (1) A global network of networks defined by a set of open standards for communicating data and information between computers. (2) A global, packet switching network of networks that links millions of computers throughout the world. (3) The set of interconnected computers that use TCP/IP.

Internet layer In the TCP/IP model, the third layer from the top responsible for routing packets.

Internet model See *TCP/IP model.*

Internet protocol (IP) The standard Internet layer TCP/IP protocol responsible for routing packets.

Internet protocol security (IPSec) A set of protocols that supports secure packet exchange at the IP level.

Internet service provider (ISP) An organization that provides access to the Internet.

Internetworking The process of linking two or more networks.

Interoperability The ability of software to function in different environments by sharing data and resources with other software.

Interorganizational system (IOS) An information system shared by two or more enterprises.

Intra-business e-commerce A form of e-commerce that applies the basic information-sharing principles of B2B e-commerce to an organization's internal value chain. Also known as business-to-employee (B2E) e-commerce. Also known as intraorganizational e-commerce.

Intranet A private corporate network that uses standard Internet protocols and interfaces.

Intrusion An attempt to break into or misuse a computer system.

Intrusion detection Procedures and techniques designed to detect an intrusion when it occurs or as soon as possible thereafter.

IP address A number that uniquely identifies a node on the Internet.

IP spoofing A system vulnerability that exploits network trust relationships to bypass security.

IPV4 The current Internet protocol standard.

IPV6 The new proposed Internet protocol standard that increases the number of address bits to 128 and adds several security features.

Island of automation An independent set of application programs, hardware, and data that support a single business function and cannot communicate with comparable resources on other islands of automation.

Key, encryption A number or code that converts a general encryption algorithm into a specific rule for encrypting and decrypting a particular message.

Key length The number of bits or characters in a key. An important measure of an encryption algorithm's strength.

Killer application An innovative application that has the potential to totally change a market or even create a new market.

Last mile problem A problem arising from the enormous speed disparity between a voice-grade line and a high-speed trunk line. The problem of providing a high-speed link between the end-user's system and an Internet access point.

Layer A program or set of programs that provides services to the layer above it and uses the services provided by the layer below it.

Layering The process of adding onto or tapping into an existing infrastructure.

Legacy application An existing application developed for an outdated platform.

Line The physical path over which a message flows.

Local Communication in which the transmitter and the receiver are in close proximity.

Local area network (LAN) A group of interconnected computers located in close proximity.

Lock-in A state in which the customer has a vested interest to stay with a company because switching to a competitor entails significant switching costs.

Logging The act of recording login attempts, transactions, and similar information on a difficult-to-change medium for later review.

Logic bomb A program that symbolically blows up in memory, often taking the contents of a hard disk, selected data, or selected software with it.

Logistics The process of planning, implementing, and controlling the efficient, effective flow and storage of goods, services, and related information from point of origin to point of consumption for the purpose of conforming to customer requirements.

Malware Harmful software.

Management (or managed) service provider (MSP) A company that manages information technology services for other companies over the Web.

Media access control (MAC) address The physical address of a network node, for example, an Ethernet card number.

Medium The physical path over which a message flows.

Message The content or intelligence being transmitted.

Metatag An HTML tag that allows a Web page designer or creator to specify information about the Web page.

Middleware Software that connects two or more server routines.

Minutiae The digitized points that represent a biometrics criterion.

Mission-critical application An application a company depends upon for its well-being.

Mobile switching station A wireless network counterpart to a plain old telephone service central office.

Model A simplified version of something complex used to analyze and solve problems or make predictions.

Monitoring The act of watching someone or something.

Moore's law A 1965 observation by Gordon Moore, one of Intel's founders, suggesting that the number of components (such as transistors) on an integrated circuit chip doubles roughly every 18 months. Because a chip's processing power is a function of the number of components, power doubles at the same rate.

Mouse-trapper A type of ad that turns off the browser's Back button, disables the pop-up window's close box, or both, leaving the victim with no way to escape the ad short of closing the browser or rebooting the system.

Network Two or more (usually more) computers or other intelligent devices linked by communication lines in a way that allows them to communicate effectively.

Network access layer The bottom TCP/IP layer where data is exchanged between a node and the physical network.

Network access point (**NAP**) An interconnection point that links the wide area networks of several network service providers (NSPs).

Network layer See *Internet layer*.

Network service provider (**NSP**) An organization that operates a national wide area network that forms part of the Internet's backbone.

Node A computer or other device on a network.

Nonrepudiation A security criterion intended to prevent the sender from denying that she sent the message.

N-tier A client/server application in which the application logic is partitioned among the clients and several specialized servers.

Open standard A standard published in detail and available to anyone.

Open systems interconnection (**OSI**) **reference model** A seven-layer model for computer-to-computer communication.

Optimize To achieve the most cost-efficient solution.

Opt in To agree to participate.

Opt out To choose not to participate.

Packet A unit of data or information transmitted over a packet switching network.

Packet sniffer A software wiretap that captures and analyzes packets.

Packet switching A data transmission technique that achieves efficient message delivery by breaking a message into small blocks called packets and transmitting the packets from multiple users simultaneously over the same line.

Partition, or **partitioning** Implementing a Web application's logic partly on the client and partly on the server.

Path name A name that identifies all the subdirectories one must navigate to get to a specific file.

Payment service An intermediary service that collects and processes payments.

Peer-to-peer network A network in which the linked computers are treated as equals with no central server to provide control.

Phreaker A person who cracks or breaks into the telephone network.

Physical layer See *network access layer*.

Ping o' death An early type of denial of service attack.

Plain old telephone service (POTS) An informal term for standard telephone service.

Plain text An original message before it is encrypted.

Platform A computing environment defined (loosely) by a set of hardware and an operating system.

Platform independence The ability of software to run on a variety of different computers under different operating systems.

Plug-in A software routine that adds functionality to a larger application.

Point of presence A point in an Internet service provider's wide area network where a user can connect with a local call and then log on to the ISP's host or server.

Point-to-point transmission A routing technique in which the signal follows a series of jumps, advancing node by node through the network.

Political feasibility A condition that occurs when a task can be done in the context of the existing or expected social and political environment.

Porn napping The act of taking over innocent-sounding or lapsed URLs or using a variation of a legitimate URL to trick Web surfers into visiting a porn site.

Port (1) A physical interface (a plug) on a computer to which you connect a device such as a peripheral. (2) In the TCP/IP model, the endpoint of a logical connection.

Portal A Web site that offers numerous services such as e-mail, search engines, news, and local information and often serves as a user's initial home page.

Port scanning The act of systematically scanning a system for open ports with exploitable weaknesses.

Post office protocol (POP) An application level protocol that supports the transfer of e-mail messages between a client and a server.

Presentation logic Web information system logic that provides the user interface, formats the data, displays the data, and accepts and validates user input.

Privacy A security criterion intended to ensure that only the sender and the receiver know the contents of a transaction. Also, freedom from the observation, intrusion, or attention of others.

Private key The nondisclosed key in an asynchronous key pair.

Private leased network A network that achieves interconnectivity by using private leased communication lines.

Protocol An agreed upon format or procedure for transmitting data between two devices. An implementation of the standard rules for passing parameters between adjacent layers.

Protocol stack A series of related protocols arranged in layers.

Proxy server An intermediate server that accepts a transaction from a user, forwards it to the appropriate server, and returns the response to the originator.

Public key In an asynchronous encryption key pair, the key that is published.

Public-key encryption An asymmetric encryption technique that uses different keys to encrypt and decrypt a message.

Public key infrastructure (PKI) The established infrastructure for assigning, distributing, and managing key pairs and digital certificates.

Pump-and-dump A type of fraud in which the perpetrator touts a weak financial asset such as a stock and then dumps the asset when the victims bid its value up.

Pyramid scheme A financial scam that depends on a steady supply of new investors to pay earlier investors.

Rabbit A program that replicates itself until no memory is left and no other programs can run.

Receiver A message's destination.

Recovery A security criterion that calls for effective backup and recovery procedures to get the system back online quickly after a security breach or a system failure has occurred.

Regional ISP An organization that operates a statewide or regional backbone and typically connects to the Internet by leasing bandwidth from a network service provider. Many local ISPs access the Internet through a regional ISP, and large organizations sometimes lease a direct broadband connection to a regional ISP.

Reintermediation The process of introducing new middlemen (intermediaries) into a process.

Relationship marketing A form of one-to-one, personalized, targeted marketing that allows a company to treat individual customers differently based on past experience, demographics, and other relevant criteria.

Remote Geographically separated.

Response time The elapsed time between a request for data and the display of that data.

Robust Able to continue functioning in extreme circumstances.

Rogue Web site A clone of a well-known Web site operated by a cybercriminal for the purpose of obtaining credit card numbers and other personal information.

Router A relatively low-cost device that connects two or more networks and routes messages between them without regard for the data content.

Routing On an unstructured network, the process of selecting the next node or the set of nodes that the signal will traverse.

Samurai A person who hacks for money.

Scalability The ability to adapt to changing demand.

Scalable Able to adapt to changing demand.

Script A set of macrolike instructions that are executed by a browser.

Script kiddie A relatively inexperienced hacker-in-training who lacks the skill or knowledge to really understand the hacker-written scripts he downloads and executes.

Seal of approval A logo that certifies a Web site meets a well-known, trusted source's online privacy standards.

Second-generation intranet An intranet that combines a considerable amount of corporate information into an interactive employee knowledge base.

Secret-key cryptography A symmetric encryption technique that uses the same key to both encrypt and decrypt a message.

Secure sockets layer (**SSL**) A protocol that runs in the context of the standard TCP/IP protocols and uses public-key encryption, a digital envelope, a digital signature, and digital certificates to authenticate and establish a secure symmetric secret key connection between a client and a server for the duration of a session.

Security A set of procedures, techniques, and safeguards designed to protect hardware, software, data, and other system resources from unauthorized access, use, modification, or theft.

Sell-side An e-procurement application that allows trading partners to connect and place orders directly on the supplier's system, a process analogous to Web-based business-to-consumer (B2C) e-commerce.

Server A computer that controls access to a resource of a service needed by a client computer.

Session The set of activities performed by a single user between logon and logoff. A relatively brief series of related transactions with a clear beginning and a clear end.

Shopping bot A bot or intelligent agent used to locate the best price for a desired product.

Signal The form in which a message moves over a communication line.

Simple network management protocol (SNMP) An application level protocol used as a network management tool.

Smurf attack A distributed denial of service attack that exploits a broadcast server.

Snoopware PC monitoring software.

Social engineering A term used among crackers and samurai for techniques that rely on weaknesses in wetware (people) rather than software.

Socket A software object that consists of an IP address plus a port number.

Spam A mass mailing of junk e-mail sent to everyone on a mailing list.

Spawner A piece of malware that enters a computer through downloaded shareware or freeware or as an attachment to an e-mail message, particularly a spam message. Once established, the software spawns its own pop-up ads that replace or compete with legitimate ads as you surf.

Spoofing A form of electronic masquerading.

Spyware Software that employs a background or back channel Internet connection to transmit information secretly from a target computer to a receiver.

State Status. The state of an executing program at any given instant is defined by a snapshot of the values of key registers and address pointers, a list of open files, and the status of any pending input or output operations.

Stateless An application or process that maintains no record of previous transactions, such as page requests.

Static page A predefined Web page that is stored on a Web site database and downloaded on request without change.

Stealth surfing The act of using a service that accepts page requests, fills them through its own proxy server, and returns them to the requester from the proxy, thus hiding the requester's identity.

Steganography The process of hiding a message to make it invisible and undetectable.

Streaming technology A technique for transmitting and playing a signal in real time by switching back and forth between two or more buffers.

Suboptimization The optimization of a single component, often at the expense of systemwide efficiency.

Supply chain A set of business processes that allow multiple companies to function as an integrated virtual organization to deliver value to consumers.

Supply chain management (SCM) A B2B e-commerce application designed to effectively manage the flow of products, information, and finances between multiple trading partners, delivering the right product at the right time in the right amount to the right place in the supply chain.

Surveillance Continual observation.

Switching The act of establishing a dedicated path linking a transmitter and a receiver for the duration of a single session, such as a single telephone call.

TCP/IP The Internet's primary packet switching protocols.

TCP/IP model A layered network model based on the OSI model.

Technical feasibility A condition that occurs if the necessary technology exists or if it is likely to exist in time to affect the outcome.

Telephone service provider A company that provides plain old telephone service.

Telephone system Today's best-known common carrier.

Telnet An application level terminal emulation protocol that allows a user to log on to a TCP/IP host and enter keyboard commands as though she were actually on that host.

Thin client A client/server application in which the server does most of the information processing.

Three-tier A client/server application in which the processing workload is distributed between the client and two servers.

Threshold The minimum acceptable score for acceptance following a test.

Tiered Internet services A layered model for accessing the Internet, with both price and content increasing with each higher layer or tier.

Time bomb A form of logic bomb that activates on a particular date or when a particular condition is met.

Time to market The elapsed time between the decision to offer a product and the availability of that product in the marketplace.

Token passing A network management technique in which an electronic token moves continuously around the network and a node is allowed to transmit a message only when it holds the token, making collisions impossible.

Topology Shape or form. A network's topology defines its connections.

Tracking The act of secretly collecting information about a person's surfing patterns.

Trade-off A compromise.

Transmission control protocol (TCP) The standard protocol used by the TCP/IP model's transport layer.

Transmitter The sender or source of a message.

Transport layer In the TCP/IP model, the second layer from the top responsible for ensuring successful end-to-end transmission of the complete message.

Trojan horse A seemingly harmless program that carries a payload and entices an unsuspecting user to try it.

Tunneling The act of encrypting each outgoing packet and encapsulating it to form a new packet that includes a header and a trailer for a special protocol understood only by the tunneling software.

Two-tier A client/server application in which all the clients (the first tier) receive services from a single server at the second tier.

Uniform resource locator (**URL**) The unique logical address of a Web page.

Value-added network (**VAN**) A semiprivate network operated by a trusted third party that offers bandwidth and other value-added services to facilitate interconnectivity among multiple organizations.

Value chain The set of integrated internal processes that combine to deliver value to a company's customers. The set of integrated internal processes that combine to transform raw materials into finished products and/or services and together define how the organization operates internally.

Vaporware Software that is announced and hyped long before it is released.

Venture capitalist An individual, partnership, or business concern that provides seed money to startups in exchange for equity or stock options.

Virtual community A portal-like site that provides many of the same services as the more well-known portals, but focuses on a particular market segment.

Virtual private network (**VPN**) A pseudoprivate network that uses public bandwidth.

Virtual value chain (**VVC**) A fully integrated digital picture of a firm's physical value chain.

Virus A program that is capable of replicating and spreading between computers by attaching itself to another program.

Virus hoax A fake virus warning.

Virus signature A code pattern that uniquely identifies a given virus.

Vulnerability A flaw or bug that allows a hacker to gain access to a system.

War dialer A program that dials all the telephone numbers in a block of potential target numbers looking for the tone that identifies a modem.

Web The World Wide Web.

Web application A client/server application that is a component of a Web information system.

Web bug A virtually invisible, single-pixel clear gif used to support tracking.

Web information system A set of programs and routines that runs on the platform defined by the Internet and the World Wide Web.

Web page The basic unit of information on the World Wide Web composed of several objects (files). A set of related files stored on a Web server's host computer and identified by a unique URL.

Web server An application program that runs on a host computer and supports creating, retrieving, and distributing pages.

Web services Intermediary-supplied e-utilities that allow incompatible application programs to interact and share information over the Internet.

Web site A set of related Web pages, most of which are stored on the Web server's host computer.

White-hat hacker A hacker who follows an unwritten code of ethics and does not intentionally cause harm.

Wide area network (WAN) A network that links geographically disbursed computers or local area networks (LANs).

Wireless A data communication medium that does not use physical wires.

Workstation An end-user computer through which a person accesses a local area network.

World Wide Web A global network of HTTP servers with a standard set of naming and linking conventions that provides access to a set of interlinked hypertext documents. An application layered on top of the Internet that provides simple, standardized protocols for naming, linking, and accessing virtually everything on the Internet.

Worm A viruslike program that is capable of spreading under its own power.

XML See *Extensible Markup Language*.

Index

B

C

FTD.com, 107, 146
FTP, *See* file transfer protocol
FUD factor, 298, 318
functional independence, 10, 11
functional orientation, 167–171

G

gateway, 45, 49
G2C e-commerce, *See*
    government-to-consumer
    e-commerce
gambling, or gaming, 320
Game Boy, 338, 339
Gateway Computers, 131
gators and gator food, 298–299
Gemstar, 336
General Mills, 201, 202
General Motors, 193
geography, 113, 115
GIF, 358
global communication network, 23
Go.com, 104
Godzillagram, 247
Google, 137, 139, 190
government-to-consumer (G2C)
    e-commerce, 150, 151
Go!Zilla, 302
graphics format, 358, 359
groupware, 189

H

hack mode, 236
hacker, or hacking, 6, 24, 233–235,
    285, 286
hand geometry, 347
Harrah's, 305
hashing, 268, 283
header, 42, 53, 54, 55, 56, 74,
    361–362
heuristic logic, 243
Hi, 242
hit, 147, 148
Home Depot, 121
home page, 71, 72, 74
honey pot, 274
hook, 132, 133

horizontal e-marketplace, 221
host, 47, 58, 71, 72, 74, 84, 85
host-to-host transport layer,
    See transport layer,
Hotjobs, 5, 145
HTML, *See* hypertext markup
    language
HTTP, *See* hypertext transfer
    protocol
hub and spoke system, 209
human engineering, 237
hyperlink, 14, 71, 72, 74, 78, 80
hypertext, 13, 14
hypertext markup language
    (HTML), 76–80, 81, 82, 86, 87,
    214, 215, 217, 309, 310
hypertext transfer protocol (HTTP),
    73, 74, 75

I

IBM, 48, 122, 155, 174, 185, 189,
    217, 344, 345
IBPP, *See* Internet bill
    presentment and payment
identity theft, 248, 316–317, 320
image file, 358–359
impact stage, 21
impression, 148
incompatibility, 174
index.html, 74
industry portal, 220
information/data logic, 177–179
information service, 153–154
information sharing, 173, 175, 184
information systems
    development, 175, 176
information systems planning, 175
information technology
    infrastructure, 175
information warfare, 250–253
infrastructure, 9, 10, 11, 14, 24,
    33–63, 351
innovation, 19, 20
insider, 235, 277
instant messaging, 272–273
integrated services
    e-marketplace, 220

integration, 108, 109, 123, 173–185
integrity, 268
Intel, 299
intellectual property, 143, 144, 339–340
intensification, 20, 21
interactivity, 81, 82
interconnection, 141
interconnectivity, 205–209
intermediary, 17, 24, 111–113, 151–155, 218–222, 341, 345
internal communication, 164, 165
International Organization for Standards (ISO), 51
inter-organizational system (IOS), 202–204, 212–217
Internet, 6–8, 13, 14, 16, 17, 23, 24, 44, 45, 47, 56, 70–72, 74, 83, 85, 92, 93, 110, 131, 133, 186, 189, 204, 207, 312, 351
Internet addressing, 57–61
Internet bill presentment and payment (IBPP), 153, 218
Internet Explorer, 71, 141
Internet infrastructure, 46–50
Internet layer, 55, 74, 75, 361
Internet model, 50–57
Internet protocol (IP), 55
Internet protocols, 49–57
Internet protocol security (IPSec), 291
Internet service provider (ISP), 46–48, 308, 314
Internet worm, 232
Internetworking, 45
Interoperability, 57
interorganizational system, 202–204, 211, 212–217
intranet, 185–192, 212, 214
intra-business e-commerce, or intra-organizational e-commerce, 22, 24, 108, 109, 123, 164–193, 200
intrusion, 240
intrusion detection, 274
IOS, *See* inter-organizational system
IP address, 58–61, 74, 361

IP header, 361
IPSec, *See* Internet protocol security
IP spoofing, 248
iris scan, 345
island of automation, 11, 12, 15, 18, 171, 174, 175, 186, 210
ISO (International Organization for Standards), 51
ISP, *See* Internet service provider

J

J2EE, 217, 344
Java, 82, 217, 344, 367
JavaScript, 82, 177, 367
JCPenney, 121
JPEG, 358
JScript, 82

K

Kak, 245
kamikaze packet, 247
key, encryption, 278
key exchange, 279, 280, 283
key length, 281–282
key recovery, 282
keystroke logging, 313
killer application, 110, 132

L

lamerz, 234
LAN, *See* local area network
last mile problem, 38–40
layer, or layering, 8–11, 23, 24, 37, 51, 87, 243
leased line, 40
leftovers, 237
legacy application, 174–176
lifetime learning, 352
line, 36
load balancing, 85
local area network (LAN), 42, 43, 61, 72, 361
lock-in, 140
log, or logging, 269, 274

two-tier client/server
application, 180–182

Notes

Notes

Notes

Notes

Notes

Notes